THE
Complete Writings of
ROGER WILLIAMS

PUBLISHER'S NOTE

All the new matter contained in this edition, including Prof. Miller's essay, will be found in VOLUME SEVEN. This arrangement was adopted in order to retain the original pagination of the first six volumes and thereby maintain the integrity of the voluminous references to the *Narragansett Edition* in the literature about ROGER WILLIAMS. The reader is directed to the inclusive Table of Contents for guidance.

THE COMPLETE WRITINGS OF ROGER WILLIAMS

VOLUME THREE

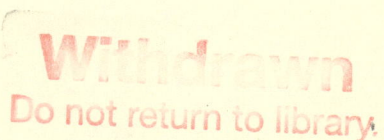

NEW YORK
RUSSELL & RUSSELL · INC
1963

THE COMPLETE WRITINGS OF ROGER WILLIAMS
Issued in Seven Volumes in a Limited Edition
of Four Hundred Sets
Published in 1963 *by Russell & Russell, Inc.*
Library of Congress Catalog Card Number: 63-11034
Printed in The United States of America

THE COMPLETE WRITINGS OF ROGER WILLIAMS
IN SEVEN VOLUMES

VOLUME I
    Biographical Introduction
        by Reuben Aldridge Guild, A.M.
    Key into the Language of America
        Edited by James Hammond Trumbull, A.M.
    Letter of MR. JOHN COTTON
    MR. COTTON's Letter Examined and Answered
        Edited by Reuben Aldridge Guild, A.M.

VOLUME II
    JOHN COTTON's Answer to ROGER WILLIAMS
    Queries of Highest Consideration
        Edited by Reuben Aldridge Guild, A.M.

VOLUME III
    Bloudy Tenent of Persecution
        Edited by Samuel L. Caldwell

VOLUME IV
    The Bloody Tenent Yet More Bloody
        Edited by Samuel L. Caldwell

VOLUME V
    GEORGE FOX Digg'd out of His Burrowes
        Edited by Rev. J. Lewis Diman

VOLUME VI
    The Letters of ROGER WILLIAMS
        Edited by John Russell Bartlett

VOLUME VII
    Publisher's Foreword
    ROGER WILLIAMS: An Essay in Interpretation
        by Perry Miller
    Christenings make Not Christians
    Experiments of Spiritual Life and Health
    The Fourth Paper Presented by Major Butler
    The Hireling Ministry None of Christs
    The Examiner—Defended in a Fair and Sober Answer

THE

BLOUDY TENENT OF PERSECUTION.

EDITED BY

SAMUEL L. CALDWELL.

EDITOR'S PREFACE.

THE work reprinted in the prefent volume was produced during the author's vifit to England in 1643–1644, and while he was engaged in obtaining the Charter. The fruit of previous ftudies and experiences, it was written at fome time during the year in which he publifhed *A Key into the Language of America, Mr. Cotton's Letter Examined and Anfwered*, and *Queries of Higheft Confideration*. Befides thefe labors, it is to be added, by his own teftimony, "that when thefe difcuffions were prepared for publike in London, his time was eaten up in attendance upon the fervice of the Parliament or City, for the fupply of the poor of the City with wood (during the ftop of coale from Newcaftle, and the mutinie of the poor for firing.) God is a moft holy witnefs, that thefe meditations were fitted for publike view in change of roomes and corners, yea fometimes (upon occafion of travel in the country concerning that bufinefs of fuell) in variety of ftrange houfes, fometimes in the fields, in the midft of travel; where he hath been forced to gather and fcatter his loofe thoughts and papers."[1] It was printed

[1] *Bloody Tenent yet More Bloody*, p. 38.

without the name of the writer or publisher. It must have passed through two impressions in the same year. For while one volume, which is literally followed in the present edition, has a table of errata, another printed in the same year, and of course afterwards, has the errata corrected, with slight changes in the type and orthography of the title page.[1] Otherwise the two correspond, page to page, and even line to line.

It is independent of his previous controversy with Cotton, though indirectly related to it, and following it by very natural consequence. It had probably been growing in his mind for years. At all events the arguments of Mr. Cotton to which it is a reply have a much earlier date, according to his own account. He says in 1647, "Mr. Williams sent me about a dozen years agoe (as I remember) a letter, penned (as he wrote) by a Prisoner in Newgate, touching persecution for Conscience sake: and intreated my judgement of it for the satisfaction of his friend."[2] This "letter" was a part,—the 6th, 7th, 8th, and 9th chapters,—of a work printed in 1620, entitled *A most Humble Supplication of the King's Majesty's Loyal Subjects, ready to testify all Civil Obedience, by the Oath of Allegiance, or otherwise, and that of Conscience; who are persecuted (only for differing in Religion) contrary to Divine and Human Testimonies: As followeth.*[3] It is signed by "your Majesty's loyal subjects unjustly called Anabaptists." According to Williams "the Authour of these

---

[1] One of the principal differences in orthography is in the substitution of *tenet* for *tenent*; the singular for the plural of the Latin *teneo*. It was probably the choice of the printer, as Williams retains his original usage eight years later in *The Bloody Tenent yet More Bloody*. Tenent, for an opinion held by more than one, is used by Sir Thomas Browne, and even as late as 1726 by Wollaston in his *Religion of Nature*, p. 111. Lond. 1726.

[2] *Bloudy Tenent Washed*, p. 1.

[3] It is reprinted by Crosby, *Hist. of Baptists*, ii. Appendix, 10–51, and in *Tracts on Liberty of Conscience, &c.* Hanserd Knollys Society, pp. 189–231.

Arguments being committed by some then in power, close prisoner to Newgate, for the witnesse of some truths of Jesus, and having not the use of Pen and Inke, wrote these Arguments in Milke, in sheets of Paper, brought to him by the Woman his Keeper, from a friend in London, as the Stopples of his Milk bottle."[1] Dr. Underhill conjectures that it must have been written by John Murton, or as Crosby calls him, Morton, who was associated with Helwisse in Holland, and after his return, in England, and against whom John Robinson directed one of his controversial works.[2]

Williams denies that this treatise was sent by him to Cotton, or that the reply was private, as Cotton alleged in complaint against its being printed in this work. He says, "To my knowledge there was no such letter or intercourse passed between Master Cotton and the discusser; but what I have heard is this: One Master Hall of Roxbury, presented the prisoners Arguments against persecution to Master Cotton, who gave this present controverted Answer; with the which Master Hall not being satisfied, he sends them unto the discusser, who never saw the said Hall, nor those Arguments in writing; (though he well remember that he saw them in print some yeers since.)"[3]

---

[1] Page 61, *infra*.
[2] *Tracts on Liberty of Cons.* 89, 187. Crosby, *History of Baptists*, i: 99, 276. Ivimey, do. i: 125. Taylor, do. i: 95. The title of Robinson's work is "A Defence of the Doctrine propounded by the Synod at Dort, against John Murton and his Associates, with the Refutation to their Answer to a writing touching baptism. By John Robinson. Printed in the year 1624." See Young, *Chron. of Pilgrims*, p. 454.
[3] *Bloody Tenent yet More Bloody*, p. 4.

I find no evidence that "Master Hall" was "a congregational minister," as is stated by Dr. Underhill in his Biographical Introduction. Probably he is the John Hall of Roxbury, noticed in Savage, *Geneal. Dict.* ii: 334, "who in the church records has prefix of respect, and I presume, was the freeman of 6 May 1635, unless he may rather be reckoned of 13 May, 1640: but as no further mention of him occurs here, perhaps he removed with the great migration to Connecticut, and was at Hartford 1644,

Williams proceeds to examine not only Cotton's Anſwer to the priſoner's Arguments, but alſo in the laſt fifty-ſix chapters, the "Treatiſe ſent to ſome of the Brethren late of Salem," to which Cotton refers at the cloſe. (p. 53.) This is called *A Model of Church and Civil Power*, and as Cotton referred his correſpondent to it as complementing what he had already written, Williams felt juſtified in aſcribing its compoſition to him "and the Miniſters of New England." Cotton however aſſerts very explicitly "that he was none of them that compoſed it."¹ Dr. Underhill infers that "the real author of it was probably Mr. Richard Mather,"² from

and at Middletown 1654, where he died 26 May 1673, aged 89." I think he is quite as likely to have been the freeman of May 14, 1634, at which date Cotton, Hooker and Stone, the three miniſters who arrived in the ſame ſhip the previous September, were admitted alſo. *Maſſachuſetts Colonial Records*, 1 : 369. If he is the ſame who died at Middletown, he alſo arrived in Boſton the ſame year (1633) with theſe divines. I am indebted to Mr. Trumbull, of Hartford, for a note in regard to him, in which he is ſaid to have died May 26, 1673, "being the 89th year of his age, and the 40th of his being in New England." "By his will (executed May 14, 1673) he gave 10 ſhillings 'towards encouraging of a reading and writing ſchool in Middletown.' So, if not himſelf a miniſter, he wiſhed his children to have 'the benefit of clergy' as far as ten ſhillings would go." He is mentioned "with prefix of reſpect" in the *Maſs. Colonial Records*, i: 241, 271.

Williams ſays that he had not ſeen the priſoner's Arguments in writing, although he had ſeen them in print "ſome yeers ſince;" but he does not ſay that Cotton's Anſwer was in print, though he ſays it "was as publike as Maſter Cottons profeſſion of the ſame tenent was and is."

The copy I have made uſe of, from the library of a gentleman in this city, has the following title : — The Controverſie concerning Liberty of Conſcience in Matters of Religion, Truly ſtated. and diſtinctly and plainly handled, By Mr. John Cotton of *Boſton* in *New England*. By way of anſwer to ſome Arguments to the contrary ſent unto him. Wherein you have, againſt all cavills of turbulent ſpirits, clearly manifeſted, wherein liberty of conſcience in matters of Religion ought to be permitted, and in what caſes it ought not, by the ſaid Mr. Cotton. *London*. Printed by *Robert Auſtin*. for Thomas *Banks*. and are to be ſold at Mrs. Breaches Shop in Weſtminſter-Hall, 1649.

Dr. Underhill ſpeaks of "the only edition known" to him, as printed in 1646. Both of theſe agree with Williams's copy in the following work.

¹ *Bloudy Tenent Waſhed*, p. 192.
² Introduction to Hanſerd Knollys Society edition of *Bloudy Tenent*, page xxxii.

the statement of Cotton Mather, that "when the Platform of Church-Discipline was agreed by a Synod of these Churches, in the year 1647, Mr. Mather's Model was that out of which it was chiefly taken."[1] But the "Model" here referred to is in all probability the one which Mather was appointed to draw up by the Synod.[2] Moreover, Cotton Mather would never have omitted this from the list of his grandfather's published works, if he could have found the least reason for ascribing it to him. And as there is no direct evidence of Mather's authorship, while the internal evidence is against it, the early date which must be given to the *Model* here examined is quite conclusive. He landed in Boston August 17, 1635.[3] But Cotton says of Williams, that "when I wrote that Letter, he (for ought I can remember) did then keepe communion with all his Brethren, and held loving acquaintance with my selfe."[4] Now Winthrop, under the same date in which he records the arrival of the ship in which Mather came, Aug. 16, 1635, informs us that Williams wrote to the church in Salem "that he could not communicate with the Churches in the bay."[5] So that the letter of Cotton must have been written before Mather reached New England, and the "treatise" must have been "sent to some of the Brethren late of Salem" even earlier than that. Williams probably did not receive a copy of the *Model* until after his banishment, although it was written and sent to Salem before that. For he says that he "*wrote*

---

[1] *Magnalia*, i: 409.

[2] "They directed three eminent persons, namely, Mr. John Cotton, Mr. Richard Mather, and Mr. Ralph Partridge, each of them to draw up a scriptural model of church government; unto the end that out of those there might be one educed, which the Synod might after the most filing thoughts upon it, send abroad." *Magnalia*, ii: 182.

[3] R. Mather's *Journal*, in Young's *Chron. of Mass.* 479.

[4] *Bloudy Tenent Washed*, p. 15.

[5] *New England*, i: 198.

on purpose to his worthy friend Mr. Sharpe (Elder of the Church of Salem, (so called) for the sight of it, who accordingly *sent it to him.*"[1]

This tract, which probably was never printed, except by extracts in *The Bloudy Tenent*, took its origin, so far as it can now be traced, from the Act of the General Court of March 4, 1634, in which they "intreate of the elders and brethren of every church within this jurisdiction, that they will consult & advise of one uniforme order of dissipline in the churches, agreeable to the Scriptures, and then to consider *howe farr the Magistrates are bound to interpose for the preservation of that uniformity* & peace of the churches."[2] This is the precise question which the *Model of Church and Civil Power* undertakes to decide,—"what bounds and limits the Lord hath set between both the administrations,"[3]—and it is the earliest matured attempt to deal with the great problem which vexed the mind of the early legislators of Massachusetts. It is valuable and deserves more attention than it has received, as an illustration of the first efforts of the New England immigrants in defining and balancing the ecclesiastical and civil jurisdictions. But Williams had learned a much shorter and surer way to solve the problem. He takes up this, and Cotton's letter, as representative of the spirit and

---

[1] *Bloody Tenent yet More Bloody*, page 291. Samuel Sharpe, who had been an Assistant of the Massachusetts Company in England, came over to Salem in 1629. He was Master-gunner of ordnance, and was also chosen ruling elder of the church. Young, *Chron. of Mass.*, 157. He died in 1658. He had occasion to feel the hand of power as well as his friend Williams. At the same meeting of the Court at which Williams was sentenced, "Mr. Sam¹. Sharpe is enjoyned to appeare att the nexte particular Court, to answere for the letter that came from the Church of Salem, *as also to bring the names of those that will justifie the same,* or else to acknowledge his offence under his owne hand for his owne particular." *Mass. Col. Records*, 1: 161.

[2] *Mass. Col. Rec.* i: 142.

[3] Preface to *Model, &c.*, p. 222, *infra*.

the principles then dominant, and uses them to set off in full contrast the principles of civil and spiritual freedom to which he had advanced. He advocates a method which Cotton and the writers of the *Model*, and the early legislators of Massachusetts thought unsafe, if indeed they did not count it wrong and impracticable. He cut the knot they were trying to untie, by simply divorcing the two jurisdictions, and remanding the civil power to its own separate sphere. His courage and his prescient wisdom time has vindicated. He dared to found his commonwealth on the principles which the prudent divines and legislators of the Massachusetts Colony feared would be the peril of the State, and the doom of Religion. All that can be said is, that with both parties equally conscientious, and faithful to their light, Williams saw farther, and had learned the true ideas of civil and ecclesiastical polity sooner than they.

And yet he was not alone, nor the first in maintaining absolute freedom in religion. Milton, at the very time that this work was issuing from the press, was printing another, in which the English language reaches the summit of eloquent prose, taking similar high and generous grounds for liberty of thought, and recognizing his fellow laborers, whose names and works were so unequal in power and fortune to his. "Now once again," he says, "by all concurrence of signs, and by the general instinct of holy and devout men, as they daily and solemnly express their thoughts, God is decreeing to begin some new and great period in his church, even to the reforming of reformation itself. Behold now this vast city, a city of refuge, the mansion-house of liberty, encompassed and surrounded with his protection; the shop of war hath not there more anvils and hammers working, to fashion out the plates and instruments of armed justice in defence of beleaguered truth, than there be pens and heads there, fitting by their ftudious lamps, mufing, fearching, revolving new notions and ideas wherewith to prefent, as with their homage and their fealty, the approaching reformation."[1]

There is no evidence that Williams was then known to Milton: although the acquaintance may have then begun, of which he writes as exifting during his fecond vifit to England.[2] Milton may have known his as one among many "pens and heads, revolving new notions and ideas," whofe writings looked towards "the approaching reformation." In this fame year, 1644, John Goodwin publifhed the work alluded to on the 165th and 185th pages of the prefent volume.[3] *The Compaffionate Samaritan, Unbinding the Confcience, &c.*, was alfo iffued in the fame year, and with Goodwin's work and *The Bloudy Tenent* were fharply criticifed in *Wholfome Severity reconciled with Chriftian Liberty*, publifhed in 1645.[4] But many years before the Baptifts had uttered their remonftrances againft the ufe of civil power in fpiritual affairs.[5] As early as 1611 they iffued a Confeffion of Faith, which fays, "that the Magiftrate is not to meddle with relig-

---

[1] *Areopagitica*, Bohn's ed. ii : 91.

[2] "The Secretary of the Council (Mr. Milton) for my Dutch I read him, read me many more languages." Letter to John Winthrop, July 12, 1654. Knowles, *Memoir*, p. 264.

[3] *M. S. to A. S. with a Plea for Liberty of Confcience in a Church Way, &c.* London. 1644.

[4] Another contemporary tract was *A Paraenetick or Humble Addreffe to the Parliament and Affembly for (not loofe) but Chiftian Libertie.* London. Printed by Mathew Simmons for Henry Overton. 1644. 4to 14 pp.

Another was *Liberty of Confcience : or the Sole meanes to obtain Peace and Truth.* Printed in the Yeare 1643.

[5] As late as 1688 Boffuet charged that with the exception of Baptifts and Socinians Proteftants held the doctrine of the Roman Church on this fubject. "Puis qu'en ce point les proteftants font d'accord avec nous. Et je ne connois parmi les chrétiens que les fociniens et les anabaptiftes qui s'oppofent à cette doctrine." *Hiftoire des Variations*, Liv. x. 56. *Œuvres*, xxviii: 62, 63.

Editor's Preface.

ion or matters of confcience, nor to compel men to this or that form of religion; becaufe Chrift is the King and Lawgiver of the church and confcience."[1]

The Hanferd Knollys Society has printed a collection of Tracts on Liberty of Confcience and Perfecution which were publifhed in England between 1614 and 1661. Three of them preceded the prefent work.[2] All of them proceeded from thofe who felt the preffure of civil power, and they contributed to the general agitation of the queftion which naturally arofe during the fittings of the Weftminfter Affembly, and the ftruggles of civil and religious factions which then divided the kingdom. They were the earlieft articulate cries of the voice whofe line has gone out through all the earth, and its words to the end of the world. Other and mightier were foon heard, with which Williams had no immediate relation, but echoing the fame notes, though not fo clear and pronounced as his. He preceded only by three years Jeremy Taylor, who fpoke from the other extreme of ecclefiaftical opinion. From the learned quiet or exile of Golden Grove in 1647 he fent forth what Williams called "an Everlafting Monumentall Teftimony to this Truth, in

---

[1] Crofby, *Hift. Eng. Bap.* I. App., 71. The parts of this Confeffion given by Crofby were collected from a work of John Robinfon, of Leyden, written in reply to it. It was written by Helwiffe, John Smith's fucceffor at Amfterdam. Crofby, i: 271. In the Appendix to his fecond volume Crofby gives the Confeffion entire; but it does not contain the fentence quoted in the text. It however omits Article XXV., which may have contained this fentence. Robinfon of courfe, could not have invented it. His reply to this fentence, which fhows how far in the rear this early and noble paftor of the Pilgrims was, is quoted in *Tracts for Liberty of Confcience*, p. 91.

[2] *Religions Peace: or A Plea for Liberty of Confcience* by Leonard Bufher Citizen of London, and Printed in the Yeare 1614.

Perfecution for Religion Judg'd and Condemn'd, &c. 1615.

A Moft Humble Supplication &c. 1620. This is the work from which the Prifoner's Arguments, pp. 1–39, *infra*, were taken.

that his excellent Discourse, of the Libertie of Prophesying."[1] With him Mr. Lecky associates Harrington and Milton as "the three principal writers who at this time represented the movement of toleration."[2] But while they gave it intellectual weight, they ought not to overshadow the earlier and

---

[1] *Bloody Tenent yet More Bloody*, Appendix, p. 317. This sentence is from a letter of seven pages "to the Cleargie of the foure great Parties," in which Williams expresses the same fears as on pp. 350, 351, of the present volume — and gives more fully their grounds — that the Independents if they had the power would use it for persecution. "Doe not all persecutours themselves zealously plead for Freedome, for Libertie, for Mercie to Men's Consciences, when themselves are in the Grates, and Pits, and under Hatches? Thus bloudie Gardiner and Bonner, yea and that bloudie Queene Mary her selfe, all plead the Freedome of their Consciences. * * Yea what excellent subscriptions to this Soule Freedome, are interwoven in many passages of the late Kings Booke (if his)? Yea and one of his Chaplaines (so cald) Doctor Jer. Taylour, what an Everlasting Monumentall Testimony did he publish to this Truth in that his excellent Discourse, of the Libertie of Prophesying?" He writes to Mrs. Sadleir in 1652–3, as follows: "My honoured Friend, since you please not to read mine, let me pray leave to request your reading of one book of your own authors. I mean the Liberty of Prophesying, penned by (so called) Dr. Jer. Taylor. In the which is excellently asserted the toleration of differing religions, yea, in a respect, that of the papists themselves, which is a new way of soul freedom, and yet is the old way of Christ Jesus, as all his holy Testament declares. I also humbly wish that you may please to read over impartially Mr. Milton's answer to the King's book." Elton's *Life*, p. 97.

The event proved the justice of Williams's judgment in regard to Taylor, as he retreated from his principles when he received promotion and his church was again ascendant. Coleridge comments on his change of opinion with considerable sharpness. "If Jeremy Taylor had not in effect retreated after the Restoration, if he had not, as soon as the church gained power, most basely disclaimed and disavowed the principle of toleration, and apologised for the publication by declaring it to have been a *ruse de guerre*, currying pardon for his past liberalism by charging and most probably slandering himself with the guilt of falsehood, treachery and hypocrisy, his character as a man would have been almost stainless." His judgment of Milton's work in comparison with Taylor's may be added. "The Liberty of Prophesying is an admirable work, in many respects, and calculated to produce a much greater effect on many than Milton's treatise on the same subject: on the other hand Milton's is throughout unmixed truth; and the man who in reading the two does not feel the contrast between the simplemindedness of the one and the *strabismus* in the other, is — in the road to preferment." *Literary Remains*, iii: 204, 250.

[2] *Hist. of Rationalism*, ii: 79, 80.

humbler pioneers, who like Williams, not only wrought out their convictions in suffering, but planted it on the everlasting grounds of reason and justice, contending not simply for toleration but for absolute liberty.

But notwithstanding all the names and the influences which were carrying forward the doctrine of spiritual liberty, this work met a harsh reception. The writer says in 1671, " 'Tis true my first book " The Bloody Tenent " was burned by the Presbyterian party (then prevailing.)"[1] The 69th question in *Necessity of Toleration in Matters of Religion*, by Samuel Richardson, " Printed in the Yeare of Jubilee 1647," is "Whether the priests were not the cause of the burning of the book, entitled " The Bloudy Tenent," because it was against persecution?"[2] This may account for the immediate appearance of a second impression. It indicates the spirit of the dominant party.[3] And yet it was not without influence. He writes eight years later:[4] " Some persons of no contemptible note nor intelligence, have by letters from England, informed the discusser, that these Images of clouts it hath pleased God to make use of to stop no small leakes

---

[1] Letter to John Cotton jr., dated Providence, 26 March, 1671. *Mass. Hist. Soc. Proceedings*, March, 1858.

[2] *Tracts on Liberty of Conscience*, 270.

[3] The attitude of the Presbyterian party towards toleration is shown by Neal, *Hist. of Puritans*, ii: 17–19. Also by Marsden, *Later Puritans*, 155. See pp. 350, 351, *infra*. Williams evidently distrusted the Independents as well as the Presbyterians, and inferred, perhaps from their affiliation with his opponents on this side of the water, that their diposition was little better. Robert Baylie, the keen and hard-headed Scotch member of the Westminster Assembly, gives countenance to his judgment. He writes, " Liberty of conscience, and toleration of all or any religion, is so prodigious an impiety, that this religious parliament cannot but abhor the very meaning of it. Whatever may be the opinions of John Goodwin, Mr. Williams, and some of that stamp, yet Mr. Burroughes, in his late Irenicum, upon many unanswerable arguments, explodes that abomination." Burroughes was one of the Five Independent Brethren in the Westminster Assembly. The quotation from Baylie I take from a note in *Tracts on Liberty of Conscience*, p. 270.

[4] *Bloody Tenent yet More Bloody*, p. 38.

of persecution, that lately begun to flow in upon diffenting confciences, and (amongft others) to Mafter Cotton's own, and to the peace and quietnefs of the Independents, which they have fo long, and fo wonderfully enjoyed."

The NARRAGANSETT CLUB now gives this work its fecond reprint. It was printed by the Hanferd Knollys Society in England in 1848, under the care of its accomplifhed Secretary, Dr. Underhill. There is a copy of each of the original impreffions in the Library of Brown Univerfity. The Club is indebted to Mr. John Carter Brown for the ufe of a copy of the firft of thefe impreffions. Copies are alfo in the Library of Harvard Univerfity, of the Maffachufetts Hiftorical Society, and in the Public Library of the City of Bofton. Amendments in the text of the prefent edition fuggefted by the Editor are placed in brackets.

S. L. C.

38 ANGELL STREET, PROVIDENCE, NOV. 13, 1867.

THE
BLOVDY TENENT,

of PERSECUTION, for cause of
CONSCIENCE, discussed, in

A Conference *betweene*

TRVTH and PEACE.

VVHO,

In all tender Affection, present to the High Court of *Parliament*, (as the *Result* of their *Discourse*) these, (amongst other *Passages*) of *highest consideration*.

Printed in the Year 1644.

First, That the blood of so many hundred thousand soules of *Protestants* and *Papists*, spilt in the *Wars* of *present* and *former Ages*, for their respective *Consciences*, is not *required* nor *accepted* by *Jesus Christ* the *Prince* of *Peace*.

Secondly, Pregnant *Scripturs* and *Arguments* are throughout the Worke proposed against the *Doctrine* of *persecution* for for *cause* of *Conscience*.

Thirdly, Satisfactorie Answers are given to *Scriptures*, and objections produced by Mr. *Calvin, Beza*, Mr. *Cotton*, and the Ministers of the New English Churches and others former and later, tending to prove the *Doctrine of persecution* for cause of *Conscience*.

Fourthly, The *Doctrine of persecution* for cause of *Conscience*, is proved guilty of all the *blood* of the *Soules* crying for *vengeance* under the *Altar*.

Fifthly, All *Civill States* with their *Officers* of *justice* in their respective *constitutions* and *administrations* are proved *essentially Civill*, and therefore not *Judges, Governours* or *Defendours* of the *Spirituall* or *Christian state* and *Worship*.

Sixtly, It is the will and command of *God*, that (since the comming of his Sonne the *Lord Jesus*) a *permission* of the most *Paganish, Jewish, Turkish*, or *Antichristian consciences* and *worships*, bee granted to *all* men in all *Nations* and *Countries*: and they are onely to bee *fought* against with that *Sword* which is only (in *Soule matters*) *able* to *conquer*, to wit, the *Sword of Gods Spirit*, the *Word* of *God*.

Seventhly, The *state* of the Land of *Israel*, the *Kings* and *people* thereof in *Peace* & *War*, is proved *figurative* and *ceremoniall*, and no *patterne* nor *president* for any *Kingdome* or *civill state* in the *world* to follow.

Eightly, *God* requireth not an *uniformity* of *Religion* to be *inacted* and *inforced* in any *civill state*; which inforced *uni-*

formity (sooner or later) is the greatest occasion of *civill Warre, ravishing* of *conscience, persecution* of *Christ Jesus* in his servants, and of the *hypocrisie* and *destruction* of *millions* of *souls*.

Ninthly, In holding an inforced *uniformity* of *Religion* in a *civill state*, wee must necessarily *disclaime* our desires and hopes of the *Iewes conversion* to *Christ*.

Tenthly, An inforced *uniformity* of *Religion* throughout a *Nation* or *civill state*, confounds the *Civill* and *Religious*, denies the principles of Christianity and civility, and that *Jesus Christ* is come in the Flesh.

Eleventhly, The permission of other *consciences* and *worships* then a state professeth, only can (according to God) procure a firme and lasting *peace*, (good *assurance* being taken according to the *wisedome* of the *civill state* for *uniformity* of *civill obedience* from all sorts.)

Twelfthly, lastly, true *civility* and *Christianity* may both flourish in a *state* or *Kingdome*, notwithstanding the *permission* of divers and contrary *consciences*, either of *Iew* or *Gentile*.

To the Right Honorable,
both Houses of the High Court of
PARLIAMENT.

Right Honourable and Renowned Patriots:

NExt to the saving of your own *soules* (in the lamentable *shipwrack* of *Mankind*) your taske (as *Christians*) is to save the *Soules*, but as *Magistrates*, the *Bodies* and *Goods* of others.

Many excellent *Discourses* have been presented to your *Fathers* hands and Yours in former and present *Parliaments:* I shall be humbly bold to say, that (in what concernes your duties as *Magistrates*, towards others) a more necessary and seasonable *debate* was never yet presented.

Two things your *Honours* here may please to view (in this Controversie of *Persecution* for cause of *Conscience*) beyond what's extant.

First the whole *Body* of this *Controversie* form'd & pitch'd in true *Battalia*.

Secondly (although in respect of my selfe it be *impar congressus*, yet in the power of that *God* who is *Maximus in Minimis*, Your Honours shall see the Controversie is discussed with men as able as most, eminent for *abilitie* and *pietie*, Mr. *Cotton*, and the *New English Ministers*.

When the *Prophets* in Scripture have given their *Coats of Armes* and *Escutchions* to *Great Men,* Your *Honours* know the *Babylonian Monarch* hath the *Lyon*, the *Perſian* the *Beare*, the *Grecian* the *Leopard*, the *Romane* a *compound* of the former 3. moſt ſtrange and dreadfull, *Dan.* 7.

Their oppreſſing, plundring, raviſhing, murthering, not only of the *bodies*, but the *ſoules* of Men are large explaining *commentaries* of ſuch ſimilitudes.

Your *Honours* have been famous to the end of the World, for your unparallel'd *wiſdome, courage, juſtice, mercie*, in the vindicating your Civill *Lawes, Liberties,* &c. Yet let it not be grievous to your *Honours* thoughts to ponder a little, why all the *Prayers* and *Teares* and *Faſtings* in this Nation have not pierc'd the *Heavens*, and quench'd theſe *Flames*, which yet who knowes how far they'll ſpread, and when they'll out!

Your *Honours* have broke the jawes of the *Oppreſſour*, and taken the prey out of their Teeth (*Iob.* 29.) For which Act I believe it hath pleaſed the moſt High *God* to ſet a *Guard* (not only of Trained Men, but) of mighty *Angels*, to ſecure your fitting and the Citie.

I feare we are not *pardoned*, though *reprieved:* O that there may be a lengthning of *Londons* tranquilitie, of the *Parliaments* ſafetie, by *mercy* to the *poore!* Dan. 4.

Right Honorable, *Soule yokes, Soule oppreſsion*, plundrings, raviſhings, &c. are of a *crimſon* and *deepeſt dye*, and I believe the chiefe of *Englands* ſins, unſtopping the Viols of *Englands* preſent ſorrowes.

This glaſſe preſents your *Honours* with *Arguments* from *Religion, Reaſon, Experience*, all proving that the greateſt yoakes yet lying upon *Engliſh necks*, (the *peoples* and Your *own*) are of a *spirituall* and *soule* nature.

All former *Parliaments* have changed thefe yoakes according to their *confciences,* (*Popifh* or *Proteftant*) 'Tis now your *Honours* turne at *helme,* and (as your *task,* fo I hope your *refolution,* not to change (for that is but to turne the wheele, which another *Parliament,* and the very next may turne againe:) but to eafe the Subjects and Your felves from a *yoake* (as was once fpoke in a cafe not unlike *Act.* 15.) which neither You nor your Fathers were ever able to beare.

Moft *Noble Senatours,* Your *Fathers* (whofe *feats* You fill) are mouldred, and mouldring their *braines,* their *tongues,* &c. to *afhes* in the pit of *rotteneffe:* They and You muft fhortly (together with two *worlds* of men) appeare at the great *Barre:* It fhall then be no griefe of heart that you have now attended to the *cries* of *Soules, thoufands oppreffed, millions ravifhed* by the *Acts* and *Statutes* concerning *Soules,* not yet *repealed.*[1]

Of *Bodies impoverifhed, imprifoned,* &c. for their *foules* beliefe, yea flaughtered on heapes for *Religions* controverfies in the *Warres* of prefent and former Ages.

"Notwithftanding the fucceffe of later times, (wherein fundry opinions have been hatched about the fubject of *Religion*) a man may clearly difcerne with his eye, and as it were touch with his finger that according to the verity of holy Scriptures, &c. mens *confciences* ought in no fort to be violated, The famous faying of a late King of Bohemia.

---

[1] The fentence continues, with a femicolon inftead of the period.

"urged or conſtrained. And whenſoever men have
"attempted any thing by this violent courſe, whether
"openly or by ſecret meanes, the iſſue hath beene
"pernicious, and the cauſe of great and *wonderfull inno-*
"*vations* in the principalleſt and mightieſt *Kingdomes*
"and *Countries*, &c.[1]

It cannot be denied to be a pious and prudentiall *act* for Your *Honours* (according to your conſcience) to call for the advice of faithfull *Councellours* in the high debates concerning Your owne, and the ſoules of others.

Yet let it not be imputed as a *crime* for any *ſuppliant* to the *God* of *Heaven* for You, if in the humble ſenſe of what their ſoules beleeve, they powre forth (amongſt others) theſe three *requeſts* at the *Throne* of *Grace*.

Firſt, That neither Your *Honours*, nor thoſe excellent and worthy perſons, whoſe advice you ſeek, limit the holy *One* of *Iſrael* to their *apprehenſions, debates, concluſions*, rejecting or neglecting the humble and faithfull ſuggeſtions of any, though as baſe as ſpittle and clay, with which ſometimes *Chriſt Ieſus* opens the *eyes* of them that are borne blinde.

Secondly, That the preſent and future *generations* of the Sons of Men may never have cauſe to ſay that ſuch a *Parliament* (as *England* never enjoyed the like) ſhould modell the *worſhip* of the *living, eternall* and *inviſible God* after the *Bias* of any earthly *intereſt*, though of the higheſt concernment under the Sunne: And yet, ſaith that learned Sir *Francis Bacon* (how ever otherwiſe perſwaded, yet thus he confeſſeth:)

Eſſay of Religion.

---

[1] Quoted alſo in *Scriptures and Reaſons*, ſee note, *infra*.

"Such as hold *pressure* of *Conscience*, are guided therein
"by some private *interests* of their owne.¹

Thirdly, What ever way of *worshipping God* Your owne *Consciences* are perswaded to walke in, yet (from any bloody *act* of violence to the consciences of others) it may bee never told at *Rome* nor *Oxford*, that the *Parliament* of *England* hath committed a greater *rape*, then if they had forced or ravished the bodies of all the women in the *World*. {It is rarely seen that ever persons were persecuted for their conscience but by such persecution they were confirmed and hardned in their conscience.}

And that *Englands Parliament* (so famous throughout all Europe and the World) should at last turne *Papists*, *Prelatists*, *Presbyterians*, *Independents*, *Socinians*, *Familists*, *Antinomians*, &c. by confirming all these sorts of Consciences, by Civill force and violence to their Consciences.

---

¹ "It was a notable observation of a wise father, and no less ingenuously confessed; *that those who held and persuaded pressure of conscience, were commonly interessed therein themselves for their own ends.*" Essay 3, Unity in Religion, ed. of 1625; Spedding's Bacon, xii: 91.

To every Courteous Reader.

While I plead the Cauſe of *Truth* and *Innocencie* againſt the bloody *Doctrine* of *Perſecution* for cauſe of *conſcience*, I judge it not unfit to give *alarme* to my ſelfe, and all men to prepare to be *perſecuted* or hunted for cauſe of *conſcience*.

Whether thou ſtandeſt charged with 10 or but 2 *Talents*, if thou hunteſt any for cauſe of *conſcience*, how canſt thou ſay thou followeſt the *Lambe* of *God* who ſo abhorr'd that practice?

If *Paul*, if *Jeſus Chriſt* were preſent here at *London*, and the *queſtion* were propoſed what *Religion* would they approve of: The *Papiſts, Prelatiſts, Presbyterians, Independents,* &c. would each ſay, Of mine, of mine.

But put the ſecond queſtion, if one of the ſeverall ſorts ſhould by *major vote* attaine the *Sword* of ſteele: what weapons doth Chriſt Jeſus authorize them to fight with in His cauſe? Doe not all men hate the *perſecutor*, and every *conſcience* true or falſe complaine of cruelty, tyranny? &c.

Two *mountaines* of crying *guilt* lye heavie upon the backes of All that name the name of *Chriſt* in the eyes of *Jewes, Turkes* and *Pagans.*

Firſt, The blaſphemies of their *Idolatrous inventions, ſuperſtitions,* and moſt *unchriſtian converſations.*

Secondly, The bloody irreligious and inhumane *oppreſſions* and *deſtructions* under the maske or vaile of the Name of *Chriſt*, &c.

O how like is the *jealous Jehovah*, the conſuming fire to end theſe preſent *ſlaughters* in a greater ſlaughter of the holy Witneſſes? *Rev.* 11.

Six yeares preaching of so much Truth of *Christ* (as that time afforded in K. *Edwards* dayes) kindles the flames of Q. *Maries* bloody *persecutions*.

Who can now but expect that after so many scores of yeares *preaching* and *professing* of more *Truth*, and amongst so many great *contentions* amongst the very best of *Protestants*, a fierie furnace should be heat, and who sees not now the *fires* kindling?

I confesse I have little hopes till those flames are over, that this Discourse against the *doctrine* of *persecution* for cause of *conscience* should passe currant (I say not amongst the *Wolves* and *Lions*, but even amongst the *Sheep* of *Christ* themselves) yet *liberavi animam meam*, I have not hid within my *breast* my *souls* belief: And although sleeping on the bed either of the pleasures or profits of sinne thou thinkest thy conscience bound to smite at him that dares to waken thee? Yet in the middest of all these *civill* and *spirituall Wars* (I hope we shall agree in these particulars.)

First, how ever the proud (upon the advantage of an higher earth or ground) or'elooke the poore and cry out *Schismatickes*, *Hereticks*, &c. shall *blasphemers* and *seducers* scape unpunished? &c. Yet there is a sorer punishment in the *Gospel* for despising of *Christ* then *Moses*, even when the despiser of *Moses* was put to death without mercie, *Heb.* 10. 28, 29. He that beleeveth not shall bee damned, *Marke* 16. 16.

Secondly, what ever Worship, Ministry, Ministration, the best and purest are practised without *faith* and true perswasion that they are the true institutions of God, they are sin, sinfull worships, Ministries, &c. And however in Civill things we may be servants unto men, yet in Divine and Spirituall things the poorest *pesant* must disdaine the service of the highest *Prince:* Be ye not the servants of men, 1 Cor. 14. [vii: 23.]

Thirdly, without search and triall no man attaines this faith and right perswasion, 1 *Thes.* 5. Try all things.

In vaine have *English Parliaments* permitted *English Bibles* in the poorest *English* houses, and the simplest man or woman to search the Scriptures, if yet against their soules perswasion from the Scripture, they should be forced (as if they lived in *Spaine* or *Rome* it selfe without the sight of a *Bible*) to beleeve as the Church beleeves.

Fourthly, having tried, we must hold fast, 1 *Thessal.* 5. upon the losse of a Crowne, *Revel.* 13. [iii: 11.] we must not let goe for all the flea bitings of the present afflictions, &c. having bought Truth deare, we must not sell it cheape, not the least graine of it for the whole World, no not for the saving of Soules, though our owne most precious; least of all for the bitter sweetning of a little vanishing pleasure.

For a little puffe of credit and reputation from the changeable breath of uncertaine sons of men.[:]

For the broken bagges of Riches on Eagles wings: For a dreame of these, any or all of these which on our death-bed vanish and leave tormenting stings behinde them: Oh how much better is it from the love of Truth, from the love of the Father of lights, from whence it comes, from the love of the Sonne of God, who is the way and the Truth, to say as he, *John* 18. 37. For this end was I borne, and for this end came I into the World that I might beare witnesse to the Truth.

A Table of the principall Contents of the Booke.

*T*Ruth *and* Peace *their rare and seldome meeting.* Page 15
2 *Great complaints of Peace.* 16
Persecutors seldome plead Christ *but* Moses *for their Authour.* 17
Strife Christian and unchristian. ibid
A threefold dolefull cry. ibid.
The wonderfull providence of God in the writing of the arguments against persecution. 18
A definition of persecution discussed. 19
Conscience will not be restrained from its owne worship, nor constrained to another. 20
A chaste soule in Gods worship, compared to a chaste wife. ibid.
Gods people have erred from the very fundamentalls of visible worship. ibid
4 *Sorts of spirituall foundations in the New Testament.* 21
The 6 fundamentalls of the Christian Religion. ibid.
The comming out of Babel not locall, but mysticall. ibid.
The great ignorance of Gods people concerning the nature of a true Church. ibid.
Common-Prayer written against by the New English Ministers. 23
Gods people have worshipped God with false worships. ibid.
God is pleased sometimes to convey good unto his people beyond a promise. ibid.
A notable speech of King James *to a great Nonconformist turned persecutor.* 24
Civill peace discussed. ibid.

The difference between Spirituall and civill state.   Page 25
Six cases wherein Gods people have been usually accounted arrogant, and peace breakers, but most unjustly   26
The true causes of breach and disturbance of civill peace.   29
A preposterous way of suppressing errours.   30
Persecutors must needs oppresse both erroneous and true consciences.   ibid.
All persecutors of Christ professe not to persecute him.   ibid.
What is meant by the Hereticke, Tit. 3.   33
The word Heretick generally mistaken.   34
Corporall killing in the Law, typing out Spirituall killing in the Gospell.   36
The cariage of a Soule sensible of mercy, towards others in their blindnesse, &c.   38
The difference between the Church, and the World wherein it is, in all places.   38
The Church and civill State confusedly made all one.   39
The most peaceable accused for peace-breaking.   40
A large Examination of what is meant by the Tares, and letting of them alone.   ibid.
Sathans subtletie about the opening of Scripture.   41
Two sorts of Hypocrites,   44
The Lord Jesus the great Teacher by Parables, and the only Expounder of them.   44
Preaching for conversion is properly out of the Church.   45
The tares proved properly to signifie Antichristians.   ibid.
Gods Kingdome on Earth the visible Church.   46
The difference between the Wheat and the Tares, as also betweene these Tares and all others.   46
A civill Magistracie from the beginning of the world.   47
The Tares are to be tolerated the longest of all sinners.   48
The danger of infection by permitting of the Tares, assoyled. ibid.

The civill Magiſtrate not ſo particularly ſpoken to in the New Teſtament as Fathers, Maſters, &c. and why. Page 50
A two-fold ſtate of Chriſtianitie; Perſecuted under the Romane Emperours, and Apoſtated under the Romane Popes. ibid.
3 Particulars contained in that prohibition of Chriſt Jeſus concerning the Tares, Let them alone, Mat. 13. 51
Accompanying with Idolaters, 1 Cor. 5. *diſcuſſed.* 52
Civill Magiſtrates never inveſted by Chriſt Jeſus with the power and title of Defenders of the Faith. 54
Gods people ever earneſt with God for an Arme of Fleſh. 55
The dreadfull puniſhment of the blind Phariſes in 4 reſpects. ibid.
The point of ſeducing, infecting, or Soule killing, examined. 57
Strange confuſions in puniſhments. 59
The blood of Soules, Acts 20. *lies upon ſuch as profeſſe the Miniſtrie: the blood of Bodies only upon the State.* ibid.
Uſurpers and Heires of Chriſt Jeſus. 60
The Civill Magiſtrate bound to preſerve the bodies of their ſubjects, and not to deſtroy them for conſcience ſake. 61
The fire from heaven, Rev. 13. 13. 2 Tim. 2. 25, 26. *examined.* 62
The originall of the Chriſtian name, Acts 11. 63
A Civill ſword in Religion makes a Nation of hypocrites, Iſa. 10 64
A difference of the true and falſe Chriſt and Chriſtians. 65
The nature of the worſhip of unbeleeving and naturall perſons. ibid.
Antoninus Pius *his famous act concerning Religion.* 66
Iſa. 24. Mic. 4. 3. *concerning Chriſts viſible Kingdome diſcuſſed.* ibid.
Acts 20. 29. *The ſuppreſſing of Spirituall wolves diſcuſſed.* 67
It is in vaine to decline the name of the head of the Church, and yet to practiſe the headſhip. 68

Titus 1. 9. 10. *discussed.* Page 69
Unmercifull and bloody doctrine. 70
The Spirituall weapons, 2 Cor. 10. 4. *discussed.* ibid.
Civill weapons most improper in Spirituall causes. 71
The Spirituall artillerie, Eph. 6. *applied.* 72
Rom. 13. *concerning Civill Rulers power in Spirituall causes, largely examined.* 73
Pauls *appeale to* Cæsar *examined.* 77
And cleared by 5 arguments. ibid.
4 *Sorts of swords.* 79
What is to be understood by evill, Rom. 13. 4. 81
Though evill be alwayes evill, yet the permission of it may sometimes be good. 83
2 *Sorts of commands both from* Moses *and Christ.* 84
The permission of divorce in Israel, Mat. 19. 17, 18. ibid.
Usury in the Civill state lawfully permitted. 85
Seducing teachers, either Pagan, Jewish, Turkish or Antichristian, may yet be obedient subjects to the Civill Laws. 86
Scandalous livers against the Civill state. 87
Toleration of Jesabel *and* Balaam, *Rev.* 2. 14, 20. *examined.* 88
The Christian world hath swallowed up Christianity. 89
Christ Jesus the deepest polititian that ever was, yet commands he a toleration of Antichristians. 91
The Princes of the world seldome take part with Christ Jesus. 93
Buchanans *item to King* James. ibid.
King James *his sayings against persecution.* ibid.
King Steven *of Poland his sayings against persecution.* 93
Forcing of conscience a soule rape. 94
Persecution for conscience hath been the launcet which hath let blood the Nations. All Spirituall whores are bloody. ibid.
Poligamie or the many-wives of the Fathers. ibid.
David *advancing of Gods worship against order.* 95

Constantine *and the good Emperours confest to have done more hurt to the Name and Crowne of Christ then the bloody* Neroes *did.* Page 95
The language of persecuters. 96
Christs Lillies may flourish in the Church, notwithstanding the weeds in the world permitted. 97
Queen Elizabeth *and King* James *their persecuting for cause of Religion examined.* ibid.
Queen Elizabeth *confessed by Mr.* Cotton *to have almost fired the world in civill combustions.* 98
The Wars between the Papists and the Protestants. ibid.
The Wars and successe of the Waldensians against three Popes. 99
Gods people victorious overcommers, and with what weapons. ibid.
The Christian Church doth not persecute, but is persecuted. ibid.
The nature of excommunication. 100
The opinion of ancient Writers examined concerning the doctrine of persecution. 101
Constraint upon conscience in Old and New England. ibid.
The Indians of New England permitted in their worshipping of devils, 102
In 2 cases a false Religion will not hurt. 103
The absolute sufficiencie of the Sword of the Spirit. 104
A Nationall Church not instituted by Christ. ibid.
Man hath no power to make Lawes, to binde conscience. 105
Hearing of the word in a Church estate a part of Gods worship. 107
Papists plea for toleration of conscience. ibid.
Protestant partiality in the cause of persecution. 108
Pills to purge out the bitter humour of persecution. ibid.
Superstition and persecution have had many votes and suffrages from Gods owne people. 109
Soul-killing discussed. ibid.

Phineas *his act discussed.* Page 111
Eliah *his slaughters examined.* ibid.
Dangerous consequences flowing from the civill Magistrates power in Spirituall cases. 114
The world turned upside downe. 114
The wonderfull answer of the Ministers of New England to the Ministers of Old. ibid.
Lamentable differences even amongst them that feare God. 115
The doctrine of persecution ever drives the most godly out of the world. 116
A Modell of Church and Civill power composed by Mr. Cotton, *and the Ministers of New England, and sent to Salem, (as a further confirmation of the bloody doctrine of persecution for cause of conscience) examined and answered.* 118
Christs power in the Church confest to be above all Magistrates in Spirituall things. 119
Isa. 49. 23. *lamentably wrested.* ibid.
The civill Commonweale, and the Spirituall Commonweale the Church not inconsistent, though independent the one on the other. 120
Christ ordinances put upon a whole city or Nation may civilize them, and moralize, but not Christianize before repentance first wrought. 121
Mr. Cottons *and the New English Ministers confession that the Magistrate hath neither Civill nor Spirituall power in Soul matters.* 122
The Magistrates and the Church (by Mr. Cottons *grounds) in one and the same cause made the Judges on the Bench, and delinquents at the Bar.* 123
A demonstrative illustration that the Magistrate cannot have power over the Church in Spirituall or Church causes. 124
The true way of the God of Peace in differences between the Church and the Magistrate. 125

The tearms Godlineſſe and Honeſty explained, 1 Tim. 2. 1. *and honeſty proved not to ſignifie in that place the righteouſnes of the ſecond Table.* Page 127
The forcing of men to Gods worſhip, the greateſt breach of civill peace. 129
The Roman Cæſars *of* Chriſts *time deſcribed.* ibid.
It pleaſed not the Lord Jeſus in the inſtitution of the Chriſtian Church to appoint and raiſe up any Civill Governours to take care of his worſhip. 130
The true cuſtodes utriuſque Tabulæ, *and keepers of the Ordinances and worſhip of Jeſus Chriſt.* ibid.
The Kings of Ægypt, Moab, Philiſtia, Aſſyria, Nineveh, were not charged with the worſhip of God, as the Kings of Judah were. 131
Maſters of families not charged under the Goſpel to force all the conſciences of their families to worſhip. 132
Gods people have then ſhined brighteſt in Godlines, when they have enjoyed leaſt quietneſſe. 134
Few Magiſtrates, few Men, ſpiritually good; yet divers ſorts of commendable Goodnes beſide ſpirituall. ibid.
Civill power originally and fundamentally in the People. Mr. Cotton *and the* New Engliſh *give the power of Chriſt into the hands of the Commonweale.* 137
Lawes concerning Religion, of two ſorts. 138
The very Indians abhor to diſturbe any Conſcience at Worſhip. 139
Canons and conſtitutions pretended Civill, but indeed Eccleſiaſticall. ibid.
A threefold guilt lying upon Civill powers, commanding the Subjects Soule in Worſhip. 143
Perſons may with leſſe ſinne be forced to marry whom they cannot love, then to worſhip where they cannot beleeve. ibid.

As the cause, so the weapons of the Beast and the Lambe are infinitely different. Page 146
Artaxerxes his Decree examined. 147
The summe of the Examples of the Gentile Kings decrees concerning Gods worship in Scripture. 149
The Doctrine of putting to death Blasphemers of Christ, cuts off the hopes of the Jewes partaking in his blood. 181
The direfull effects of fighting for Conscience. 151
Errour is confident as well as Truth. 152
Spirituall prisons. 153
Some Consciences not so easily healed and cured as men imagine. 154
Persecuters dispute with Hereticks, as a tyrannicall Cat with the poore Mouse: And with a true Witnes, as a roaring Lyon with an innocent Lambe in his paw. 155
Persecuters endure not the name of Persecuters. 156
Psal. 101 concerning cutting off the wicked, examined. 158
No difference of Lands and Countries, since Christ Jesus his comming. ib.
T*he New English separate in America, but not in Europe.* 159
Christ Jesus forbidding his followers to permit Leaven in the Church, doth not forbid to permit Leaven in the World. 160
The Wall (Cant. 8. 9.) *discussed.* 161
Every Religion commands its professors to heare only its own Priests or Ministers. 162
Jonah his preaching to the Ninevites discussed. 162
Hearing of the Word discussed. ibid.
Eglon his rising up to Ehuds message, discussed. ibid.
A two-fold Ministrie of Christ: First, Apostolicall, properly converting. Secondly, Feeding or Pastorall. 162
T*he* New English *forcing the people to Church, and yet not to Religion (as they say) forcing them to be of no Religion all their dayes* 163

The Civill State can no more lawfully compell the Consciences of men to Church to heare the Word, then to receive the Sacraments. Page 164
No president in the Word, of any people converting and baptizing themselves. 166
True conversion to visible Christianitie, is not only from sins against the second Table, but from false Worships also. ibid.
The Commission, Mat. 28 discussed. 167
The Civill Magistrates not betrusted with that Commission. ibid.
Jehosaphat, 2 Chron. 17. a figure of Christ Jesus in his Church, not of the Civill Magistrate in the State. 168
The maintenance of the Ministrie, Gal. 6. 6. examined. ibid.
Christ Jesus never appointed a maintenance of the Ministrie from the impenitent and unbelieving. 169
They that compell men to heare, compell them also to pay for their hearing and conversion. ibid.
Luc. 14. Compell them to come in, examined. ibid.
Naturall men can neither truly worship nor mainteine it. 170
The Nationall Church of the Jewes might well be forced to a setled maintenance: but not so the Christian Church. 171
The maintenance which Christ hath appointed his Ministrie in the Church. 172
The Universities of Europe causes of universall sins and plagues: yet Schooles are honourable for tongues and Arts. 173
The true Church is Christs Schoole, and Believers his Scholars. ibid.
Mr. Ainsworth excellent in the Tongues, yet no Universitie man. 174
K. Henry the 8. set down in the Popes chaire in England. 175
Apocrypha, Homilies, and Common Prayer precious to our forefathers. ib.
Reformation proved fallible. 176

The president of the Kings of Israel & Judah largely examined. Page 178

The Persian Kings example make strongly against the doctrine of Persecution. 179

1. *The difference of the Land of Canaan from all lands and countries, in 7 [8] particulars.* ibid.

2. *The difference of the people of Israel from all other peoples, in 7 particulars.* 183

Wonderfull turnings of Religion in England *in twelve yeares revolution.* 185

The Pope not unlike to recover his Monarchy over Europe, before his downfall. ibid.

Israel Gods only Church might well renew that Nationall Covenant and ceremoniall worship, which other Nations cannot doe. 187

The difference of the Kings and Governours of Israel from all Kings and Governours of the world, in 4 particulars. 188

5 *Demonstrative arguments proving the unsoundnesse of the maxime, viz. The Church and Commonweale are like* Hypocrates *twins.* 189

A sacrilegious prostitution of the name Christian. 192

David *immediately inspired by God in his ordering of Church affairs.* 193

Solomons *deposing of* Abiathar, 1 Kings 2. 26, 27. *discussed.* 194

The liberties of Christs Churches in the choice of her officers. 195

A civill influence dangerous to the State liberties. ibid.

Jehosaphats *fast examined.* ibid.

God will not wrong Cæsar, *and* Cæsar *should not wrong God.* 196

The famous acts of Josiah *examined.* ibid.

Magistracie in generall from God, the particular formes from the people. ibid.

Israel confirmed in a Nationall Covenant by revelations, signes and miracles, but not so any other Land. ibid.

Kings and Nations often plant and often plucke up Religions. Page 197
A Nationall Church ever subject to turne and returne. ibid.
A woman, Papissa, *or head of the Church.* ibid.
The Papists neerer to the truth, concerning the governour of the Church, then most Protestants. 198
The Kingly power of the Lord Jesus troubles all the Kings and Rulers of the World. ibid.
A twofold exaltation of Christ. ibid.
A monarchicall and Ministeriall power of Christ. 199
3 Great competitours for the Ministeriall power of Christ. ibid.
The Pope pretendeth to the Ministeriall power of Christ, yet upon the point chalengeth the Monarchicall also. ibid.
3 Great factions in England *striving for the Arme of Flesh.* 200
The Churches of the separation ought in humanity, and subjects liberty, not to be oppressed, but at least permitted. 201
7 Reasons proving that the Kings of Israel and Judah can have no other but a Spirituall Antitype. 202
Christianitie addes not to the nature of a Civill Commonweale; nor doth want of Christianitie diminish it. 203
Most strange, yet most true consequences from the Civill Magistrates being the Antitype of the Kings of Israel and Judah. ibid.
If no Religion but what the Commonweale approve; then no Christ, no God, but at the pleasure of the World. 204
The true Antitype of the Kings of Israel and Judah. ibid.
4. The difference of Israels Statutes and Lawes from all others in 3 particulars. ibid.
5. The difference of Israels Punishments & Rewards from all others. 205
Temporall prosperitie most proper to the Nationall state of the Jewe. ibid.

The Excommunication in Israel. Page 206
The corporall stoning in the Law typed out spirituall stoning in the Gospel. ibid.
The wars of Israel typicall and unparalleld, but by the Spirituall wars of Spirituall Israel. ibid.
The famous typicall captivitie of the Jewes. 207
Their wonderfull victories. 208
The mysticall Army of white troopers. 209
Whether the Civill state of Israel was presidentiall. ibid.
Great unfaithfulnesse in Magistrates to cast the burthen of judging and establishing Christianitie upon the Commonweale. 210
Thousands of lawfull Civill Magistrates, who never heare of Jesus Christ. 211
Nero and the persecuting Emperours not so injurious to Christianity, as Constantine *and others, who assumed a power in Spirituall things.* ibid.
They who force the conscience of others, cry out of persecution, when their owne are forced. 212
Constantine *and others wanted not so much affection, as information of judgement.* ibid.
Civill Authoritie giving and lending their Hornes to Bishops dangerous to Christs truth. ibid.
The Spirituall power of Christ Iesus, compared in Scripture to the incomparable horne of the Rhinocerot. 213
The nursing Fathers and Mothers, Isa. 49. ibid.
The civill Magistrate owes 3 things to the true Church of Christ. 214
The civill Magistrate owes 2 things to false Worshippers. 214
The rise of High Commissions. 215
Pious Magistrates & Ministers consciences are perswaded for that, which other as pious Magistrates & Ministers consciences condemn. 215

An apt similitude discussed concerning the Civill Magistrate. Page 216
A grievous charge against the Christian Church and the King of it. 222
A strange Law in New England formerly against excommunicate persons. ibid.
A dangerous doctrine against all Civill Magistrates. 223
Originall sin charged to hurt the Civill state. ibid.
They who give the Magistrate more then his due, are apt to disroabe him of what is his. 224
A strange double picture. 226
The great priviledges of the true Church of Christ. 227
2 Similitudes illustrating the true power of the Magistrate. ibid.
A marvelous chalenge of more power under the Christian, then under the Heathen Magistrate. 229
Civill Magistrates, derivatives from the fountains or bodies of people. 230
A beleeving Magistrate no more a Magistrate then an unbeleeving. ibid.
The excellencie of Christianity in all callings. ibid.
The Magistrate like a Pilot in the Ship of the Commonweale. 231
The tearmes Heathen and Christian Magistrates. ibid.
The unjust and partiall liberty to some consciences and bondage unto all others. 232
The commission Matth. 28. 19, 20. *not proper to Pastors and teachers, least of all to the Civill Magistrate.* 233
Unto whom now belongs the care of all the Churches, &c. ibid.
Acts 15. *commonly misapplied.* 234
The promise of Christs presence Mat. 18. *distinct from that* Mat. 28. 235
Church administrations firstly charged upon the Ministers thereof. 236

Queen Elizabeths *Bishops truer to their principles then many of a better spirit and profession.* Page 237

Mr. Barrowes *profession concerning Queen* Elizabeth. ibid.

The *inventions of men swarving from the true essentialls of civill and Spirituall Commonweales.* 239

A great question viz. *whether only Church members, that is godly persons in a particular Church estate, be only eligible into the Magistracie.* ib.

The *world being divided into* 30 *parts,* 25 *never heard of Christ.* 240

Lawfull civill states where Churches of Christ are not. ibid.

Few Christians Wise and noble and qualified for affaires of State. ibid.

SCRIPTURES AND REASONS

written long since by a *Witnesse* of Iesus Christ, close *Prisoner* in *Newgate*, against *Persecution* in cause of *Conscience*; and sent some while since to Mr. *Cotton*, by a Friend who thus wrote:

In the multitude *of* Councellours *there is safety: It is therefore humbly desired to be instructed in this point: viz.*

Whether Persecution *for cause of* Conscience *be not against the Doctrine of* Iesus Christ *the* King of Kings. *The Scriptures and Reasons are these.*

Because *Christ* commandeth that the *Tares* and *Wheat* (which some understand are those that walke in the *Truth*, and those that walke in *Lies*) should be *let alone* in the *World*, and not *plucked* up untill the *Harvest*, which is the end of the *World*, Matth. 13. 30. 38. &c.

The same commandeth *Matth.* 15. 14. that they that are *Blinde* (as some interpret, led on in false *Religion*, and are offended with him for teaching true *Religion*) should be *let alone*, referring their punishment unto their falling into the *Ditch*.

Againe, *Luke* 9. 54, 55. hee reproved his *Disciples* who would have had *Fire* come downe from Heaven and devoure those *Samaritanes* who would not receive Him, in these words: Ye know not of what *Spirit* ye are, the fon of Man is not come to deftroy *Mens lives*, but to fave them.

4   *Paul* the Apoftle of our Lord teacheth, 2 *Tim.* 24. 2. That the fervant of the Lord muft not *ftrive*, but muft be *gentle* toward *all Men*, fuffering the Evill Men, inftructing them with *meekneſſe* that are contrary minded, proving if *God* at any time will give them *repentance*, that they may acknowledge the Truth, and come to *amendment* out of that fnare of the *devill*, &c.

5   According to thefe bleſſed *Commandements*, the holy *Prophets* foretold, [2] that when the *Law* of *Moſes* (concerning *Worſhip*) fhould ceafe, and *Chriſts Kingdome* be eftablifhed, *Eſa.* 2. 4. *Mic.* 4. 3, 4. They fhall breake their *Swords* into *Mathookes*, and their *Speares* into *Sithes*. And *Eſa.* 11. 9. Then fhall none hurt or deftroy in all the *Mountaine* of my Holineſſe, &c. And when he came, the fame he *taught* and *practiſed*, as before: fo did his *Diſciples* after him, for the *Weapons* of his *Warfare* are not *carnall* (faith the Apoftle) 2 *Cor.* 10. 4.

But he chargeth ftraitly that his Difciples fhould be fo far from perfecuting thofe that would not bee of their Religion, that when they were *perſecuted* they fhould *pray* (*Matth.* 5.) when they were *curſed* they fhould *bleſſe*, &c.

And the Reafon feemes to bee, becaufe they who now are *Tares*, may hereafter become *Wheat* ; they who are now *blinde*, may hereafter *ſee* ; they that now *reſiſt* him, may hereafter *receive* him ; they that are now in the *devils ſnare*, in *adverſeneſſe* to the *Truth*, may hereafter come to *repentance* ; they that are now *blaſphemers* and *perſecutors* (as *Paul* was) may in time become *faithfull* as he ; they that are now *idolators* as the *Corinths* once were (1 *Cor.* 6. 9.) may hereafter become *true worshippers* as they; they that are now *no people* of *God*, nor under *mercy* (as the Saints fometimes were, 1 *Pet.* 2. 20.) may hereafter become the people of *God*, and obtain *mercy*, as they.

Some come not till the 11. houre, *Matth.* 20. 6. if thofe that come not till the *laft houre* fhould be *deftroyed*, becaufe they come not at the *firft*, then fhould they never come but be prevented.

All which *premifes* are in all humility referred to your godly wife *confideration*.

Becaufe this *perfecution* for caufe of *confcience* is againft II. the *profeffion* and *practice* of *famous Princes*.

Firft, you may pleafe to confider the fpeech of *King James*, in his *Majefties Speech at Parliament*, 1609.[1] He faith, it is a fure *Rule* in *divinity*, that God never loves to plant his *Church* by *violence* and *bloodfhed*.

And in his *Highneffe Apologie*, pag. 4. [2] fpeaking of fuch *Papifts* that tooke the Oath, thus:[1]

"I gave good proofe that I intended no *perfecution* "againft them for *confcience* caufe, but onely defired to "bee fecured for *civill obedience*, which for *confcience* "caufe they are bound to performe.

And pag. 60. [22] fpeaking of *Blackwell*[2] (the Arch-

---

[1] *The Workes of the Moft High and Mightie Prince James.* Publifhed by James, Bifhop of Winton, &c. London, 1616, p. 544. do. p. 248.

[2] George Blackwell, a Roman Catholic divine, was commiffioned to act as archprieft over the fecular clergy in England by Cardinal Cajetan, March 7, 1598, in order to meet fome of the difficulties arifing from the lack of a Romifh epifcopate, and was confirmed and approved by a bull from Pope Clement VIII, April 6, 1599. He took the oath of allegiance enacted in confequence of the Gunpowder Plot, and openly expreffed his approbation of it, though Paul V. had condemned it. His fuperiors at Rome could not endure his attempts to induce Roman Catholics to take the oath, and he was fuperfeded in 1508. Rofe, Biog. Dict., IV; Wood's Athenæ Oxonienfes, ii: 122.

priest) his *Majesty* faith,[1] "It was never my intention to "lay any thing to the said *Arch-Priests* charge (as I "have never done to any) for *cause of conscience*. And in his *Highnesse Exposition* on *Revel*. 20. printed 1588. and after [in] 1603. his *Majesty* writeth thus:[2] "Sixthly, "the compassing of the *Saints* [3] and the *besieging* of "the *beloved City*, declareth unto us a certaine *note* of a "*false Church*, to be *Persecution*, for they come to seeke "the *faithfull*, the *faithfull* are them that are sought: "the *wicked* are the *besiegers*, the *faithfull* are the "*besieged*.

Secondly, the saying of *Stephen* King of *Poland*:[3] "I "am *King* of *Men*, not of *Consciences*, a Commander of "*Bodies*, not of *Soules*.

Thirdly, the *King* of *Bohemia* hath thus written:

"And notwithstanding the successe of the later times "(wherein sundry *opinions* have beene hatched about the "subject of *Religion*) may make one clearly discerne "with his *eye*, and as it were to touch with his *Finger*, "that according to the veritie of *Holy Scriptures*, and a "*Maxime* heretofore told and maintained, by the ancient "Doctors of the *Church*; That *mens consciences* ought "in no sort to bee *violated, urged,* or *constrained*; and "whensoever men have attempted any thing by this "*violent course*, whether openly or by secret meanes, the "issue hath beene *pernicious*, and the cause of great

---

[1] *The Workes of the Most High and Mightie Prince James*, p. 268.
[2] *The Workes of the Most High and Mightie Prince James*, p. 79.
[3] Stephen Bathori was King of Poland 1575–1586. Though a convert to the Roman Church he used no intolerance towards his Protestant subjects. He said, "I reign over persons; but it is God who rules the conscience. Know that God has reserved three things to himself; the creation of something out of nothing, the knowledge of futurity, and the government of the conscience." *Lardner's Cabinet Cyclopedia, Poland*, p. 167.

"and wonderfull *Innovations* in the principalleſt and "mightieſt *Kingdomes* and *Countries* of all Chriſten-"dome.

And further his *Majeſty* ſaith: "So that once more "we doe profeſſe before *God* and the *whole World*, that "from this time forward wee are firmly reſolved not to "*perſecute* or *moleſt*, or ſuffer to be *perſecuted* or *moleſted*, "any perſon whoſoever for *matter of Religion*, no not "they that profeſſe *themſelves* to be of the *Romiſh Church*, "neither to trouble or diſturbe them in the exerciſe of "their *Religion*, ſo they live conformable to the *Lawes* "of the *States*, &c.[1]

And for the practice of this, where is *perſecution* for cauſe of *conſcience* except in *England* and where *Popery* reignes, [?] and there neither in all places, as appeareth by *France*, *Poland*, and other places.

Nay, it is not practiſed amongſt the *Heathen* that acknowledge not the *true God*, as the *Turke*, *Perſian*, and others.

Thirdly, becauſe *perſecution* for cauſe of conſcience is condemned by the ancient and later *Writers*, yea and *Papiſts* themſelves.

3 *Rea.*

---

[1] This paragraph, quoted alſo in the Addreſs to Parliament, p. 7, is from the manifeſto iſſued by the Elector Palatine, Frederick the Fifth, who had been elected King of Bohemia againſt Ferdinand the Second, Archduke of Auſtria and Emperor of Germany, at the beginning of the Thirty Years War. Schiller, *Thirty Years War*, Book I. James the Firſt, whoſe daughter he married, was entirely oppoſed to his taking the crown, and refuſed to recogniſe him. Hume, *Hiſtory of England*, Chap. 48. It was in the ſame year (1620) in which he was defeated that this "Humble Supplication" from which theſe "Scriptures and Reaſons" are taken was printed. The Commons had boldly declared their ſympathy with his misfortunes, and ſo circumſtances gave ſignificance to opinions uttered by one who was confidered a repreſentative of the Proteſtant cauſe, and which were ſo much in advance of thoſe of James. Brandt, *The Hiſtory of the Reformation in and about the Low Countries*, iv: lib. 52, p. 200.

Hilarie againſt *Auxentius*[1] ſaith thus: The *Chriſtian Church* doth not *perſecute*, but is *perſecuted*. And lamentable it is to ſee the great folly of theſe times, and to ſigh at the fooliſh opinion of this world, in that men thinke by humane aide to helpe *God*, and with worldly pompe and power to undertake to defend the *Chriſtian Church*. I aske you *Biſhops*, what helpe uſed the *Apoſtles* in the publiſhing of the *Goſpel*? with the aid of what power did they preach *Chriſt*, and converted the *Heathen* from their *idolatry* to *God*? When they were in *priſons*, and lay in *chaines*, did they praiſe and give thankes to God for any *dignities, graces*, [4] and *favours* received from the *Court*? Or do you thinke that *Paul* went about with *Regall Mandates*, or *Kingly authority*, to gather and eſtabliſh the *Church* of *Chriſt*? ſought he *protection* from *Nero, Veſpaſian*?

The *Apoſtles* wrought with their *hands* for their owne *maintenance*, travailing by *land* and *water* from *Towne* to *Citie*, to preach *Chriſt*: yea the more they were *forbidden*, the more they *taught* and preached *Chriſt*. But now alas, *humane helpe* muſt *aſſiſt* and *protect* the *Faith*, and give the ſame countenance to and by vaine and *worldly honours*.[2] Doe men ſeek to defend the *Church of Chriſt*? as if hee by his power were unable to performe it.

The ſame againſt the *Arrians*.[1]

The *Church* now, which formerly by induring *miſery* and *impriſonment* was knowne to be a *true Church*, doth

---

[1] S. Hilarii Opera, Lib. I, Contra Arianos vel Auxentium, Cap. 3, 4, pp. 465, 466; Venetiis, 1749.

[2] This ſentence may be read with a period after "countenance," the remaining words being connected with the following interrogation: or by changing the order of the words, thus, "and give countenance to the ſame by vaine and worldly honours."

now terrifie others by *imprifonment, banifhment,* and *mifery,* and boafteth that fhe is highly efteemed of the *world,* when as the true *Church* [fhe] cannot but be hated of the fame.

Tertull. ad Scapulam :[1] It agreeth both with *humane reafon,* and *naturall equity,* that every man *worfhip* God uncompelled, and beleeve what he will; for it neither hurteth nor profiteth any one another mans *Religion* and *Beleefe :* Neither befeemeth it any *Religion* to compell another to be of their *Religion,* which willingly and freely fhould be imbraced, and not by conftraint : for as much as the *offerings* were required of thofe that freely and with good will offered, and not from the *contrary.*

Jerom. in proœm. lib. 4. in Jeremiam.[2] *Herefie* muft be cut off with the *Sword* of the *Spirit :* let us ftrike through with the *Arrowes* of the *Spirit* all *Sonnes* and *Difciples* of mif-led *Hereticks,* that is, with *Teftimonies* of holy *Scriptures.* The flaughter of *Hereticks* is by the word of God.

Brentius[3] upon 1 *Cor.* 3. No man hath power to make or give Lawes to *Chriftians,* whereby to binde their *confciences ;* for willingly, freely, and uncompelled, with a ready defire and cheerfull minde, muft thofe that come, run unto *Chrift.*

Luther in his Booke of the *Civill Magiftrate*[4] faith;

[1] Tertulliani Opera, Tom. 1, Cap. 2, p. 152, Antverpiæ, 1583; Lib'ry of Fathers, Tertullian, i: 143, Oxford, 1842.

[2] S. Hieronymi Opera, in prœmium lib. 4, in Jeremiam, pp. 615–616, Parifiis, 1704. Only the firft member of this fentence is found in the place cited. "*Quod fi cavendum nobis eft, ne veterem lædere videamur neceffitudinem, fi fuperbiffimam hærefim fpirituali mucrone truncemus.*"

[3] The works of Brentius, 8 vols. folio, Tubingen, 1575–1590, are not within the Editor's reach, nor on the catalogues of any of the public libraries of the country, fo far as examined.

[4] Luther's Sämtliche Schriften, herausgegeben J. G. Walch, 10ʳ Theil, 452. Halle. 1744.

The *Lawes* of the *Civill Magiſtrates* government extends no further then over the *body* or *goods*, and to that which is *externall*: for over the *ſoule God* will not ſuffer any man to *rule*: onely he *himſelfe* will rule there. Wherefore whoſoever doth undertake to give *Lawes* unto the *Soules* and *Conſciences* of Men, he uſurpeth that *government* himſelfe which appertaineth unto *God*, &c.

Therefore upon 1 *Kings* 5.[1] In the building of the *Temple* there was no *ſound* of *Iron* heard, to ſignifie that *Chriſt* will have in his *Church* a *free* and a *willing* People, not compelled and conſtrained by *Lawes* and *Statutes*.

5] Againe he ſaith upon *Luk.* 22.[2] It is not the true *Catholike Church*, which is defended by the *Secular Arme* or humane Power, but the *falſe* and *feigned Church*, which although it carries the *Name* of a *Church* yet it denies the power thereof.

And upon *Pſal.* 17.[3] he ſaith: For the true *Church* of *Chriſt* knoweth not *Brachium ſæculare*, which the *Biſhops* now adayes, chiefly uſe.

Againe, in *Poſtil. Dom.* 1. *poſt Epiphan.*[4] he ſaith: Let not *Chriſtians* be *commanded*, but *exhorted*: for, He that willingly will not doe that, whereunto he is friendly exhorted, he is no *Chriſtian*: wherefore they that doe compell thoſe that are not willing, ſhew thereby that they are not *Chriſtian Preachers*, but *Worldly Beadles*.

Againe, upon 1 *Pet.* 3.[5] [ii: 17] he ſaith: If the

---

[1] Schriften, x: 438.
[2] Schriften, xiii: 2818. Auſlegung des Evangelii am Bartholomews Tag, Luke xxii: 24–30. "God will keep and govern his Church only by his Word, and not by human power." It may be that the reference is to ſome other paſſage.
[3] This paſſage is not found in his explanation of the 117th Pſalm, Theil 4^r, 1261.
[4] Schriften, xii: 429. Auſlegung der Epiſtel am erſten Sonntage nach Epiphania.
[5] Schriften, ix: 740. Auſlegung der erſten Ep. Petri, cap. 2, v. 17.

C*ivill Magiſtrate* ſhall command me to believe thus and thus: I ſhould anſwer him after this manner: *Lord*, or *Sir*, Looke you to your C*ivill* or *Worldly Government*, Your Power extends not ſo farre as to command any thing in *Gods Kingdome:* Therefore herein I may not heare you. For if you cannot beare it, that any ſhould uſurpe *Authoritie* where you have to Command, how doe you thinke that *God* ſhould ſuffer you to thruſt him from his Seat, and to ſeat your ſelfe therein?

Laſtly, the Papiſts, the *Inventors of Perſecution*, in a wicked Booke of theirs ſet forth in *K. James* his *Reigne*, thus:

Moreover, the *Meanes* which *Almighty God* appointed his Officers to uſe in the Converſion of *Kingdomes* and *Nations*, and People, was *Humilitie, Patience, Charitie*; ſaying, Behold I ſend you as *Sheepe* in the midſt of *Wolves*, Mat. 10. 16. He did not ſay, Behold I ſend you as *Wolves* among *Sheepe*, to kill, impriſon, ſpoile and devoure thoſe unto whom they were ſent.

Againe *verſ.* 7. he ſaith: They to whom I ſend you, will deliver you up into *Councells*, and in their *Synagogues* they will ſcourge you; and to *Preſidents* and to *Kings* ſhall you be led for my ſake. He doth not ſay: You whom I ſend, ſhall deliver the people (whom you ought to convert) unto *Councells*, and put them in Priſons, and lead them to *Preſidents*, and *Tribunall Seates*, and make their *Religion Felony* and *Treaſon*.

Againe he ſaith, *verſ.* 32. When ye enter into an Houſe, ſalute it, ſaying, Peace be unto this Houſe: he doth not ſay, You ſhall ſend *Purſevants* to ranſack or ſpoile his Houſe.

Againe he ſaid, *John* 10. The good *Paſtour* giveth

his life for his Sheep, the *Thiefe* commeth not but to steale, kill and destroy. He doth not say, The *Theefe* giveth his life for his Sheep, and the Good *Pastour* 6] commeth not but to steale, kill and destroy.

So that we holding our peace, our *Adversaries* themselves speake for us, or rather for the Truth.

To answer some maine *Objections*.

And first, that it is no *prejudice* to the *Common wealth*, if *Libertie of Conscience* were suffred to such as doe feare *God* indeed, as is or will be manifest in such mens lives and conversations.

Abraham abode among the *Canaanites* a long time, yet contrary to them in *Religion*, Gen. 13. 7. & 16. 13. Againe he sojourned in *Gerar*, and K. *Abimelech* gave him leave to abide in his Land, *Gen.* 20. 21. 23. 24. [xx, xxi: 33. 34.]

Isaack also dwelt in the same Land, yet contrary in *Religion*, Gen. 26.

Jacob lived 20 yeares in one House with his Unkle *Laban*, yet differed in *Religion*, Gen. 31.

The people of *Israel* were about 430 yeares in that infamous land of *Egypt*, and afterwards 70 yeares in *Babylon*, all which time they differed in *Religion* from the States, *Exod.* 12. & 2 *Chron.* 36.

Come to the time of *Christ*, where *Israel* was under the *Romanes*, where lived divers Sects of *Religion*, as *Herodians, Scribes* and *Pharises, Saduces* and *Libertines, Thudæans* and *Samaritanes*, beside the Common Religion of the *Jewes, Christ* and his *Apostles*. All which differed from the Common *Religion* of the State, which was like the Worſhip of *Diana*, which almoſt the whole world then worſhipped, *Acts* 19. 20. [27.]

All theſe lived under the Government of *Cæſar*, being nothing hurtfull unto the *Common-wealth*, giving unto *Cæſar* that which was his. And for their *Religion* and Conſciences towards God, he left them to themſelves, as having no Dominion over their *Soules* and *Conſciences*. And when the Enemies of the Truth raiſed up any *Tumults*, the wiſedome of the *Magiſtrate* moſt wiſely appeaſed them, *Acts* 18 14. & 19. 35.

The *Answer* Of Mr. Iohn

Cotton of *Boston* in *New-England*,
To the aforesaid Arguments against
Persecution for Cause of *Conscience*.

Professedly mainteining *Persecution for Cause of Conscience*.

The *Question* which you put, is, Whether *Persecution* for cause of *Conscience*, be not against the *Doctrine* of *Jesus Christ* the *King of Kings*.

Now by *Persecution* for Cause of *Conscience*, I conceive you meane, either for professing some point of *Doctrine* which you believe in Conscience to be the Truth, or for practising some *Worke* which in *Conscience* you believe to be a *Religious Duty*.

Now in Points of *Doctrine* some are *fundamentall*, without right beliefe whereof a Man cannot be *saved*: Others are *circumstantiall* or lesse principall, wherein Men may differ in judgement, without prejudice of *salvation* on either part.

In like sort, in Points of *Practice*, some concerne the waightier Duties of the *Law*, as, What *God* we worship, and with what kinde of *Worship*; whether such, as if it be *Right*, fellowship with *God* is held; if *Corrupt*, fellowship with Him is lost.

Againe, in Points of *Doctrine* and *Worship* lesse Principall: either they are held forth in a meeke and *peaceable* way, though the Things be *Erroneous* or unlawfull:

Or they are held forth with such *Arrogance* and *Impetuousnesse*, as tendeth and reacheth (even of it selfe) to the disturbance of *Civill Peace*.

Finally, let me adde this one distinction more: When we are persecuted for *Conscience* sake, It is either for *Conscience* rightly informed, or for erronious and blind *Conscience*.

These things premised, I would lay down mine Answer to the Question in certaine *Conclusions*.

1. First, it is not not lawfull to persecute any for *Conscience* sake *Rightly informed*; for in *persecuting* such, *Christ* himselfe is persecuted in them, *Acts* 9. 4.

2. Secondly, for an *Erronious* and *blind Conscience*, (even in fundamentall [8] and weighty Points) It is not lawfull to persecute any, till after *Admonition* once or twice: and so the Apostle directeth, *Tit.* 3. 10. and giveth the Reason, that in *fundamentall* and principall points of Doctrine or Worship, the Word of *God* in such things is so cleare, that hee cannot but bee convinced in *Conscience* of the dangerous Errour of his way, after once or twice *Admonition*, wisely and faithfully dispensed. And then if any one persist, it is not out of *Conscience*, but against *his Conscience*, at the Apostle saith, *vers.* 11. He is subverted and sinneth, being condemned of Himselfe, that is, of his owne *Conscience*. So that if such a Man after such Admonition shall still *persist* in the Errour of his way, and be therefore punished; He is not *persecuted* for Cause of *Conscience*, but for sinning *against* his Owne *Conscience*.

3. Thirdly, In things of lesser *moment*, whether Points of *Doctrine* or *Worship*, If a man hold them forth in a Spirit of Christian *Meeknesse* and *Love* (though with

Zeale and *Conſtancie*) he is not to be *perſecuted*, but *tolerated*, till *God* may be pleaſed to manifeſt his Truth to him, *Phil.* 3. 17. *Rom.* 14. 1, 2, 3, 4.

But if a Man hold forth or profeſſe any *Errour* or falſe way, with a *boyſterous* and *arrogant* ſpirit, to the diſturbance of *Civill peace*, he may juſtly be puniſhed according to the qualitie and meaſure of the *diſturbance* cauſed by him.

4.

Now let us conſider of your *Reaſons* or *Objections* to the contrary.

Your firſt head of *Objections* is taken from the *Scripture*.

Object. 1. Becauſe Chriſt commandeth to let alone the *Tares* and *Wheat* to grow together unto the *Harveſt*, Mat. 13. 30. 38.

Anſw. *Tares* are not *Briars* and *Thornes*, but partly *Hypocrites*, like unto the *Godly*, but indeed *Carnall*, as the *Tares* are like to *Wheat*, but are not *Wheat*. Or partly ſuch Corrupt Doctrines or Practices as are indeed unſound, but yet ſuch as come very neere the Truth, (as *Tares* doe to the *Wheat*) and ſo neere, that Good men may be taken with them, and ſo the Perſons in whom they grow, cannot be rooted out, but good will be rooted up with them. And in ſuch a caſe *Chriſt* calleth for *Toleration*, not for *penall proſecution*, according to the 3. Concluſion.

Object. 2. In *Math*. 15. 14. *Chriſt* commandeth his Diſciples to let the *Blind* alone till they fall into the *ditch*; therefore he would have their puniſhment deferred till their finall *deſtruction*.

Anſw. He there ſpeaketh not to *publique officers*, whether in *Church* or *Common-weale*, but to his private

Disciples, concerning the *Pharises*, over whom they had had no power. And the Command he giveth to let [9] them alone, is spoken in regard of troubling themselves or regarding the offence, which they tooke at the wholesome D*octrine* of the *Gospell:* As who should say, Though they be offended at this Saying of mine, yet doe not you feare their *Feare*, nor bee troubled at their offence, which they take at my *Doctrine*, not out of sound Judgement, but out of their *Blindnesse*. But this maketh nothing to the Cause in hand.

Ob. In *Luk.* 9. 54 55. *Christ* reproveth his *Disciples*, who would have had fire come downe from *Heaven* to consume the *Samaritanes*, who refused to receive Him.

Obj. And *Paul* teacheth *Timothy*, not to strive, but to be gentle towards All men, suffering evill patiently.

Answ. Both these are *Directions* to *Ministers* of the *Gospell* how to deale (not with *obstinate offenders* in the *Church*, that sinne against Conscience, but) either with Men without, as the *Samaritanes* were, and many unconverted *Christians* in *Crete*, whom *Titus* (as an *Evangelist*) was to seeke to convert: Or at best with some *Jewes* or *Gentiles* in the *Church*, who though carnall, yet were not convinced of the errour of their Way: And 'tis true, it became not the Spirit of the *Gospell* to convert Aliens to the Faith of *Christ* (such as the *Samaritanes* were) by *Fire* and *Brimstone*; nor to deale harshly in publique Ministrie or private Conference with all such contrary minded men, as either had not yet entred into *Church-Fellowship*, or if they had, yet did hitherto sinne of *Ignorance*, not against *Conscience*.

But neither of both these Texts doe hinder the Ministers of the Gospell to proceed in a Church-way against

Church-members, when they become *Scandalous offenders*, either in *Life* or *Doctrine:* much leffe doe they fpeake at all to Civill *Magiftrates*.

Ob. 5. From the *prediction* of the *Prophets*, who foretold that *Carnall Weapons* fhould ceafe in the dayes of the *Gofpell*, Ifa. 2. 4. & 11. 9. Mic. 4. 3. 4. And the *Apoftle* profeffeth, The weapons of our *Warfare* are not *carnall*, 2 Cor. 10. 4. And *Chrift* is fo farre from perfecuting thofe that would not be of his *Religion*, that he chargeth them, when they are perfecuted themfelves, they fhould *pray*, and when they are *curfed* they fhould *bleffe*. The reafon whereof feemeth to be, that they who are now *Perfecuters* and wicked perfons, may become true *Difciples* and *Converts*.

Anfw. Thofe *predictions* in the *Prophets* doe onely fhew, Firft, with what kind of *Weapons* he will fubdue the *Nations* to the Obedience of the Faith of the *Gofpell*, not by *Fire* and *Sword*, and *Weapons* of Warre, 10] but by the Power of his *Word* and Spirit, which no man doubteth of.

Secondly, thofe *predictions* of the *Prophets* fhew what the meeke and peaceable *temper* will be of all the true Converts to *Chriftianity*, not *Lions* or *Leopards*, &c. not cruell *oppreffors*, nor malignant *oppofers*, or *biters* of one another. But doth not forbid them to drive ravenous *Wolves* from the *fheepfold*, and to reftraine them from devouring the Sheepe of *Chrift*.

And when *Paul* faith, The weapons of our *warfare* are not *carnall* but *fpirituall*, he denyeth not *civill weapons of Juftice* to the Civill *Magiftrate*, Rom. 13. but onely to *Church officers*. And yet the weapons of fuch officers he acknowledgeth to be fuch, as though they be *spirituall,* yet are ready to take *vengeance* of all *disobedience,* 2 *Cor.* 10. 6. which hath reference (amongst other Ordinances) to the cenfure of the C*hurch* againft *fcandalous offenders.*

3. When C*hrift* commandeth his D*ifciples* to bleffe them that curfe them and perfecute them, he giveth not therein a rule to *publick officers,* whether in C*hurch* or *Commonweale,* to fuffer notorious finners, either in *life* or *doctrine,* to paffe away with a *bleffing* : But to private C*hriftians* to fuffer *perfecution* patiently, yea and to pray for their *perfecutors.*

Againe, it is true, Chrift would have his D*ifciples* to bee farre from perfecuting (for that is a *finfull oppreffion* of Men for *righteoufneffe* fake) but that hindreth not but that he would have them execute upon all *difobedience* the *judgement* and *vengeance* required in the Word, 2 *Cor.* 10. 6. *Rom.* 13. 4.

4. Though it be true that wicked perfons now may by the grace of *God* become true D*ifciples* and *Converts,* yet we may not doe evill that good may come thereof: And evill it would bee to tolerate notorious evill doers, whether *feducing teachers* or *fcandalous livers.* C*hrift* had fomething againft the *Angel* of the C*hurch* of *Pergamus* for tolerating them that held the *doctrine* of *Balaam,* and againft the C*hurch* of *Thiatira* for tolerating *Jefabel* to teach and feduce, *Rev.* 2. 14. 20.

Your fecond Head of *Reafons* is taken from the *profeffion* and *practice* of famous *Princes,* King *James, Stephen* of *Poland,* King of *Bohemia.*

Whereunto a treble anfwer may briefly be returned.

Firft, we willingly acknowledge, that none is to be perfecuted at all, no more then they may be oppreffed for righteoufneffe fake.

Againe, we acknowledge that none is to be punished for his *conscience*, though mif-informed, as hath been said, unleffe his *errour* be *fundamentall*, [11] or feditiously and turbulently promoted, and that after due conviction of his *conscience*, that it may appeare he is not punished *for his conscience*, but for finning *against his conscience*.

Furthermore, we acknowledge none is to be *constrained* to beleeve or profeffe the true *Religion* till he be convinced in judgement of the *truth* of it : but yet restrained he may [be] from blafpheming the *truth*, and from feducing any unto pernicious errours.

2. Wee anfwer, what *Princes* profeffe or practife, is not a rule of *conscience:* they many times tolerate that in point of *State policy*, which cannot juftly be tolerated in point of true *Christianity*.

Againe, *Princes* many times tolerate offendours out of very *neceffity*, when the offenders are either too many, or too mighty for them to punish, in which refpect D*avid* tolerated *Joab* and his *murthers*, but *against his will*.

3. We anfwer further, that for thofe three Princes named by you, who tolerated *Religion*, we can name you more and greater who have not tolerated *Heretickes* and *Schifmatickes*, notwithftanding their pretence of *conscience*, and arrogating the Crowne of *Martyrdome* to their fufferings.

Constantine the Great at the requeft of the Generall *Councell of Nice*, banifhed *Arrius* with fome of his fellowes. *Sozom. lib.* 1. *Ecclef. Hift. cap.* 19. 20.[1] The

---

[1] Bibliotheca Patrum, tom. vii, p. 387, London, 1677; Sozomen, *Eccl. History*, Bagfter, London, 1846, pp. 37, 38; Gibbon, *Decline and Fall*, chap. xxi, p. 317, London, 1835; Stanley, *Eastern Church*, Lecture iv, p. 240, Am. Ed.

same *Conſtantine* made a ſevere Law againſt the *Donatiſts*.[1] And the like proceedings againſt them were uſed by *Valentinian, Gratian,* and *Theodoſius,* as *Auguſtine* reporteth in *Epiſt.* 166.[2] Only *Julian* the *Apoſtate* granted liberty to *Heretickes* as well as to *Pagans,* that he might by tolerating all *weeds* to grow, choake the vitals of *Chriſtianity,*[3] which was alſo the practice and ſin of *Valens* the *Arrian.*

Queene *Elizabeth,* as famous for her *government* as any of the former, it is well knowne what Lawes ſhe made and executed againſt *Papiſts*. Yea and King *James* (one of your own witneſſes) though he was ſlow in proceeding againſt *Papiſts* (as you ſay) for *conſcience* ſake, yet you are not ignorant how ſharply and ſeverely he puniſhed thoſe whom the malignant world calleth *Puritanes,* men of more *conſcience* and better faith then he tolerated.

I come now to your third and laſt argument, taken from the judgement of ancient and later *Writer*s, yea even of *Papiſts* themſelves, who have condemned *perſecution* for conſcience ſake.

You begin with *Hilary,* whoſe teſtimony we might admit without any prejudice to the truth :. for it is true, the Chriſtian *Church* doth not [12] perſecute, but is perſecuted. But to excommunicate an *Hereticke,* is not

---

[1] Euſebii Pamphili, *Eccl. Hiſt.*, De Vita Conſtantini, lib. ii, cap. 66. This however he repealed. "In a reſcript addreſſed to the Vicar Verinus, in North Africa, he granted to the Donatiſts full liberty to act according to *their own* convictions, declaring that this was a matter which belonged to the judgment of God." Neander, *Church Hiſtory,* Torrey's Tranſlation, ii, 193.

[2] S. Aug. Opera, tom. ii, (105) Ad Donatiſtas, pp. 299, 300, Pariſiis, 1679.

[3] Neander, *The Emperor Julian and his Generation,* tr. by Cox, Sect. IV, p. 122. "Julian gave all parties among the Chriſtians equal liberty, with the hope that by their mutual contentions they would deſtroy one another."

to persecute; that is, it is not to punish an innocent, but a culpable and damnable person, and that not for *conscience*, but for persisting in *errour* against light of *conscience*, whereof it hath beene convinced.

It is true also what he saith, that neither the *Apostles* did, nor may we propagate [the] *Christian Religion* by the Sword: but if *Pagans* cannot be won by the *Word*, they are not to be compelled by the *Sword*. Neverthelesse this hindreth not, but if they or any others should *blaspheme* the true *God*, and his true *Religion*, they ought to be severely punished; and no lesse doe they deserve, if they *seduce* from the truth to damnable *Heresie* or *Idolatry*.

Your next Writer (which is *Tertullian*) speaketh to the same purpose in the place alledged by you. His intent is onely to restraine *Scapula* the *Romane Governour* of *Africa* from the *persecution* of *Christians*, for not offering sacrifice to their *gods*: And for that end fetcheth an argument from the Law of *Naturall Equity*, not to compell any to any *Religion*, but to permit them either to beleeve willingly, or not to beleeve at all. Which wee acknowledge, and accordingly permit the *Indians* to continue in their *unbeleefe*. Neverthelesse it will not therefore be lawfull openly to tolerate *the worship of devils* or *Idols*, or the *seduction* of any from the *truth*.

When *Tertullian* saith, Another mans *Religion* neither hurteth nor profiteth any; it must be understood of *private worship* and *Religion* professed in private: otherwise a false *Religion* professed by the Members of a *Church*, or by such as have given their *Names* to *Christ*, will be the *ruine* and *desolation* of the *Church*, as appeareth by the threats of Chrift to the *Churches* of *Afia, Revel.* 2.

Your next Authour *Hierom* croffeth not the *truth*, nor advantageth not your *caufe:* for we grant what he faith, that *Herefie* muft bee cut off with the Sword of the *Spirit*. But this hindreth not, but that being fo cut downe, if the *Hereticke* ftill perfift in his *Herefie*, to the *feduction* of others, he may be cut off by the *civill fword*, to prevent the *perdition* of others. And that to bee *Hieromes* meaning appeareth by his note upon that of the Apoftle, [A *little Leaven* leaveneth the whole *lumpe*] therefore (faith he)[1] a *fparke* as foone as it appeareth, is to be extinguifhed, and the *Leaven* to be removed from the reft of the *dough, rotten peeces* of flefh are to be cut off, and a *fcabbed beaft* is to be driven from the fheep-fold: left the *whole houfe, maffe of dough, body* and *flocke*, be fet on fire with the *fparke*, bee fowred with the *Leaven*, be putrified with the [13] *rotten flefh*, perifh by the *fcabbed beaft*.

Brentius (whom you next quote) fpeaketh not to your *Caufe*. We willingly grant him and you, that Man hath no power to make *Lawes,* to bind *Confcience*. But this hindreth not, but that Men may fee the Lawes of *God* obferved, which doe bind Confcience.

The like Anfwer may be returned to *Luther,* whom you next alleadge. Firft, that the *Government* of the *Civill Magiftrate* extendeth no further then over the *Bodies* and *Goods* of their Subjects, not over their *Soules:* And therefore they may not undertake to give *Lawes* to the *Soules* and *Confciences* of Men.

Secondly, that the *Church of Chrift* doth not ufe the

---

[1] S. Hieronymi Opera, tom. iv, 291, Parifiis, 1706.

Arme of *Secular Power* to compell men to the *Faith*, or profeſſion of the *Truth*; for this is to be done by *Spirituall weapons*, whereby *Chriſtians* are to be *exhorted*, not *compelled*.

But this hindreth not that *Chriſtians* ſinning againſt *light* of *Faith* and *Conſcience*, may juſtly be cenſured by the *Church* with *Excommunication*, and by the *Civill Sword* alſo, in caſe they ſhall corrupt others to the perdition of their *Soules*.

As for the *Teſtimony* of the *Popiſh Book*, we weigh it not, as knowing (whatſoever they ſpeake for *Toleration of Religion*, where themſelves are under *Hatches*) when they come to ſit at *Sterne*, they judge and practiſe quite contrary, as both their *Writings* and *Judiciall proceedings* have teſtified to the World theſe many yeares.

To ſhut up this Argument from *Teſtimonie* of *Writers*. It is well known, *Auguſtine* retracted this Opinion of yours, which in his younger times he had held, but in after *riper age* reverſed and refuted, as appeareth in the ſecond Book of his *Retractations*, chap. 5. and in his Epiſtles 48. 50. And in his 1. Book againſt *Parmenianus*, cap. 7. he ſheweth, that if the *Donatiſts* were puniſhed with death, they were juſtly puniſhed. And in his 11 Tractate upon *John*, They murther, ſaith he, *Soules*, and themſelves are afflicted in *Body*: They put men to *everlaſting death*, and yet they complaine when themſelves are put to ſuffer *temporall death*.[1]

---

[1] S. Aug. Opera, Retractationum lib. ii, cap. v, tom. i, p. 43, Eps. 93, 185. Ad Vincentium and De Correctione Donatiſtarum, tom. ii, 230, 643. Contra Epiſtolam Parmeniani, lib. i, cap. 8, tom. ix, 19. In Johannis Evang. cap. 2, Tr. xi, 15, tom. iii, pars. 2, 383. This change of opinion in St. Auguſtine in regard to the employment of force in religion is well preſented by Neander, *Church Hiſtory*, ii, 214–217. "It was by Auguſtine, then, that a theory was

Optatus in his 3. book,[1] juſtifieth *Macharius*, who had put ſome *Hereticks* to death ; that he had done no more herein then what *Moſes, Phineas,* and *Elias* had done before him.

Bernard in his 66 Sermon *in Cantica :*[2] Out of doubt (ſaith he) it is better that they ſhould be reſtrained by the Sword of Him, who beareth not the Sword in vaine, then that they ſhould be ſuffred to draw many [14] others into their *Errour.* For he is the *Miniſter of God* for *Wrath* to every evill doer.

Calvins judgement is well knowne, who procured the death of *Michael Servetus* for pertinacie in *Hereſie,* and defended his fact by a Book written of that Argument.[3]

Beza alſo wrote a Booke *de Hæreticis Morte plectendis,* that *Hereticks* are to be puniſhed with *Death.*[4] *Aretius* likewiſe tooke the like courſe about the Death of *Valentinus Gentilis,* and juſtified the Magiſtrates proceeding againſt him, in an Hiſtory written of that Argument.[5]

propoſed and founded, which tempered though it was, in its practical application, by his own pious, philanthropic ſpirit, neverthelefs contained the germ of that whole ſyſtem of ſpiritual deſpotiſm, of intolerance and perſecution, which ended in the tribunals of the inquiſition."

[1] S. Optati Opera, p. 75, Pariſiis, 1679.
[2] S. Bernardi Opera, i, tom. 4, p. 1499, Pariſiis, 1680.
[3] Calvini Opera, tom. viii, p. 510, Amſterdam, 1667.
[4] Beza Tract. Theol. tom. 1, p. 85, edit. 1582. (Underhill.) *De Hæreticis a Civili Magiſtratu Puniendis, Opuscula,* p. 85, Geneva, 1658.
[5] Valentini gentilis juſto capitis (an. 1566) ſupplicio Bernæ affecti brevis hiſtoria, etc. Généve, 1567.

A Short Hiſtory of Valentinus Gentilis the Tritheiſt. Tryed, condemned and put to Death by the Proteſtant Reformed City and Church of Bern in Switzerland, for aſſerting the Three Divine Perſons of the Trinity to be Three Diſtinct, Eternal Spirits, &c. Wrote in Latin by Benedictus Aretius, a Divine of that Church : and now tranſlated into Engliſh for the uſe of Dr. Sherlock. London, 1696.

For an account of Gentilis ſee *Bayle's Dictionary,* iii, p. 153, art. *Gentilis.* R. Wallace, *Antitrinitarian Biography,* 1, 352. C. C. Sand, *Bibliotheca Anti-trinitariorum,* p. 26. Jac. Spon, *Hiſtoire de Généve,* Liv. iii.

Finally, you come to anfwer fome maine Objections, as you call them, which yet are but one, and that one objecteth nothing againft what we hold. It is (fay you) no prejudice to the Common-wealth, if Libertie of Confcience were fuffred to fuch as feare God indeed, which you prove by the examples of the Patriarchs and others.

But we readily grant you, Libertie of Confcience is to be granted to men that feare God indeed, as knowing they will not perfift in Herefie, or turbulent Schifme, when they are convinced in Confcience of the finfulneffe thereof.

But the Queftion is, Whether an Heretick after once or twice Admonition (and fo after conviction) or any other fcandalous and heynous offender, may be tolerated, either in the Church without Excommunication, or in the Common-wealth without fuch punifhment as may preferve others from dangerous and damnable infection.

Thus much I thought needfull to be fpoken, for avoyding the Grounds of your Errour.

I forbeare adding Reafons to juftifie the Truth, becaufe you may finde that done to your hand, in a Treatife fent to fome of the Brethren late of *Salem*, who doubted as you[1] doe.

The Lord Jefus lead you by a Spirit of Truth into all Truth, through Jefus Chrift.

[1] "Writing to one Mr. Hall," fays Williams in a note to this fentence in *The Bloody Tenent yet more bloody*, p. 290. The "treatife" is "A Model of Church and Civil Power" which is "examined and anfwered" in the fecond part of this work, Chap. lxxxii. By whom it was "fent to fome of the Brethren late of Salem," is a point difputed between Cotton and Williams. Williams had added to the title, following the above hint of Cotton's, "Compofed by Mr. Cotton and the Minifters of New England, and fent to the Church at Salem." *Bloudy Tenent*, p.

118. Cotton replied that this was "a double falſhood." "For Mr. Cotton, I know, that he was none of them that compoſed it." "Howſoever this Modell came to Salem, the Miniſters ſay, it was not ſent by them." *Bloudy Tenent Waſhed*, p. 192. "Againſt this bluſtering charge of double falſhood," Williams, after quoting this cloſing paragraph of Cotton's anſwer to the priſoner's arguments, ſays, "To my knowledge it was reported (according to this hint of Mr. Cotton's) that from the Miniſters of the Churches (pretended) ſuch a Modell compoſed by them was ſent to Salem: Hereupon it was that the Diſcuſſer wrote on purpoſe to his worthy friend Mr. Sharpe (elder of the Church of Salem (ſo called) for the ſight of it, who accordingly ſent it to him." *The Bloody Tenent yet more bloody*, p. 291.

A Reply to the aforesaid Answer of *Mr. Cotton*.

In a Conference betweene *TRVTH and PEACE*.

CHAP. I.

Truth. IN what *darke corner* of the World (*sweet Peace*) are *we two* met? How hath this present evill *World* banished *Me* from all the Coasts & Quarters of it? and how hath the Righteous *God* in judgement taken *Thee* from the *Earth*, Rev. 6. 4.

Peace. 'Tis lamentably true (*blessed Truth*) the *foundations* of the *World* have long been out of course: the *Gates* of *Earth* and *Hell* have conspired together to intercept our joyfull *meeting* and our holy *kisses:* With what a wearied, *tyred Wing* have I flowne over *Nations, Kingdomes, Cities, Townes*, to finde out precious *Truth?* <small>Truth and Peace rarely and seldom meete.</small>

Truth. The like enquiries in my flights and travells have I made for *Peace*, and still am told, she hath left the *Earth*, and fled to *Heaven*.

Peace. Deare *Truth*, What is the *Earth* but a *dungeon of darknesse*, where *Truth* is not?

Truth. And what's the *Peace* thereof but a fleeting *dreame*, thine *Ape* and *Counterfeit?*

Peace. O where's the Promife of the *God* of *Heaven*, that *Righteoufnes* and *Peace* fhall *kiffe* each other?

Truth. Patience (fweet *Peace*) thefe *Heavens* and *Earth* are growing *Old,* and fhall be changed like a *Garment,* Pfal. 102. They fhall melt away, and be burnt up with all the *Works* that are therein; and the moft high *Eternall Creatour,* fhall glorioufly create *New Heavens* and *New Earth,* wherein dwells *Righteoufneffe,* 2 Pet. 3. Our *kiffes* then fhall have their *endleffe* date of pure and fweeteft ioyes? till then both *Thou* and *I* muft hope, and wait, and beare the furie of the *Dragons* wrath, whofe *monftrous Lies* and *Furies* fhall with himfelfe be caft into the *lake* of *Fire,* the *fecond death,* Revel. 20.

Peace. Moft precious *Truth,* thou knoweft we are both purfued and [16] laid [in wait] for: Mine *heart* is full of fighes, mine *eyes* with teares: Where can I better vent my full oppreffed *bofome,* then into *thine,* whofe faithfull *lips* may for thefe few houres revive my drooping wandring *fpirits,* and here begin to *wipe Teares* from mine eyes, and the eyes of my deareft *Children?*

Truth. Sweet daughter of the *God* of *Peace,* begin; powre out thy *forrowes,* vent thy *complaints:* how joyfull am I to improve thefe precious Minutes to revive our *Hearts,* both thine and mine, and the hearts of all that *love* the *Truth* and *Peace,* Zach. 8.

Peace. Deare *Truth,* I know thy *birth,* thy *nature,* thy *delight.* They that know thee, will *prize* thee farre above themfelves and lives, and *fell themfelves* to *buy thee.* Well fpake that famous *Elizabeth* to her famous *Attorney* Sir *Edward Coke* :[1] Mr. *Attourney*, goe on as thou haſt begun, and ſtill plead, not *pro Domina Regina*, but *pro Domina Veritate*.

Truth. 'Tis true, my *Crowne* is high, my *Scepter*'s ſtrong to breake down *ſtrongeſt holds*, to throw down higheſt *Crownes* of all that plead (though but in thought) againſt me. Some few there are, but oh how few are valiant for the *Truth*, and dare to *plead my Cauſe*, as my *Witneſſes* in *ſack-cloth*, Revel. 11. While all mens *Tongues* are bent like *Bowes* to ſhoot out lying words againſt Me!

Peace. O how could I ſpend *eternall dayes* and *endleſſe dates* at thy holy feet, in liſtning to the precious Oracles of thy mouth! All the Words of thy mouth are *Truth*, and there is no *iniquity* in them; Thy *lips* drop as the hony-combe. But oh! ſince we muſt part anon, let us (as thou ſaidſt) improve our *Minutes*, and (according as thou promiſedſt) revive me with

---

[1] Sir Edward Coke was a patron of Williams in his youth. During Williams's ſecond viſit to England, 1652–4, he begun a correſpondence with Mrs. Sadleir, Coke's daughter, and in his firſt letter ſays of him, "How many thouſand times have I had honourable and precious remembrance of his perſon, and the life, the writings, the ſpeeches, and the examples of that glorious light. And I may truly ſay, that beſide my natural inclination to ſtudy and activity, his example, inſtruction and encouragement, have ſpurred me on to a more than ordinary, induſtrious, and patient courſe in my whole courſe hitherto." To this letter Mrs. Sadleir put the following note: "This Roger Williams, when he was a youth, would in ſhort hand, take ſermons and ſpeeches in the Star Chamber, and preſent them to my dear father. He, ſeeing ſo hopeful a youth, took ſuch a liking to him that he ſent him in to Sutton's Hoſpital [now the Charter Houſe] and he was the ſecond that was placed there: full little did he think that he would have proved ſuch a rebel to God, the king and his country. I leave his letters, that if ever he has the face to return into his native country, Tyburn may give him welcome." Elton, *Life of Roger Williams*, pages 90, 100. He had ſent a copy of the *Bloudy Tenent* to Mrs. Sadleir, which ſhe refuſed to read.

thy words, which are sweeter then the honey and the honey-combe.

CHAP. II.

2 great complaints of Peace.

DEare *Truth*, I have two sad *Complaints*: First, the most sober of thy *Witnesses*, that dare to *plead* thy *Cause*, how are they charged to be *mine Enemies, contentious, turbulent, seditious*?

Secondly, Thine *Enemies*, though they speake and raile against thee, though they outragiously *pursue, imprison, banish, kill* thy faithfull *Witnesses*, yet how is all vermillion'd o're for *Justice* 'gainst the *Hereticks*? Yea, if they kindle coales, and blow the flames of *devouring Warres*, that leave neither *Spirituall* nor *Civill State*, but burns up *Branch* [17] and *Root*, yet how doe all pretend an *holy War*? He that *kills*, and hee that's *killed*, they both cry out, It is for *God*, and for their *conscience*.

Persecutors seldom plead Christ, but Moses for their Author.

Tis true, nor one nor other seldome dare to plead the mighty Prince *Christ Jesus* for their *Authour*, yet both (both *Protestant* and *Papist*) pretend they have spoke with *Moses* and the *Prophets*, who all, say they (before *Christ* came) allowed such *holy persecutions, holy Warres* against the enemies of holy *Church*.

Truth. Deare Peace (to ease thy first *complaint*) tis true, thy dearest *Sons*, most like their mother, *Peace-keeping, Peace-making* Sons of *God*, have borne and still must beare the *blurs* of *troublers* of *Israel*, and turners of the *World* upside downe. And tis true againe, what *Salomon* once spake: The *beginning* of *strife* is as when one letteth out *Water*, therefore (faith he) leave off *contention* before it be medled with. This *Caveat* fhould keepe the *bankes* and *fluces* firme and ftrong, that *ftrife*, like a *breach of waters*, breake not in upon the fons of men.

Yet *ftrife* muft be diftinguifhed: It is *neceffary* or *unneceffary, godly* or *ungodly, Chriftian* or *unchriftian*, &c. Strife diftinguifhed

It is *unneceffary, unlawfull, difhonourable, ungodly, unchriftian*, in moft cafes in the world, for there is a *pofsibility* of keeping *fweet Peace* in moft cafes, and if it be *pofsible*, it is the expreffe command of God that *Peace* be kept, *Rom.* 13. 1. Ungodly ftrife.

Againe, it is *neceffary, honourable, godly*, &c. with *civill* and earthly *weapons* to *defend* the *innocent*, and to *refcue* the oppreffed from the violent *pawes* and *jaws* of oppreffing perfecuting *Nimrods, Pfal.* 73. *Job* 29. 2. Godly ftrife.

It is as *neceffary*, yea more *honourable, godly*, and *Chriftian*, to *fight* the *fight* of *faith*, with *religious* and *fpirituall Artillery*, and to *contend earneftly* for the *faith* of *Jefus*, once delivered to the *Saints* againft all *oppofers*, and the *gates* of *earth* and *hell*, *men* or *devils*, yea againft *Paul* himfelfe, or an *Angell* from *heaven*, if he bring any other *faith* or *doctrine*, *Jude verf.* 4. *Gal.* 1. 8.

Peace. With the *clafhing* of fuch *Armes* am I never *wakened.* Speake once againe (deare Truth) to my fecond *complaint* of bloody *perfecution*, and devouring *wars*, marching under the colours of upright *Juftice*, and holy *Zeale*, &c. A threefold dolefull cry. Chrifts worfhip is his bed, Cant. 1. 16

Truth. Mine eares have long beene filled with a threefold dolefull *Outcry*.

Falſe worſhip therefore is a falſe bed.

Firſt, of one hundred forty foure thouſand *Virgins* (*Rev.* 14.) forc'd and raviſht by *Emperours*, *Kings*, and *Governours* to their beds of *worſhip* and *Religion*, ſet up (like *Abſaloms*) on high in their ſeverall *States* and *Countries*.

The cry of the ſoules under the Altar.

18] Secondly, the cry of thoſe precious *ſoules* under the *Altar* (*Rev.* 6.) the *ſoules* of ſuch as have beene perſecuted and ſlaine for the teſtimony and *witneſſe* of *Jeſus*, whoſe *bloud* hath beene ſpilt like *water* upon the *earth*, and that becauſe they have held faſt the *truth* and *witneſſe* of *Jeſus*, againſt the *worſhip* of the *States* and *Times*, compelling to an *uniformity* of State *Religion*.

Theſe *cries* of *murthered Virgins* who can ſit ſtill and heare? Who can but run with zeale inflamed to prevent the *deflowring* of *chaſte ſoules*, and ſpilling of the *bloud* of the *innocent*? *Humanity* ſtirs up and prompts the *Sonnes* of men to draw *materiall ſwords* for a *Virgins chaſtity* and *life*, againſt a *raviſhing murtherer*? And *Piety* and *Chriſtianity* muſt needs awaken the *Sons of God* to draw the *ſpirituall ſword* (the Word of *God*) to preſerve the *chaſtity* and *life* of *ſpirituall Virgins*, who abhorre the ſpirituall *defilements* of *falſe worſhip*, *Rev.* 14.

A cry of the whole earth.

Thirdly, the *cry* of the *whole earth*, made *drunke* with the *bloud* of its *inhabitants*, ſlaughtering each other in their *blinded zeale*, for *Conſcience*, for *Religion*, againſt the *Catholickes*, againſt the *Lutherans*, &c.

What fearfull *cries* within theſe twenty years of hundred *thouſands* men, women, children, fathers, mothers, husbands, wives, brethren, ſiſters, old and young, high and low, *plundred*, *raviſhed*, *ſlaughtered*, *murthered, famished?* And hence these cries, that men fling away the *spirituall sword and spirituall artillery* (in *spirituall* and *religious* causes) and rather trust for the suppressing of each others *God, Conscience,* and *Religion* (as they suppose) to an *arme* of *flesh,* and *sword* of *steele?*

Truth. Sweet *Peace,* what hast thou there?

Peace. Arguments against *persecution* for cause of *Conscience.*

Truth. And what there?

Peace. An *Answer* to such *Arguments,* contrarily maintaining such *persecution* for *cause* of *Conscience.*

Truth. These *Arguments* against such *persecution,* and the *Answer* pleading for it, written (as *Love* hopes) from godly *intentions, hearts,* and *hands,* yet in a marvellous different *stile* and *manner.* The *Arguments* against *persecution* in *milke,* the *Answer* for it (as I may say) in *bloud.* _{The wonderfull providéce of God in the writing of the Arguments against persecution in Milke.}

The *Authour* of these *Arguments* (against *persecution*) (as I have beene informed) being committed by *some* then in power, *close prisoner* to *Newgate,* for the witnesse of some *truths* of *Jesus,* and having not the use of *Pen* and *Inke,* wrote these *Arguments* in *Milke,* in sheets of Paper, brought to him by the *Woman* his *Keeper,* from a friend in *London,* as the *stopples* of his *Milk bottle.*

19] In such Paper written with *Milk* nothing will appear, but the way of reading it by *fire* being knowne to this *friend* who received the Papers, he transcribed and kept together the Papers, although the *Author* himselfe could not correct, nor view what himselfe had written.

It was in *milke*, tending to foule *nourishment*, even for *Babes* and Sucklings in *Christ*.

It was in *milke*, fpiritually *white*, pure and innocent, like thofe *white horfes* of the *Word* of *truth* and *meekneffe*, and the *white Linnen* or *Armour* of *righteoufneffe*, in the *Army* of *Jefus*. Rev. 6. & 19.

It was in *milke*, foft, meeke, peaceable and gentle, tending both to the *peace* of *foules*, and the *peace* of *States* and Kingdomes.

<small>The Anfwer writ in Bloud.</small>   *Peace.* The *Anfwer* (though I hope out of milkie pure intentions) is returned in *bloud: bloudy* & flaughterous *conclufions; bloudy* to the *fouls* of all men, forc'd to the *Religion* and *Worfhip* which every civil State or Common-weale agrees on, and compells all fubjects to in a diffembled *uniformitie*.

Bloudy to the *bodies*, firft of the holy *witneffes* of *Chrift Jefus*, who teftifie againft fuch invented worfhips.

Secondly, of the *Nations* and Peoples flaughtering each other for their feverall refpective Religions and Confciences.

CHAP. III.

Truth. IN the Anfwer Mr. *Cotton* firft layes downe feverall *diftinctions* and *conclufions* of his owne, tending to prove perfecution.

Secondly, *Anfwers* to the *Scriptures*, and *Arguments* propofed againft *perfecution*.

<small>The firft diftinction difcuffed.</small>   *Peace.* The firft diftinction is this: By perfecution for caufe of *Confcience*, " I conceive you meane " either for profeffing fome point of *doctrine* which

"you beleeve in *conscience* to be the *truth*, or for "*practising* some worke which you beleeve in con-"*science* to be a *religious* dutie.

Truth. I acknowledge that to molest any person, *Jew* or *Gentile*, for either professing *doctrine*, or practising *worship* meerly *religious* or spirituall, it is to persecute him, and such a person (what ever his *doctrine* or *practice* be true or *false*) suffereth persecution for *conscience*. <small>Definition of persecution discussed.</small>

But withall I desire it may bee well observed, that this *distinction* is not full and complete: For beside this that a man may be persecuted [20] because he holdeth or practiseth what he beleeves in *conscience* to be a *Truth*, (as *Daniel* did, for which he was cast into the *Lyons* den, *Dan.* 6.) and many thousands of *Christians*, because they durst not cease to *preach* and *practise* what they beleeved was by *God* commanded, as the *Apostles* answered (*Acts* 4. & 5.) I say besides this a man may also be persecuted, because hee dares not be *constrained* to yeeld obedience to such *doctrines* and *worships* as are by men invented and appointed. So the three famous *Jewes* were cast into the fiery furnace for refusing to fall downe (in a *non-conformity* to the whole conforming world) before the golden *Image*, Dan. 3. 21. So thousands of *Christs witnesses* (and of late in those bloudy *Marian* dayes) have rather chose to yeeld their *bodies* to all sorts of *torments*, then to subscribe to *doctrines*, or practise *worships*, unto which the States and Times (as *Nabuchadnezzar* to his golden *Image*) have compelled and urged them. <small>Conscience will not be restrained from its own worship, nor constrained to another.</small>

A chaste *wife* will not onely abhorre to be restrained

<small>A chaste soule in Gods worship like a chast wife.</small> from her *husbands bed,* as adulterous and polluted, but also abhor (if not much more) to bee constrained to the *bed* of a *stranger.* And what is abominable in *corporall,* is much more loathsome in *spirituall whoredome* and defilement.

The Spouse of *Christ Jesus* who could not finde her soules beloved in the *wayes* of his *worship* and *Ministery, (Cant.* 1. 3. and 5. Chapters) abhorred to turne aside to other *Flockes, Worships, &c.* and to imbrace the bosome of a false *Christ, Cant.* 1. 8.

CHAP. IV.

<small>The second distinction discussed.</small> *Peace.* THe second distinction is this.
In points of Doctrine some are fundamentall, without right beleefe whereof a man cannot be saved: others are circumstantiall and lesse principall, wherein a man may differ in judgement without prejudice of salvation on either part.

<small>Gods people may erre from the very fundamentals of visible worship.</small> *Truth.* To this *distinction* I dare not subscribe, for then I should everlastingly condemne thousands, and ten thousands, yea the whole *generation* of the *righteous,* who since the falling away (from the first primitive *Christian* state or *worship*) have and doe erre fundamentally concerning the true *matter, constitution, gathering* and *governing* of the *Church:* and yet farre be it from any pious *breast* to imagine that they are not saved, and that their soules are not bound up in the bundle of *eternall life.*

We reade of foure sorts of spirituall or Christian *foundations* in the *New Testament.*

<small>4 sorts of</small> 21] First, the *Foundation* of all *foundations,* the Cor-

ner-stone it selfe, the *Lord Jesus*, on whom all depend, *Persons*, *Doctrine*, *Practices*, 1 Cor. 3. ^{spirituall Foundations.}

2. *Ministeriall foundations.* The *Church* is built upon the *foundation* of the *Apostles* and *Prophets,* Ephes. 2. 20.

3. The *foundation* of future rejoycing in the fruits of *Obedience,* 1 *Tim.* 6.

4. The *foundation* of *Doctrines,* without the knowledge of which, there can be no true profession of *Christ,* according to the first *institution, Heb.* 6. The *foundation* or *principles* of *Repentance* from dead works, *Faith* towards *God*, the Doctrine of *Baptisme, Laying on of Hands,* the *Resurrection,* and *Eternall Judgement.* In some of these, to wit, those concerning *Baptismes*, & *Laying on of Hands, Gods* people will be found to be ignorant for many hundred yeares: and I yet cannot see it proved that *light* is risen, I mean the *light* of the first *institution*, in practice.¹ ^{ςτοιχεῖα θεμέλιοι. The sixe Foundations of the Christian Religion or Worship.}

Gods people in their persons, *Heart-waking,* (Cant. 5. 2.) in the life of *personall grace*, will yet be found fast asleep in respect of *publike Christian Worship.*

Gods people (in their *persons*) are *His*, most deare and precious: yet in respect of the *Christian Worship* they are mingled amongst the *Babylonians*, from ^{Comming out of Babell, not}

---

¹ The doctrine of laying on of hands was early adopted in some of the Baptist churches of Rhode Island. "About the year 1653 or '54, there was a division in the Baptist Church at Providence, about the right of laying on of hands, * * * * but laying on of hands at length generally obtained," Callender, *Historical Discourse,* 114; Comer's Ms. Diary, Staples, *Annals of Providence,* 410; Backus, *Church History of New England,* iii, 217. The adherents of this practice formed an Association of Churches about 1670, which still continues, though now quite small. "They have eighteen or twenty churches, sixteen ordained ministers, and about three thousand members." Appleton's *Amer. Cyclopedia,* xiv.

whence they are called to come out, not *locally* (as locall but myſticall. ſome have ſaid) for that belonged to a materiall and locall *Babell*, (and, literall *Babell* and *Jeruſalem* have now no difference, *John* 4. 21.) but *ſpirituall*, and myſtically to come out from her ſins and *Abominations*.

If Mr. *Cotton* maintaine the true *Church* of *Chriſt* to conſiſt of the true *matter* of *holy perſons* call'd out from the World; and the true *forme* of *Union* in a *Church-Covenant*; And that alſo, neither *Nationall*, *Provinciall*, nor *Dioceſan* Churches are of *Chriſts inſtitution*: how many Thouſands of *Gods* people of all ſorts, (*Clergie* and *Laitie*, as they call them) will they finde both in former and later times, captivated in ſuch *Nationall, Provinciall*, and *Dioceſan* Churches? yea and ſo far from living in, yea or knowing of any The great Ignorance of Gods people concerning the Nature of the true Church. ſuch *Churches* (for matter and forme) as they conceive now only to be true, that untill of late yeares, how few of *Gods* people knew any other *Church* then the *Pariſh Church* of dead ſtones or timber? It being a late marvailous *light* revealed by *Chriſt Jeſus* the Sun of *Righteouſneſſe*, that his people are a *Company* or *Church* of living ſtones, 1 *Pet*. 2. 9.

Mr. *Cotton* & all the Halfe Seperates, halting between true & falſ Churches, and conſequently, not yet clear in And however his own *Soule*, and the ſoules of many others (precious to *God*) are perſwaded to ſeparate from *Nationall, Provinciall*, and *Dioceſan Churches*, and to aſſemble into particular *Churches*: yet ſince [22] there are no *Pariſh Churches* in *England*, but what are made up of the *Pariſh* bounds within ſuch and ſuch a compaſſe of *houſes*; and that ſuch *Churches* have beene and are in conſtant dependance on, and ſubordination to the *Nationall Church*:

how can the *New-English particular Churches* joyne with the *Old English Parish Churches* in so many Ordinances of *Word, Prayer, Singing, Contribution, &c.* but they must needs confesse, that as yet their Soules are farre from the *knowledge* of the *foundation* of a true *Christian Church*, whose matter must not only be living stones, but also separated from the *rubbish* of *Antichristian confusions* and *desolations*. the fundamentall matter of a Christiā Church.

CHAP. V.

Peace. WIth lamentation I may adde: How can their Soules be cleare in this *foundation* of the true *Christian* matter, who persecute and oppresse their own (acknowledged) Brethren presenting Light unto them about this Point? But I shall now present you with Mr. *Cottons* third *distinction*. " In point of Practice (saith he) some concerne the " weightier duties of the Law, as, What God we " worship, and with what kind of Worship: whether " such, as if it be Right, fellowship with God is held, " if false, fellowship with God is lost.

Truth. It is worth the inquirie, what kind of *Worship* he intendeth; for *Worship* is of various signification: whether in generall acceptation he meane the *rightnesse* or *corruptnesse* of the *Church*, or the *Ministry* of the *Church*, or the Ministrations of the *Word, Prayer, Seales, &c.* The true Ministrie a Fundamentall.

And because it pleaseth the *Spirit* of *God* to make the *Ministry* one of the *foundations* of the *Christian Religion*, (*Heb.* 6. 12.) and also to make the *Ministrie* of the *Word* and *Prayer* in the *Church*, to be two speciall works (even of the Apostles themselves) *Acts* 6. 2. I shall desire it may be well considered in the feare of *God*.

The New English Ministers examined.

First, concerning the *Ministery* of the *Word;* The *New-English Ministers,* when they were new elected & ordained *Ministers* in *New-Engläd,* must undeniably grant, that at that time they were no *Ministers,* notwithstanding their profession of standing so long in a true *Ministry* in *Old England,* whether received from the Bishops (which some have maintained true) or from the People, which Mr. *Cotton* & others better liked,[1] and which *Ministrie* was always accounted perpetuall and indelible: I apply, and aske, Will it not follow, that if their new *Ministry* and *Ordination* be true, the former was false? and if false, that in the [23] exercise of it (notwithstanding *abilities, graces, intentions, labours,* and (by Gods gracious, unpromised, & extraordinary blessing) some *successe*) I say, will it not according to this distinction follow, that according to visible *rule, Fellowship* with *God* was lost?

Common Prayer cast off, & written against by the New-English.

Secondly, concerning *Prayer*; The *New-English Ministers* have disclaimed and written against that *worshipping* of God by the *Common* or set formes of *Prayer,* which yet themselves practised in *England,* notwithstanding they knew that many servants of God in great sufferings witnessed against such a *Ministrie* of the *Word,* and such a *Ministrie* of *Prayer.*[2]

Peace. I could name the *persons, time* and *place,*

---

[1] "The Church of Brethren hath the power, priviledges and liberty to choose their officers." *The Keyes of the Kingdom of Heaven,* p. 12. Cf. *The Way of the Churches,* Chap. 2, Sect. 6–9.

[2] Cotton's views on this subject have already been considered by Professor Diman in a note to Cotton's *Answer,* &c., *Publications of Narr. Club,* ii, 162.

when some of them were faithfully admonished for using of the *Common prayer*, and the Arguments presented to them, then seeming weake, but now acknowledged sound: yet at that time they satisfied their hearts with the practice of the *Author* of the *Councell* of *Trent*, who used to read only some of the choicest selected Prayers in the *Masse-booke*, (which I confesse was also their own practice in their using of the *Common-Prayer*.)¹ But now according to this *distinction*, I ask whether or no fellowship with *God* in such prayers was lost.

¹ " I know no such faithfull admonishers, as presented to us in England, arguments against the Common Prayer, * * * though such a thing possibly may be true, howsoever forgotten. But this I am perswaded to be utterly false, that any of us satisfied our hearts with the practise of the Author of the Councell of Trent, &c." Cotton, *The Bloudy Tenent Washed*, page 8.

" Possibly Master Cotton may call to minde, that the discusser (riding with himself and one other of precious memorie (Master Hooker) to and from Sempringham) presented his argument from Scripture, why he durst not joyn with them in their use of Common Prayer; and all the answer that yet can be remembred the discusser received from Master Cotton, was, that he selected the good and best prayers in his use of that book, as the Author of the Councel of Trent was used to do, in his using of the Masse-book." *The Bloody Tenent yet more bloody*, p. 12.

Sempringham, a seat of the Clintons, Earls of Lincoln, and of a Priory of Cistercians, is a small parish near Folkingham, in Lincolnshire, about eighteen miles from Boston, where Cotton was rector. Rapin, *History of England*, i, 254; Camden, *Britannia*, 464; Allen, *History of County of Lincoln*, ii, 285.

Thomas Hooker, who is probably referred to, was minister at Chelmsford in Essex, 1626–1630, and came to this country in the same ship with Cotton in 1633. *Mather's Magnalia*, I, 304. There is possibly a clue here to Williams's life previous to his coming to America, which might be followed with advantage.

Father Paul Sarpi, the historian of the Council of Trent, in many things showed his independence of the Holy See and provoked its enmity. Father Courayer, who translated his History into French, says that " Sarpi was a Catholic in general, and sometimes a Protestant in particulars. He observed every thing in the Romish religion which could be practiced without superstition." An account of his life is prefixed to Brent's translation of his History, London, 1676. There is a discriminating notice of Sarpi, and of his biographies, by Rev. James Martineau, in the *Westminster Review*, April, 1838.

Truth. I could particularize other *exercises* of *Worſhip*, which cannot be denied (according to this *diſtinction*) to be of the *waightier points* of the *Law*, to wit, [What *God* we *worſhip*, and with what kind of *worſhip*:] wherein fellowſhip with *God* (in many of our unclean and abominable *Worſhips*) hath been loſt. Only upon theſe premiſes I ſhall obſerve. Firſt, that *Gods* people, even the *ſtandard-bearers* and *leaders* of them (according to this diſtinction) have worſhipped *God* (in their ſleepy *ignorance*) by ſuch a kind of *Worſhip*, as wherein *fellowſhip* with *God* is loſt; yea alſo this it is poſſible for them to do, after much *light* is riſen againſt ſuch *Worſhip*, and in particular, brought to the eyes of ſuch *holy* and *worthy* perſons.

<small>*Gods* people have worſhipped God with falſe worſhips.</small>

Secondly, there may be inward and ſecret *fellowſhip* with *God* in falſe *Miniſteries* of *Word* and *Prayer*, (for that to the eternall prayſe of *Infinite Mercy* beyond a word or promiſe of *God* I acknowledge) when yet (as the diſtinction ſaith) in ſuch *worſhip* (not being *right*) *fellowſhip* with *God* is loſt, and ſuch a *ſervice* or *miniſtration* muſt be lamented and forſaken.

<small>It pleaſeth God ſometimes, beyond his promiſe, to convey bleſſings & comfort to His, in falſe worſhips.</small>

Thirdly, I obſerve that *Gods people* may live and die in ſuch kindes of *worſhip*, notwithſtanding that *light* from *God* publikely and privately, hath beene preſented to them, able to convince: yet not reaching to [24] their *conviction* and forſaking of ſuch wayes, contrary to a *concluſion* afterward expreſt, to wit, [That *fundamentals* are ſo cleere, that a man cannot but be convinced in *Conſcience*, and therefore that ſuch a perſon not being convinced, he is *condemned of himſelfe*, and may be *perſecuted* for ſinning againſt his *conſcience*.]

<small>Fundamentals of Chriſtian worſhip not ſo eaſie and ſure.</small>

Fourthly, I obferve that in fuch a maintaining a clearneffe of *fundamentals* or waightier *points*, and upon that ground a perfecuting of men, becaufe they finne againft their *confciences*, Mr. *Cotton* meafures that to *others*, which himfelfe when he lived in fuch *practices*, would not have had meafured to himfelfe. As firft, that it might have beene affirmed of him, that in fuch *practices* he did finne againft his *confcience*, having fufficient light fhining about him.

Secondly, that hee fhould or might lawfully have beene cut off by *death* or *banifhment*, as an *Hereticke*, finning againft his owne *confcience*.

And in this refpect the Speech of King *Iames* was notable to a great *Non-conformitant* converted (as is faid by King *James*) to *conformity*, and counfelling the *King* afterward to perfecute the *Non-conformifts* even unto *death*: Thou *Beaft* (quoth the *King*) if I had dealt fo with thee in thy *non-conformity*, where hadft thou beene? A notable fpeech of K. *Iames* to a great non-conformift, turned perfecuter.

CHAP. VI.

Peace. THe next *diftinction* concerning the manner of *perfons* holding forth the aforefaid *practices* (not onely the *waightier duties* of the *Law*, but points of *doctrine* and *worfhip* leffe principall.) The 4. diftinctió difcuffed.

"Some (faith he) hold them forth in a *meeke* and
" *peaceable* way: fome with fuch *arrogance* and *impet-*
" *uoufneffe*, as of it felfe tendeth to the difturbance of
" *civill peace*.

Truth. In the examination of this *diftinction* we fhall difcuffe,

What civill peace is.

First, what is *civill Peace*, (wherein we shall vindicate thy name the better.)

Secondly, what it is to hold forth a Doctrine or Practice in this *impetuousnesse* or *arrogancy*.

First, for *civill peace*, what is it but *pax civitatis*, the peace of the Citie, whether an *English* City, *Scotch*, or *Irish* Citie, or further abroad, *French*, *Spanish*, *Turkish* City, &c.

Thus it pleased the Father of *Lights* to define it, *Ierem*. 29. 7. Pray for the *peace* of the *City*; which *peace* of the *City*, or *Citizens*, so compacted in a *civill* way of *union*, may be intire, unbroken, safe, &c. notwithstanding so many thousands of *Gods people* the *Jewes*, were there in *bondage*, and would neither be *constrained* to the *worship* of the Citie *Babell*, nor restrained from so much of the *worship* of the true *God*, as they then could practice, as is plaine in the practice of the 3 Worthies, *Shadrach*, *Misach*, and *Abednego*, as also of *Daniel*, *Dan*. 3. & *Dan*. 6. (the peace of the C*i*ty or *Kingdome*, being a far different Peace from the Peace of the *Religion* or Spirituall *Worship*, maintained & professed of the Citizens. This *Peace* of their *Worship* (which *worship* also in some Cities being various) being a false Peace, *Gods people* were and ought to be *Nonconformitants*, not daring either to be *restrained* from the *true*, or *constrained* to *false Worship*, and yet without *breach* of the Civill or *Citie-peace*, properly so called.

Gods people must be Nonconformitants to Evill.

Peace. Hence it is that so many glorious and flourishing *Cities* of the World maintaine their *Civi*.*l* peace, yea the very *Americans* & wildest *Pagans* keep the peace of their *Towns* or *Cities*; though neither

The difference between Spirituall

in one nor the other can any man prove a true *Church* and Civill Peace. of God in thofe places, and confequently no fpirituall and heavenly peace: The Peace *fpirituall* (whether true or falfe) being of a higher and farre different nature from the Peace of the place or people, being meerly and effentially *civill* and *humane*.

Truth. O how loft are the fonnes of men in this point? To illuftrate this: The *Church* or *company* of *worfhippers* (whether true or falfe) is like unto a Body or Colledge of *Phyfitians* in a *Citie*; like unto a *Corporation, Society,* or *Company* of *Eaft-Indie* or *Turkie-Merchants*, or any other *Societie* or *Company* in *London*: which Companies may hold their *Courts*, keep their *Records*, hold *difputations*; and in matters concerning their *Societie*, may diffent, divide, breake into *Schifmes* and *Factions*, fue and implead each other at the *Law*, yea wholly breake up and diffolve into pieces and nothing, and yet the *peace* of the *Citie* not be in the leaft meafure impaired or difturbed; becaufe the *effence* or being of the *Citie*, and fo the *well-being* and *peace* thereof is effentially diftinct from thofe The difparticular *Societies*; the *Citie-Courts*, *Citie-Lawes*, ference be- tween the *Citie-punifhments* diftinct from theirs. The *Citie* was Spirituall before them, and ftands abfolute and intire, when and Civill fuch a *Corporation* or *Societie* is taken down. For State. inftance further, The *City* or *Civill ftate* of *Ephefus* was effentially diftinct from the *worfhip* of *Diana* in the Citie, or of the *whole city*. Againe, the *Church* of *Chrift* in *Ephefus* (which were Gods people, converted and call'd out from the *worfhip* of that *City* unto *Chriftianitie* or *worfhip* of *God* in *Chrift*) was diftinct from both.

The Civil State, the Spirituall estate, and the Church of Chrift diftinct in Ephefus.

26] Now suppose that *God* remove the *Candlestick* from *Ephefus*, yea though the *whole Worship* of the *Citie of Ephefus* should be altered: yet (if men be true and honestly ingenuous to *Citie-covenants, Combinations* and *Principles*) all this might be without the least impeachment or infringement of the Peace of the *City* of *Ephefus*.

Thus in the Citie of *Smirna* was the Citie it selfe or Civill estate one thing, The Spirituall or Religious state of *Smirna*, another; The Church of *Chrift* in *Smirna*, distinct from them both; and the *Synagogue* of the *Jewes*, whether literally *Jewes* (as some thinke) or mystically, false *Christians*, (as others) called the *Synagogue* of *Sathan*, Revel. 2. distinct from all these. And notwithstanding these spirituall oppositions in point of *Worship* and *Religion*, yet heare we not the least noyse (nor need we, if Men keep but the Bond of *Civility*) of any *Civil breach*, or *breach* of *Civill peace* amongst them: and to persecute Gods people there for Religion, that only was a breach of Civilitie it selfe.

CHAP. VII.

Peace. NOw to the second Quærie, What it is to hold forth Doctrine or Practice in an arrogant or impetuous way?

The Anfwerer too obfcure in generalls.
Truth. Although it hath not pleased Mr. *Cotton* to declare what is this *arrogant* or *impetuous* holding forth of *Doctrine* or *Practice* tending to disturbance of *Civill peace*, I cannot but expresse my sad and sorrowfull obfervation, how it pleafeth *God* to leave him,

as to take up the common reproachfull *accufation* of the *Accufer* of *Gods* children; to wit, that they are arrogant and impetuous: which charge (together with that of *obftinacie, pertinacie, pride, Troublers* of the Citie, &c.) *Sathan* commonly loads the meekeft of the *Saints* and *Witneffes* of *Jefus* with. *{Gods meekeft fervants ufe to be counted arrogant and impetuous.}*

To wipe off therefore thefe fowle *blurs* and *afperfions* from the faire and beautiful face of the *Spoufe* of *Jefus*, I fhall felect and propofe 5 or 6 cafes, for which *Gods witneffes* in all Ages and Generations of Men, have been charged with *arrogance, impetuoufnes*, &c. and yet the *God* of *Heaven*, and *Iudge* of all men, hath gracioufly difcharged them from fuch crimes, and maintained and avowed them for his *faithfull* and *peaceable* fervants. *{6 cafes wherein Gods people have been bold & zealous, yet not arrogant.}*

Firft, *Gods* people have *proclaimed, taught, difputed* for divers months together, a *new Religion* and *Worfhip*, contrary to the *Worfhip* projected [27] in the *Towne, City*, or *State*, where they have lived, or where they have travelled, as did the *Lord Jefus Himfelfe* over *all Galile*, and the *Apoftles* after Him in all places, both in the *Synagogues* and *Market-places*, as appeares *Acts* 17. 2. 17. *Acts* 18. 48. [4. 8.] Yet this no *Arrogance* nor *Impetuoufneffe*. *{Chrift Jefus and his Difciples teach publikely a new Doctrine, fundamentally differently different from the Religion profeffed.}*

Secondly, Gods *fervants* have been *zealous* for their Lord and *Mafter*, even to the very faces of the Higheft, and concerning the perfons of the Higheft, fo far as they have oppofed the *Truth* of God: So *Eliah* to the face of *Ahab*, It is not *I*, but *thou*, and thy *Fathers* houfe that troubleft *Ifrael:* So the Lord *Jefus* concerning *Herod*, Goe tell that *Fox*: So *Paul*, God delivered me from the mouth of the *Lion*; and to *{Gods fervants zealous and bold to the faces of the Higheft. Gods people conftantly im-}*

Ananias, Thou *whited wall*, and yet in all this no *Arrogance*, nor *Impetuousnesse*.

<small>moveable to death.</small>

Thirdly, *Gods people* have been *immoveable, constant* and *resolved* to the *death*, in refusing to submit to false *Worships*, and in *preaching* and *professing* the true *worship*, contrary to expresse command of *publicke Authority*: So the three *famous Worthies* against the command of *Nebuchadnezzar*, and the uniforme *conformity* of all *Nations* agreeing upon a false *worship*, *Dan.* 3. So the Apostles (*Acts* 4 and 5 chap.) and so the witnesses of *Jesus* in all ages, who loved not their lives to the *death* (*Rev.* 12.) not regarding sweet *life* nor bitter *death*, and yet not *Arrogant*, nor *Impetuous*.

<small>Gods people ever maintained Christ Jesus the only Lord and King to the conscience.</small>

Fourthly, *Gods people* since the comming of the *King* of *Israel*, the *Lord Jesus*, have openly and constantly profest, that no Civill *Magistrate*, no *King* nor *Cæsar* have any power over the *Soules* or *Consciences* of their Subjects, in the matters of God and the *Crowne* of *Jesus*, but the *Civill Magistrates* themselves; yea *Kings* and *Keisars* are bound to subject their owne soules to the *Ministery* and *Church*, the *Power* and *Government* of this *Lord Iesus*, the *King* of *Kings*. Hence was the charge against the *Apostles* (false in *Civill*, but true in *spiritualls*) that they affirmed that there was another *King*, one Iesus, *Acts* 17. 7. And indeed, this was the great charge against the *Lord Iesus* H*imself*, which the *Iews* laid against Him, and for which he suffered Death, as appears by the Accusation written over His Head upon the Gallows, *Iohn* 9. 19. *Iesus of Nazareth King of the Iewes*.

This was and is the summe of all true preaching of the Gospell or glad newes, *viz.* That God anointed Jesus to be the sole King and Governour of all the Israel of God in spirituall and soule causes, *Psal.* 2. 6. *Acts* 2. 36. Yet this Kingly power of His he resolved not to manage [28] in His owne Person, but Ministerially in the hands of such Messengers which he sent forth to preach and baptise, and to such as beleeved that word they preached, *Iohn* 17. And yet here no *Arrogance* nor *Impetuousnesse*.

_{That Christ is King alone over conscience is the sum of all true preaching}

5. *Gods people* in delivering the Minde and Will of God concerning the Kingdomes and Civill States where they have lived, have seemed in all shew of common sense and rationall policie (if men looke not higher with the eye of faith) to endanger and overthrow the very Civill State, as appeareth by all *Jeremies* preaching and counsell to King *Zedechia*, his Princes and people, insomuch that the charge of the Princes against *Jeremiah* was, that he discouraged the Army from fighting against the Babylonians, and weakned the Land from its own defence, and this charge in the eye of reason, seemed not to be unreasonable or unrighteous, *Jer.* 37. 38. chapters, and yet in *Jeremy* no *Arrogance* nor *Impetuousnesse*.

_{Gods people have seemed the disturbers of Civill State.}

6. Lastly, *Gods people* by their preaching, disputing, &c. have beene (though not the cause) yet accidentally the occasion of great contentions and divisions, yea tumults and uproares in Townes and Cities where they have lived and come, and yet neither their Doctrine nor themselves *Arrogant* nor *Impetuous*, however so charged: For thus the Lord Jesus discovereth mens false and secure suppositions, *Luke* 11. 51. *Sup-*

_{Gods word and people the occasion of tumults.}

pose ye that I am come to give peace on the earth? I tell you nay, but rather division, for from hence forth shall there be five in one house divided, three against two, and two against three, the father shall be divided against the sonne, and the sonne against the father, &c. And thus upon the occasion of the Apostles preaching, the Kingdome and Worship of God in Christ, were most commonly uproares and tumults, where ever they came: For instance, those strange and monstrous uproares at *Iconium*, at *Ephesus*, at *Jerusalem*, Acts 14. 4. Acts 19. 29. 40. Acts 21. vers. 30, 31.

CHAP. VIII.

Peace. IT will be said (deare *Truth*) what the Lord Jesus and his Messengers taught was *Truth*, but the question is about Errour.

Truth. I answer, this distinction now in discussion, concernes not *Truth*, or Errour, but the manner of holding forth or divulging.

The instances proposed carry a great shew of impetuousnesse, yet all are pure and peaceable.

29] I acknowledge that such may bee the way and manner of holding forth, (either with railing or reviling, daring or chalenging speeches, or with force of Armes, Swords, Guns, Prisons, &c.) that it may not only tend to breake, but may actually breake the civill peace, or peace of the Citie.

Yet these instances propounded are cases of great opposition and spirituall hostility, and occasions of breach of civill peace: and yet as the borders (or matter) were of gold: so the speckes (or manner

Cantic. 1.) were of silver: both matter and manner, pure, holy, peaceable, and inoffenfive.

Moreover, I anfwer, that it is poffible and common for perfons of foft and gentle nature and fpirits to hold out falfhood with more feeming meekneffe and peaceableneffe, then the Lord Jefus or his fervants did or doe hold forth the true and everlafting Gofpell. So that the anfwerer would be requefted to explain what he means by this arrogant and impetuous holding forth of any doctrine, which very manner of holding forth tends to breake civill peace, and comes under the cognifance and correction of the Civill Magiftrate: Left hee build the Sepulchre of the Prophets, and fay, If we had been in the Pharifes daies, the Romane Emperours dayes, or the bloody *Marian* dayes, we would not have been partakers with them in the blood of the Prophets, *Mat.* 23. 30. who were charged with arrogance and impetuoufneffe.

CHAP. IX.

2. *Ob. Peace.* IT will here be faid, Whence then arifeth civill diffentions and uproares about matters of Religion?

Truth. I anfwer: When a Kingdome or State, Towne or Family, lyes and lives in the guilt of a falfe God, falfe Chrift, falfe worfhip: no wonder if fore eyes be troubled at the appearance of the light, be it never fo fweet: No wonder if a body full of corrupt humours be troubled at ftrong (though wholfome) Phyfick?[:] If perfons fleepy and loving to fleepe

The true caufe of tumults at the preaching of the Word.

be troubled at the noise of shrill (though silver) alarums: No wonder if *Adonijah* and all his company be amazed and troubled at the sound of the right Heyre [heir] King *Salomon*, 1 *King*. 1.[:] If the Husbandmen were troubled when the Lord of the Vineyard sent servant after servant, and at last his onely Sonne, and they beat, and wounded, and kill'd even the Sonne himselfe, because they meant themselves to seize upon the inheritance, unto which they had no right, *Matth*. 21. 38. [30] Hence all those tumults about the Apostles in the *Acts*, &c. whereas good eyes are not so troubled at light; vigilant and watchfull persons loyall and faithfull, are not so troubled at the true, no nor at a false Religion of Jew or Gentile.

<small>A preposterous way of suppressing errours.</small> Secondly, breach of civil peace may arise, when false and idolatrous practices are held forth, & yet no breach of civil peace from the doctrine or practice, or the manner of holding forth, but from that wrong and preposterous way of suppressing, preventing, and extinguishing such doctrines or practices by weapons of wrath and blood, whips, stockes, imprisonment, banishment, death, &c. by which men commonly are perswaded to convert Heretickes, and to cast out uncleane spirits, which onely the finger of God can doe, that is the mighty power of the Spirit in the Word.

<small>Light only can expell fogs and darknesse.</small> Hence the Towne is in an uproare, and the Country takes the Alarum to expell that fog or mist of Errour, Heresie, Blasphemy, (as is supposed) with Swords and Guns; whereas tis Light alone, even Light from the bright shining Sunne of Righteous-

nesse, which is able, in the soules and consciences of men to dispell and scatter such fogges and darknesse.

Hence the Sons of men, (as *David* speakes in another case, *Psal.* 39.) disquiet themselves in vaine, and unmercifully disquiet others, as (by the helpe of the Lord) in the sequell of this discourse shall more appeare.

CHAP. X.

Peace. NOw the last distinction is this: " Persecu-"tion for Conscience, is either for a rightly "informed conscience, or a blinde and erroneous "conscience.

Answ. Truth. Indeed both these consciences are perfecuted: but lamentably blinde and erronious will these consciences shortly appear to be, which out of zeale for God (as is pretended) have persecuted either. And heavie is the doome of those blinde Guides and Idoll Shepherds (whose right eye Gods finger of jealousie hath put out) who flattering the ten Hornes or worldly Powers, perswade them what excellent and faithfull service they performe to God, in persecuting both these consciences: either hanging up a rightly informed conscience, and therein the Lord Jesus himselfe, betweene two malefactors, or else killing the erroneous and the blinde, like *Saul* (out of zeale to the Israel [31] of God) the poore Gibeonites, whom it pleased God to permit to live: and yet that hostility and cruelty used against them (as the repeated judgement yeare after yeare upon the whole Land after told them) could not be pardoned, untill the

Persecutors oppresse both true and erroneous consciences.

death of the perfecutor *Saul* [and] his fons had appeafed the Lords difpleafure, 2 *Sam.* 21.

CHAP. XI.

Peace. AFter explication in thefe Diftinctions, it pleafeth the Anfwerer to give his refolution to the queftion in foure particulars.

Firft, that he holds it not lawfull to perfecute any for confcience fake rightly informed, for in perfecuting fuch (faith he) Chrift himfelf is perfecuted: for which reafon, truly rendred, he quotes *Act.* 9. 4. *Saul, Saul, why perfecuteft thou me?*

Truth. He that fhall reade this Conclufion over a thoufand times, fhall as foone finde darkneffe in the bright beames of the Sunne, as in this fo cleare and fhining a beame of Truth, *viz.* That Chrift Jefus in his Truth muft not be perfecuted.

Yet this I muft aske (for it will be admired by all fober men) what fhould be the caufe or inducement to the Anfwerers mind to lay down fuch a Pofition or Thefis as this is, *It is not lawfull to perfecute the Lord Jefus.*

Search all Scriptures, Hiftories, Records, Monuments, confult with all experiences, did ever *Pharaoh, Saul, Ahab, Jezabel,* Scribes and Pharifes, the Jewes, *Herod,* the bloudy *Neroes, Gardiners, Boners,* Pope or Devill himfelfe, profeffe to perfecute the Son of God, Jefus as Jefus, Chrift as Chrift, without a mask or covering?

No, faith *Pharaoh,* the Ifraelites are idle, and therefore fpeake they of facrificing: *David* is rifen up in a conspiracy against *Saul*, therefore persecute him: Naboth hath blasphemed God and the King, therefore stone him: *Christ* is a seducer of the people, a blasphemer against God, and traytor against *Cæsar*, therefore hang him: Christians are schismaticall, factious, hereticall, therefore persecute them: The Devill hath deluded *John Hus*, therefore crown him with a paper of Devils, and burne him, &c.

_{All persecutors of Christ professe not to persecute him.}

Peace. One thing I see apparently in the Lords over-ruling the pen of this worthy Answerer, *viz.* a secret whispering from heaven to him, that (although his soules ayme at Christ, and hath wrought much for [32] Christ in many sincere intentions, and Gods mercifull and patient acceptance) yet he hath never left the Tents of such who think they doe God good service in killing the Lord Jesus in his servants, and yet they say, if we had beene in the dayes of our Fathers in Queene *Maries* dayes, &c. we would never have consented to such persecution: And therefore when they persecute Christ Jesus in his truths or servants, they say, Doe not say you are persecuted for the Word for Christ his sake, for we hold it not lawfull to persecute Iesus Christ.

_{All persecutors of Christ, professe not to persecute him.}

Let me also adde a second; So farre as he hath beene a Guide (by preaching for persecution) I say, wherein he hath beene a Guide and Leader, by misinterpreting and applying the Writings of Truth, so far I say his owne mouthes and hands shall judge (I hope not his persons, but) his actions, for the Lord Jesus hath suffered by him, *Act.* 9. 3. and if the Lord Jesus himselfe were present, himselfe should suffer that in his owne person, which his servants witnessing his Truth doe suffer for his sake.

CHAP. XII.

Peace. THeir second Conclusion is this: "It is not "lawfull to persecute an erroneous and "blinde conscience, even in fundamentall and weighty "points, till after admonition once or twice, *Tit.* 3. "11. and then such consciences may be persecuted, "because the Word of God is so cleare in fundamen- "tall and weighty points, that such a person cannot "but sin against his conscience, and so being con- "demned of himselfe, that is, of his conscience, hee "may be persecuted for sinning against his owne "conscience.

Truth. I answer, in that great battell betweene the Lord Jesus and the Devill, it is observable that Sathan takes up the weapons of Scripture, and such Scripture which in shew and colour was excellent for his purpose: but in this 3. of *Titus*, as *Salomon* speakes of the Birds of heaven, *Prov.* 1. a man may evidently see the snare; and I know the time is comming wherein it shall bee said, Surely in vaine the Net is laid in the sight of the Saints (heavenly Birds.)

So palpably grosse and thicke is the mist and fog which Sathan hath raised about this Scripture, that he that can but see men as trees in matters of Gods worship, may easily discerne what a wonderfull deepe sleepe Gods people are fallen into concerning the visible Kingdome of Christ, in so much that this third of *Titus* which through fearfull pro- [33] phanations, hath so many hundred years been the pretended Bulwark and defence of all the bloudy Wolves, dens of Lions, and mountains of Leopards, hunting and devouring the Witnesses of Jesus, should now be the refuge and defence of (as I hope) the Lambes and little ones of Jesus, yet (in this point) so preaching and practising so unlike to themselves, to the Lord Jesus, and lamentably too like to His and their Persecutors.

CHAP. XIII.

Peace. Bright *Truth*, since this place of *Titus* is such a pretended Bulwark for persecuting of Hereticks, & under that pretence of persecuting all thy followers, I beseech you by the bright beames of the Sun of Righteousnesse, scatter these mists, and unfold these particulars out of the Text:

First, What this Man is that is an Hereticke.

Secondly, How this Hereticke is condemned of himselfe.

Thirdly, What is this first and second Admonition, and by whom it is supposed to be given.

Fourthly, What is this rejecting of Him, and by whom it is supposed this Rejection was to be made.

Truth. First, What is this Heretick? I find him commonly defined to be such an one as is obstinate in Fundamentalls, and so also I conceive the Answerer seems to recent[1] him, saying, That the Apostle renders this reason, why after once and twice Admonition, he ought to be persecuted, because in fundamentall and principall points of Doctrine and Worship, the

_{What is meant by Hereticke in *Titus.*}

---

[1] *Resent*, which in its earlier meaning carried the idea of its Latin root,— to perceive, to feel, to regard. For instances, see Richardson, *Dictionary*, Trench, *Glossary of English Words*, &c., p. 170.

Word of God is fo cleare, that the Hereticke cannot but be convinced in his owne Confcience.

But of this reafon, I finde not one tittle mentioned in this Scripture; for although he faith fuch an one is condemned of himfelfe, yet he faith not, nor will it follow that fundamentalls are fo cleare, that after firft and fecond Admonition, a perfon that fubmits not to them is condemned of himfelf, any more then in leffer points. This 11 verfe hath reference to the former verfes. *Titus* an Evangelift, a Preacher of glad Newes, abiding here with the Church of Chrift at Creet, is required by *Paul* to avoid, to reject, and to teach the Church to reject Genealogies, difputes, and unprofitable queftions about the Law: Such a like charge it is as he gave to *Timothy*, left alfo an Evangelift at Ephefus, 1 *Tim*. 1. 4.

34] If it fhould be objected what is to be done to fuch contentious, vain ftrivers about Genealogies and queftions unprofitable? The Apoftle feems plainly to anfwer, Let him be once and twice admonifhed.

Ob. Yea, but what if once and twice admonition prevaile not?

The Apoftle feems to anfwer, $\alpha\iota\rho\varepsilon\tau\iota\varkappa\grave{o}\nu\ \alpha\nu\vartheta\rho\omega\pi o\nu$, and that is, the man that is willfully obftinate after fuch once and twice admonition, Reject him.

With this Scripture agrees that of 1 *Tim*. 6. 4, 5. where *Timothy* is commanded to withdraw himfelfe from fuch who dote about queftions and ftrife of words.

All which are points of a lower and inferiour nature, not properly falling within the tearms or notions of thofe ($\varsigma o\iota\chi\varepsilon\tilde{\iota}\alpha$) firft principles and ($\theta\varepsilon\mu\varepsilon\lambda\acute{\iota}o\iota\varsigma$)

foundations of the Chriſtian Profeſſion, to wit, Repentance from dead workes, Faith towards God, the doctrine of Baptiſmes, and of laying on of hands, the Reſurrection, and eternall Judgement, *Heb.* 6. 2. &c.

Concerning theſe Fundamentalls (although nothing is ſo little in the Chriſtian Worſhip, but may be referred to one of theſe ſix, yet) doth not *Paul* to *Timothy* or *Titus* ſpeake in thoſe places by me alledged, or of any of theſe, as may evidently appeare by the context and ſcope?

The beloved Spouſe of Chriſt is no receptacle for any filthy perſon, obſtinate in any filthyneſſe againſt the purity of the Lord Jeſus, who hath commanded his people to purge out the old leaven, not only greater portions, but a little leaven which will leaven the whole lumpe; and therefore this Hereticke or obſtinate perſon in theſe vaine and unprofitable queſtions, was to be rejected, as well as if his obſtinacie had been in greater matters.

Againe, if there were a doore or window left open to vaine and unprofitable queſtions, and ſinnes of ſmaller nature, how apt are perſons to cover with a ſilken covering, and to ſay, Why, I am no *Hereticke* in *Fundamentalls*, ſpare me in this or that *little* one; this or that *opinion* or *practice*, theſe are of an inferiour *circumſtantiall* nature? &c. The word Hereticke generally miſtaken.

So that the *coherence* with the former verſes, and the *ſcope* of the *Spirit of God* in this and other like *Scriptures* being carefully obſerved, this *Greek* word *Hereticke* is no more in true *Engliſh* and in Truth, then an *obſtinate* or *wilfull* perſon in the *Church* of

Creet, ftriving and contending about thofe unprofitable *Queftions* and *Genealogies*, &c. and is not fuch a *monfter* intended in this place, as moft *Interpreters* run upon, to wit, [wit] One *obftinate* in *Fundamentalls*,[1] and as the *Anfwerer* makes the [35] *Apoftle* to write in fuch *Fundamentalls* and *principall points*, wherein the Word of *God* is fo cleare that a man cannot but be convinced in *confcience*, and therefore is not perfecuted for matter of *confcience*, but for finning againft his *confcience*.

CHAP. XIV.

Peace. NOw in the fecond place, What is this *Self-condemnation?*

Truth. The *Apoftle* feemeth to make this a ground of the *rejecting* of fuch a perfon, becaufe he is *fubverted* and *finneth*, being *condemned* of himfelfe: It will appear upon due fearch that this *felfe-condemning* is not here intended to be in Hereticks (as men fay) in fundamentalls only, but as it is meant here, in men obftinate in the leffer Queftions, &c.

First, he is *fubverted* or turned crooked, ἐξέςραπται, a word oppofite to *ftreightneffe* or *rightneffe*: So that the fcope is, as I conceive, upon true and faithfull *admonition* once or twice, the pride of *heart*, or heat

---

[1] The beft recent commentators fuftain Williams in this view. "The term αἱρέσεις occurs but twice in St. Paul's Epiftles. In neither cafe does the word feem to imply fpecially 'the open efpoufal of any *fundamental* error,' but more generally, 'divifions in church matters,' poffibly, of a fomewhat matured kind. Thus then, αἱρετικος ἄνθρωπος will here be one who gives rife to such divifions by erroneous teaching, not neceffarily of a fundamentally heterodox nature, but of the kind juft defcribed, verfe 9." Bifhop Ellicott, *Commentary on Paftoral Epiftles, in loco.*

of *wrath*, drawes a *vaile* over the *eyes* and *heart*, so that the *soule* is turned loosed and[1] from the checks of *truth*.

Secondly, he *sinneth*, ἁμαρτανει, that is, being *subverted* or turned aside; he *sinneth* or wanders from the path of *Truth*, and is *condemned* by *himselfe* αυτοκάταχριτος, that is, by the secret *checkes* and *whisperings* of his owne *conscience*, which will take *Gods* part against a mans selfe, in smiting, accusing, &c. *Checks of conscience.*

Which checks of *conscience* we finde even in *Gods* owne dear people, as is most admirably opened in the 5 of *Cant.* in those sad, drowsie and unkinde *passages* of the *Spouse* in her *answer* to the *knocks* and *calls* of the *Lord Jesus*; which Gods people in all their awakening acknowledge how sleightly they have listned to the checks of their owne *consciences*. This the *Answerer* pleaseth to call sinning against his *conscience*, for which he may lawfully be persecuted, to wit, for sinning against his *conscience*.

Which *conclusion* (though painted over with the *vermillion* of *mistaken Scripture*, and that *old dreame* of *Jew* and *Gentile*, that the *Crowne* of *Jesus* will consist of outward *materiall gold*, and his *sword* be made of *iron* or *steele*, executing judgement in his *Church* and *Kingdome* by *corporall punishment*) I hope (by the assistance of the Lord Jesus) to manifest it to be the overturning and rooting up the very *foundation* and [36] *roots* of all true *Christianity*, and absolutely denying the *Lord Jesus* the Great *Anointed* to be yet come in the Flesh.

[1] " And " should precede " loosed."

CHAP. XV.

THis will appeare, if we examine the two laſt *Quæries* of this place of *Titus:* to wit,

Firſt, What this *Admonition* is?

Secondly, What is the *Rejection* here intended? *Reject* him.

Firſt then, *Titus*, unto whom this *Epiſtle* & theſe *directions* were written, (and in him to all that ſucceed him in the like work of the *Goſpell* to the Worlds end) he was no *Miniſter* of the *Civill State*, armed with the *majeſtie* and *terrour* of a *materiall ſword*, who might for *offences* againſt the *civill ſtate*, inflict *puniſhments* upon the *bodies* of men, by *impriſonments, whippings, fines, baniſhment, death*. *Titus* was a Miniſter of the *Goſpel* or *Glad tidings*, armed onely with the *Spirituall ſword* of the *Word of God*, and ſuch *Spirituall weapons* as (yet) through *God* were mighty to the caſting down of *ſtrong holds*, yea every *high thought* of the *higheſt head* and *heart* in the world, 2 Cor. 10. 4.

What is the firſt & second admonition.

Therefore theſe firſt and ſecond Admonitions were not *civill* or *corporall* puniſhments on mens *perſons* or *purſes*, which the *Courts* of Men may lawfully inflict upon *Malefactors:* but they were the *reprehenſions, convictions, exhortations*, and *perſwaſions* of the Word of the *Eternall God*, charged home to the *Conſcience*, in the name and preſence of the *Lord Jeſus*, in the middeſt of the *Church*. Which being deſpiſed and not hearkned to, in the laſt place followes *rejection*; which is not a *cutting off* by *heading, hanging, burning*, &c. or an *expelling* of the *Country*

What the rejecting of the Heretick was.

and *Coasts:* neither [of] which (no nor any lesser *civill* punishment) *Titus* nor the Church at *Crete* had any power to exercise. But it was that dreadfull cutting off from that visible *Head* and *Body*, *Christ Jesus* and his *Church*; that *purging* out of the *old leaven* from the *lumpe* of the *Saints*; the putting away of the *evill* and wicked person from the holy *Land* and Commonwealth of *Gods Israel*, 1 Cor. 5. where it is observable, that the same word used by *Moses* for putting a malefactor to *death* in typicall *Israel*, by *sword*, *stoning*, &c. Deut. 13. 5. is here used by *Paul* for the *spirituall killing* or *cutting off* by *Excommunication*, 1 Cor. 5. 13. Put away that evill person, &c.

<small>Corporall killing in the Law, typing out Spirituall killing by Excommunication in the Gospell.</small>

Now I desire the Answerer, and any, in the holy awe and feare of *God* to consider, That

37] From whom the *first* and *second Admonition* was to proceed, from them also was the *rejecting* or casting out to proceed, as before.

But not from the Civill *Magistrate* (to whom *Paul* writes not this *Epistle*, and who also is not bound once and twice to admonish, but may speedily punish, as he sees cause, the persons or purses of *Delinquents* against his *Civill* State :) but from *Titus* the *Minister* or *Angel* of the *Church*, and from the *Church* with him, were these *first* and *second Admonitions* to proceed; And

Therefore at last also this *Rejecting*, which can be no other but a *casting* out, or *excommunicating* of him from their Church-societie.

Indeed, this *rejecting* is no other then that *avoyding* which *Paul* writes of to the *Church* of *Christ* at *Rome*, Rom. 16. 17. which avoyding (however wofully perverted by some to prove persecution) belonged to the *Governours* of *Christs Church* & *Kingdome* in *Rome,* and not to the *Romane Emperour* for him to rid and avoyd the *World* of them, by bloody and cruell *Persecution.*

CHAP. XVI.

The third Conclusiõ discussed.

Peace. THe third Conclusion is; In points of lesser moment, there ought to be a *Toleration.*
Which though I acknowledge to be the Truth of God, yet 3 things are very observable in the manner *Sathans* of laying it down; for *Sathan* useth excellent *arrowes policie.* to bad *markes,* and sometimes beyond the *intent,* and hidden from the eye of the *Archer.*

The Answerer granteth a Toleration.

First (saith he) such a person is to be tolerated, till God may be pleased to reveale his Truth to him.

Truth. This is well observed by you; for indeed this is the very *ground* why the *Apostle* calls for meekenesse and gentlenesse toward *all* men, and toward such as oppose themselves, 2 *Tim.* 2. because there is a *peradventure* or *it may be*; It *may be* God may give them *Repentance.* That *God* that hath shewen *Patience* mercy to one, may shew *mercy* to another: It may be *to be used* that *eye-salve* that anointed *one mans* eye who was *toward the oppo-* *blinde* and opposite, may anoint another as *blinde* and *site.* opposite: He that hath given *Repentance* to the *husband,* may give it to his *wife,* &c.

Hence that *Soule* that is lively and sensible of *mercy* received to it selfe in former *blindnesse,* opposition and enmitie against God, cannot but be patient and gentle toward the *Jewes,* who yet deny the *Lord Jesus*

38] to be come, and juſtifie their *Fore-fathers* in mur- | The car-
thering of him: Toward the *Turkes*, who acknowl- | riage of a Soule ſen-
edge *Chriſt a great Prophet*, yet affirme [him] leſſe than | ſible of
Mahomet. Yea to all the ſeverall ſorts of *Antichriſ-* | mercy, toward
tians, who ſet up many a *falſe Chriſt* in ſtead of him. | other ſin-
And laſtly to the *Pagans* and *wildeſt* ſorts of the ſons | ners in their blind
of men, who have not yet heard of the *Father*, nor | neſſe and
the *Son*. And to all theſe ſorts, *Jewes*, *Turkes*, *Anti-* | oppoſi-
chriſtians, *Pagans*, when they oppoſe the light pre- | tion.
ſented to them; In ſenſe of its own former oppoſition, and that *God* peradventure may at laſt give
repentance: I adde, ſuch a Soule will not onely be
patient, but earneſtly and conſtantly pray for all ſorts
of men, that out of them *Gods* elect may be called to
the fellowſhip of *Chriſt Jeſus*. And laſtly, not only
pray, but endeavour (to its utmoſt abilitie) their participation of the ſame *grace* and *mercy*.

That great *Rock* upon which ſo many gallant Ships
miſcarrie, viz. That ſuch perſons, falſe *Prophets*,
Hereticks, *&c.* were to be put to death in *Iſrael*, I
ſhall (with Gods aſſiſtance) remove: as alſo that fine
ſilken covering of the *Image*, viz. that ſuch perſons
ought to be put to *death* or *baniſhed*, to prevent the
infecting and *ſeducing* of others, I ſhall (with Gods
aſſiſtance) in the following diſcourſe pluck off.

Secondly, I obſerve from the Scriptures he quoteth | The An-
for this *Toleration*, (*Phil.* 3. & *Rom.* 14.) how cloſely, | ſwerer có-
yet I hope unadviſedly, he makes the *Churches* of | founds the Churches
Chriſt at *Philippi* and *Rome*, all one with the Cities | in Philip-
Philippi and *Rome*, in which the *Churches* were, and to | pi and Rome
whom onely *Paul* wrote. As if what theſe *Churches* | with the
in *Philippi* and *Rome* muſt tolerate amongſt them- | Cities Phi-

lippi and Rome. selves, that the Cities *Philippi* and *Rome* must tolerate in their *citizens:* and what these *Churches* must not tolerate, that these Cities *Philippi* and *Rome* must not tolerate within the compasse of the City, State and Jurisdiction.

Truth. Upon that ground, by undeniable consequence, these Cities *Philippi* and *Rome* were bound not to tolerate themselves, that is, the Cities and Citizens of *Philippi* and *Rome*, in their own Civill life and being, but must kill or expell themselves from their own Cities, as being Idolatrous *worshippers* of other gods then the true *God* in *Jesus Christ*.

Difference between the Church and the World. But as the *Lilie* is amongst the *Thornes*, so is Christs *Love* among the *Daughters*: and as the *Apple-tree* among the *Trees* of the *Forrest*, so is her *Beloved* among the Sons: so great a difference is there between the *Church* in a Citie or Country, and the *Civill state*, *City* or Country in which it is.

39] No lesse then (as *David* in another case, *Psal.* 103. as far as the *Heavens* are from the *Earth*) are they that are truly *Christs* (that is, anointed truly with the Spirit of *Christ*) [different] from many thousands who love not the *Lord Iesus Christ*, and yet are and must be permitted in the World or Civill State, although they have no right to enter into the gates of *Jerusalem* the *Church* of God.

The Church and Civill State confusedly made all one. And this is the more carefully to bee minded, because when ever a *toleration* of others *Religion* and *Conscience* is pleaded for, such as are (I hope in truth) *zealous* for *God*, readily produce plenty of *Scriptures* written to the *Church*, both before and since *Christs* comming, all commanding and pressing the putting forth of the *uncleane*, the cutting off the *obstinate*, the purging out the *Leaven*, rejecting of *Heretickes*. As if becaufe *briars*, *thornes*, and *thiftles* may not be in the *Garden* of the *Church*, therefore they muft all bee pluckt up out of the *Wildernesse*: whereas he that is a *Briar*, that is, a *Jew*, a *Turke*, a *Pagan*, an *Antichristian* to day, may be (when the Word of the *Lord* runs freely) a member of *Jesus Christ* to morrow cut out of the wilde *Olive*, and planted into the true.

Peace. Thirdly, from this *toleration* of perfons but holding *lesser errours*, I obferve the *unmercifulnesse* of fuch *doctrines* and *hearts*, as if they had forgotten the *Blessednesse*, *Blessed* are the mercifull, for they fhall obtaine mercy, *Math.* 5. He that is fleightly and but a little hurt, fhall be *suffered*, and meanes vouchfafed for his *cure*: But the deepe *wounded sinners*, and *leprous*, *ulcerous*, and thofe of *bloudy issues* twelve yeares together, and thofe which have been bowed down 38. years of their *life*, they muft not be fuffered untill peradventure God may give them *repentance*; but either it is not lawfull for a *godly Magistrate* to rule and governe fuch a people (as fome have faid) or elfe if they be under *government*, and reforme not to the *State Religion* after the firft and fecond *admonition*, the *Civill Magistrate* is bound to perfecute, &c.

Truth. Such perfons have need, as *Paul* to the *Romanes*, Chap. 12. 1. to be befought by the mercy of God to put on *bowels* of *mercy* toward fuch as have neither wronged them in *body* or *goods*, and therefore juftly fhould not be punifhed in their *goods* or perfons.

<small>Perfecutors have forgotten the bleffedneffe promifed to the mercifull, Math. 5.</small>

CHAP. XVII.

Peace. I Shall now trouble you (deare Truth) but with one conclusion more, which is this: *viz.* That if a man hold forth errour with [40] a *boysterous* and *arrogant* spirit, to the disturbance of the civill Peace, he ought to be punished, &c.

Truth. To this I have spoken too, confessing that if any man commit ought of those things which *Paul* was accused of (*Act.* 25. 11.) he ought not to be spared, yea he ought not, as *Paul* saith, in such cases to refuse to dye.

<small>What persons are guilty of breach of civil peace</small> But if the *matter* be of another *nature*, a spirituall and divine *nature*, I have written before in many cases, and might in many more, that the *Worship* which a State professeth may bee *contradicted* and *preached* against, and yet no breach of *Civill Peace*. And if a *breach* follow, it is not made by such *doctrines*, but by the boysterous and violent opposers of them.

<small>The most peaceable wrongfully accused of peace-breaking.</small> Such persons onely breake the *Cities* or *Kingdomes* peace, who cry out for *prison* and *swords* against such who crosse their *judgement* or *practice* in *Religion*. For as *Josephs* mistris accused *Joseph* of *uncleannesse*, and calls out for civill violence against him, when *Joseph* was chaste, and her *selfe* guilty: So commonly the meeke and *peaceable* of the earth are traduced as *rebells, factious, peace-breakers*, although they deale not with the *State* or *State-matters*, but *matters* of *divine* and *spirituall* nature, when their *traducers* are the onely *unpeaceable*, and guilty of *breach* of *Civill Peace*.

Peace. We are now come to the second part of the *Answer,* which is a particular examination of such *grounds* as are brought against such *persecution.*

The first sort of grounds are from the *Scriptures.*

CHAP. XVIII.

First, *Matth.* 13. 30, 38. because *Christ* commandeth to let alone the *Tares* to grow up together with the *Wheat,* untill the *Harvest.* _{The examination of what is meant by the Tares, and the command of the L. Jesus to let them alone.}

Unto which he answereth: That *Tares* are not *Bryars* and *Thornes,* but partly *Hypocrites,* like unto the *godly,* but indeed *carnall* (as the *Tares* are like to *Wheat,* but are not *Wheat,*) or partly such corrupt *doctrines* or *practices* as are indeed unsound, but yet such as come very near the truth (as *Tares* do to the *Wheat*) and so neer that *good* men may be taken with them, and so the persons in whom they grow cannot bee rooted out, but good *Wheat* will be rooted out with them. In such a case (saith he) *Christ* calleth for *peaceable toleration,* and not for *penall prosecution,* according to the third Conclusion.

41] *Truth.* The *substance* of this *Answer* I conceive to be first *negative,* that by *Tares* are not meant persons of another *Religion* and *Worship,* that is (saith he) they are not *Briars* and *Thornes.* _{The Answerers fallacious exposition that Tares signifie either Persons, Doctrines or Practices.}

Secondly, *affirmative,* by *Tares* are meant either *persons,* or *doctrines,* or *practices*; *persons,* as *hypocrites,* like the *godly*: *doctrines* or *practices* corrupt, yet like the *truth.*

For answer hereunto I confesse that not onely those worthy *witnesses* (whose memories are sweet with all that feare God) *Calvin*,[1] *Beza*, &c. but of later times many conjoyne with this worthy *Anſwerer*, to ſatisfie themſelves and others with ſuch an *Interpretation*.

<small>The Anſwerer barely affirming a moſt ſtrange interpretation.</small>

But alas, how darke is the ſoule left that deſires to walke with God in holy feare and trembling, when in ſuch a waighty and mighty point as this is, that in matters of *conſcience* concerneth the ſpilling of the *bloud of thouſands*, and the *Civill Peace* of the *World* in the taking up *Armes* to ſuppreſſe all falſe *Religions!* when I ſay no *evidence* or *demonſtration* of the *Spirit* is brought to prove ſuch an *interpretation*, nor *Arguments* from the place it ſelfe or the Scriptures of truth to confirme it; but a bare Affirmation that theſe *Tares* muſt ſignifie *perſons*, or *doctrines* and *practices*.

<small>Sathans ſubtletie about the opening of Scripture.</small>

I will not imagine any deceitfull purpoſe in the Anſwerers thoughts in the propoſall of theſe three, *perſons, doctrines*, or *practices*, yet dare I confidently avouch that the *Old Serpent* hath deceived their precious ſoules, and by *Tongue* and *Pen* would deceive

---

[1] "Quare hic meo judicio ſimplex eſt parabolæ ſcopus. Quamdiu in hoc mundo peregrinatur Eccleſia, bonis et ſinceris in ea permixtos fore malos et hypocritas, ut ſe patientia arment filii Dei, et inter offendicula, quibus turbari poſſent, retineant infractam fidei conſtantiam. Eſt autem aptiſſima comparatio, quum Dominus Eccleſiam vocat agrum ſuum, quia ejus ſemen ſunt fideles. Quanquam autem Chriſtus poſtea ſubjicit, mundum eſſe agrum dubium tamen non eſt, quin proprie hoc nomen ad Eccleſiam aptare voluerit, de qua exorſus fuerat ſermonem. Sed quoniam paſſim aratrum ſuum ducturus erat per omnes mundi plagas, ut ſibi agros excoleret in toto mundo ac ſparget vitæ ſemen, per ſynecdochen ad mundum tranſtulit, quod parti tantum magis quadrabat. Nunc videndum eſt, quid per *triticum* intelligat, et quid per *zizania*. Non poteſt hic de doctrina exponi, quaſi dixiſſet, ubi ſeminatur Evangelium, ſtatim corrumpi et adulterari pravis figmentis: nunquam enim vetuiſſet Chriſtus, in tali corruptela purganda ſtrenue ſatagere. Neque enim ut in hominum moribus, quæ corrigi nequeunt vitia, tolerari oportet, ita liceret impios errores ferre, qui fidei puritatem inficiunt. Deinde nominatim Chriſtus filios maligni zizania eſſe dicens dubitationem tollit." Johannis Calvini *Commentarii*, ii, 14, ed. A. Tholuck.

the foules of others by such a *method* of dividing the word of *truth*. A threefold *Cord,* and so a threefold *Snare* is strong, and too like it is that one of the three, either *Persons, Doctrines,* or *Practices* may catch some feet.

CHAP. XIX.

Peace. THe place then being of such great importance as concerning the *truth of God,* the *bloud of thousands,* yea the bloud of *Saints,* and of the Lord *Jesus* in them, I shall request your more diligent search (by the Lords holy assistance) into this Scripture.[1] [*Truth.*] I shall make it evident, that by these Tares in this Parable are meant *persons* in respect of their *Religion* and way of *Worship, open* and *visible professours,* as bad as *briars* and *thornes*; not onely suspected *Foxes,* but as bad as those *greedy Wolves* which *Paul* speakes of, *Acts* 20. who with perverse and evill *doctrines* labour spiritually to devoure the *flocke,* and to draw away Disciples after them, whose mouthes must be stopped, and yet no carnall

---

[1] This parable, to which so much importance is here ascribed, ten chapters being devoted to it, has for ages been the battle-ground of a controversy to which this between Williams and Cotton is allied. The Donatists who were the Separatists of the fourth and fifth centuries, held with Williams, and all who contend for the entirely spiritual and regenerate character of the churches, that, as our Lord says, "the field" is not the *Church* but the *world,* and that it is no reason for receiving or allowing ungodly men in the church because they were not to be rooted out of the world. Trench, *Notes on the Parables,* p. 74; Neander, *Church History,* ii : 205, 207. Williams however turns it here not to the decision of the question of church-discipline, but against the use of civil force with such. He was strict and exclusive in regard to toleration even of such as observed "popish Christmas, Easter, Whitsuntide, and other superstitious popish festivals," (p. 42,) but liberal for all outside of the church and not voluntarily under its discipline.

42] *force* or *weapon* to be used against them, but their *mischiefe* to bee resisted with those mighty *weapons* of the holy *Armoury* of the Lord *Jesus*, wherein there hangs a *thousand shields*, Cant. 4.

That the *Lord Iesus* intendeth not *doctrines* or *practices* by the *tares* in this Parable is cleare: for

First, the *Lord Iesus* expresly interpreteth the *good seed* to be *persons*, and those the children of the *Kingdome*; and the *tares* also to signifie *Men*, and those the *children* of the *Wicked one*, ver. 38.

<small>Toleration in Rom. 14. considered.</small> Secondly, such corrupt *doctrines* or *practices* are not to bee tolorated now as those *Iewish* observations (the *Lords* owne *Ordinances*) were for a while to be permitted, *Rom.* 14. Nor so long as till the Angels the *Reapers* come to reape the Harvest in the end of the *world*. For can we thinke that because the tender Consciences of the *Iewes* were to be tendred in their *differences* of *meats*, that therefore persons must now bee tolerated in the *Church* (for I speake not of the *Civill State*) and that to the worlds end, in superstitious forbearing and forbidding of *flesh* in *Popish Lents*, and *superstitious Fridayes, &c.* and that because they were to be tendred in their observation of *Iewish Holidayes*, that therefore untill the *Harvest* or *Worlds end*, persons must now be tolerated (I meane in the <small>Toleratió of Jewish ceremonies for a time upon some grounds</small> *Church*) in the observation of Popish *Christmas, Easter, Whitsontide*, and other superstitious Popish *Festivals?*

I willingly acknowledge, that if the members of a *Church of Christ* shall upon some *delusion* of *Sathan* kneele at the *Lords Supper*,[1] keep *Christmas*, or any

---

[1] The objections of the Puritans to this practice are stated in Neal, *History of the Puritans*, i, 246, 247, Am. Ed. They were, in brief, that the Sacrament was

other Popish *observation*, great tendernesse ought to bee used in winning his soule from the errour of his way: and yet I see not that persons so practising were fit to be received into the Churches of Christ now, as the *Iewes* weake in the Faith, (that is, in the Liberties of *Christ*) were to be received, *Rom.* 14. 1. And least of all (as before) that the *toleration* or *permission* of such ought to continue till *Doomes day*, or the end of the *world*, as this Parable urgeth the *Toleration*; Let them alone untill the *Harvest*.

<small>in the Jewish Church proves not toleration of Popish and Antichristian Ceremonies in the Christian Church, although in the State.</small>

CHAP. XX.

AGaine, *Hypocrites* were not intended by the *Lord Iesus* in this famous Parable.

First, the Originall word ζιζάνια, signifying all those *Weeds* which spring up with the *Corne*, as *Cockle, Darnell, Tares,* &c. seemes to imply such a kinde of people as commonly and generally are knowne to bee [43] manifestly different from, and opposite to the true *worshippers* of *God*, here called the *children* of the *Kingdom*; as these *weeds, tares, cockle, darnell,* &c. are commonly and presently knowne by every *husbandman* to differ from the *wheat*, and to be opposite, and contrary, and hurtfull unto it.

<small>Tares proved not to signifie hypocrites Hence were the witnesses of Christ *Wickliff* and others in H. 4. his reigne called Lollards (as some say) from *Lolia*,</small>

---

not so received originally, the Apostles not kneeling when in the corporeal presence of Christ; that the practice arose from the notion of transubstantiation; that it is of "very late antiquity," and that it is contrary to the nature of the Lord's Supper.

It was Cotton's refusal to conform to this ceremony which led to his being informed against in the High Commission. Neal, *Puritans*, i, 317. He says "When the Bishop of Lincoln Diocesse (Dr. *Mountaigne*) offered me liberty upon once kneeling at the Sacrament with him the next Lord-day after, I durst not accept his offer of liberty upon once kneeling." *Way of Congregational Churches Cleared*, p. 19.

weeds known well enough, hence taken for signe of barrenesse Infelix Lolium & steriles dom inantur avenæ:[1] others conceive they were so called from one Lollard,[2] &c. but all Papists accounted

Now whereas it is pleaded that these *tares* are like the *wheat*, and so like that this *confimilitude* or likenesse is made the ground of this *interpretation*, viz. That *tares* must needs signifie *hypocrites*, or *doctrines*, or *practices*, who are like Gods children, Truth, &c.

I answer, first, The *Parable* holds forth no such thing, that the likenesse of the *tares* should deceive the servants to cause them to suppose for a time that they were good *wheat*, but that as soone as ever the *tares* appeared, ver. 26. the *servants* came to the *housholder* about them, ver. 27. the Scripture holds forth no such time wherein they doubted or suspected what they were.

Peace. It may be said they did not appeare to be *tares* untill the *corne* was in the blade, and put forth its fruit.

---

[1] Virgil, *Georgics*, i, 154.

[2] "The derivation of the name from the pretended founder of a sect, Walter Lollhard, who is said to have been a German, is fabulous; that from *lolium*, darnel or cockle-weed, which stigmatizes the people themselves or their doctrine as tares among wheat, is also erroneous and unfounded. The only correct derivation, and the one of late universally accepted, is from the old German *lollen* or *lullen*—to sing softly, which last word is still common in English, mainly in "lullabies," while the German *lallen* is allied to it. The name, probably suggested by the low, suppressed singing and devotional exercises in conventicles, was coined to designate a close, religious communion of unchurchly and heretical tendencies; in this sense it came into use in popular as well as in church parlance. Then in Wicliffe's time, a Cistercian monk, Heinrich Grumpe, Master of Theology, applied it to Wickliffe's followers in some polemical lectures which he gave at Oxford, about the year 1382. And in the years 1387–1389, the name was already used in official episcopal documents, in such a way, however, that it is plain that it was first current as a popular expression, and was only afterward adopted into official speech; and here it received an impress in which the primary, undefined, broad meaning of Low-German origin was entirely lost, and the exclusive and specific English reference to Wicliffe's followers and to his doctrine, took its place." Herzog, *Real-encyclopädie für protestantische theologie und kirche;* Art. *Lollarden,* viii, 458.

Truth. I anfwer, *The one appeared as foone as the other, for fo the word clearly carries it, that the *feed* of both having been fowne, when the *wheat* appeared and put forth its blade and fruit, the *tares* alfo were as early, and put forth themfelves as appeared alfo.

<sub>them as Tares be-caufe of their profeffion.
*The falfe and counterfeit Chriftians appeare as foon as the true and faithfull.</sub>

Secondly, there is fuch a *diffimilitude* or *unlikeneffe*, I fay fuch a *diffimilitude*, that as foone as *tares* and *wheat* are fprung up to blade and fruit, every *hufbandman* can tell which is *wheat*, and which are *tares* and *cockle*, &c.

Peace. It may be faid true: So when the *hypocrite* is manifefted, then all may know him, &c. but before *hypocrites* be manifefted by *fruits* they are unknowne.

[*Truth.*] I anfwer, fearch into the *Parable*, and aske when was it that the *fervants* firft complained of the *tares* to the *houfholder*, but when they appeared or came in fight, there being no *interim*, wherein the fervants could not tell what to make of them, but doubted whether they were *wheat* or *tares*, as the Anfwerer implies.

Secondly, when was it that the *houfholder* gave charge to let them alone, but after that they appeared, and were known to be *tares*, which fhould imply by this *interpretation* of the *Anfwerer*, that when men are difcovered and knowne to be *Hypocrites*, yet ftill fuch a *generation* of *Hypocrites* in the *Church* muft be let alone and tolerated untill the *harveft* or end of the world, which is contrary to all *order*, *piety* and *fafety* in the *Church* of the *Lord Jefus*, as doubtleffe the *Anfwerers* will grant; [44] fo that thefe Tares being notorioufly knowne to be different from the Corne, I conclude that they cannot here be intended

_{Hypocriticall Chriftians.}

_{The Tares cannot fig-}

nifie Hyp- by the *Lord Jesus* to signifie secret *Hypocrites,* but
ocrites. more open and apparent Sinners.

CHAP. XXI.

Two sorts of Hypocrites: 1. In the Church as *Iudas, Simon Magus* and these must be tolerated untill discovered, and no longer. 2. Hypocrites in the world which are false Christians, false Churches, & these the Lord Iesus wil have let alone unto Harvest.

THe second reason why these *tares* cannot signifie *hypocrites* in the *Church,* I take from the *Lord Jesus* His own *Interpretation* of the *field* (in which both *wheat* and *tares* are sowne, which saith he is the *World,* out of which God chooseth and calleth His *Church.*

The *World* lyes in *wickednesse,* is like a *Wildernesse* or a *Sea* of *wilde Beasts* innumerable, *fornicators, covetous, Idolaters,* &c. with whom *Gods people* may lawfully converse and cohabit in *Cities, Townes,* &c. else must they not live in the *World,* but goe out of it, In which *world* as soone as ever the *Lord Jesus* had sowne the *good seed,* the *children* of the *Kingdome,* true *Christianity,* or the true *Church;* the *Enemy Sathan* presently in the *night* of *security, Ignorance* and *Errour* (whilest men slept) sowed also these *tares* which are *Antichristians* or *false Christians.* These *strange Professours* of the Name of *Jesus,* the *Ministers* and *Prophets* of *God,*[1] beholding they are ready to runne to *Heaven* to fetch *fiery judgements* from thence to consume these strange *Christians,* and to pluck them by the *roots* out of the world: But the Son of Man, the *meek Lamb* of God (for the *Elect* sake which must be gathered out of *Jew* and *Gentile, Pagan, Antichistian*) commands a permission of them in the *World,* untill the time of the end of the *World,* when

---

[1] Let the comma follow "beholding," and *dele* the comma after "Jesus."

the *Goats* and *Sheep*, the *Tares* and *Wheat* shall be eternally separated each from other. *(The Field by most, generally,*

Peace. You know some excellent *Worthies* (dead and living) have laboured to turne this *Field* of the *World* into the *Garden* of the *Church*. *but falsely interpreted the Church.)*

Truth. But who can imagine that the *Wisdome* of the *Father*, the *Lord Jesus Christ*, would so open this *Parable* (as He professedly doth) as that it should be close shut up, and that one *difficulty* or *locke* should be opened by a greater and harder, in calling the *World* the *Church*? contrary also to the way of the Light and Love that is in Jesus, when he would purposely teach and instruct His scholars [; also] contrary to the nature of *Parables* and *similitudes*. *(The Lord Iesus the great teacher by Parables, and the only expounder of them.)*

And lastly, to the nature of the *Church* or *Garden* of *Christ*.

CHAP. XXII.

IN the former *Parable* the Lord *Jesus* compared the *Kingdome* of *Heaven* to the sowing of *Seed*. The true *Messengers* of *Christ* are the [45] *Sowers*, who cast the *Seed* of the *Word* of the *Kingdome* upon foure *sorts* of ground, which foure *sorts* of *ground* or *hearts* of men, cannot be supposed to be of the *Church*, nor will it ever be proved that the *Church* consisteth of any more sorts or natures of ground properly, but *one*, to wit, the *honest* and *good* ground, and the proper worke of the *Church* concernes the flourishing and prosperity of this sort of ground, and not the other *unconverted* three sorts, who it may be seldome or never come neare the *Church* unlesse they be forced *(The scope of the Parable. Foure sorts of ground or hearers of the word in the world and but one properly in the Church, the rest seldome come or accidentally to hear) the word in the Church, which word ought to be fitted for the feeding of the Church or flocke: preaching for conversion is properly out of the Church.*

by the *Civill sword*, which the *patterne* or first *sowers* never used, and being forced they are put into a way of *Religion* by such a course, if not so, they are forced to live without a *Religion*, for one of the two must necessarily follow, as I shall prove afterward.

In the *field* of the *World* then are all those *sorts* of ground, *high way hearers, stony* and *thorny* ground hearers, as well as the *honest* and good ground; and I suppose it will not now be said by the Answerer, that those three sorts of *bad* grounds were *hypocrites* or *tares* in the *Church*.

Now after the Lord *Jesus* had propounded that great *leading Parable* of the *Sower* and the *Seed*, He is pleased to propound this *Parable* of the *Tares*, with admirable *coherence* and sweet *consolation* to the honest and good ground, who with glad and honest hearts having received the *word* of the *Kingdome*, may yet seem to be discouraged and troubled with so many *Antichristians* and false *Professours* of the *Name* of *Christ*. The Lord *Jesus* therefore gives *direction* concerning these *tares*, that unto the end of the World successively in all the *sorts* and *generations* of them they must be (not approved or countenanced, but) let alone or *permitted* in the *World*.

The scope of the Parable of the Tares.

Secondly, he gives to His owne *good seed* this *consolation*, that those heavenly *Reapers* the *Angells* in the *harvest* or end of the *World*, will take an order and course with them, to wit, they shall binde them into *bundles*, and cast them into the *everlasting burnings*, and to make the cup of their *consolation* run over: He addes vers. 4. Then, then at that time shall the *Righteous* shine as the *Sun* in the *Kingdome* of their *Father*.

The Lord Iesus in this Parable of the Tares gives direction and consolation to His servants.

These *tares* then neither being erronious *doctrines*, nor corrupt *practises*, nor *hypocrites* in the true *Church* intended by the Lord Jesus in this Parable; I shall in the third place (by the helpe of the same Lord Jesus) evidently prove that these *tares* can be no other sort of sinners, but false *worshippers, Idolaters*, and in particular properly, *Antichristians*. The Tares proved properly to signifie Antichristians.

46] CHAP. XXIII.

First then, these Tares are such sinners as are opposite and contrary to the *children* of the *Kingdome* visibly so declared and manifest, ver. 38. Now the Kingdome of *God* below, is the *visible Church* of Christ Jesus, according to *Matth.* 8. 12. The children of the *Kingdome* which are threatned to be cast out, seeme to be the *Jewes*, which were then the onely *visible Church* in Covenant with the Lord, when all other *Nations* followed other *gods* and *worships*. And more plaine is that fearefull *threatning, Matth.* 21. 43. The *Kingdome* of *God* shall be taken from you, and given to a *Nation* that will bring forth the fruits thereof. Math. 8. 12. Math. 21. 43. Gods kingdome on Earth the visible Church.

Such then are the *good seed, good wheat, children of the Kingdome*, as are the *disciples, members* and *subjects* of the Lord *Jesus Christ* his *Church & Kingdom*: and therefore consequently such are the *tares*, as are opposite to these, *Idolaters, Will-worshippers*, not truly but fasly submitting to *Jesus*: and in especiall, the children of the *wicked* one, visibly so appearing. Which wicked one I take not to be the *Devill*; for the Lord *Jesus* seemes to make them distinct: The difference between the

<small>Wheat & the Tares, as also between these Tares and all other.</small> He that sowes the good seed (saith he) is the *Son* of *man*, the *field* is the *World*, the good seed are the *Children* of the *Kingdome*, but the *Tares* are the *children* of the *wicked*, or wickednesse, the *enemy* that sowed them, is the *Devill*.

The Originall here, τῦ πονηρῦ, agrees with that, *Luk*. 11. 4. Deliver us, ἀπο τ͠ πονηρῦ, from evill or *wickednesse*; opposite to the children of the *Kingdome* and the *righteousnesse* thereof.

CHAP. XXIV.

Peace. IT is true, that all *drunkards*, *thieves*, *uncleane persons*, &c. are opposite to *Gods children*.

Truth. Answ. Their opposition here against the *children* of the *Kingdome*, is such an opposition as properly fights against the *Religious state* or Worship of the *Lord Jesus Christ*.

Secondly, it is manifest, that the Lord Jesus in this parable intends no other sort of sinners, unto whom he saith, Let them alone, in *Church* or *State*; for then he should contradict other holy and blessed o̱rdinances for the punishment of offenders both in *Christian* and *Civill State*.

<small>Civill Magistracie from the beginning of the World.</small> First, in *Civill state*, from the beginning of the World, God hath [47] armed *Fathers*, *Masters*, *Magistrates*, to punish evill doers, that is, such of whose actions *Fathers*, *Masters*, *Magistrates* are to judge, and accordingly to punish such sinners as transgresse against the good and peace of their Civill state, *Families*, *Townes*, *Cities*, *Kingdomes*: their *States*, *Governments*, *Governours*, *Lawes*, *Punishments* and *Weapons*

<small>Offenders against the Civill lawes not</small>

being all of a *Civill nature*; and therefore neither *disobedience* to *parents* or *magistrates*, nor *murther* nor *quarrelling*, *uncleannesse* nor *laciviousnesse*, *stealing* nor *extortion*, neither ought of that kinde ought to be let alone, either in lesser or greater *families, townes, cities, kingdomes*, Rom. 13. but seasonably to be suppreſt, as may beſt conduce to the *publike safetie*. to be perpetually tolerated.

Againe secondly, in the *Kingdome* of *Chriſt Ieſus*, whoſe *kingdome, officers, lawes, puniſhments, weapons*, are ſpirituall and of a Soule-nature, he will not have *Antichriſtian idolaters, extortioners, covetous, &c.* to be let alone, but the *uncleane* and *lepers* to be thruſt forth, the old *leaven* purged out, the *obſtinate* in ſinne ſpiritually *ſtoned* to *death*, and put away from Iſrael; and this by many degrees of gentle *admonition* in *private* and *publique*, as the caſe requires. Nor offenders in the Church of Chriſt Jeſus to be ſuffred.

Therefore if neither *offenders* againſt the *civill Lawes, State* and *peace* ought to be let alone; nor the *Spirituall eſtate*, the *Church* of *Ieſus Chriſt* ought to beare with them that are *evill*, Revel. 2. I conclude, that theſe are ſinners of another nature, *Idolaters, Falſe-worſhippers, Antichriſtians*, who without diſcouragement to true Chriſtians muſt be let alone and permitted in the world to grow and fill up the meaſure of their ſinnes, after the *image* of him that hath ſowen them, untill the great Harveſt ſhall make the *difference*.

CHAP. XXV.

THirdly, in that the *officers* unto whom theſe *Tares* are referred, are the *Angels* the heavenly *Reapers* at the laſt day, it is cleare as the *light*, that (as before)

The Bloudy Tenent.

The great Reapers are the Angels. these *Tares* cannot signifie *Hypocrites* in the *Church*, who when they are discovered and seen to be *Tares* opposite to the good fruit of the good seed, are not to be let alone to the *Angels* at Harvest or end of the world, but purged out by the *Governors* of the *Church*, and the whole *Church* of *Christ*. Againe, they cannot be offenders against the *civill state* and Common welfare, whose dealing with is not suspended unto the comming of the *Angels*, but [is committed] unto Men, [48] who (although they know not the Lord *Jesus Christ*, yet) are lawfull *Governours* and *Rulers* in *Civill things*.

Accordingly in the 4. and last place, in that the plucking up of these *tares* out of this *field* must bee let alone unto the very *harvest* or end of the *world*, it is apparent from thence, that (as before) they could not signifie *hypocrites* in the *Church*, who when they are discovered to be so, (as these *tares* were discovered to be *tares*) are not to be suffered (after the first and second Admonition) but to be rejected, and every Brother that walketh disorderly to be withdrawen or separated from: So likewise no offendour against the *Civill state*, by *robbery*, *murther*, *adultery*, *oppression*, *sedition*, *mutinie*, is for ever to be connived at, and to enjoy a perpetuall *toleration* unto the *Worlds end*, as these *tares* must.

The Tares to be tolerated the longest of any sinners. *Moses* for a while held his peace against the *sedition* of *Korah*, *Dathan*, and *Abiram*. *David* for a season tolerated *Shimei*, *Joab*, *Adonijah*; but till the *Harvest* or end of the World, the *Lord* never intended that any but these *spirituall* and *mysticall Tares* should be so permitted.

CHAP. XXVI.

NOw if any imagine that the time or date is long, that in the meane feafon they may doe a *world* of *mifchiefe* before the *Worlds end*, as by infection, &c.

The danger of infection by thefe tares affoyled.

Truth. Firft, I anfwer, that as the *civill State* keepes it felfe with a *civill Guard,* in cafe thefe *Tares* fhall attempt ought againft the *peace* and *welfare* of it, let fuch *civill offences* be punifhed, and yet as *Tares* oppofite to *Chrifts Kingdome,* let their *Worfhip* and *Confciences* be tolerated.

Lamentable experience hath proved this true of late in Europe, and lamentably true in the flaughter of fome hundred thoufands of the Englifh.

Secondly, the *Church* or *fpirituall State, City,* or *Kingdome* hath *lawes,* and *orders,* and *armories,* (whereon there hang a thoufand *Bucklers, Cant.* 4.) *Weapons* and *Ammunition,* able to break down the ftrongeft *Holds,* 1 *Cor.* 10. and fo to defend it felfe againft the very *Gates* of *Earth* or *Hell.*

Thirdly, the *Lord* himfelf knows who are his, & his *foundation* remaineth fure, his *Elect* or chofen cannot perifh nor be finally deceived.

Laftly, the *Lord Iefus* here in this Parable layes downe two *Reafons*, able to content and fatisfie our *hearts*, to beare patiently this their *contradiction* and *Antichriftianity*, and to permit or let them alone.

Firft, let the good Wheat bee pluckt up and rooted up alfo out of this *Field* of the *World,* [:] if fuch *combuftions* and *fightings* were, as to pluck up all the falfe profeffours of the name of *Chrift,* the *good wheat* alfo 49] would enjoy little peace, but be in danger to bee pluckt up and torne out of this world by fuch bloody *ftormes and tempefts.*

And therefore as *Gods people* are commanded, *Ier.* 29. to pray for the peace of *materiall Babell*, wherein they were captivated, and 1 *Tim.* 2. to pray for all men, and fpecially *Kings and Governors*, that in the peace of the *civill State* they may have peace.[:] So contrary to the opinion and practice of moft (drunke with the Cup of the *Whores fornication*) yea, and of *Gods* owne people faft afleepe in *Antichriftian Dalilahs* laps, *obedience* to the command of *Chrift* to let the *tares* alone, will prove the onely meanes to preferve their Civill Peace, and that without obedience to this command of Chrift, it is impoffible (without great tranfgreffion againft the *Lord* in carnall policy, which will not long hold out) to preferve the *civill* peace.

Befide, Gods people the good Wheat are generally pluckt up and perfecuted, as well as the vileft idolaters, whether Jewes or Antichriftians, which the Lord Jefus feemes in this *Parable* to foretell.

The great & dreadfull Harveft.

The fecond *Reafon* noted in the *Parable* which may fatisfie any man from wondring at the *patience* of *God*, is this: when the *world* is ripe in finne, in the finnes of *Antichriftianifme* (as the Lord fpake of the finnes of the *Amorites, Gen.* 12.) then thofe holy and mighty *Officers* and *Executioners*, the *Angels*, with their fharpe and cutting *fickles* of eternall vengeance, fhall downe with them, and bundle them up for the *everlafting burnings*.

Then fhall that Man of Sin, 2. *Theff*. 2. be confumed by the breath of the mouth of the *Lord Iefus*, and all that *worfhip* the *Beaft* and his picture, and receive his *mark* into their *forehead* or their *hands*, fhall drink of the Wine of the *wrath of God* which is poured out without mixture into the Cup of his *indignation,* and he shall be tormented with *fire and brimstone* in the presence of the holy *Angels,* and in the presence of the *Lambe,* and the smoake of their *torment* shall ascend up for ever and ever, *Rev.* 14. 10. 11.

CHAP. XXVII.

Peace. YOu have beene larger in vindicating this Scripture from the violence offered unto it, because as I said before, it is of such great consequence, as also because so many excellent *hands* have not *rightly divided* it, to the great misguiding of many *precious feet,* which [50] otherwise might have beene turned into the paths of more *peaceablenesse* in *themselves* and towards *others.*

Truth. I shall be briefer in the *Scriptures* following. *Peace.* Yet before you depart from this, I must crave your patience to satisfie one *Objection,* and that is; These servants to whom the *Housholder* answereth, seem to be the *Ministers* or *Messengers* of the *Gospel,* not the *Magistrates* of the *civill State,* and therfore this charge of the Lord Jesus is not given to *Magistrates* to let alone *false worshippers* and *idolaters.* *The charge of Christ Jesus, Let alone the Tares, was not spoken to Magistrates, Ministers of the civill state, but to Ministers of the Gospel.*

Againe, being spoken by the *Lord Iesus* to his *Messengers,* it seemes to concern *Hypocrites* in the *Church,* as before was spoken, and not *false worshippers* in the *State* or *World.*

Truth. I answer, first, I beleeve I have sufficiently and abundantly proved, that these *tares* are not *offenders* in the *civill State.* Nor secondly, *Hypocrites* in *The civill Magistrate not so particularly spoken to as Fathers and Masters in the New Testament, and why. Eph. 5. 6. Col. 3. 4. &c.*

the *Church*, when once discovered so to bee, and that therefore the *Lord Iesus* intends a grosser kinde of *Hypocrites*, professing the name of *Churches* and *Christians* in the field of the *World* or *Commonwealth*.

Secondly, I acknowledge this command [Let them alone] was expresly spoken to the *Messengers* or *Ministers* of the *Gospel*, who have no *civill power* or *authority* in their hand, and therefore not to the *civill Magistrate, King,* or *Governour,* to whom it pleased not the *Lord Iesus* by *himselfe* or by his *Apostles* to give particular *Rules* or *directions* concerning their *behaviour* and carriage in Civill *Magistracy,* as they have done expresly concerning the duty of *fathers, mothers, children, masters, servants,* yea and of *Subjects* towards *Magistrates, Ephes. 5. & 6. Colos. 3. & 4. &c.*

A twofold state of Christianity, the persecuted under the Roman Emperors, and the Apostate ever since.

I conceive not the reason of this to be (as some weakly have done) because the Lord Jesus would not have any *followers* of his to hold the place of *civill Magistracy,* but rather that he foresaw, and the *Holy Spirit* in the *Apostles* foresaw how few *Magistrate*s, either in the first persecuted, or apostated state of Christianity would imbrace his yoake: in the persecuted state, Magistrates hated the very name of Christ or Christianity: In the state apostate some few Magistrates (in their persons holy and precious, yet) as concerning their places, as they have professed to have beene Governours or Heads of the Church, have beene so many false Heads, and have constituted so many false visible Christs.

Thirdly, I conceive this charge of the Lord Jesus to his *Messengers* the *Preachers* and *Proclaimers* of his minde, is a sufficient declaration [51] of the minde of the *Lord Iesus*, if any *civill Magistrate* should make question what were his *duty* concerning *spirituall* things.

The *Apostles*, and in them all that succeed them, being commanded not to pluck up the *Tares*, but let them alone, received from the *Lord Iesus* a threefold charge.

Christs Messengers receive a threefold charge in that prohibition of Christ, Let them alone.

First, to let them alone, and not to plucke them up by prayer to *God* for their present temporall *destruction*.

Jeremie had a Commission to plant and build, to pluck up and destroy *Kingdomes*, *Ier.* 1. 10. therefore hee is commanded not to pray for that people whom God had a purpose to pluck up, *Jer.* 14. 11. and he plucks up the whole *Nation* by *prayer*, *Lament.* 3. 66. Thus *Elijah* brought fire from *heaven* to consume the *Captaines* and the *fifties*, 2 *King* 1. and the *Apostles* desired also so to practise against the *Samaritanes*, *Luc.* 9. 54. but were reproved by the *Lord Jesus*. For contrarily, the *Saints* and *Servants* and *Churches* of *Christ* are to pray for *all men*, especially for all *Magistrates* (of what sort or *Religions* soever) and to seeke the peace of the City (what ever City it be) because in the peace of the place of Gods people have peace also, *Jer.* 29. 7. 2. *Tim.* 2. *&c.*

Gods people not to pray for the present ruine and destruction of idolaters, although their persecutors, but for their peace and salvation.

Secondly, *Gods Messengers* are herein commanded not to prophesie or denounce a *present destruction* or *extirpation* of all false *professours* of the name of *Christ*, which are *whole Townes, Cities,* and *Kingdomes* full.

Jeremy did thus pluck up *Kingdomes* in those fearfull Prophecies hee poured forth against all the *Nations* of the *World*, throughout his Chap. 24. 25.

26. &c. as did alſo the other Prophets in a meaſure, though none comparably to *Ieremy* and *Ezekiel*.

<small>The word of God rightly denounced plucks up kingdoms.</small> Such *denunciations* of preſent temporall *judgements* are not the *Meſſengers* of the *Lord Ieſus* to poure forth. Tis true, many ſore and fearfull *plagues* are poured forth upon the *Romane Emperours* and *Romane Popes* in the *Revelation*, yet not to their utter *extirpation* or *plucking* up untill the *Harveſt*.

<small>Gods Miniſters are not to provoke Magiſtrates to perſecute Antichriſtians.</small> Thirdly, I conceive Gods *Meſſengers* are charged to let them alone and not pluck them up, by exciting and ſtirring up Civill Magiſtrates, Kings, Emperours, Governours, Parliaments, or Generall Courts or Aſſemblies, to puniſh and perſecute all ſuch perſons out of their Dominions and Territories, as worſhip not the true God according to the revealed will of God in *Chriſt Ieſus*. Tis true, *Elijah* thus ſtirred up *Ahab* to kill all the Prieſts and Prophets of *Baal*, but that was in that *figurative* ſtate of the Land of Canaan (as I have already and ſhall further [52] manifeſt) not to be matcht or paralleld by any other *State*, but the *ſpirituall State* or *Church* of Chriſt in all the world, putting the falſe *Prophets* and *Idolaters* ſpiritually to death by the two-edged ſword and power <small>1 Pet. 2.9. 1 Cor. 5.</small> of the *Lord Ieſus*, as that *Church of Iſrael* did corporally.

<small>Companying with idolaters, 1 Cor. 5. diſcuſſed.</small> And therefore ſaith *Paul* expreſly, 1. *Cor.* 5. 10. we muſt goe out of the world, in caſe we may not company in civill converſe with Idolaters, &c.

Peace. It may be ſaid, ſome ſorts of ſinners are there mentioned, as Drunkards, Raylers, Extortioners, who are to bee puniſhed by the Civill Sword, why not Idolaters alſo? for although the Subject may lawfully converse, buy and sell, and live with such, yet the *Civill Magistrate* shall neverthelesse be justly blamed in suffering of them.

Truth. I answer, the Apostle in this Scripture speakes not of permission of either, but expresly showes the difference betweene the *Church* and the *World*, and the lawfulnesse of conversation with such persons in *civill things*, with whom it is not lawfull to have converse in *spirituals:* secretly withall foretelling, that Magistrates and People, whole States and Kingdomes should bee Idolatrous and Antichristian, yet with whom notwithstanding the Saints and Churches of God might lawfully cohabit, and hold *civill converse and conversation*. {Lawfull converse with idolaters in civill, but not in spirituall things.}

Concerning their permission of what they judge Idolatrous, I have and shall speake at large.

Peace. Oh how contrary unto this command of the *Lord Jesus* have such as have conceived themselves the true Messengers of the *Lord Iesus*, in all ages, not let such Professours and Prophets alone, whom they have judged *Tares*, but have provoked Kings and Kingdomes (and some out of good intentions and zeale to God) to prosecute and persecute such even unto death? Amongst whom Gods people (the *good wheat*) hath also beene pluckt up, as all Ages and Histories testifie, and too too oft the World laid upon bloody heapes in *civill* and *intestine desolations* on this occasion. All which would bee prevented, and the greatest breaches made up in the peace of our owne or other Countries, were this command of the Lord Jesus obeyed, to wit, to let them alone untill the Harvest. {Dangerous and ungrounded zeale.}

CHAP. XXVIII.

[*Truth.*] I Shall conclude this controverſie about this *Parable* in this briefe *ſum* and *recapitulation* of what hath beene ſaid. I hope by the evident 53] demonſtration of Gods Spirit to the conſcience I have proved, Negatively,

Firſt, that the *Tares* in this *Parable* cannot ſignifie *Doctrines* or *Practices* (as was affirmed) but *Perſons*.

Secondly, the *Tares* cannot ſignifie Hypocrites in the Church either undiſcovered or diſcovered.

Thirdly, the *Tares* here cannot ſignifie *Scandalous Offenders* in the Church.

Fourthly, nor ſcandalous offenders in *life* and *converſation* againſt the *Civill ſtate*.

Fifthly, The field in which theſe *Tares* are ſowne, is not the *Church*.

Againe affirmatively: Firſt, the *Field* is properly the *World*, the *Civill State* or *Common-wealth*.

Secondly, The *Tares* here intended by the Lord *Ieſus*, are *Antichriſtian idolaters*, oppoſite to the good ſeed of the *Kingdome*, true *Chriſtians*.

Thirdly, the *miniſters* or *meſſengers* of the Lord *Ieſus* ought to let them alone to live in the world, and neither ſeeke by *prayer* or *propheſie* to pluck them up before the *Harveſt*.

Fourthly, this permiſſion or ſuffering of them in the field of the *World*, is not for hurt, but for common good, even for the good of the good Wheat, the people of *God*.

Laſtly, the *patience* of *God* is, and the *patience* of *Men* ought to be exerciſed toward them, and yet notwithstanding their *doome* is fearfull at the *harvest*, even *gathering*, *bundling*, and *everlasting burnings* by the mighty hand of the *Angels* in the end of the World.

CHAP. XXIX.

Peace. THe second Scripture brought against such persecution for cause of *Conscience*, is *Matth.* 15. 14. where the *Disciples* being troubled at the *Pharises* cariage toward the Lord *Jesus* and his *doctrines*, and relating how they were offended at him, the Lord *Jesus* commandeth his *Disciples* to let them alone, and gives this reason, that the *blinde* lead the *blinde*, and both should fall into the *ditch*. _{Matth.15. 14, the second Scripture controverted in this cause.}

Unto which, Answer is made, "That it makes "nothing to the Cause, because it was spoken to his "private *Disciples*, and not to publique Officers in "*Church* or *State:* and also, because [54] it because "it was spoken in regard of not troubling themselves, "or regarding the offence which the *Pharises* tooke.

Truth. I answer, (to passe by his *assertion* of the *privacie* of the *Apostles*) in that the Lord *Jesus* commanding to let them alone, that is, not onely not be offended themselves, but not to meddle with them; it appeares it was no *ordinance* of *God* nor *Christ* for the *Disciples* to have gone further, and have complained to, and excited the Civill *Magistrate* to his duty: which if it had been an Ordinance of *God* and *Christ*, either for the vindicating of Chrifts doctrine, or the *recovering* of the *Pharises*, or the *pre-* _{Christ Jesus never directed his Disciples to the civill Magistrate for}

<small>help in his caufe.</small> *ferving* of others from *infection*, the Lord Iefus would never have commanded them to omit that which fhould have tended to thefe holy ends.

CHAP. XXX.

Peace. IT may be faid, that neither the *Romane Cæfar* nor *Herod*, nor *Pilate* knew ought of the true *God*, or of *Chrift*; and it had been in vaine to have made complaint to them who were not fit and *competent*, but *ignorant* and *oppofite* Iudges.

<small>Pauls appealing to Cæfar.</small> *Truth.* I anfwer firft, this removes (by the way) that *ftumbling block* which many fall at, to wit, *Pauls* appealing to *Cæfar*; which fince he could not in common fenfe doe unto *Cæfar* as a competent *Iudge* in fuch cafes, and wherein he fhould have alfo denied his own Apoftlefhip or office, in which regard (to wit in matters of Chrift) he was higher then *Cæfar* himfelfe: it muft needs follow, that his *appeale* was meerly in refpect of his *Civill wrongs*, and falfe accufations of *fedition, &c.*

<small>Civill Magiftrates never appointed by God, Defenders of the Faith of Jefus. Every one is bound to put forth him felfe to his utmoft power in Gods bufi-</small> Secondly, if it had been an Ordinance of *God*, that all *Civill Magiftrates* were bound to judge in caufes *fpirituall* or *Chriftian*, as to fuppreffe *herefies*, defend the *faith* of *Iefus*; although that *Cæfar, Herod, Pilate* were wicked, ignorant and oppofite, yet the *Difciples* and the *Lord Chrift* himfelfe had been bound to have performed the duty of faithfull Subjects, for the preventing of further evill, and the clearing of themfelves, and fo to have left the matter upon the *Magiftrates* care and confcience, by complaining unto the Magiftrate againft fuch evils; for every perfon is

bound to goe fo far as lies in his power for the pre- *neffe; &*
venting and the redreffing of evill; and where it ftops *where it ftops, the*
in any, and runs not cleere, there the guilt, like filth *guilt will*
or mud, will lie. *lie.*

Thirdly, had it been the holy purpofe of God to *Chrift*
have eftablifhed the [55] *doctrine* and *kingdome* of his *could have eafily been*
Son this way, fince his comming, he would have fur- *furnifhed*
nifhed *Common-weales, Kingdomes, Cities,* &c. then *with godly*
and fince, with fuch temporall *Powers* and *Magif-* *Magif- trates, if*
trates as fhould have been excellently fit and com- *he had fo*
petent: for he that could have had legions of Angels, *appointed*
if he fo pleafed, could as eafily have been, and ftill
be furnifhed with legions of good and gracious Magiftrates to this end and purpofe.

CHAP. XXXI.

IT is generally faid, that God hath in former rimes, and doth ftill, and will hereafter ftirre up Kings and Queenes, &c.

I anfwer, that place of *Ifa.* 49. 23. will appeare to be far from proving fuch Kings and Queenes Iudges of Ecclefiafticall caufes: and if not Iudges, they may not punifh.

In Spirituall things, themfelves are fubject to the Church, and cenfures of it, although in Civill refpects fuperior. How fhall thofe Kings and Queenes be fupreme Governours of the Church, and yet lick the duft of the Churches feet? as it is there expreft.

Thirdly, Gods Ifrael of old were earneft with God *Gods Ifrael earn-*
for a King, for an Arme of Flefh, for a King to pro- *eft with*

God for an Arme of Flesh, which God gives in his anger, and takes away in his wrath.

tect them, as other Nations had. Gods Ifrael ftill have ever been reftleffe with God for an Arme of flesh.

God gave them *Saul* in his anger, and took him away in his wrath: And God hath given many a *Saul* in his Anger, that is, an Arm of Flesh in the way of his Providence, (though I judge not all perfons whom *Saul* in his Calling typed out, to be of *Sauls* fpirit) for I fpeake of a State and outward vifible Power only.

I adde, God will take away fuch ftayes on whom Gods people reft, in his wrath, that King *David*, that is, *Chrift Iefus* the *Antitype*, in his own *Spirituall* power in the hands of the Saints, may fpiritually and for ever be advanced.

The punifhment of blind Pharifes, though let alone, yet is greater then any corporall punifhment in the world, in 4 refpects.

And therefore I conclude, it was in one refpect that the *Lord Iefus* faid, Let them alone, becaufe it was no Ordinance for any *Difciple* of *Iefus* to profecute the *Pharifes* at *Cæfars* Bar.

Befide, let it be ferioufly confidered by fuch as plead for prefent *corporall punifhment*, as conceiving that fuch finners (though they breake not Civill peace) fhould not efcape unpunifhed, I fay, let it be confidered, though for the prefent their punifhment is deferred, yet the *punifhment* inflicted on them will be found to amount to an higher pitch [56] then any *corporall punifhment* in the *World* befide, and that in thefe foure refpects.

CHAP. XXXII.

FIrst by just judgement from God, *false teachers* are starke *blinde*, Gods *sword* hath strucke out the right *eye* of their *minde* and *spirituall understanding*, ten thousand times a greater punishment then if the *Magistrate* should command both the *right* and *left eye* of their *bodies* to bee bored or pluckt out, and that in so many fearfull respects if the blindnesse of the *soule* and of the *body* were a little compared together, whether we looke at that want of *guidance*, or the want of *joy* and *pleasure*, which the light of the eye affordeth; or whether we looke at the *damage, shame, deformity* and *danger*, which *blindnesse* brings to the outward man, and much more true in the *want* of the former, and *miserie* of the latter in spirituall and soule blindnesse to all *eternity*.
<small>The eye of the soul struck out is worse then for both right and left eye of the body to be strucke out tenne thousand times</small>

Secondly, how fearfull is that wound that no *Balme* in *Gilead* can cure? How dreadfull is that blindnesse which for ever to all eye-salve is incurable? For if persons be wilfully and desperately obstinate (after light shining forth) let them alone saith the *Lord*. So spake the *Lord* once of *Ephraim*, *Ephraim* is joyned to *Idolls*, let him alone, *Hos.* 7. what more lamentable condition then when the *Lord* hath given a poor sinner over as a hopelesse *patient*, incurable, which we are wont to account a sorer affliction, then if a man were torne and rack'd, &c.
<small>Some soules incurable, whom not only corporall but spirituall physicke can nothing availe.</small>

And this I speake not that I conceive that all whom the *Lord Jesus* commands His servants to passe from, and let alone, to permit and tolerate (when it is in their power corporally to molest them)

I say that all are thus incurable, yet that sometimes that word is spoken by Christ Jesus to His servants to be patient, for neither can corporall or spirituall Balme or Physicke ever heale or cure them.

<small>The bottomlesse pit or ditch into which the spiritually blind fall.</small> Thirdly, their end is the *Ditch*, that bottomlesse pit of everlasting *separation* from the holy and sweet Presence of the *Father* of *Lights*, *Goodnesse* and *Mercy* it selfe, *endlesse*, *easelesse*, in *extremity*, *universality*, and *eternity* of *torments*, which most direfull and lamentable downefall, should strike an holy fear & trembling into all that see the *Pit*, whither these blinde Pharises are tumbling, and cause us to strive (so far as hope may be) by the spirituall eye-salve of the Word of *God* to heale and cure them of this their soule-destroying blindnesse.

Fourthly, of those that fall into this dreadfull *Ditch*, both leader and followers, how deplorable in more especiall manner is the *leaders* case, [57] upon whose necke the *followers* tumble, the ruine not only of his owne soule, being horrible, but also the ruine of the followers soules eternally galling and tormenting.

Peace. Some will say these things are indeed full of horrour, yet such is the state of all sinners and of many Malefactours, whom yet the State is bound to punish, and sometimes by *death* it selfe.

Truth. I answer, The Civill Magistrate beareth not the sword in vaine, but to cut off *Civill offences*, yea and the offendours too in case: But what is this to a blinde *Pharisee*, resisting the *Doctrine* of *Christ*, who happily may be as good a subject, and as peaceable and profitable to the *Civill State* as any, and for his spirituall offence against the *Lord Jesus*, in denying Him to be the true *Chrift*, he fuffereth the vengeance of a *dreadfull judgement* both prefent and eternall, as before.

CHAP. XXXIII.

Peace. YEa but it is faid that the blinde *Pharifes* mifguiding the fubjects of a *Civill State*, greatly finne againſt a *Civill State*, and therefore juſtly fuffer *civill puniſhment*; for ſhall the *Civill Magiſtrate* take care of *outſides* only, to wit, of the bodies of men, and not of foules, in labouring to procure their everlaſting welfare? *Soul killing the chiefeſt murder. No Magiſtrate can execute true juſtice in killing foule for foule, but Chriſt Jefus who by typicall death in the Law, typed out ſpirituall in the Goſpel.*

Truth. I anfwer, It is a *truth*, the miſchiefe of a blinde *Pharifes* blinde *guidance* is greater then if he acted Treaſons, Murders, &c. and the loſſe of one foule by his ſeduction is a greater miſchiefe then if he blew up Parliaments, and cuts the throats of Kings or Emperours, ſo pretious is that invaluable Jewell of a Soul, above all the preſent lives and bodies of all the men in the world! and therefore a firme Juſtice calling for *eye* for *eye*, *tooth* for *tooth*, *life* for *life*; calls alſo *ſoule* for *ſoule*, which the blind-guiding ſeducing *Phariſee* ſhall ſurely pay in that dreadfull Ditch, which the Lord Jeſus ſpeakes of, but this ſentence againſt him the Lord Jeſus only pronounceth in His *Church*, His *ſpirituall judicature*, and executes this *ſentence* in part at preſent and hereafter to all eternity: Such a *ſentence* no *Civill Judge* can paſſe, ſuch a *Death* no *Civill ſword* can inflict.

I anſwer ſecondly, *Dead men* cannot be infected, the *civill ſtate*, the *world*, being in a naturall ſtate *A great miſtake in moſt to conceive that dead men, that is, foules dead in fin may be infected by falſe doctrine.*

dead in sin (what ever be the *State Religion* unto which *persons* are forced) it is impossible it should be infected: Indeed the *living*, the *beleeving*, the *Church* and *spirituall state*, that and that onely is capable of *infection*; for whose helpe we shall presently [58] see what *preservatives*, and *remedies* the *Lord Jesus* hath appointed.

<small>All naturall men being dead in sin, yet none die everlastingly but such as are thereunto ordained.</small> Moreover as we see in a *common plague* or *infection* the names are taken how many are to dye, and not one more shall be strucke, then the destroying *Angel* hath the names of. So here, what ever be the soule *infection* breathed out from they lying lips of a *plague-sicke Pharisee*, yet the names are taken, not one *elect* or chosen of *God* shall perish, *Gods sheep* are safe in His *eternall hand* and *counsell*, and he that knowes his *materiall*, knows also his *mysticall stars*, their *numbers*, and calls them every one by *name*, none fall into the *Ditch* on the blinde *Pharises* backe, but such as were *ordained* to that *condemnation*, both *guid* and *followers*, 1 *Pet.* 2. 8. *Jude* 4. The *vessells* of *wrath* shall breake and split, and only they to the praise of *Gods* eternall *justice, Rom.* 9.

CHAP. XXXIV.

Peace. BUt it is said, be it granted that in a *common plague* or *infection* none are smitten and dye but such as are appointed, yet it is not only every mans duty, but the common duty of the Magistrate to prevent *infection*, and to preserve the *common health* of the place; likewise though the number of the *Elect* be sure, and *God* knowes who are His, yet hath

He appointed meanes for their *preservation* from *perdition*, and from *infection*, and therefore the *Angel* is blamed for suffering *Balaams* doctrine, and *Jesabel* to seduce Christ Jesus His servants, *Rev.* 2. *Tit.* 3. 10. *Rom.* 16. 17.

Truth. I answer, Let that Scripture and that of *Titus* reject an *Hereticke*, and *Rom.* 16. 17. avoid them that are *contentious*, &c. let them, and all of like nature be examined, and it will appeare that the great and good *Physitian Christ Jesus*, the *Head* of the *Body*, and *King* of the *Church* hath not been unfaithfull in providing spirituall *antidotes* and *preservatives* against the spirituall *sicknesses, sores, weaknesses, dangers* of his *Church* and people; but he never appointed the *civill sword* for either *antidote* or *remedy*, as an *addition* to those *spiritualls*, which he hath left with his *wife*, his *Church* or People. The Lord Jesus hath not left his Church without spirituall antidotes and remedies against infection.

Hence how great is the *bondage*, the *captivity* of Gods owne People to *Babylonish* or *confused mixtures* in Worship, and unto worldly and earthly policies to uphold *State Religions* or *Worships*, since that which is written to the *Angel* and *Church* at *Pergamus*, shall be interpreted as sent to the Governour and City of *Pergamus*, and that which is sent to *Titus*, and the Church of Christ at *Creet* must be delivered to the civill officers and City thereof. The Miserable bondage Gods people live in.

59] But as the *Civill Magistrate* hath his charge of the *bodies* and *goods* of the *subject*: So have the *spirituall Officers, Governours* and *overseers* of *Christs City* or *Kingdome*, the charge of their *souls*, and *soule safety*; Hence that charge of *Paul* to *Tim.* 1 *Tim.* 5. 20. Them that sinne *rebuke* before all, that others may learne to *fear*. This is in the Church of Chrift a fpirituall meanes for the *healing* of a *foule* that hath finned, or taken *infection*, and for the preventing of the infecting of others, that others may learne to feare, &c.

CHAP. XXXV.

Peace. IT is faid true that *Titus* and *Timothy*, and fo the Officers of the *Church* of *Chrift* are bound to prevent *foule infection:* But what hinders that the Magiftrate fhould not be charged alfo with this duty?

<small>The Kings and Queens of England Governours of the Church.</small>

Truth. I anfwer, many things I have anfwered, and more fhall; at prefent I fhall only fay this: If it be the *Magiftrates* duty or office, then is he both a *Temporall* and *Ecclefiafticall* officer; contrary to which moft men will affirme: and yet we know the policie of our owne Land and Country hath eftablifhed to the *Kings* and *Queens* thereof, the fupreme *heads* or *governours* of the *Church* of *England*.

<small>Strange confufion in punifhments.</small>

That *doctrine* and *diftinction* that a *Magiftrate* may punifh an *Heretick* civilly will not here availe; for what is *Babel* if this be not confufedly to punifh *corporall* or *civill offences* with *fpirituall* or *Church cenfures* (the offendour not being a member of it) or to punifh *foule* or *fpirituall* offences with *corporall* or *temporall weapons* proper to *Delinquents* againft the temporall or *civill ftate*.

<small>Woe were it with the civill Magiftrate if the bloud of foules (befide the ordinary care of the</small>

Laftly, woe were it with the *civill Magiftrate* (and moft intolerable *burthens* do they lay upon their backs that teach this *doctrine*) if together with the common care and charge of the *Commonwealth* (the peace and safety of the *Towne, City, State* or *Kingdome*) the bloud of every foule that perifheth fhould cry againft him, unleffe he could fay with *Paul, Acts* 20. (in fpirituall regards) I am clear from the *bloud* of all men, that is the bloud of *foules,* which was his charge to looke after, fo far as his *preaching* went, not the bloud of *bodies* which belongeth to the *civill Magiftrate.* _{bodies and goods of the fubject)fhould cry againft him.}

I acknowledge he ought to cherifh (as a fofterfather) the *Lord Jefus* in his *truth,* in his *Saints,* to *cleave* unto them *himfelfe,* and [60] to *countenance* them even to the *death,* yea alfo to breake the teeth of the *Lions,* who offer Civill violence and injury unto them. _{The Magiftrates duties toward the Church the Spoufe of Chrift.}

But, to fee all his Subjects *Chriftians,* to keepe fuch *Church* or *Chriftians* in the purity of worfhip, and fee them doe their *duty,* this belongs to the *Head* of the *Body Chrift Jefus,* and fuch fpirituall Officers as he hath to this purpofe deputed, whofe right it is according to the true paterne : *Abimelech, Saul, Adonijah, Athalia* were but ufurpers : *David, Salomon, Joafh,* &c. they were the true *heires* and *types* of *Chrift Jefus* in His true *Power* and *Authority* in His Kingdome. _{Ufurpers and true heires of the fpirituall Crowne of Jefus.}

CHAP. XXXVI.

Peace. **T**He next Scripture brought againft fuch perfecution is *Luke* 9. 54, 55. where the Lord Jefus reproved His Difciples, who would have had fire come downe from Heaven, and devoure thofe _{Luke 9. 54. 55 difcuffed.}

Samaritanes that would not receive Him in thefe words: You know not of what *fpirit* you are, the Son of Man is not come to *deftroy* mens lives, but to *fave* them.

With this Scripture Mr. *Cotton* joynes the fourth, and anfwers both in one, which is this, 2 *Tim.* 2. 24. The fervant of the *Lord* muft not ftrive, but muft be gentle toward all men, fuffering the *evill men*, inftructing them with *meekneffe* that are contrary minded and *oppofe* themfelves, proving if *God* peradventure will give them *repentance* that they may acknowledge the *truth*, and that they may recover themfelves out of the fnare of the *Divell* who are taken *captive* by him at his *will*.

Unto both thefe *Scriptures* it pleafeth him thus to anfwer: " Both thefe are *directions* to *Minifters* of the
" *Gofpel* how to deale (not with obftinate offendors
" in the *Church* who fin againft *confcience*, but) either
" with *men* without as the *Samaritanes* were, and
" many unconverted *Chriftians* in *Creet*, whom *Titus*
" (as an Evangelift) was to feek to convert:

An excellent faying of perfecutors themfelves.
" Or at beft with fome *Jewes* or *Gentiles* in the
" Church, who though carnall, yet were not con-
" vinced of the errour of their way: And it is true it
" became not the Spirit of the *Gofpel* to convert Aliens
" to the *Faith* (fuch as the *Samaritanes* were) by fire
" and brimftone, nor to deale harfhly in *publicke Min-*
" *iftery* or private conference with all fuch feverall
" minded men as either had [61] not yet entred into
" *Church fellowfhip*, or if they had did hitherto fin
" of *ignorance*, not againft *Confcience:* But neither of
" both thefe Texts doe hinder the *Minifter* of the

" *Gospel* to proceed in a *Church* way against *Church* " *members*, when they become scandalous offenders " either in *life* or *doctrine*, much lesse doe they speake " at all to the *Civill Magistrate*.[1]

CHAP. XXXVII.

Truth. THis perplexed and ravelled *Answer*, where in so many things and so doubtfull are wrapt up and intangled together, I shall take in pieces.

First, concerning that of the *Lord Jesus* rebuking his *Disciples* for their rash and ignorant bloudy *zeale* (*Luc.* 9.) desiring *corporall destruction* upon the *Samaritanes* for refusing the *Lord Jesus*, &c. the *Answerer* affirmeth, that hindreth not the *Ministers* of the *Gospell* to proceed in a *Church* way against scandalous offenders, which is not here questioned, but maintained to bee the holy will of the *Lord*, and a sufficient censure and punishment, if no civill offence against the *Civill State* be committed.

The Answerer when he should speake to toleration in the State, runnes to punishments in the Church, which none can deny.

Secondly (saith hee) " Much lesse doth this speake " at all to the Civill *Magistrate.*

---

[1] This paragraph is quoted literally from Cotton's Letter, see p. 9. But Cotton, for some reason, denies its literal accuracy, which Williams affirms. "The matter of this Answer, it is likely enough was given by me: for it suiteth with mine own apprehensions, both then and now. But some expressions in laying it downe, I doe not owne, nor can I finde any Copie under my owne hand-writing, that might testifie, how I did expresse myselfe, especially in a word or two, wherein the *Discusser* observeth (in *chap.* 38.) some haste, and light, and sleepy attention. But if the *Discusser* can shew the same under mine owne hand (as it is not impossible) I shall be willing (by God's help) both to acknowledge it, and my haste in it." *The Bloody Tenent Washed*, pp. 74, 75. "It is at hand for Master *Cotton* or any to see that *copy* which he gave forth and corrected in some places with his own hand, and every word *verbatim* here published." *The Bloody Tenent yet More Bloody*, p. 114.

Where I observe that he implyes that beside the censure of the Lord *Jesus*, in the hands of his *spirituall governours*, for any spirituall evill in *life* or *doctrine*, the *Civill Magistrate* is also to inflict *corporall punishment* upon the contrary minded: whereas

First, if the *Civill Magistrate* be a *Christian*, a *Disciple* or follower of the meeke *Lambe* of *God*, he is bound to be far from destroying the *bodies of men*, for refusing to receive the Lord *Jesus Christ*, for otherwise hee should not know (according to this speech of the *Lord Iesus*) what *spirit* he was of, yea and to be ignorant of the sweet end of the comming of the *Son of Man*, which was not to destroy the *bodies of Men*, but to save both *bodies* and *soules*, *vers.* 55. 56.

Secondly, if the *Civill Magistrate*, being a *Christian*, gifted, *prophesie* in the *Church*, 1 *Corinth.* 1. 14. although the *Lord Iesus Christ*, whom they in their owne persons hold forth, shall be refused, yet they are here forbidden to call for fire from *heaven*, that is, to procure or inflict any corporall *judgement* upon such *offenders*, remembring the end of the *Lord Iesus* his comming, not to *destroy* mens lives, but to *save* them.

62] Lastly, this also concernes the *conscience* of the *Civill Magistrate*, as he is bound to preserve the *civill peace* and quiet of the *place* and people under him, he is bound to suffer no man to breake the *Civill Peace*, by laying hands of *violence* upon any, though as vile as the *Samaritanes* for not receiving of the Lord *Iesus Christ*.

It is indeed the *ignorance* and blind *zeale* of the second *Beast*, the *false Prophet*, *Rev.* 13. 13. to perswade the *civill Powers* of the earth to persecute the *Saints*, that is, to bring fiery *judgements* upon men in a *judiciall way*, and to pronounce that such *judgements* of *imprisonment, banishment, death*, proceed from Gods righteous *vengeance* upon such *Hereticks*. So dealt divers *Bishops* in *France*, and *England* too in Queene *Maries* dayes with the Saints of God at their putting to death, declaiming against them in their Sermons to the people, and proclaiming that these persecutions even unto death were Gods *just judgements from heaven upon these Hereickes*.

<small>Fire from heaven. What the fire from heaven is which the falsf Prophet bringeth downe</small>

CHAP. XXXVIII.

Peace. Doubtlesse such fiery spirits (as the Lord Jesus said) are not of God: I pray speake to the second place out of *Timothy, 2. Epist. 25. 26.*

<small>2 Tim. 3. 25. 26. examined.</small>

Truth. I acknowledge this instruction to be meeke and patient, &c. is properly an instruction to the *Ministers* of the Gospel. Yet divers Arguments from hence will truly and fairly be collected, to manifest and evince how farre the *civill Magistrate* ought to bee from dealing with the *civill sword* in *spirituall cases*.

And first (by the way) I desire to aske, What were these *unconverted Christians* in *Crete*, which the Answerer compareth with the *Samaritanes*, whom *Titus* (saith he) as an *Evangelist* was to seek to convert; and whether the *Lord Iesus* have any such Disciples and Followers, who yet are visibly in an *unconverted estate*. O that it may please the *Father of mercies,* the *Father of lights,* to awaken and open the eyes of all that feare before him, that they may see whether this be the *Language of Canaan,* or the Language of Aſhdod.

<small>A quære what the Anſwerer meanes by his unconverted Chriſtian in Crete.</small>
What is an *unconverted Chriſtian* but in truth an *unconverted Convert?* that is in Engliſh one *unturned turned: unholy holy: Diſciples* or *Followers* of *Ieſus* not following of him: In a word, that is *Chriſtians* or anointed by *Chriſt, Antichriſtians* not anointed with the Spirit of *Ieſus Chriſt.*

<small>The originall of Chriſtians.</small>
63] Certaine it is, ſuch they were not unto whom the Spirit of *God* gives that name, *Act.* 11. And indeed whither can this tend but to uphold the *blaſphemy* of ſo many as ſay they are *Iewes,* that is, *Chriſtians,* but are not? *Rev.* 2. But as they are not *Chriſtians* from *Chriſt,* but from the *Beaſt* and his *Picture,* ſo their proper name from *Antichriſt,* is *Antichriſtians.*

<small>The Anſwerer yet in the unconverted Churches and worſhips.</small>
How ſad yet and how true an *evidence* is this, that the ſoule of the Anſwerer (I ſpeake not of his inward ſoule and perſon, but of his worſhip) hath never yet heard the call of the *Lord Ieſus,* to come out from thoſe unconverted *Churches,* from that unconverted *Antichriſtian Chriſtian* world, and ſo from *Antichriſt Belial,* to ſeeke fellowſhip with *Chriſt Ieſus,* and his converted *Chriſtians, Diſciples* after the firſt patterne.

<small>Gods people ſleepy in the matters of Chriſts Kingdome Cant. 5.2.</small>
Againe, I obſerve the *haſte* and light *attention* of the Anſwerer to theſe Scriptures (as commonly the ſpirits of *Gods children* in matters of *Chriſts Kingdome* are very *ſleepy*) for theſe perſons here ſpoken of were not (as he ſpeakes) unconverted *Chriſtians* in *Crete,* whom *Titus* as an *Evangeliſt* was to convert, but they

were such *opposites* as *Timothy* (to whom *Paul* writes this Letter at *Ephesus*) should meet withall.[1]

CHAP. XXXIX.

Peace. BUt what is there in this Scripture of *Timothy* alledged concerning the civill *Magistracy?*

Truth. I argue from this place of *Timothy* in particular, thus.

First, if the *civill Magistrates* bee *Christians,* or members of the *Church,* able to *prophesie in the Church of Christ,* then I say as before, they are bound by this command of *Christ* to suffer opposition to their *doctrine,* with *meekenesse* and *gentlenesse,* and to be so farre from striving to subdue their *opposites* with the *civill sword,* that they are bound with *patience* and *meekenesse* to wait if *God* peradventure will please to grant *repentance* unto their opposites.

1 Cor. 14. Patience and meeknesse required in all that open Christs mysteries.

So also it pleaseth the Answerer to acknowledge in these words:

"It becomes not the *Spirit* of the *Gospel* to con-

---

[1] Cotton says in regard to the points made by Williams in this Chapter, "It must lye upon the Discussers credit, whether I used at all such a phrase or no: Sure I am, I cannot hitherto (after much seeking) find mine owne hand-written copy, which might cleare the mistake, both of *Creet* for *Ephesus,* and unconverted Christians for unconverted Persons." "The Transcript, which with much seeking, I found, hath it, instead of unconverted Christians in *Creete,* unconverted Persons in *Ephesus.*" The *Bloody Tenent Washed,* pp. 77. 78. He however, defends the phrase "unconverted Christians," alleging in its behalf the doctrine that unconverted children of Church-members are also members of the Church. "I have not yet learned, (nor doe I thinke, I ever shall) that the children of believing Parents borne in the Church, are all of them Pagans, and no Members of the Church: or that being Members of the Church (and so holy) that they are all of them truly converted." p. 78.

"vert *Aliens* to the Faith (such as the *Samaritanes*, "and the unconverted *Christians* in *Crete*) with *Fire* "and *Brimstone*.

Secondly, be they *oppositions within*, and *Church members* (as the Answerer speakes) become *scandalous* in *doctrine*, (I speake not of [64] *scandals* against the *civill State*, which the *civill Magistrate* ought to punish) it is the *Lord* onely (as this Scripture to *Timothy* implyes) who is able to give them *repentance*, and recover them out of *Sathans* snare: to which end also he hath appointed those holy and dreadfull *censures* in his *Church* or *Kingdome*. True it is, the *Sword* may make (as once the *Lord* complained, *Isa.* 10.) a whole *Nation* of *Hypocrites:* But to recover a *Soule* from *Sathan* by *repentance*, and to bring them from *Antichristian doctrine* or *worship*, to the *doctrine* or *worship Christian*, in the least true *internall* or *externall* submission, that only works the *All-powerfull God*, by the *sword* of the Spirit in the hand of his *Spirituall officers*.

<small>The civill Sword may make a Nation of Hypocrites & Antichristians, but not one Christian.</small>

<small>Wonderfull changes of Religion in England.</small> What a most wofull proofe hereof have the *Nations* of the Earth given in all *Ages?* And to seeke no further then our *native* Soyle, within a few scores of yeeres, how many wonderfull *changes* in *Religion* hath the *whole Kingdome* made, according to the *change* of the *Governours* thereof, in the severall *Religious* which they themselves imbraced! *Henry* the 7. finds and leaves the *kingdome* absolutely *Popish*. *Henry* the 8. casts it into a *mould* half *Popish* halfe *Protestant*. *Edward* the 6. brings forth an *Edition* all *Protestant*. Queene *Mary* within few yeares defaceth *Edwards* worke, and renders the *Kingdome* (after her Grand-

father *Hen.* 7. his pattern) all *Popish.* *Maries* short life and *Religion* ends together: and *Elizabeth* reviveth her Brother *Edwards* Modell, all Protestant: And some eminent *Witnesses* of Gods Truth against *Antichrist*, have enclined to believe, that before the downfall of that *Beast*, England must once againe bow down her faire Neck to his proud usurping yoake and foot.

Englands changes in point of Religion.

Peace. It hath been *Englands* sinfull shame, to fashion & change their *Garments* and *Religions* with wondrous *ease* and *lightnesse*, as a *higher Power*, a *stronger Sword* hath prevailed; after the ancient patterne of *Nebuchadnezzars* bowing the whole world in one most solemne *uniformitie* of *worship* to his *Golden Image*, Dan. 3.

CHAP. XL.

BUt it hath been thought, or said, Shall *oppositions* against the *Truth* escape unpunished? will they not prove mischievous, &c.

Truth. I answer (as before) concerning the blinde Guides (in [65] case there be no *Civill offence* committed) the *Magistrates*, & all men that by the mercy of God to themselves discerne the *miserie* of such *Opposites*, have cause to lament and bewaile that fearfull condition wherein such are entangled, to wit, in the *snares* & *chains* of *Satan*, with which they are so invincibly caught and held, that no power in *Heaven* or *Earth*, but the Right hand of the *Lord* in the meeke and gentle dispensing of the *Word* of *Truth*, can release and quit them.

The miserie of opposites against the Truth.

Those many *false Chrifts* (of whom the Lord Jefus forewarnes, *Mat.* 24.) have futably their falfe *bodies, faith, fpirit, Baptifme,* as the Lord Jefus, hath his true *body, faith, fpirit,* &c. *Ephef.* 4. correfpondent alfo are their *weapons,* and the *fucceffe,* iffue, or operation of them. A *carnall weapon* or *fword* of *fteele* may produce a *carnall repentance,* a fhew, an outfide, an *uniformitie* through a State or *Kingdome:* But it hath pleafed the Father to exalt the *Lord Jefus* only, to be a Prince (armed with *power* and meanes fufficient) to give *repentance* to *Ifrael,* Acts 5. 31.

<small>A difference between the true and falfe Chrift and Chriftians.</small>

Accordingly an *unbelieving* Soule being dead in finne (although he be changed from one *worfhip* to another, like a dead man fhifted into feverall changes of *apparell*) cannot pleafe *God,* Heb. 11. and confequently, whatever fuch an *unbelieving* & *unregenerate* perfon acts in *Worfhip* or *Religion,* it is but finne, Rom. 14. *Preaching* finne, *praying* (though without beads or booke) finne; *breaking of bread,* or *Lords fupper* finne, yea as odious as the oblation of Swines *blood,* a Dogs *neck,* or *killing of a Man,* Ifa. 66.

<small>The worfhip of unbelieving unregenerate perfons.</small>

But *Faith* it is that *gift* which proceeds alone from the *Father* of Lights, *Phil.* 1. 29. and till he pleafe to make his *light* arife and open the eyes of blind finners, their foules fhall lie faft afleep (and the fafter, in that a *fword* of fteele compells them to a *worfhip* in *hypocrifie*) in the dungeons of *fpirituall darkneffe* and *Sathans flavery.*

<small>The danger & mifchiefe of a civill fword in Soule matters, which makes the civill Magiftrate deeply guilty of all thofe</small>

Peace. I adde, that a *civill fword* (as wofull experience in all ages hath proved) is fo far from bringing or helping forward an *oppofite* in *Religion* to *repentance,* that *Magiftrates* finne grievoufly againft the *worke* of *God* and *blood* of Soules, by such proceedings. Because as (commonly) the suffrings of *false* and *Antichristian Teachers* harden their *followers*, who being blind, by this meanes are occasioned to tumble into the *ditch of Hell* after their *blind leaders*, with more inflamed zeale of lying confidence. So secondly, *violence* and a *sword of steele* begets such an *impression* in the sufferers, [66] that certainly they conclude (as indeed that *Religion* cannot be true which needs such *instruments* of *violence* to uphold it so) that *Persecutors* are far from soft and gentle commiseration of the *blindnesse* of others. To this purpose it pleased the *Father* of *Spirits*, of old, to constraine the *Emperour* of *Rome*, *Antoninus Pius*, to write to all the *Governours* of his *Provinces* to forbeare to persecute the *Christians*, because such dealing must needs be so far from converting the *Christians* from their way, that it rather begat in their mindes an opinion of their *crueltie*, &c.[1]

evils which he aims to suppresse. That cannot be a true Religion, which needs carnall weapons to uphold it. Persecutors beget a perswasion of their cruel tie in the hearts of the persecuted. Antoninus Pius his golden act.

CHAP. XLI.

Peace. THe next Scripture against such *persecution*, is that of the *Prophet*, *Isa.* 2. 4. together with *Mic.* 4. 3. they shall break their *swords* into *plough-shares*, and their *speares* into *pruning-hookes*,

Isa. 2. 4.
Mic. 4. 3.
Isa. 11. 9.
concerning Christs

---

[1] Eusebii Pamphili *Ecc. Hist*. Lib. iv. cap. 13, Cantabrigiæ, 1720; Justini Martyris *Opera*, tom. 1, p. 100, Parisiis, 1636. In *The Bloody Tenent yet more Bloody*, p. 126, Williams quotes this edict "related by that praise-worthy Master John Speade out of Eusebius." It is also quoted in Milner, *Church Hist*. 1 : 181. It is "now generally given up as spurious." Milman, *History of Christianity*, ii : 158. "Any man moderately acquainted with Roman history will see at once from the style and tenor that it is a clumsy forgery." George Long, *Thoughts of M. Aurelius Antoninus*, page 24.

Isa. 11. 9. There shall none hurt or destroy in all the *mountaine* of my *Holinesse.*

<small>peaceable Kingdom discussed.</small>

Unto which it pleased Mr. *Cotton* to say, "That " these *predictions* doe onely shew, first, with what " kinde of *weapons* he should subdue the *Nations* to " the *obedience* of the *faith* of the *Gospell*, not by *fire* " and *sword*, and weapons of *War*, but by the power " of the *Word* and *Spirit* of God, which, saith he, no " man doubts of.

"Secondly, those *predictions* of the *Prophets* shew, " what the *meeke* and *peaceable* temper will be of all " true *converts* to *Christianity*; not *Lyons* or *Leopards*, " not *cruell oppressors* nor *malignant opposers* or *biters* " one of another: but doth not forbid them to drive " ravenous *wolves* from the *sheep-fold*, and to restraine " them from devouring the *sheep* of *Christ.*

<small>Mr. Cottons excellent interpretation of those Prophecies.</small>

Truth. In this first excellent and truly Christian *Answer*, me thinks the *Answerer* may heare a voyce from *Heaven*, Out of thine owne mouth will I judge thee: For what can be said more heavenly by the tongues of *Men* and *Angels*, to shew the *heavenly meek temper* of all the *Souldiers* of the *Lambe of God*, as also to set forth what are the *Spirituall weapons* and *ammunition* of the holy war and battle of the *Gospell* and *Kingdome* of *Jesus Christ*, for the subduing of the *Nations* of the World unto him.

<small>His doctrine and practice condemned by that interpretation.</small>

Peace. And yet out of the same mouth (which should not be, saith *James*) proceeds *good* and *evill*, *sweet* and *sowre*; for he addes: But this doth not forbid them to drive *ravenous wolves* from the 67] sheepfold, and to restraine them from devouring the sheepe of *Christ.*

Truth. In these words (according to the judgement here maintained by him) he fights against the former *truth* (to wit, that by *spirituall weapons Christ Jesus* will subdue the *Nations* of the *Earth* to the *obedience* of the *Gospel*) for by driving away these *Wolves* hee intends not onely the *resistance* and *violence* which the *Shepherds* of *Christ* ought spiritually to make, but the *civill resistance* of the *materiall Swords, Staves Guns, &c.* Whence I argue, that same power that forceth the evill (or Wolves) out, forceth the good (the Sheepe) in; for of the *same* or *like* things is the *same* or *like* reason; as the same *arme of flesh* that with a *staffe* beats off a *Wolfe*, with a *Rod* and *Hooke* brings in the *Sheepe:* the same *dog* that assaulteth and teareth the *Wolfe*, frighteth and forceth in the *straggling Sheep.*

<small>Spirituall and mysticall Wolves.</small>

CHAP. XLII.

Peace. BVt for the clearer opening of this *mystery*, I pray explicate that Scripture where the *Spirit of God* is pleased to use this similitude of *Wolves*, *Acts* 20. 29. out of which (keeping to the Allegory) I shall propose these Quæries.

First, what Wolves were these *Paul* warnes of?

Truth. Answ. Wolves *literally* he will not say: Nor secondly, *persecutors* of the *Flock*, such as the *Romane Emperours* were, [or] Magistrates under him.

Therefore (thirdly) such as brought other *Religions* and *Worships*, as the *Spirit of God* opens it, *vers.* 30. Such as amongst themselves should speake *perverse things*, as many *Antichrists* did, and especially *The*

<small>Act. 20. 29 opened.</small>

<small>What those Wolves were. Act. 20. 29</small>

Antichrift. And I aske whether or no such as may hold forth other *Worships* or *Religions*, (*Iewes*, *Turkes*, or *Antichriftians*) may not be peaceable and quiet *Subjects*, loving and helpfull *neighbours*, faire and juft *dealers*, true and loyall to the *civill government*? It is cleare they may from all *Reafon* and *Experience* in many flourifhing *Cities* and *Kingdomes* of the World, and fo offend not againft the *civill State* and *Peace*; nor incurre the punifhment of the *civill fword*, notwithftanding that in *fpirituall* and *myfticall account* they are ravenous and greedy *Wolves.*

Peace. 2. I quære to whom *Paul* gave this charge to watch againft them, *verf.* 31.

68] *Truth.* They were not the *Magiftrates* of the *City* of *Ephefus*, but the *Elders* or *Minifters* of the *Church of Chrift* (his myfticall flock of fheepe) at *Ephefus:* Vnto them was this *charge* of *watching* given, and fo confequently of driving away thefe *Wolves.*

Charges directed to Minifters of the fpirituall kingdome, fafly applyed to the Magiftrates of the civill. No word of Chrift to the civill Magiftrate to feed his flock, but

And however that many of thefe *charges* and *exhortations* given by that *One Shepherd Chrift Iefus* to the *Shepherds* or *Minifters* of *Churches*, be commonly attributed and directed (by the Anfwerer in this difcourfe) to the *civill Magiftrate*; yet I defire in the feare and holy prefence of God it may bee inquired into, whether in all the *Will* or *Teftament* of *Chrift* there bee any fuch *word* of *Chrift* by way of *command, promife*, or *example*, countenancing the Governors of the *civill State* to meddle with thefe *Wolves*, if in *civill* things *peaceable* and *obedient*.

Peace. Truly if this charge were given to the Magiftrates at *Ephefus*, or any Magiftrates in the World,

doubtleffe they muft bee able to difcerne and deter-
mine (out of their owne *official abilities* in thefe fpirit-
uall Law queftions) who are fpirituall *Sheep*, what is
their *food*, what their *poifon*, what their *properties*,
who their *Keepers*, &c.   So on the contrary who are
Wolves, what their *properties*, their *haunts*, their
affaults, the manner of taking, &c. fpiritually: (and
this befide the care and ftudy of the Civill Lawes,
and the difcerning of his owne proper Civill *Sheep*,
obedient Sheepe, &c. as alfo wolvifh oppreffors, &c.
whom he is bound to punifh and fuppreffe)

<small>to his Minifters, who (if true) have fpirituall power fufficient againft fpirituall Wolves.</small>

Truth. I know that Civill Magiftrates (in fome places) have declined the name of *Head* of the Church, and *Ecclefiafticall* Judge, yet can they not with good confcience decline the *name*, if they doe the *worke*, and performe the *office* of determining and punifhing a meerly fpirituall *Wolfe*.

<small>Magiftrates decline the name of Head of the Church, and yet practife the headfhip or government.</small>

They muft be fufficiently alfo able to judge in all *fpirituall* caufes, and that with their owne, and not with other mens eyes, (no more then they doe in *civill caufes*) contrary to the common practice of the Governours and Rulers of Civill States, who often fet up that for a *Religion* or *Worfhip* to God, which the *Clergie* or Churchmen (as men fpeake) fhall in their Confciences agree upon.

And if this be not fo, to wit, that *Magiftrates* muft not be *Spirituall Judges* (as fome decline it in the title, Supreme Head and Governour) why is *Gallio* wont to be exclaimed againft for refufing to be a *Iudge* in fuch matters as concerned the *Iewifh worfhip* and *Religion?* How is he cenfured for a *Prophane perfon*, without *confcience*, [69] &c. in that he would bee no *Iudge* or *Head*? (for that is all one in point of Government.)

<small>The Elect shall not be devoured.</small> *Peace.* In the third place I quærie whether the *Father* who gave, and the *Sonne* who keepes the Sheepe, bee not greater then all? Who can pluck these Sheepe the *Elect* out of his hand, which answers that common objection of that danger of devouring, although there were no other weapons in the world appointed by the Lord Jesus. But

CHAP. XLIII.

<small>Christ Jesus furnisheth his Shepherds with power sufficient to drive away Wolves.</small> Fourthly, I ask, Were not these *Elders* or *Ministers* of the *Church* of *Ephesus* sufficiently furnished from the *Lord Iesus* to drive away these mysticall and spirituall Wolves?

Truth. True it is, against the inhumane and uncivill violence of Persecutors, they were not, nor are *Gods children* able and provided: but to resist, drive away, expell, and kill spirituall & mysticall *Wolves* by the *word* of the *Lord*, none are fit to be Chrifts Shepherds <small>Tit. 1. 9. 10. opened.</small> who are not able, *Tit.* 1. 9. 10. 11. The *Bishop* or *Overseer* must be able by sound *doctrine* both to exhort and to convince the Gainsayers: which Gainsayers to be by him convinced, that is, overcome or subdued (though it may be in themselves ever obstinate) they were I say as greedy *Wolves* in *Crete*, as any could be at *Ephesus:* for so saith *Paul* vers. 10. they were unruly and vaine talkers, deceivers, whose mouthes must bee stopped, who subverted whole houses; and yet *Titus* (and every ordinary Shepherd of a flocke of *Christ*) had ability sufficient to defend the flock from spirituall and mysticall *wolves* without the helpe of the Civill Magistrate.

Peace. In this respect therefore me thinks we may fitly allude to that excellent answer of *Iob* to *Bildad* the *Shuhite, Iob* 26. How hast thou helped him that is without power? How savest thou the *arme* that hath no strengh? How hast thou counselled him that hath no *wisedome?* how hast thou plentifully declared the thing as it is?

^{— marginal: Job. 26. 1, 2.}

5. Lastly, I ask, whether (as men deale with Wolves) these *wolves* at *Ephesus* were intended by *Paul* to be killed, their braines dasht out with stones, staves, halberts, guns, &c. in the hands of the Elders of Ephesus, &c?

Truth. Doubtlesse (comparing spirituall things with spirituall) [70] all such mysticall wolves must spiritually and mystically so be slain. And the *Witnesses* of *Truth,* Revel. 11. speake fire, and kill all that hurt them, by that *fierie* Word of *God,* and that two-edged *sword* in their hand, *Psal.* 149.

But oh what streames of the *blood* of Saints have been and must be shed (untill the *Lambe* have obtained the Victorie, *Revel.* 17.) by this unmercifull (and in the state of the New *Testament,* when the *Church* is spread all the World over) most *bloody doctrine,* viz. The *wolves* (Hereticks) are to be driven away, their braines *knockt* out and *kill'd,* the poore sheepe to be preserved for whom Christ died, &c.

^{— marginal: Unmercifull and bloody doctrine.}

Is not this to take *Christ Jesus,* and make him a temporall *King* by force? *John* 6. 15. Is not this to make his *Kingdome* of this *world,* to set up a *civill* and temporall *Israel,* to bound out new *Earthly holy*

Lands of *Canaan,* yea and to set up a *Spanish Inquisition* in all parts of the *World,* to the speedy destruction of thousands, yea of millions of Soules, and the frustrating of the sweet *end* of the comming of the *Lord Iesus,* to wit, to save *mens soules* (and to that end not to destroy their *bodies*) by his own blood?

CHAP. XLIV.

<small>John 6. 15
2 Cor. 10.
4. discussed.</small> *Peace.* THe next Scripture produced against such Persecution, is 2 *Cor.* 10. 4. The *weapons* of our *warfare* are not *carnall*, but mighty through God to the pulling down of strong holds, casting down *imaginations*, and every high thing that exalteth it selfe against the *knowledge of God*, and bringing into *captivity* every thought to the obedience of *Christ*, and having in a readinesse to avenge all *disobedience, &c.*

Unto which it is answered, "When *Paul* saith, "The *weapons* of our *warfare* are not *carnall*, but "*spirituall*: he denieth not *civill* weapons of *Justice* "to the *civill Magistrate*, Rom. 13. but only to "*Church-officers*: and yet the *weapons* of *Church* "*officers* he acknowledgeth to be such, as though they "be *spirituall*, yet are ready to take *vengeance* on all "*disobedience*, 2 Cor. 10. 6. which hath reference, "amongst other *Ordinances*, to the censures of the "*Church* against *scandalous offenders*.

Truth. I acknowledge that herein the Spirit of God denieth not [71] *civill weapons* of *justice* to the *Civill Magistrate,* which the Scripture he quotes, *Rom.* 13. abundantly testifie.

Yet withall I must aske, why he here affirmeth

the Apostle denies not *civill weapons* of Justice to the *civill Magistrate?* of which there is no question, unlesse that (according to his scope of proving *perfecution* for *conscience*) he intends withall, that the *Apostle* denies not *civill weapons* of *justice* to the Civill Magistrate in *Spirituall* and *Religious* causes: The contrary whereunto (the Lord assisting) I shall evince, both from this very Scripture, and his owne observation, and lastly by that 13 of the Romanes, by himselfe quoted.

First then from this *Scripture* and his owne *Observation*: The *weapons* of *Church officers* (faith he) are such, which though they be *spirituall*, are ready to take vengeance on all *disobedience*; which hath reference (faith he) amongst other Ordinances, to the Censures of the *Church* against scandalous offenders.

I hence observe, that there being in this Scripture held forth a two-fold state, a *Civill state* and a *Spirituall*, Civill officers and *spirituall*, *civill weapons* and *spirituall weapons*, *civill vengeance* and *punishment*, and a *spirituall vengeance* and *punishment*: although the Spirit speakes not here expresly of *Civill Magistrates* and their *civill weapons*, yet these States being of different Natures and Considerations, as far differing as Spirit from *Flesh*, I first observe, that *Civill weapons* are most improper and unfitting in matters of the *Spirituall state* and *kingdome*, though in the *Civill state* most proper and sutable.

The difference of the civill & spirituall estate.

Civill weapons most improper in spirituall causes: fitly exemplified by that similitude, 2 Cor. 10.4.

CHAP. XLV.

FOr (to keepe to the *fimilitude* which the *Spirit* ufeth, for inftance) To batter downe a *ftrong hold, high wall, fort, tower* or *caftle,* men bring not a firft and fecond *Admonition,* and after obftinacie, *Excommunication,* which are *fpirituall weapons* concerning them that be in the *Church:* nor *exhortation* to *Repent* and be *baptized,* to beleeve in the Lord Jefus, &c. which are proper weapons to them that be without, &c. But to take a *ftrong hold,* men bring *Canons, Culverins, Saker,*[1] *Bullets, Powder, Mufquets, Swords, Pikes,* &c. and thefe to this end are weapons effectuall and proportionable.

<small>Spirituall weapons, only effectuall in fpirituall & foule caufes.</small> 72] On the other fide, to batter downe *Idolatry, falfe worfhip, herefie, fchifme, blindneffe, hardneffe,* out of the *foule* and *fpirit,* it is vaine, improper, and unfutable to bring thofe *weapons* which are ufed by *perfecutors, ftocks, whips, prifons, fwords, gibbets, ftakes,* &c. (where thefe feem to prevaile with fome Cities or Kingdomes, a ftronger force fets up againe, what a weaker pull'd downe) but againft thefe *fpirituall ftrong holds* in the foules of men, *Spirituall Artillery* and *weapons* are proper, which are mighty through *God* to fubdue and bring under the very *thought* to *obedience,* or elfe to binde faft the foule with *chaines* of *darkneffe,* and locke it up in the *prifon* of *unbeleefe* and hardneffe to *eternity.*

---

[1] "(1) The peregrine hawk.
(2) A piece of ordnance of three inches and a half bore, weight of fhot five pounds and a half. According to Harrifon the weight of the Saker was 1500 lbs." J. O. Halliwell, *Dictionary of Archaic and Provincial Words.* 2: 702.

2. I observe that as *civill weapons* are improper in this businesse, and never able to effect ought in the *soule:* So (although they were proper, yet) they are *unnecessary*, for if as the *Spirit* here saith (and the *Answerer* grants) *spirituall weapons* in the hand of *Church officers* are able and ready to take *vengeance* on all disobedience, that is *able* and mighty, sufficient and ready for the *Lords* worke either to *save* the soule, or to *kill* the soule of whomsoever, be the party or parties opposite, in which respect I may againe remember that speech of *Job*, How hast thou helped him that hath no power? *Job* 26.

Civill weapons not only improper, but unnecessary in spirituall causes.

Peace. Offer this (as *Malachie* once spake) to the Governours the *Kings* of the *Earth*, when they besiege, beleagure, and assault great Cities, Castles, Forts, &c. should any subject pretending his service bring store of *pins, sticks, strawes, bulrushes*, to beat and batter downe *stone walls*, mighty Bulwarkes, what might his expectation and reward be, but at least the censure of a man distract, beside himselfe? &c.

No earthly Kings or Governours will be so served, as we pretend to serve the King of Kings.

Truth. What shall we then conceive of His *displeasure*, (who is the *chiefe* or *Prince* of the *Kings* of the earth, and rides upon the *Word* of *Truth* and *meeknesse*, which is that *white Horse, Rev.* 6. and *Rev.* 19. with His holy *witnesses* the *white Troopers* upon *white horses*) when to His *helpe* and *aid* men bring and adde such *unnecessary, improper* and weake munition?

Psal. 45. The white Troopers.

Will the *Lord Jesus* (did He ever in His owne Person practice, or did he appoint to) joyne to His *Breastplate* of *Righteousnesse*, the *breastplate* of *iron* and *steele?* to the *Helmet* of *righteousnesse* and *salva-*

Spirituall Ammunition. Eph. 6. applied

tion in *Christ*, an helmet and crest of *iron, brasse*, or *steel*, a target of wood to His shield of Faith? [to] His two *edged sword* comming forth of the mouth of *Jesus*, the *materiall sword*, the worke of Smiths 73] and Cutlers? or a girdle of shooes leather to the girdle of truth, &c. Excellently fit and proper is that *alarme* and *item*, *Psal*. 2. Be *wise* therefore O ye *Kings* (especially those ten *Horns*, *Rev*. 17.) who under pretence of fighting for C*hrist Jesus* give their power to the *Beast* against *Him*, and be warned ye *Judges* of the Earth : *Kisse the Son*, that is with *subjection* and *affection*, acknowledge Him only the *King* and *Judge of soules* (in that power bequeathed to His *Ministers* and *Churches*) lest if His wrath be kindled, yea but a little, then *blessed* are they that *trust in* Him.

Materiall and Spirituall Artillery unfitly joyned together.

An alarme to civill or earthly Rulers.

CHAP. XLVI.

Concerning the civill Rulers power in spirituall causes discust.

Peace. NOw in the second place concerning that Scripture, *Rom*. 13. which it pleaseth the *Answerer* to quote, and himselfe, and so many excellent servants of God have insisted upon to prove such *persecution* for *Conscience*; how have both he and they *wrested* this Scripture (not as *Peter* writes of the *wicked*, to their *eternall*, yet) to their owne and others *temporall destruction* by Civill *wars* and *combustions* in the world?

My humble request therefore is to the Father of *Lights*, to send out the bright *beames* of the *Sun* of *Righteousnesse*, and to scatter the mist which that old *serpent*, the great *jugler Sathan*, hath raised about this holy Scripture, and my request to you (divine

Truth) is for your care and paines to inlighten and cleare this Scripture.

Truth. Firſt then upon the ſerious *examination* of this whole Scripture it will appeare that from the ninth verſe of 12 Chap. to the end of this whole 13 Chap. the Spirit handles the duties of the Saints in the carefull obſervation of the ſecond Table in their civil converſation, or walking towards men, and ſpeaks not at all of any point or matter of the firſt Table concerning the *Kingdome* of the *Lord Jeſus*.

Rom. 13. ſpeakes not at all of ſpirituall but civill affaires.

For, having in the whole Epiſtle handled that great point of free *Juſtification* by the free *Grace* of *God* in *Chriſt*, in the beginning of the 12 Chap. he exhorts the *Beleevers* to give and dedicate themſelves unto the Lord both in *ſoule* and *body*, and unto the 9 verſe of the 12 Chap. he expreſſely mentioneth their *converſation* in the *Kingdome* or *Body* of *Chriſt Jeſus*, together with the ſeverall Officers thereof.

And from the 9 ver. to the end of the 13 he plainly diſcourſeth of [74] their civill converſation, and walking, one toward another, and with all men, from whence he hath faire occaſion to ſpeake largely concerning their ſubjection to *Magiſtrates* in the 13 Chap.

The ſcope of Rom. 13.

Hence it is that verſe 7 of this 13 Chap. *Paul* exhorts to performance of *love* to all men (*Magiſtrates and ſubjects*) verſe 7. 8. Render therefore to all their due, *tribute* to whom *tribute* is due, *cuſtome* to whom *cuſtome*, *feare* to whom *feare*, *honour* to whom *honour*. Owe nothing to any man, but to *love* one another, for he that *loveth* another hath fulfilled the Law.

Love to man, the duty of the whole ſecond Table.

How love fulfilleth the Law.

If any man doubt (as the Papifts fpeak) whether a man may perfectly fulfill the *Law*; every man of found judgement is ready to anfwer him that thefe words [He *that loveth hath fulfilled the Law*]¹ concerneth not the whole *Law* in the firft Table, that is the *worſhip* and *Kingdome* of *God* in *Chriſt*.

Secondly, That the Apoſtle ſpeaks not here of perfect obſervation of the ſecond Table without failing in word or act toward men, but layes open the ſumme and ſubſtance of the *Law*, which is *love*, and that he that walkes by the rule of *love* toward all *men* (*Magiſtrates and ſubjects*) he hath rightly attained unto what the *Law* aimes at, and ſo in *Evangelicall obedience* fulfills and keeps the *Law*.

Hence therefore againe in the 9 verſe having diſcourſed of the 5 Command in this point of *Superiours*, he makes all the reſt of the Commandements of the ſecond Table, which concerne our *walking* with man (viz. *Thou ſhalt not kill, Thou ſhalt not commit adultery, Thou ſhalt not ſteale, Thou ſhalt not beare falſe witneſſe, Thou ſhalt not covet:* and if there be any other Commandement, to be briefly comprehended in this ſaying, namely, *Thou ſhalt love thy neighbour as thy ſelfe.*

And verſe 10 *Love* worketh no ill to his neighbour, therefore *love* is the fulfilling of the Law, that is (as before) the *Law* concerning our *civill converſation* toward All men, *Magiſtrates* or *Governours,* and fellow-ſubjects of all conditions.

---

¹ The brackets are in the original text.

CHAP. XLVII.

Peace. Although the Scripture is sufficient to make the *man of God perfect*, and the *foole wife* to *salvation*, and our *faith* in *God* must be only founded upon the *Rocke Chrift*, and not upon [75] the *fand* of mens *judgements* and *opinions*: Yet as *Paul* alledgeth the *judgement* and fayings of *unbeleevers* for their *conviction* out of their owne *tenets* and *grants*: So I pray you to fet downe the words of one or two (not unbeleevers in their *perfons*, but excellent and pretious *fervants* and *witneffes* of *God* in their times, whofe *names* are fweet and pretious to all that *feare God*) who although their *judgement* ran in the *common ftreame, viz.* That *Magiftrates* were keepers of the 2 *Tables, defendors* of the *Faith* againft *Hereticks*, and notwithftanding what ever they have written for defence of their *judgements*, yet the *light* of *truth* fo evidently fhined upon their *foules* in this Scripture, that they abfolutely denied the 13 of the *Romanes* to concerne any matter of the firft *Table*.

<small>Rom. 13 fo interpreted even by them that held perfecution for confcience.</small>

Truth. Firft, I fhall produce that excellent fervant of *God, Calvin*, who upon this 13 to the *Romanes* writes;[1] *Tota autem hæc difputatio eft de civilibus præfecturis: It ag fruftra inde facrilegam fuam tyrannidem ftabilire moliuntur qui Dominatum in confcientias exerceant:* But (faith he) this whole *difcourfe* concerneth *civill Magiftrates*, and therefore in vaine doe they who exercife *power* over *confciences*, goe about from this place to eftablifh their *facrilegious tyranny*.

<small>Calvins judgement of Rom. 13.</small>

---

[1] Johannis Calvini *Commentarii*, edit. A. Tholuck, v: 200.

Peace. I know how far moſt men (and eſpecially the ſheep of *Ieſus* will flie from the thought of exerciſing tyranny over *conſcience*) that happily they will diſclaime the dealing of all with *mens conſciences:* Yet if the Acts and Statutes which are made by them concerning the worſhip of God be attended to; their profeſſion (and that out of zeale according to the patterne of that *ceremoniall* and figurative ſtate of *Iſrael*) to ſuffer no other Religion nor worſhip in their Territories, but *one*; their *profeſſion* and *practice* to defend their *Faith* from reproach and blaſphemy of *Hereticks* by *Civill weapons*, and all that from this very 13 of the *Romanes*; I ſay if theſe particulars and others be with feare and trembling in the preſence of the moſt High examined; the wonderfull *deceit* of their owne *hearts* ſhall appeare unto them, and how *guilty* they will appeare to be of wreſting this Scripture before the Tribunall of the moſt High.

Truth. Again *Calvin* ſpeaking concerning fulfilling of the *Law* by *love*, writes thus on the ſame place:[1] *Sed Paulus in totam Legem non reſpicit, tantum de officiis loquitur, quæ nobis erga proximû demândantur alege:* That is, *Paul* hath not reſpect unto the whole *Law*, he ſpeaks [76] only of thoſe duties which the Law commands towards our neighbours, and it is manifeſt, that in this place by our *neighbours* hee meanes *high* and *low, Magiſtrates* and *ſubjects*, unto whom we ought to walke by the rule of *love*, paying unto every one their due.

Againe, *Cæterùm Paulus hic tantùm meminit ſecunde Tabulæ quiâ de ea tantum erat quæſtio:*[2] But *Paul* here

<small>Gods people loath to be found, yet proved perſecutors.</small>

---

[1] *Commentarii,* v: 201.   [2] *Commentarii,* v: 201.

only mentioneth the second *Table*, becaufe the queftion was only concerning that.

And againe, *Quod autem repetit complementum legis effe dilectionem, intellige (ut prius) de ea legis parte quod hominum focietatem fpectat: Prior enim legis tabula quæ eft de cultu Dei minimè hic attingitur*.¹ But in that he repeateth that *love* is the fulfilling of the *Law*, underftand as before, that he fpeakes of that part of the *Law* which refpects *humane fociety*; for the firft Table of the *Law* which concerneth the Worfhip of God is not in the leaft manner here touched. ^{Calvin confeffeth that the firft Table concerning Gods worfhip, is not here in Rom. 13. touched.}

After *Calvin*, his fucceffour in *Geneva* that holy and learned *Beza* upon the word Ἀνακεφαλαιωται, if there be any other Commandement it is fummed up in this, Thou fhalt love thy *neighbour* as thy *felfe*, writes thus: *Tota lex nihil aliud quàm amorem Dei & proximi præcipit, fed tamen cum Apoftolus hoc loco de mut nis hominum officiis differat, legis vocabulum ad fecundam Tabulam reftringendane puto.*² ^{Beza upon Rom. 13.}

The whole Law (faith he) commands nothing elfe but the *love* of *God*, and yet neverthelefſe fince the *Apoftle* in this place difcourfeth of the *duties* of men one *toward* another, I thinke this terme *law* ought to be reftrained to the fecond Table.

CHAP. XLVIII.

Peace. I Pray now proceed to the fecond Argument from this Scripture againft the ufe of *civill weapons* in *matters of Religion* and fpirituall worfhip.

---

¹ *Commentarii*, v: 202.   ² Bezæ, Nov. Teft. in loco, edit. Londini, 1585. (Underhill.)

Truth. The Spirit of God here commands fubjection and obedience to *higher Powers,* even to the *Romane Emperours* and all fubordinate *Magiftrates;* and yet the Emperours and Governours under them were ftrangers from the life of God in Chrift, yea moft averfe and *oppofite,* yea *cruell* and bloody Perfecutors of the name and Followers of *Jefus:* and yet unto thefe is this *fubjection* and *obedience* [77] commanded. Now true it is, that as the *civill Magiftrate* is apt not to content himfelfe with the *majefty* of an *earthly Throne, Crowne, Sword, Scepter,* but to feat himfelfe in the *Throne* of *David* in the *Church:* So *Gods* people (and it may be in *Pauls* time) confidering their high and glorious *preferment* and *priviledges* by *Jefus Chrift,* were apt to be much tempted to defpife Civill Governours, efpecially fuch as were ignorant of the Son of God, and perfecuted him in his fervants.

Paul writes not to the Romane Governors to defend the truth, and to punifh hereticks.

Now then I argue, if the *Apoftle* fhould have commanded this *fubjection* unto the *Romane Emperours* and *Romane Magiftrates* in fpirituall caufes, as to *defend* the *truth* which they were no way able to *difcerne,* but *perfecuted,* (and upon truft from others no Magiftrate (not perfwaded in his owne *confcience*) is to take it.) Or elfe to punifh Hereticks, whom then alfo they muft *difcerne* and *judge,* or elfe condemne them as the *Jewes* would have *Pilate* condemne the *Lord Jefus* upon the *fentence* of others, I fay if *Paul* fhould have (in this Scripture) put this worke upon thefe *Romane Governours,* and commanded the *Churches of Chrift* to have yeelded *fubjection* in any fuch matters, he muft (in the judgement of all men) have put out the eye of *Faith* and *Reafon* and *Senfe* at once.

CHAP. XLIX.

Peace. IT is said by some, Why then did *Paul* himselfe, *Act*. 25. appeale to *Cæsar*, unlesse that *Cæsar* (though he was not, yet) he ought to have beene a fit *Judge* in such matters?

Truth. I answer, if *Paul* in this *Appeale* to *Cæsar*, had referred and submitted simply and properly the cause of *Christ*, his *Ministry* and *Ministration* to the *Romane Emperours* Tribunall, knowing him to be an *Idolatrous stranger* from the *true God*, and a *Lion*-like bloody *persecutor* of the *Lord Iesus*, the *Lambe* of *God*, I say let it be considered whether or no he had committed these 5. *Evils*.

Pauls appeale to Cæsar discussed.

If Paul had appealed to Cæsar in spirituall things, he had committed 5. evils.

The first against the dimmest light of *Reason* in appealing to *darknesse* to judge *light*, to *unrighteousnesse* to judge *righteousnesse*, the *spiritually blinde*, to judge and end the controversie concerning *heavenly colours*.

Secondly, against the cause of *Religion*, which if condemned by every inferiour *Idolater*, must needs bee condemned by the *Cæsars* themselves, who (*Nabuchadnezzar*-like) set up their *State-images* or [78] *Religions*, commanding the *Worlds uniformity* of *worship* to them.

Thirdly, against the holy State and Calling of the *Christians* themselves, who (by virtue of their subjection to *Christ*) even the least of them are in *spirituall* things above the highest *Potentates* or *Emperours* in the world, who continue in *enmity* against, or in an *ignorant naturall* state without *Christ Jesus*. This honour or high *exaltation* above all his *Holy ones*, to binde (not literally but spiritually) their *Kings* in Chaines, and their *Nobles* in Linkes of Iron, *Psal.* 49.

Fourthly, against his owne *Calling, Apostleship,* or office of *Ministery,* unto which *Cæsar* himselfe and all *Potentates* (in spirituall and soule matters) ought to have submitted: and unto which in controversies of *Christs Church* and *Kingdome, Cæsar* himself ought to have *appealed,* the *Church* of God being built upon the foundation of the *Apostles* and *Prophets, Ephes.* 2. 20.

<small>Emperours themselves, if Christians subject to the Apostles and Churches in spirituall things.</small>
And therefore in case that any of the *Romane Governours,* or the *Emperour* himselfe had beene humbled and converted to *Christianity,* by the preaching of *Christ,* were not they themselves bound to subject themselves unto the power of the *Lord Iesus* in the hands of the Apostles and Churches, and might not the Apostles and Churches have refused to have baptized or washed them into the profession of *Christ Iesus,* upon the apprehension of their unworthinesse?

Or if received into *Christian Fellowship,* were they not to stand at the Bar of the *Lord Iesus* in the *Church,* concerning either their *opinions* or *practices,* were they not to be cast out and delivered unto *Sathan* by the power of the *Lord Iesus,* if after once and twice *admonition* they persist obstinate, as faithfully and impartially, as if they were the meanest in the *Empire:* Yea, although the Apostles, the Churches, the Elders or Governours thereof were poore and meane despised persons in civill respects, and were themselves bound to yeeld all faithfull and loyall *obedience* to such Emperours and Governours in Civill things.

Were they not (if *Christians*) bound themselves to

have submitted to those spirituall decrees of the Apostles and Elders, as well as the lowest and meanest members of *Christ*, *Act*. 16? And if so, how should *Paul* appeale in *spirituall* things to *Cæsar*, or write to the *Churches* of *Iesus* to submit in *Christiau* or *Spirituall* matters?

Fifthly, if *Paul* had appealed to *Cæsar* in spirituall respects, hee [79] had greatly prophaned the holy name of *God* in holy things, in so improper and vaine a *prostitution* of *spirituall* things to carnall and *naturall* judgements, which are not able to comprehend *spirituall* matters, which are alone spiritually discerned, 1 *Cor*. 2.

And yet *Cæsar* (as a *civill* supreme *Magistrate*) ought to defend *Paul* from Civill *violence*, and *slanderous accusations* about *sedition, mutiny, civill disobedience, &c*. And in that sense who doubts but *Gods people* may appeale to the Romane *Cæsar*, an Egyptian *Pharaoh*, a Philistian *Abimelecke*, an Assyrian *Nabuchadnezzar*, the great *Mogol*, *Prester Iohn*, the great *Turke*, or an Indian *Sachim*?

<small>Lawfull appeales in civill things to Civill Magistrates.</small>

CHAP. L.

Peace. WHich is the third Argument against the *civill Magistrates* power in *spirituall* and soule matters out of this Scripture, *Rom*. 13?

Truth. I dispute from the nature of the Magistrates *weapons, vers*. 4. He hath a *sword* (which hee beares not in vaine) delivered to him, as I acknowledge from *Gods appointment* in the free consent and choice of the *subjects* for common good.

The Bloudy Tenent.

We muſt diſtinguiſh of *ſwords.*

<small>Foure ſorts of ſwords mentioned in the New Teſtament.</small>

We finde foure ſorts of *ſwords* mentioned in the *New Teſtament.*

Firſt, the *ſword* of *perſecution,* which *Herod* ſtretched forth againſt *Iames, Act.* 12.

Secondly, the *ſword* of *Gods Spirit,* expreſly ſaid to be the *Word of God, Epheſ.* 6. A *ſword* of two *edges* caried in the *mouth* of *Chriſt, Rev.* 1. which is of ſtrong and mighty *operation,* piercing betweene the *bones* and the *marrow,* betweene the *ſoule* and the *ſpirit, Heb.* 4.

Thirdly, the great *ſword* of *War* and Deſtruction, given to him that rides that terrible *Red Horſe* of *War,* ſo that he takes *Peace* from the *Earth,* and men kill *one another,* as is moſt lamentably true in the *ſlaughter* of ſo many hundred thouſand ſoules within theſe few yeares in ſeverall parts of *Europe,* our owne and others.

None of theſe 3 *ſwords* are intended in this *Scripture:*

<small>The Civill Sword.</small>

Therefore, fourthly, there is a *Civill ſword,* called the Sword of *Civill juſtice;* which being of a *materiall civill nature,* for the *defence* of *Perſons, Eſtates, Families, Liberties* of a *City* or *Civill State,* and the *ſuppreſſing* of *uncivill* or injurious perſons or actions by ſuch *civill puniſhment,* It cannot according to its utmoſt reach and capacitie [80] (now under *Chriſt,* when all *Nations* are meerly *civill,* without any ſuch typicall holy reſpect upon them, as was upon *Iſrael* a *Nationall Church*) I ſay, cannot extend to *ſpirituall* and *Soul-cauſes,* Spirituall and Soule *puniſhment,* which belongs to that *ſpirituall ſword* with two edges, the *foule-piercing* (in *foule-faving* or *foule-killing*) the Word of God.

CHAP. LII.

Truth. A Fourth Argument from this Scripture I take in the 6. verse, from *Tribute, cuftome, &c.* which is a meerly *civill Reward* or *Recompence* for the *Magiftrates* worke. Now as the *wages* are, such is the *worke :* But the *wages* are meerely *civill, Cuftome, Tribute, &c.* not the *contributions* of the Saints or *Churches* of *Chrift* (proper to the *Spirituall* and *Chriftian ftate*) and such *work* only muft the *Magiftrate* attend upon, as may properly deferve such *civill wages*, reward or recompence. _{Tribute, Cuftome, &c. meerly civill recompences for civill work.}

Laftly, that the *Spirit of God* never intended to direct or warrant the *Magiftrate* to ufe his Power in *fpirituall* affaires and *Religions* worfhip: I argue, from the *terme* or *title* it pleafeth the wifedome of God to give fuch *Civill officers*, to wit, (verf. 6.) *Gods Minifters*. _{Magiftrates called by God Gods Minifters.}

Now at the very firft blufh, no man denies a double *Minifterie*.

The one appointed by *Chrift Jefus* in his *Church*, to *gather*, to *governe*, *receive in*, *caft out*, and order all the affaires of the *Church*, the *Houfe, Citie* or *Kingdome* of *God*, Ephef. 4. 1 Cor. 12. _{The fpirituall Miniftery.}

Secondly, a Civill *Miniftery* or *office*, meerely *humane* and *civill*, which Men agree to conftitute (called therefore an humane *creation*, (1 Pet. 2.) and is as true and lawfull in thofe Nations, Cities, Kingdomes, &c. which never heard of the true *God*, nor his holy _{The civill Miniftery or fervice.}

Sonne *Iesus*, as in any part of the World beside, where the Name of *Iesus* is most taken up.

From all which *premises*, viz. that the scope of the *Spirit of God* in this Chapter is to handle the matters of the *second Table* (having handled the matters of the *first*, in the 12.) since the Magistrates of whom *Paul* wrote, were naturall, ungodly, persecuting, and yet lawfull Magistrates, and to be obeyed in all lawfull Civill things.

Since all *Magistrates* are *Gods Ministers*, essentially *civill*, bounded [81] to a *civill* work, with *civill weapons* or instruments, and paid or rewarded with *civill* rewards. From all which, I say, I undeniably collect, that this *Scripture* is generally mistaken, and wrested from the scope of Gods Spirit, and the nature of the place, and cannot truly be alleadged by any for the Power of the *Civill Magistrate* to be exercised in *spirituall* and *Soule-matters*.

CHAP. LII.

<small>What is to be understood by Evill, Rom. 13 4.</small>

Peace. Against this I know many object out of the 4. verse of this Chapter, that the *Magistrate* is to avenge or punish *Evill:* from whence is gathered, that *Heresie*, false *Christs*, false *Churches*, false *Ministeries*, false *Seales*, being evill, ought to be punished Civilly, &c.

Truth. I answer, that the word κακον᾽ is generally opposed to *Civill Goodnesse* or *Virtue* in a *Commonwealth*, and not to *Spirituall Good* or *Religion* in the *Church*.

Secondly, I have proved from the scope of the

place, that here is not intended *Evill* againſt the *Spirituall* or *Chriſtian Eſtate*, handled in the 12 Chap. but *Evill* againſt the *Civill State*, in this 13. properly falling under the cognizance of the *Civill Miniſter* of *God*, the *Magiſtrate*, and puniſhable by that *civill ſword* of his, as an *incivilitie*, *diſorder*, or breach of that *civill order*, *peace* and *civility*, unto which all the Inhabitants of a *City*, *Town*, or *Kingdome* oblige themſelves.

Peace. I have heard that the *Elders* of the *New-Engliſh Churches*, (who yet out of this 13 *Rom.* maintaine Perſecution) grant that the *Magiſtrate* is to preſerve the *peace* and welfare of the *State*, and therefore that he ought not to puniſh ſuch ſinnes as hurt not his *peace*. In particular, they ſay, the *Magiſtrate* may not puniſh *ſecret ſinnes* in the *Soule:* Nor ſuch ſinnes as are yet handling in the *Church* in a *private* way: Nor ſuch ſinnes which are private in *Families*; and therefore they ſay, the *Magiſtrate* tranſgreſſeth to proſecute complaints of *children* againſt their *parents*, *ſervants* againſt *maſters*, *wives* againſt *huſbands*, (and yet this proper to the Civill State) Nor ſuch ſinnes as are between the *Members* and *Churches* themſelves.

And they confeſſe, that if the *Magiſtrate* puniſh, and the *Church* puniſh, there will be a greater Rent in their *Peace*.

82] *Truth.* From thence (ſweet *Peace*) may we well obſerve,

Firſt, the *Magiſtrate* is not to puniſh all *Evill*, according to this their *confeſſion*.

The diſtinction of *private* and *publike Evill* will

Some give to the Magiſtrate what is not his, and take from him *that which is proper to him.* not here availe, becaufe fuch as urge that terme *Evill*, viz. that the Magiftrate is to punifh *Evill*, urge it ftrictly, *eo nomine*, becaufe *Herefie, Blafphemie, falfe Church, falfe Minifterie* is *evill*, as well as Diforder in a Civill State.

Secondly, I obferve, how they take away from the *Magiftrate* that which is proper to his cognifance, as the *complaints* of *fervants, children, wives*, againft their *parents, mafters, husbands*, &c. (*Families* as families, being as ftones which make up the common building, and are properly the object of the *Magiftrates* care, in refpect of Civill Government, Civill order and obedience.)

CHAP. LIV.

Peace. I Pray now (laftly) proceed to the *Authours* Reafon why *Chrifts* Difciples fhould be fo far from perfecuting, that they ought to bleffe them that curfe them, and pray for them that perfecute them, becaufe of the *freeneffe* of *Gods grace*, and the *deepeneffe* of his *Councels*, calling them that are *Enemies, Perfecutors, No people*, to become *meeke Lambes*, the *fheep* and *people* of *God*, according to 1 *Pet.* 2. 20. You which were not a *people*, are now a *people, &c.* and *Matth.* 20. 6. Some come at the *laft houre*, which if they were cut off becaufe they came not *fooner*, would be prevented, and fo fhould *never* come.

Unto this *Reafon* the *Anfwerer* is pleafed thus to reply:

Firft in generall; We muft not doe *Evill*, that Good may come thereof.

Secondly, in particular, he affirmeth, "that it is "evill to tolerate *seditious evill doers, seducing Teachers,* "*scandalous livers:* and for proof of this he quotes "*Chrifts* reproofe to the *Angel* of the *Church* at *Per-* "*gamus*, for tolerating them that hold the *doctrine* of "*Balaam*; and againft the *Church* of *Thiatyra*, for "tolerating *Jesabel* to teach and seduce, *Revel.* 2. 14. "20.

Toleration difcuffed. Upon this point hath Mr. John Goodwin excellently of late difcourfed

Truth. I anfwer, firft, by affenting to the generall Propofition, that it is moft true, like unto Chrift Jefus himfelfe, a fure *foundation*, 1 Cor. 3. Yet what is built upon it, I hope (by Gods affiftance) to [83] make it appeare is but *hay* and *ftubble, dead* and *withered*, not fuiting that *golden foundation*, nor pleafing to the Father of *mercies*, nor *comfortable* to the Soules of men.

It is *evill* (faith he) to tolerate notorious evill doers, feducing Teachers, fcandalous livers.

In which fpeech I obferve 2 evills:

Firft that this *Propofition* is too large and generall, becaufe the *Rule* admits of *exception*, and that according to the will of *God*.

1. It is true, that *Evill* cannot alter its nature, but it is alway *Evill*, as *darkneffe* is alway *darkneffe*, yet

2. It muft be remembred, that it is one thing to *command*, to *conceale*, to *councell*, to *approve Evill*, and another thing to *permit* and *fuffer Evill* with *protefta-tion* againft it, or *diflike* of it, at leaft without *approbation* of it.

Evill is always Evill, yet permiffion of it may in cafe be good.

Laftly, this *fufferance* or *permiffion* of *Evill* is not for its own fake, but for the fake of *Good*, which puts a refpect of *Goodneffe* upon fuch *permiffion*.

Hence it is, that for *Gods* owne *Glorie* fake (which

<small>Gods wonderfull toleration.</small> is the highest *Good*) he endures, that is, *permits* or *suffers* the *Vessels of Wrath*, Rom. 9. And therefore although he be of pure eyes, and can behold no iniquitie, yet his pure eyes patiently and quietly beholds and permits all the *idolatries* and *prophanations*, all the *thefts* and *rapines*, all the *whoredomes* and *abominations*, all the *murthers* and *poysonings*; and yet I say, for his *glory* sake he is patient, and long permits.

Hence for his peoples sake (which is the next Good in his Son) he is oftentimes pleased to permit and suffer the wicked to enjoy a longer *reprive*. Therefore he gave *Paul* all the *lives* that were in the ship, Acts 27.

Therefore he would not so soone have destroyed *Sodome*, but granted a longer *permission*, had there been but 10 righteous, Gen. 19. Therefore, *Jerem.* 5. had he found some to have stood in the *gap*, he would have spared others. Therefore gave he *Jesabel* a time or space, Revel. 2.

Therefore for his Glory sake hath he permitted longer *great sinners*, who afterward have perished in their season, as we see in the case of *Ahab*, the *Ninevites* and *Amorites*, &c.

<small>Deut. 24.</small> Hence it pleased the *Lord* not onely to permit the many *evills* against his owne honourable ordinance of *Mariage* in the world, but was pleased after a wonderfull manner to suffer that sin of many [84] wives in *Abraham, Jacob, David, Salomon*, yea with some expression which seeme to give *approbation*, as 2 Sam. 12.

Peace. It may be said, this is no *patterne* for us, because *God* is above Law, and an absolute *Soveraigne.*

Truth. I anfwer, although wee finde him fometime difpenfing with his Law, yet we never finde him deny himfelfe, or utter a *falfhood*: And therefore when it croffeth not an abfolute *Rule* to *permit* and tolerate (as in the cafe of the permiffion of the *foules* and *confciences* of all men in the world, I have fhewne and fhall fhew further it doth not) it will not hinder our being *holy* as hee is holy in all manner of converfation.

CHAP. LIV.

Peace. IT will yet bee faid, it pleafeth *God* to permit Adulteries, Murthers, Poifons: *God* fuffers men like *fifhes* to devoure each other, *Habac.* 1. the *wicked* to flourifh, *Ier.* 12. yea fends the Tyrants of the world to deftroy the *Nations*, and *plunder* them of their riches, *Ifa.* 10. Should men doe fo, the world would be a *Wildernesse*, and befide we have command for *zealous execution* of Juftice impartially, fpeedily.

Truth. I anfwer, we finde two forts of *commands* both from *Mofes* and from *Chrift*, the two great Prophets and Meffengers from the living *God*, the one the type or figure of the later: *Mofes* gave pofitive Rules both *fpirituall* and *civill*, yet alfo hee gave fome not *pofitive* but *permiffive* for the common good: So the Lord *Iefus* expoundeth it.

Two forts of commands both by Mofes and Chrift.

For, whereas the *Pharifes* urged it, that *Mofes* commanded to give a *Bill of Divorcement* and to put away: the Lord *Iefus* expoundeth it, *Mofes* for the hardneffe of your heart *fuffered or permitted, Math.* 19. 17, 18.

Math. 16. 17. 18.

The permission of divorce in Israel.

This was a *permissive command* universall to all *Israel*, for a *generall good*, in preventing the continuall fires of Diffentions & Combuftions in families (yea it may be Murthers, Poyfons, Adulteries) which that people (as the wifedome of *God* forefaw) was apt out of the *hardneffe* of their *heart* to break out into, were it not for this *preventing permiffion*.

Hence it was that for a further *publike good* fake, and the publike fafety, *David* permitted *Ioab*, a notorious malefactor, and *Shimei* [85] and *Adonijah, &c.* And *civill States* and *Governours* in like cafes have and doe permit and fuffer what neither *David* nor any *civill Governour* ought to doe or have done, were it not to prevent the hazard of the *whole*, in the fhedding of much *innocent blood* (together with the *nocent*) in *civill combuftions*.

Peace. It may be faid, *Ioab, Shimei, Adonijah, &c.* were only (as it were) reprived for a time, and proves only that a feafon ought to be attended for their punifhment.

Truth. Anfw. I anfwer, I produce not thefe inftances to prove a permiffion of Tares (Antichriftians, Heretikes) which other Scriptures abundantly prove, but to make it cleare (againft the *Anfwerers allegation*, that even in the *civill State* permiffion of notorious evill doers, even againft the *civill State*, is not difapproved by *God* himfelfe, and the wifeft of his fervants in its feafon.

CHAP. LV.

Truth. I Proceed. Hence it is that some Generals of Armies, and Governours of Cities, Townes, &c. doe, and (as those former instances prove) lawfully permit some evill persons and practices: As for instance, in the *civill State, Usury*, for the preventing of a *greater evill* in the *civill Body*, as *stealing, robbing, murthering, perishing* of the poore, and the hindrance or stop of *commerce* and dealing in the *Commonwealth*. Just like *Physicians*, wisely permitting noysome *humours*, and sometimes *diseases*, when the *cure* or *purging* would prove more dangerous to the *destruction* of the *whole*, a *weake* or *crazy* body, and specially at such a time. ^{*Usurie in a Commonweale or Civill State lawfully permitted.*}

Thus in many other instances it pleased the *Father of lights,* the *God of Israel,* to permit that people, especially in the matter of their demand of a *King,* (wherein he pleaded that himselfe as well as *Samuel* was rejected.)

This *ground,* to wit, for a *common good* of the *whole,* is the same with that of the *Lord Iesus* commanding the *Tares* to be permitted in the *World,* because otherwise the *good wheat* should be indangered to be rooted up out of the *Field* or *World* also, as well as the *Tares:* and therefore for the good sake the Tares, which are indeed *evill*, were to be permitted: Yea and for the generall good of the *whole world,* the field it selfe, which for want of this obedience to that command of *Christ,* hath beene and is laid waste and desolate, with the fury [86] and rage of *civill War,* professedly raised and maintained (as all States professe for the ^{*Permission of the Tares in the field of the world for a twofold good. 1. Of the good Wheat. 2. Of the whole world, the field it selfe.*}

maintenance of one *true Religion* (after the patterne of that typicall land of *Canaan*) and to suppresse and pluck up these Tares of *false Prophets* and false Professors, *Antichristians, Heretickes, &c.* out of the world.

Hence *illæ lachrymæ*: hence *Germanies, Irelands,* and now *Englands* teares and dreadfull *desolations,* which ought to have beene, and may bee for the future (by obedience to the command of the *Lord Iesus,* concerning the permission of Tares to live in the *world,* though not in the *Church*) I say ought to have beene, and may bee mercifully prevented.

CHAP. LVI.

Peace. I Pray descend now to the second *evill* which you observe in the *Answerers position, viz.* that it would bee *evill* to tolerate notorious *evill doers, seducing teachers, &c.*

Truth. I say, the *evill* is, that he most improperly and confusedly joynes and couples *seducing teachers* with *scandalous livers.*

Peace. But is it not true that the world is full of *seducing teachers,* and is it not true that *seducing teachers* are *notorious evill doers?*

Truth. I answer: far be it from me to deny either: and yet in two things I shall discover the great *evill* of this joyning and coupling *seducing teachers, and scandalous livers* as one adequate or proper object of the Magistrates care and worke to supresse and punish.

First, it is not an *Homogeneall* (as we speake) but an *Heterogeneall* commixture or joyning together of things moſt different in kindes and natures, as if they were both of one conſideration.

For who knowes not but that many *ſeducing teachers*, either of the *Paganiſh, Iewiſh, Turkiſh,* or *Antichriſtian* Religion, may be clear and free from *ſcandalous offences* in their life, as alſo from *diſobedienee* to the Civill Lawes of a State? Yea the *Anſwerer* himſelfe hath elſewhere granted, that if the Lawes of a *Civill State* be not broken, the *Peace* is not broken. Seducing teachers, either Pagan, Jewiſh or Antichriſtian, may yet be obedient ſubjects to the Civill lawes.

Againe, who knowes not that a *ſeducing teacher* properly ſinnes againſt a *Church* or Spirituall eſtate and Lawes of it, and therefore ought moſt properly and onely to bee dealt withall in ſuch a way, and by ſuch weapons as the *Lord Ieſus* himſelfe hath appointed 87] *gainſayers, oppoſites* and *diſobedients* (either within his Church or without) to be *convinced, repelled, reſiſted,* and *ſlaine* withall.

Whereas *ſcandalous offendours* againſt *Parents,* againſt *Magiſtrates* in the 5 Command, and ſo againſt the *life, chaſtity, goods* or *good name* in the reſt, is properly tranſgreſſion againſt the Civill State and Commonweale, or the worldly ſtate of Men: And therefore conſequently if the World or Civill State ought to be preſerved by *Civill Government* or *Governours;* ſuch ſcandalous offendours ought not to be tolerated, but ſuppreſt according to the wiſdome and prudence of the ſaid *Government*. Scandalous livers againſt the Civill ſtate who they are.

Secondly, as there is a fallacious conjoyning and confounding together perſons of ſeverall kindes and natures, differing as much as Spirit and Fleſh, Heaven and Earth each from other. So is there a ſilent and implicite *juſtification* to all the unrighteous and *cruell* Mr. *Cottons* tenent juſtifies all the cruell proceedings againſt

Chrst and Christians *proceedings* of *Jews* and *Gentiles* against all the Prophets of God, the *Lord Jesus* Himselfe, and all His Messengers and Witnesses, whom their Accusers have ever so coupled and mixed with notorious evill *doers and scandalous livers.*

Elijah was a *troubler* of the *State*; *Jeremy* weakned the hand of the people: yea *Moses* made the people neglect their worke: the *Jewes* built the Rebellious and bad City: the three Worthies regarded not the command of the King: *Chrift Jesus* deceived the people, was a *conjurer* and a *trayter* against *Cæsar* in being King of the Jewes (indeed He was so spiritually over the true Jew the Christian) therefore He was numbred with *notorious evill doers*, and nailed to the Gallowes between two Malefactours.

Hence *Paul* and all true Messengers of *Jesus Chrift* are esteemed seducing and seditious teachers and turners of the World upside downe: Yea and to my knowledge (I speake with honourable respect to the *Answerer*, so far as he hath laboured for many Truths of *Chrift*) the *Answerer* himselfe hath drunke of this cup to be esteemed a *seducing Teacher.*

CHAP. LVII.

Peace. Yea but he produceth Scriptures against such *toleration*, and for *persecuting* men for the cause of *conscience*: "*Chrift* (saith he) had something "against the *Angel* of the Church of *Pergamus* for "tolerating them that held the doctrine of *Balaam*, 88] "and against the Church of *Thiatira* for tolera- "ting *Iesabel* to teach and seduce, *Rev.* 2. 14. 20.

Truth. I may anſwer with ſome admiration and aſtoniſhment how it pleaſed the *Father* of *lights*, and moſt jealous God to darken and vaile the eye of ſo pretious a man, as not to ſeek out and propoſe ſome Scriptures (in the proofe of ſo weighty an aſſertion) as at leaſt might have ſome colour for an influence of the Civill Magiſtrate in ſuch caſes: for

Firſt, he ſaith not that Chriſt had ought againſt the City *Pergamus*, (where Sathan had his throne *Rev.* 2.) but againſt the *Church* at *Pergamus*, in which was ſet up the Throne of Chriſt.

<small>Toleration. Rev.2. 14, 20. examined.</small>

Secondly, Chriſts Charge is not againſt the Civill Magiſtrate of *Pergamus*, but the Meſſenger or Miniſtry of the Church in *Pergamus*.

Thirdly, I confeſſe ſo far as *Balaams* or *Ieſabels* doctrine maintained a liberty of *corporall fornication*, it concerned the City of *Pergamus* and *Thiatira*, and the *Angel* or *Officers* of thoſe Cities to ſuppreſſe not only ſuch *practices*, but ſuch *Doctrines* alſo, as the *Roman Emperour* juſtly puniſhed *Ovid* the Poet, for teaching the wanton Art of Love, leading to and uſhering on *laciviouſneſſe* and *uncleanneſſe*.

4. Yet ſo far as *Balaams* teachers or *Ieſabel* did ſeduce the members of the Church in *Pergamus* or *Thiatira*, to the worſhip of the *Idolaters* in *Pergamus* or *Thiatira* (which will appear to be the caſe) I ſay ſo far I may well and properly anſwer, as himſelfe anſwered before thoſe Scriptures, brought from *Luc.* 9. & 2 *Tim.* 2. to prove *patience* and *permiſſion* to men oppoſite, *viz.* " Theſe *Scriptures* (ſaith he) are " *directions* to *Miniſters* of the Goſpel, and in the end " of that paſſage he addes, Much leſſe doe they ſpeake " at all to *Civill Magiſtrates.*

Fifthly, Either these *Churches* and the *Angels* thereof had power to suppresse these doctrines of *Balaam*, and to suppresse *Iesabel* from teaching, or they had not:

That they had not cannot be affirmed, for *Christs Authority* is in the hands of his *Ministers* and *Churches*, *Matth.* 16. & 18. & 1 *Cor.* 5.

If they had *power*, as must be granted, then I conclude *sufficient power* to suppresse such persons, who ever they were that maintained *Balaams* doctrine in the Church at *Pergamus*, although the very [89] *Magistrates* themselves of the City of *Pergamus*, (if Christians) and to have suppressed *Iesabel* from teaching and seducing in the *Church* had she been *Lady*, *Queen*, or *Empresse*, if there were no more but teaching without hostility: And if so, all *power and authority* of *Magistrates* and *Governours* of *Pergamus* and *Thiatira*, and all submitting or appealing to them, in such cases, must needs fall as none of *Christs* appointment.

Lastly, From this perverse wresting of what is writ to the *Church* and the Officers thereof, as if it were written to the *Civill State* and the Officers thereof; all may see how since the *Apostacie* of *Antichrist*, the *Christian World* (so called) hath swallowed up *Christianity*, how the *Church* and *civill State*, that is the *Church* and the *World* are now become one *flocke* of *JesusChrist*; *Christs sheepe*, and the *Pastors* or *Shepherds* of them, all one with the severall unconverted, *wilde* or *tame* Beasts and Cattell of the *World* and the *civill* and earthly *governours* of them: The *Christian Church* or *Kingdome* of the Saints, that *stone* cut out of the *mountaine* without hands, *Daniel* 2. now made

[sidenote: Christ Ministers & Churches have power sufficient from Christ to suppresse Balaam and Iesabel seducing to false worship.]

[sidenote: The Christian world hath swallowed up Christianity.]

all one with the mountaine or Civill State, the *Roman Empire*, from whence it is cut or taken: *Chrifts lilies, garden* and *love*, all one with the *thornes*, the *daughers* and *wildernesse* of the *World*, out of which the *Spouse* or *Church* of *Chrift* is called, and amongst whom in *civill things* for a while here below, she must necessarily be mingled and have converse, unlesse she will goe out of the *World* (before *Chrift Jesus* her *Lord* and *Husband* send for her home into the Heavens, 1 Cor. 5. 10.)

CHAP. LVIII.

Peace. Having thus (by the help of *Chrift*) examined those *Scriptures* or writings of *truth*, brought by the Author against *Persecution*, and cleared them from such vailes & mists wherewith Mr. *Cotton* hath endeavored to obscure & darken their light: I pray you now (by the same gracious assistance) proceed to his answer to the second head of Reasons from the profession of *famous Princes* against *persecution* for *conscience*, K. *James*, *Steven* of *Poland*, K. of *Bohemia*, unto whom the Answerer returneth a treble answer. *The second head of Reasons against such persecution, viz. the profession of famous Princes, K. James, Steven of Poland, and K. of Bohemia.*

"First, saith he, We willingly acknowledge that
"none is to be *persecuted* at all no more then they
"may be *oppressed* for *righteousnesse* sake.

90] "Againe, we acknowledge that none is to be
"punished for his *conscience* though misinformed (as
"hath been said) unlesse his Error be *fundamentall* or
"*seditiously* and *turbulently* promoted, and that after
"due *conviction* of his *conscience*, that it may appeare

"he is not punished for his *conscience*, but for sinning "against his *conscience*.

"Furthermore, we acknowledge none is to be *con-*"*strained* to beleeve or professe the true *Religion*, till "he be convinced in judgement of the *truth* of it, "but yet *restrained* he may be from *blaspheming* the "*truth*, and from seducing any unto *pernicious error*.

Isa. 40 6.
2 Pet. 2.

Truth. This first answer consists of a *repetition* and *enumeration* of such *grounds* or *conclusions*, as Mr. Cotton in the entrance of this Discourse laid downe, and I beleeve that (through the helpe of God) in such replies as I have made unto them, I have made it evident what weak *foundations* they have in the Scriptures of truth; as also that, when such *conclusions* (excepting the first) as *grasse*, and the *flower* of the *grasse* shall fade, that holy Word of the *Lord*, which the Author against such persecution produced, and I have cleared, shall stand for ever, even when these Heavens and Earth are burnt.

Peace. His second answer is this: "What Princes "professe and practice is not a *rule* of *conscience:* They "many times tolerate that in point of *State-policie*, "which cannot justly be tolerated in point of true "Christianity.

"Againe, Princes many times tolerate offendours "out of very necessity, when the offendors are either "too many or too mighty for them to punish, in "which respect *David* tolerated *Joab* and his mur-"ders, but against his will.

CHAP. LIX.

VNto those excellent and famous speeches of those Princes worthy to be written in *golden letters* or *rows* of *Diamonds* upon all the gates of all the Cities and Palaces in the World, the Answerer (without any particular reply) returnes two things.

Truth. First, that Princes profession and practice is no rule of *conscience*: unto this as all men will subscribe, so may they also observe how the Answerer deales with Princes.

<small>Mr. Cottons unquall dealing with Princes.</small>

One while they are the nursing Fathers of the Church, not only to feed, but also to correct, and therefore consequently bound to [91] judge what is true *feeding* and *correcting*: and consequently *all men* are bound to submit to their *feeding* and *correcting*.

Another while, when Princes crosse Mr. *Cottons* judgement and practice, then it matters not what the *profession* and *practice* of Princes is; for (saith he) their *profession* and *practice* is no Rule to *Conscience*.

I aske then, unto what *Magistrates* or *Princes* will themselves or any so perswaded submit, as unto *keepers* of both *Tables*, as unto the *Antitypes* of the *Kings* of *Israel* and *Judah*, and nursing *Fathers* and *Mothers* of the *Church*?

First, will it not evidently follow, that by these Tenents they ought not to submit to any Magistrates in the world in these cases, but to Magistrates just of their owne *conscience*: and

Secondly, that all other *Consciences* in the world (except their owne) must be persecuted by such their Magistrates?

And lastly, is not this to make Magistrates but *steps* and *stirrops* to afcend and mount up into their *rich* and *honourable Seats* and *Saddles*; I meane great and fetled maintenances, which neither the *Lord Jesus*, nor any of his firft *Messengers*, the true *patternes*, did ever know?

CHAP. LX.

Truth. IN the fecond place hee faith that *Princes* out of *State policy* tolerate what fuits not with *Chriftianity*, and out of State *necessity* tolerate (as *David* did *Joab*) againft their wils.

To which I anfwer,

<small>The Anfwerer acknowledgeth a necessity of fome toleration.</small> Firft, that although with him in the firft I confesse that *Princes* may tolerate that out of *State policy* which will not ftand with *Chriftianity*, yet in the fecond he muft acknowledge with me, that there is a *necessity* fometime of *State Toleration*, as in the cafe of *Ioab*, and fo his former *affirmation* generally laid downe [*viz.* that it is evill to tolerate *feducing Teachers*, or *fcandalous livers*] was not duly waighed in the *Balance* of the *Sanctuary*, and is too light.

<small>Chrift Jefus the deepeft politician that ever was, and yet he commands a toleration of</small> Secondly, I affirme that that State policy and State necessity, which (for the *peace* of the *State* and preventing of Rivers of *civill Blood*) permits the *Confciences* of men, will bee found to agree moft punctually with the *Rules* of the beft *Politician* that ever the *World* faw, the *King* of *Kings*, and *Lord* of *Lords*, in comparifon of whom [92] *Salomon* himfelfe had but a *drop* of *wifedome*, compared to *Chrifts* Ocean,

and was but a *Farthing Candle* compared with the *All* and *Ever glorious Son of Righteousnesse*. ^{Antichristians.}

That absolute Rule of this great *Politician* for the peace of the *Field*, which is the *World*, and for the good and peace of the *Saints*, who must have a *civill* being in the *World*, I have discoursed of in his *command* of *permitting* the *Tares*, that is, *Antichristians* or false *Christians* to be in the *Field* of the *World*, growing up together with the true *Wheat*, true *Christians*.

CHAP. LXI.

Peace. His third Answer is this:

"For those three *Princes* named by you "who tolerated *Religion*, we can name you more and "greater who have not tolerated *Hereticks* and *Schis-* "*matickes*, notwithstanding their pretence of Con- "science, and their arrogating the *Crowne* of *Martyr-* "*dome* to their sufferings.

"*Constantine* the Great at the request of the *Gen-* "*erall Councell* at *Nice*, banished *Arrius*, with some "of his *Fellowes, Sozom, lib.* 1. *Eccles. hist. cap.* 19. 20.

"The same *Constantine* made a severe Law against "the *Donatists*: and the like proceedings against "them were used by *Valentinian, Gratian,* and *Theo-* "*dosius*, as *Augustine* reports in *Ep.* 166. Onely *Julian* "the *Apostate* granted liberty to *Hereticks*, as well "as to *Pagans*, that he might by tolerating all weeds "to grow, choake the *vitals* of *Christianity*: which "was also the practice and sinne of *Valens* the *Arrian*.

"*Queene Elizabeth,* as famous for her *Government*

"as most of the former, it is well knowne what
"Lawes she made and executed against *Papists*: yea
"and *K. James* (one of your owne *Witnesses*) though
"he was slow in proceeding against *Papists* (as you
"say) for Conscience sake, yet you are not ignorant
"how sharply and severely he punished those whom
"the *malignant* World calls *Puritans*, men of more
"*Conscience* and better *Faith* then the *Papists* whom
"he tolerated.

The Princes of the world seldome take part with Christ.

Truth. Unto this I answer: First, that for mine owne part I would not use an *argument* from the number of *Princes*, witnessing in profession of practice against *Persecution* for cause of *Conscience*, [93] for the *truth* and *faith* of the Lord *Jesus* must not bee received with respect of *faces*, be they never so high, princely and glorious.

Precious *Pearles* and *Jewels*, and farre more precious *Truth* are found in muddy shells and places. The rich *Mines* of *golden Truth* lye hid under *barren* hills, and in *obscure* holes and *corners*.

Princes not persecuting are very rare.

The most *High* and *Glorious God* hath chosen the *poore* of the *World*: and the *Witnesses* of *Truth* (Rev. 11.) are cloathed in *sackcloth*, not in *Silke* or *Sattin*, *Cloth of Gold*, or *Tissue*: and therefore I acknowledge, if the number of *Princes* professing *persecution* bee considered, it is rare to finde a *King, Prince*, or *Governour* like *Christ Iesus* the *King* of *Kings*, and *Prince* of the *Princes* of the Earth, and who tread not in the steps of *Herod* the *Fox*, or *Nero* the *Lyon*, openly or secretly persecuting the name of the *Lord Iesus*; such were *Saul, Ieroboam, Ahab*, though under a maske or pretence of the name of the *God of Israel*.

To that purpose was it a noble speech of *Buchanan*, [*Buchanans Item to King Iames.*] who lying on his *death-bed* sent this *Item* to King *Iames*: Remember my humble service to his *Majestie*, and tell him that *Buchanan* is going to a place where few *Kings* come.

CHAP. LXII.

Truth. SEcondly, I observe how inconsiderately (I hope not willingly) he passeth by the *Reasons* and *Grounds* urged by those three *Princes* for their practices; for as for the bare examples of *Kings* or *Princes*, they are but like *shining Sands*, or *guilded Rockes*, giving no solace to such as make wofull *shipwrack* on them.

In *K. Iames* his Speech he passeth by that *Golden Maxime* in D*ivinity*, that *God* never loves to plant his *Church* by *Blood*. [*King Iames his sayings against persecution.*]

Secondly, that *Civill Obedience* may be performed from the *Papists*.

Thirdly, in his observation on *Revel.* 20. that true and certaine note of a *false Church*, to wit, *persecution*: The wicked are *besiegers*, the *faithfull* are *besieged*.

In *K. Steven* of *Poland* his Speech, hee passeth by the true difference betweene a *Civill* and a *Spirituall Government*: I am (said *Steven*) a *Civill Magistrate* over the *bodies* of men, not a *spirituall* over their *soules*. [*King Steven of Poland his speech against Persecution.*]

94. Now to confound these, is *Babel*; and Jewish it is to seek for *Moses*, and bring him from his grave (which no man shall finde, for *God* buried him) in setting up a *Nationall state* or *Church* in a land of

Canaan, which the great *Messiah* abolished at his comming.

<small>Forcing of Conscience is a Soule rape.</small>

Thirdly, he passeth by in the speech of the King of *Bohemia*, that *foundation* in *Grace* and *Nature*, to wit, that *Conscience* ought not to be violated or forced: and indeed it it is most true, that a *Soule* or *spirituall Rape* is more abominable in *Gods* eye, then to force and ravish the Bodies of all the Women in the World.

<small>Persecution for conscience, the Launcet that letteth blood Kings & Kingdomes.</small>

Secondly, that most lamentably true *experience* of all Ages, which that *King* observeth, viz. that *persecution* for cause of Conscience hath ever proved pernicious, being the causes of all those wonderfull *innovations* of, or changes in the *Principalities* and mightiest *Kingdomes* of *Christendome*. He that reads the *Records* of *Truth* and *Time* with an impartiall eye, shall finde this to be the *Launcet* that hath pierc'd the veines of *Kings* and *Kingdomes*, of *Saints* and *Sinners*, and fill'd the *streames* and *Rivers* with their *blood*.

<small>All spirituall Whores are bloody</small>

Lastly, that Kings observation of his own time, viz. that *Persecution* for cause of *Conscience*, was practised most in *England*, and such places where *Popery* raigned, implying (as I conceive) that such practises commonly proceed from that great *whore* the *Church of Rome*, whose *Daughters* are like their *Mother*, and all of a *bloody nature*, as most commonly all *Whores* be.

CHAP. LXIII.

NOw thirdly, in that the Answerer observeth, that amongst the *Romane Emperours*, they that did not persecute, were *Julian* the *Apostate*, and *Valens* the *Arrian*; whereas the good Emperours, *Constantine*, *Gratian*, *Valentinian*, and *Theodosius*, they did persecute the *Arrians*, *Donatists*, &c.

Answ. It is no new thing for *godly* and eminently godly men, to performe *ungodly actions*: nor for *ungodly* persons, for wicked ends to act what in it selfe is *good* and righteous. The Godly sometimes evill actors and the Ungodly good actors.

Abraham, Iacob, David, Salomon, &c. (as well as *Lamech, Saul,* &c.) lived in constant transgression against the *institution* of so holy and so ratified a *Law* of *Mariage,* &c. and this not against the *light* and checks of *conscience*, (as other sinnes are wont to be recorded [95] of them) but according to the dictate and perswasion of a *Resolved* Soule and *Conscience*. Poligamie or the many wives of the Fathers.

David out of *zeale* to *God,* with 30 thousand of *Israel,* and Majesticall *solemnity,* carries up the *Arke,* contrary to the *Order* God was pleased to appoint: the issue was both *Gods* and *Davids* great offence, 2 *Sam.* 6. Davids advancing of Gods Worship against Gods Order.

David in his zeale would build an *house* to entertaine his *God!* what more pious? and what more (in shew) seriously consulted, when the Prophet *Nathan* is admitted Councellour? 2 *Sam.* 7.

And probable it is, that his slaughter of *Uriiah* was not without a good *end*, to wit, to prevent the dishonour of *Gods* name, in the discoverie of his Adulterie with *Bathsheba*: yet *David* was holy and precious to *God* still, (though like a *jewell* fallen into the dirt) whereas K. *Ahab,* though acting his fasting & *humiliation*, was but *Ahab* still, though his Act (in it selfe) was a *duty*, and found successe with *God*.

CHAP. LXIV.

Peace. I Have often heard that *Historie* reports, and I have heard that Mr. *Cotton* himselfe hath affirmed it, that *Christianitie* fell asleep in *Constantines* bosome, and the laps and bosomes of those Emperours professing the name of *Christ*.

Truth. The unknowing zeale of *Constantine* and other Emperours, did more hurt to *Christ Iesus* his Crowne and Kingdome, then the raging fury of the most bloody *Neroes*. In the *persecutions* of the later, *Christians* were sweet and fragrant, like spice pounded and beaten in morters: But those *good* Emperours, persecuting some erroneous persons, *Arrius, &c.* and advancing the professours of some Truths of Christ (for there was no small number of *Truths* lost in those times) and maintaining their *Religion* by the materiall Sword, I say by this meanes *Christianity* was *ecclipsed*, and the Professors of it fell asleep, *C*ant. 5. *Babel* or *confusion* was usher'd in, and by degrees the *Gardens* of the *Churches* of *Saints* were turned into the *Wildernesse* of whole *Nations*, untill the *whole World* became *Christian* or *Christendome*, *Revel.* 12. & 13.

Doubtlesse those holy men, *Emperours* and *Bishops*, intended and aimed right, to exalt *Christ:* but not attending to the Command of *Christ Iesus*, to permit the *Tares* to grow in the *field* of the *World*, [96] they made the *Garden* of the *Church*, and *Field* of the *World* to be all one; and might not onely sometimes in their zealous mistakes persecute *good wheat* in stead of *Tares*, but also pluck up thousands of those pre-

Marginal notes: Constantine and the good Emperours are confest to have done more hurt to the name and crown of the Lord Jesus, then the persecuting Neroes &c. — The Garden of the Church and Field of the World made all one by Antichristianisme.

cious *stalkes* by *commotions* and *combustions* about *Religion*, as hath been since practised in the great and wonderfull changes wrought by such *Wars* in many great and mighty States and Kingdomes, as we heard even now in the Observation of the *King* of *Bohemia*.[1]

CHAP. LXV.

Peace. DEare *Truth*, before you leave this passage concerning the *Emperours*, I shall desire

---

[1] By a misarrangement a few chapters immediately preceding this passed through the press in the Editor's absence, and without his supervision. Some omitted notes may be inserted here.

The confusion in numbering Chaps. LI.–LIV. is in the original edition. On p. 165 there is reference to a work of Rev. John Goodwin. It was published in London in 1644, the same year with *The Bloudy Tenent*, and was entitled "M. S. to A. S. with a Plea for Libertie of Conscience in a Church Way, &c." He was "a Republican, an Independent and a thorough Arminian; he had been Vicar of Coleman-Street, whence he was ejected, in the year 1645, by the Committee for plundered Ministers, because he refused to baptize the children of his parishioners promiscuously and to administer the Sacrament to his whole parish." Neal's *Puritans*, ii: 45.

On page 173, the Author says "the Roman Emperour justly punished Ovid the Poet, for teaching the wanton Art of Love." When Ovid was fifty years old he was ordered into exile by an imperial edict in which his having published the *Art of Love* was the only reason given. This is regarded by scholars as a mere pretext, and many conjectures have been offered in regard to the real cause. By some writers it is ascribed to an intrigue with Julia, daughter of Augustus; by others to the discovery by Ovid of incestuous connection of Augustus with his daughter or grand-daughter; by some to his having seen Livia in the bath; by M. Villenave, in a theory which has been received with much favor, it has been supposed that Ovid was the victim of a *coup d' état;* and by a late English writer that he was the accidental witness of some crime of Julia, grand-daughter of Augustus. These solutions of the question are fully considered by Mr. Dyer in *The Classical Museum*, iv: xix.; also in Smith's *Dict. of Rom. Biog.* iii. art. *Ovidius*.

The anecdote of George Buchanan, the great Scotch Latinist, which is related on p. 181, is also found in Bayle's *Dictionary*, ii: 183, *note*. "I have heard a Scotch Lord say that when Buchanan was asked on his deathbed, whether he did not repent of what he had written against the authority of Kings, and in particular against the honor of Mary, Queen of Scots, he answered, I am going to a place where there are not many Kings."

you to glance your eye on this not unworthy obfervation, to wit, how fully this worthy *Anfwerer* hath learned to fpeake the roaring *language* of *Lyon-like Perfecution,* far from the *purity* and *peaceableneffe* of the *Lambe,* which he was wont to expreffe in *England.* For thus he writes:

"More and greater *Princes* then thefe you mention "(faith he) have not tolerated *Hereticks* and *Schif-* "*maticks,* notwithftanding their pretence of Con- "fcience, and their arrogating the Crown of Martyr- "dome to their fuffrings.

Truth. Thy tender *eare* and *heart* (fweet *Peace*) endures not fuch *language:* 'Tis true, that thefe termes, *Hereticks* (or wilfully obftinate) and *Schifmaticks* (or Renders) are ufed in Holy Writ: 'tis true alfo, that fuch pretend *confcience,* and challenge the *crowne* of *Martyrdome* to their *fuffrings:* Yet fince (as King *Iames* fpake in his [Marke of a falfe Church][1] on *Revel.* 20.) the Wicked perfecute and befiege, and the Godly are perfecuted and befieged; this is the common clamour of *Perfecuters* againft the *Meffengers* and *Witneffes* of *Iefus* in all Ages, *viz.* You are *Hereticks, Schifmaticks, factious, feditious, rebellious.* Have not all *Truths witneffes* heard fuch reproaches? You pretend *confcience;* You fay you are perfecuted for *Religion;* You will fay you are *Martyrs?*

Oh it is hard for *Gods children* to fall to *opinion* and *practice* of *Perfecution,* without the ready learning the *language* thereof: And doubtleffe, that Soule that can fo readily fpeake *Babels* language, hath caufe to

The language of Perfecuters, the wolves and hunters of the World.

---

[1] *The Workes of the Moft High and Mightie Prince James,* p. 79 ante p. 32.

fear that he hath not yet in point of Worſhip left the Gates or Suburbs of it.

Peace. Againe, in blaming *Iulian* and *Valens* the *Arrian,* for [97] "tolerating all weeds to grow, he "notes their ſinfull end, that thereby they might "choake the *vitals* of *Chriſtianity*; and ſeemes to "conſent (in this and other paſſages foregoing and "following on a ſpeech of *Jerome*) that the weeds of "*falſe Religions* tolerated in the world, have a power "to choake and kill true Chriſtianity in the Church.

Truth. I ſhall more fully anſwer to this on *Jeromes* ſpeech, and ſhew that if the weeds be kept out of the *Garden* of the *Church,* the Roſes and Lilies therein will flouriſh, notwithſtanding that weeds abound in the *Field* of the *Civill State.* When *Chriſtianity* began to be choaked, it was not when *Chriſtians* lodged in cold *Priſons,* but Downe beds of *eaſe,* and perſecuted others, &c.

Chriſts Lilies may flouriſh in his Church, notwithſtanding the abundance of weeds (in the world) permitted.

CHAP. LXVI.

Peace. HE ends this paſſage with approbation of Q. *Elizabeth* for perſecuting the *Papiſts,* and a *reproofe* to King *James* for his perſecuting the Puritans, &c.

Truth. I anſwer, if *Queene Elizabeth* according to the *Anſwerers Tenent* and Conſcience, did well to perſecute according to her conſcience, King *James* did not ill in perſecuting according to his: For Mr. *Cotton* muſt grant, that either King *James* was not fit to be a King, had not the eſſentiall *qualifications* of a *King,* in not being able rightly to judge who ought

The perſecution of Queen Elizabeth and King Iames compared together.

to be perfecuted, and who not, or elfe he muft confeffe that *King James* and all *Magiftrates* muft perfecute fuch whom in their *Confcience* they judge worthy to be perfecuted.

I fay it againe (though I neither approve Queen *Elizabeth* or K. *James* in fuch their perfecutions, yet) fuch as hold this Tenent of perfecuting for *Confcience*, muft alfo hold that *Civill Magiftrates* are not effentially fitted and qualified for their function and office, except they can difcerne clearly the difference betweene fuch as are to be punifhed and perfecuted, and fuch as are not.

Or elfe if they be effentially qualified, without fuch a religious fpirit of difcerning, and yet muft perfecute the *Hereticke*, the *Schifmaticke*, &c. muft they not perfecute according to their confcience and perfwafion. And then doubtleffe (though he bee excellent for *Civill Government*) may he eafily, as *Paul* did ignorantly, perfecute the *Son* of *God*, in ftead of the *Son* of *perdition*.

98] Therefore (laftly) according to *Chrift Jefus* his command, *Magiftrates* are bound not to perfecute, and to fee that none of their fubjects be perfecuted and oppreffed for their *confcience* and *worfhip*, being otherwife fubject and peaceable in Civill Obedience.

CHAP. LXVII.

IN the fecond place I anfwer and aske, what *glory* to *God*, what *good* to the *foules* or *bodies* of their *fubjects* fhall *Princes*, did thefe Princes bring in perfecuting? &c.

Peace. Mr. *Cotton* tells us in his discourse upon the third *Violl*, that *Queene Elizabeth* had almost *fired* the *world* in *civill combustions* by such her persecuting: "For, though hee bring it in to another end, yet he "confesseth that it raised all *Christendome* in *combus-* "*tion*, raised the Warres of 88. and the S*panish Inva-* "*sion:* and he addes (both concerning the *English* "Nation and the D*utch*) that if *God* had not born "witnesse to his people, and their *Laws*, in defeating "the *intendments* of their *enemies* against both the "*Nations*, it might have beene the *ruine* of them "both."[1]

In his opening of the 7 Viols, in print, Mr. Cotton confesseth that Queen Elizabeth her persecuting the Papists, had almost ruined the English Nation.

Truth. That those *Lawes* and *Practices* of Queene *Elizabeth* raised those *combustions* in *Christendome* I deny not: That they might likely have cost the *ruine* of *English* and *Dutch* I grant.

That it was *Gods* gracious worke in defeating the *Intendments* of their *enemies* I thankfully acknowledge. But that *God* bore witnesse to such *persecutions* and *lawes* for such *persecutions* I deny, for

The Wars betweene the Papists and the Protestants.

First, *event* and *successe* come alike to *all*, and are no *Arguments* of *love* or *hatred*, *&c.*

Secondly, the *Papists* in their warres have ever yet had both in *Peace* and *War victory* and *dominion*; and therefore (if *successe* be the measure) *God* hath borne witnesse unto them.

It is most true what *Daniel* in his 8. and 11. and 12. Chapters, and *Iohn* in his *Revel.* 11. 12. and 13. Chapters write of the great *successe* of *Antichrist* against *Christ Iesus* for a time appointed.

---

[1] *The Powring out of the Seven Vials; or an Exposition of the* 16. *Chapter of the Revelation, with an application of it to our Times.* The third Vial, p. 7. Lond. 1642.

Eventus omnis belli incertus. Succeſſe was various betweene *Charles* the fift and ſome *German Princes*: *Philip* of *Spaine* and the *Low Countries*: The *French King* and his Proteſtant Subjects, ſometimes loſing, ſometimes winning, interchangeably.

The wars and ſucceſſe of the Waldenſian witneſſes againſt three Popes and their popiſh Armies. But moſt memorable is the famous hiſtory of the *Waldenſes* and *Albingenſes*, thoſe famous *Witneſſes* of *Jeſus Chriſt*, who riſing from [99] *Waldo* at *Lyons* in *France* (1160.) ſpread over *France*, *Italy*, *Germany*, and almoſt all *Countries*, into thouſands and ten thouſands, making *ſeparation* from the *Pope* and *Church* of *Rome*. Theſe fought many *Battels* with various ſucceſſe, and had the aſſiſtance and protection of divers great *Princes* againſt three ſucceeding *Popes* and their *Armies*, but after mutuall *ſlaughters* and miſeries to both ſides, the finall *ſucceſſe* of *victory* fell to the *Popedome* and *Romiſh Church* in the utter extirpation of thoſe famous *Waldenſian witneſſes*.

Gods people victorious overcommers, and with what weapons. *Gods* ſervants are all *overcommers* when they war with *Gods* weapons in *Gods cauſe* and *Worſhip:* and *Revel.* 2. and 3. Chapters, ſeven times is it recorded, To him that *overcommeth* in *Epheſus*, To him that *overcommeth* in *Sardis*, &c. and *Revel.* 12. *Gods* ſervants overcame the *Dragon* or *Devill* in the *Romane Emperours* by three weapons, The *blood* of the *Lambe*, The *word* of their *Teſtimony*, and The not loving of their *lives* unto the *death*.

CHAP. LXVIII.

The third head of Argu- *Peace.* THe *Anſwerer* in the next place deſcends to the third and laſt *Head* of *Arguments* produced by the *Authour*, taken from the *judgement* of *ancient* and later *Writers*, yea even of the *Papists* themselves, who have condemned *persecution* for *conscience* sake: some of which the *Answerer* pleaseth to answer, and thus writeth.

ments from ancient and later writers.

"You begin with *Hilarie*, whose *testimony* without "*prejudice* to the *Truth* we may admit: For it is "true, the *Christian Church* doth not *persecute*, but "is *persecuted*.

The Christian Church doth not persecute, but is persecuted.

"But to *excommunicate* an *Hereticke* is not to *per-* "*secute*, that is, it is not to punish an *innocent*, but a "*culpable* and *damnable* person, and that not for *con-* "*science*, but for persisting in *errour* against light of "*conscience*, whereof he hath beene convinced.

Truth. In this *Answer* here are two things.

First, his *confession* of the same *Truth* affirmed by *Hilarius*, to wit, that the *Christian Church* doth not *persecute*, but is *persecuted:* suting with that foregoing *observation* of King *Iames* from *Rev.* 20.

Peace. Yet to this he addes a *colour* thus: which, saith he, wee may admit without prejudice to the *truth*.

Truth. I answer, If it bee a *marke* of the *Christian Church* to bee *persecuted*, and of the *Antichristian* or false *Church* to persecute, then those *Churches* cannot be truly *Christian* (according to the first [100] *institution*) which either *actually* themselves, or by the *Civill* power of *Kings* and Princes given to them (or procured by them to fight for them) doe *persecute* such as dissent from them or be opposite against them.

Persecuting Churches cannot be Chrifts Churches.

Peace. Yea, but in the second place he addeth,

that to *excommunicate* an *Heretick,* is not to *persecute,* but to punish him for sinning against the light of his own *conscience,* &c.

Truth. I answer, if this worthy *Answerer* were throughly awaked from the *Spouses* spirituall *slumber,* (*Cant.* 5.) and had recovered from the *drunkennesse* of the *great whore,* who intoxicateth the *Nations,* Revel. 17. It is impossible that he should so answer: for

The nature of excommunication. First, who questioneth, whether to *excommunicate* an *Heretick,* (that is, an *obstinate Gainsayer*) as we have opened the word upon *Tit.* 3.) I say, who questioneth whether that be to *persecute?* *Excommunication* being of a *spirituall nature,* a *Sentence* denounced by the *Word* of *Christ Jesus* the Spirituall *King* of his *Church*; and a Spirituall *killing* by the most sharpe two-edged Sword of the Spirit, in delivering up the person excommunicate to *Sathan.* Therefore who sees not that his *Answer* comes not neere our *Question?*

Peace. In the *Answerers* second *conclusion* (in the entrance of this Discourse) he proves *persecution* against an *Heretick* for sinning against his *conscience,* and quotes *Tit.* 3. 10. which only proves (as I have there made it evident) a Spirituall *rejecting* or *excommunicating* from the *Church* of God, and so comes not neer the question.

Here again he would prove *Churches* charged to be false, because they persecute: I say he would prove them not to be false, because they persecute not: for, saith he, *Excommunication* is not *Persecution.* Whereas the *Question* is (as the whole *discourse,* and *Hilaries* own amplification of the matter in this speech, and the *practice* of all Ages testifies) whether it be not a false *Church* that doth persecute other *Churches* or *Members* (opposing her in Spirituall and Church matters, not by Excommunications, but by *imprisonments, stocking, whipping, fining, banishing, hanging, burning, &c.* notwithstanding that such persons in *Civill obedience* and subjection are unreproveable.

What persecution or hunting is.

Truth. I conclude this passage with *Hilarius* and the *Answerer,* That the *Christian Church* doth not *persecute*; no more then a *Lilie* doth scratch the *Thornes,* or a *Lambe* pursue and teare the *Wolves,* or a *Turtle dove* hunt the *Hawkes* and *Eagles,* or a *chaste and modest* [101] *Virgin* fight and scratch like *whores* and *harlots*.

Chrifts Spouse no scratcher or fighter.

And for punishing the *Heretick* for sinning against his *conscience* after *conviction,* which in the second *conclusion* he affirmeth to be by a *civill sword* I have at large there answered.

CHAP. LXIX.

Peace. IN the next place he selecteth one passage out of *Hilarie,* (although there are many golden passages there exprest against the use of *Civill* Earthly Powers in the Affaires of *Christ.*) The passage is this:

"It is true also what he saith, that neither the
" *Apostles* nor We may propogate *Christian Religion*
" by the *Sword:* but if *Pagans* cannot be won by the
" *Word,* they are not to be compelled by the *Sword:*
" Neverthelesse this hindreth not (saith he) but if

Who cannot be won by the Word, must not be compelled

by the Sword.

"they or any other fhould *blafpheme* the true *God* "and his true *Religion*, they ought to be feverely pun- "ifhed: and no leffe doe they deferve, if they *feduce* "from the *Truth* to damnable *Herefie* or *Idolatrie*.

Truth. In which Anfwer I obferve, firft his Agreement with *Hilarie*, that the *Chriftian Religion* may not be propagated by the *Civill Sword*.

Unto which I reply, and aske then what meanes this paffage in his firft anfwer to the former fpeeches of the *Kings*, viz. "We acknowledge that none is to "be *conftrained* to beleeve or profeffe the *true Religion*, "till he be convinced in judgement of the Truth of "it: implying 2 things.

Firft, that the *Civill Magiftrate*, who is to conftraine with the *Civill Sword*, muft judge all the *Confciences* of their Subjects, whether they be convinced or no.

Secondly, when the *Civill Magiftrate* difcerns that his Subjects *confciences* are convinced, then he may conftraine them *vi & armis*, hoftily.

Conftraint upon Confciences in Old and New England.

And accordingly, the *Civill State* and *Magiftracie* judging in *fpirituall things*, who knowes not what *conftraint* lies upon all *confciences* in *Old* and *New England*, to come to *Church*, and pay *Church duties*,[1]

[1] "By 1 Eliz. c. 2 (g), it was provided, that every inhabitant of the realm or dominion fhall diligently and faithfully, having no lawful or reafonable excufe to be abfent, endeavour themfelves to refort to their parifh church or chapel accuftomed, or, upon feafonable let, to fome ufual place where common prayer fhall be ufed, on Sundays or holidays, upon penalty of forfeiting for every non-attendance twelve pence, to be levied by the Church Wardens to the ufe of the poor." This and other penal laws in regard to religious opinions was abolifhed by the ftatute 9 and 10 Vict. c. 59. Stephen, *Commentaries on the Laws of England*, iii: 51.

"Whereas complainte hath bene made to this Court that dyvers perfons within this jurifdiction doe vfually abfent themfelves from church meetings vpon the Lords day, power is therefore giuen which is upon the point (though with a *sword* of a finer gilt and trim in *New England*) nothing else but that which he confesseth *Hilarie* saith true, should not be done, to wit, a *propagation* of *Religion* by the *Sword*. 102] Againe, although he confesseth that *propagation* of *Religion* ought not to be by the *sword*: yet he maintaineth the use of the *sword*, when persons (in the *judgement* of the *Civill State*, for that is implied)

to any two Assistants to heare and sensure, either by styne or imprisonm^t, (att their discrecōn) all misdemean^{rs} of that kinde committed by any inhabitant within this jurisdiction." *Mass. Colonial Records*, i: 140. March, 1634-5. cf. *Records* i: 240, Sept. 1638.

To the assertion in the text Cotton replies: "I know no constraint at all, that lieth upon the consciences of any in *New-England*, to come to Church: Least of all do I know, that any are constrayned to pay Church-duties in *New Englâd*. Sure I am, none in our Town, neither Church-members, nor other, are constrained to pay any Church duties at all. What they pay they give voluntarily, each one with his owne hand, without any constraint at all." *Bloudy Tenent Washed*, p. 146. Cotton's assertion in regard to Boston is sustained by Winthrop, *New England*, i: 355. "Mr. Cotton preaching out of the 8 of Kings, 8, taught, that their Magistrates are forced to provide for the maintenance of ministers, etc. when the Churches are in a declining condition. There he showed, that the ministers' maintenance should be by voluntary contribution, etc."

But Williams rejoins, "If Mr. *Cotton* be *forgettful*, sure he can hardly be *ignorant* of the *Lawes* and *Penalties* extant in *New England* that are (or if *repealed* have been) against such as absent themselves from *Church Morning* and *Evening*, and for *Non-payment* of Church-duties, although no Members.

"For a *Freedome* of *Not paying* in his *Towne*, it is to their *commendation* and *Gods praise*, who hath shewed him and others more of his holy *Truth*: Yet who can be ignorant of the Sessments upon all in other Townes, of the many *Suits* and *Sentences* in *Courts* (for Non-payment of *Church-Duties*) even against such as are no Church Members?" *The Bloody Tenent yet more Bloody*, p. 216.

Lechford's testimony also goes somewhat against Cotton's general denial: "At some places they make a rate upon every man, as well within, as not of the Church, residing with them, towards the Churches occasions; and others are beholding, now and then, to the generall Court, to study wayes to enforce the maintenance of the Ministerie." *Plain Dealing*, p. 19. To this may be added two sentences from Winthrop's journal in 1642: "The churches held a different course in raising the Minister's maintenance. Some did it by way of taxation, which was very offensive to some." *New England*, ii: 112.

blaspheme the true *God,* and the true *Religion,* and also seduce others to damnable *Heresie* and *Idolatrie.* Which because he barely affirmeth in this place, I shall defer my Answer unto the after *Reasons* of Mr. *Cotton* and the Elders of New English Churches; where Scriptures are alleadged, and in that place (by *Gods* assistance) they shall be examined and answered.

CHAP. LXX.

Tertullian his speech discussed.

Peace. THe *Answerer* thus proceeds: "Your next "*Writer* is *Tertullian,* who speaketh to "the same purpose in the place alleadged by you. "His intent is only to restraine *Scapula* the Roman "Governour of *Africa,* from persecuting the *Chris-* "*tians,* for not offering *sacrifice* to their *Gods:* and "for that end, fetcheth an *Argument* from the Law "of *Naturall equity,* not to compell any to any *Religion,* "but *permit* them to believe or not to believe at all.

"Which we acknowledge; and accordingly we "judge, the English may *permit* the *Indians* to con-"tinue in their *unbeliefe:* neverthelesse it will not "therefore be lawfull to *tolerate* the *worship* of *Devils* "or *Idols,* to the seduction of any from the *Truth.*

Truth. Answ. In this passage he agrees with *Tertullian,* and gives instance in *America* of the English permitting the Indians to continue in their *unbeleefe:*

The Indians of New England permitted by the English not

yet withall he affirmeth it not lawfull to tolerate *worshipping* of *Devils,* or *seduction* from the *Truth.*

I answer, that in *New England* it is well known that they not onely *permit* the *Indians* to continue in their unbeliefe, (which neither they, nor all the

Ministers of *Christ* on *Earth*, nor *Angels* in *Heaven* can helpe, not being able to worke beleefe) but they also permit or tolerate them in their *Paganish worship*, which cannot be denied to be a *worshipping* of *Devils*, as all false Worship is.[1] only to continue in their unbeleef (which they cannot cure)

And therefore consequently according to the same practice, did they walke by *Rule* and *impartially*, not onely the *Indians*, but their C*ountrymen*, *French*, *Dutch*, *Spanish*, *Persians*, *Turkes*, *Iewes*, &c. should also be permitted in their *Worships*, if correspondent in *civill obedience*. but also in their false worship which they might by the civil sword restraine.

103] *Peace.* He addes further, when *Tertullian* saith, That another mans *Religion* neither hurteth nor profiteth any; It must be understood of *private worship* and *Religion* professed in private: otherwise a false Religion professed by the members of the *Church*, or by such as have given their *names* to *Christ*, will be the *ruine* and *desolation* of the *Church*, as appeareth by the threats of *Christ* to the Churches, *Revel.* 2.

Truth. I answer (passing by that unsound *distinction* of *members* of the *Church*, or those that have given their *Names* to *Christ*, which in point of visible *profession* and *Worship* will appear to be all one) it is plaine,

First, that *Tertullian* doth not there speake of private, but of publike Worship and Religion.

Secondly, Although it be true in a *Church* of *Christ*, that a false *Religion* or *Worship* permitted, will hurt,

---

[1] This Cotton denies, (*Bloudy Tenent Washed*, p. 147,) and Williams reaffirms. "It is most true, that the Monahiggan-éucks, Mishawoméucks, Pautuckséucks and Cawsumséucks (who professe to sub- mit to the *English*) continue in their publike Paganish Worship of Devills, I say *openly* and *constantly*." *Bloody Tenent yet more Bloody*, p. 218.

according to thofe threats of *Chrift*, Revel. 2. Yet in 2 cafes I believe a falfe *Religion* will not hurt (which is moft like to have been *Tertullians* meaning.)

<small>In 2 cafes a falfe Religion will not hurt the true Church, or the State.</small>

Firft, a falfe *Religion* out of the *Church* will not hurt the *Church*, no more then *weedes* in the *Wildernefſe* hurt the inclofed *Garden*, or *poyſon* hurt the *body* when it is not touched or taken, yea and *antidotes* are received againſt it.

Secondly, a falfe *Religion* and *Worſhip* will not hurt the *Civill State*, in cafe the *worſhippers* breake no *civill Law:* and the *Anſwerer* (elſwhere) acknowledgeth, that the *civill Lawes* not being broken, *civill Peace* is not broken: and this only is the Point in Queſtion.

CHAP. LXXI.

Peace. YOur next Authour (faith he) *Jerome*, croffeth not the "Truth, nor advantagerh your "Cauſe; for we grant what he faith, that Herefie "muſt be cut off with the fword of the Spirit: but "this hinders not, 'but being fo cut down, if the "Heretick will perfiſt in his Herefie, to the feduc-"tion of others, he may be cut off alfo by the Civill

<small>The feducing or infecting of others difcuffed.</small>

"Sword, to prevent the perdition of others. And "that to be *Jeromes* meaning, appeareth by his note "upon that of the Apoſtle, [A little Leaven leaveneth "the whole lumpe] Therefore (faith he) a fparke as "foon as it appeareth, is to be extinguiſhed, and "the leaven to be removed from the reſt of the 104] "dough; Rotten pieces of fleſh are to be cut

"off, and a scabbed beast is to be driven from the
"sheepfold; lest the whole House, Body, masse of
"Dough, and Flock, be set on fire with the sparke,
"be putrified with the rotten flesh, sowred with the
"leaven, perish by the scabbed beast.

Truth. I answer, first, he granteth to *Tertullian*,[1] that *Heresie* must be cut off with the *sword* of the *Spirit:* yet withall he maintaineth a cutting off by a second Sword, the *sword* of the *Magistrate*; and conceiveth that *Tertullian*[1] so meanes, because he quoteth that of the Apostle, *A little leaven leaveneth the whole lumpe.*

The Answerer trusteth not to the sword of the Spirit only in Spirituall causes.

Answ. It is no Argument to prove that *Tertullian*[1] meant a *civill sword,* by alleadging 1 Cor. 5. or Gal. 5. which properly and only approve a cutting off by the *sword* of the *Spirit* in the *Church,* and the purging out of the *leaven* in the *Church* in the Cities of Corinth and Galatia.

And if *Tertullian*[1] should so meane as himselfe doth, yet

First, that grant of his, that *Heresie* must be cut off with the sword of the *Spirit*, implies an absolute sufficiencie in the *sword* of the *Spirit* to cut it down, according to that mighty operation of Spirituall weapons, (2 Cor. 10. 4.) powerfully sufficient either to convert the Heretick to God, and subdue his very thoughts into subjection to *Christ,* or else spiritually to slay and execute him.

The absolute sufficiencie of the sword of the Spirit.

Secondly, it is cleare to be the meaning of the *Apostle,* and of the Spirit of *God,* not there to speake to the *Church* in *Corinth* or *Galatia,* or any other

---

[1] Thus in the original text, but an evident misprint for *Jerome*.

Church, concerning any other *dough*, or *houſe*, or *body*, or *flock*, but the *dough*, the *body*, the *houſe*, the *flock* of *Chriſt* his *Church:* Out of which ſuch *ſparks*, ſuch *leaven*, ſuch *rotten fleſh* and *ſcabbed ſheep* are to be avoided.

<small>The Church of Chriſt to be kept pure.</small>

Nor could the eye of this worthy *Anſwerer* ever be ſo obſcured, as to run to a *Smiths* ſhop for a Sword of *iron* and *ſteale* to helpe the Sword of the *Spirit*, if the *Sun of Righteouſneſſe* had once been pleaſed to ſhew him, that a *Nationall Church* (which elſewhere he profeſſeth againſt) a *ſtate* Church (whether *explicite*, as in *Old England*, or *implicite*, as in *New*) is not the *Inſtitution* of the Lord *Jeſus Chriſt*.

<small>A Nationall Church not inſtituted by Chriſt Jeſus.</small>

The *Nationall typicall State-Church* of the *Jewes* neceſſarily called for ſuch weapons: but the *particular Churches* of *Chriſt* in all parts of the World, conſiſting of *Jewes* or *Gentiles*, is powerfully able by the *ſword* of the Spirit to *defend* it ſelfe, and *offend* Men or Devils, although the *State* or *Kingdome* (wherein ſuch a *Church* or *Churches* [105] of *Chriſt* are gathered) have neither carnall *ſpeare* nor *ſword*, &c. as once it was in the *Nationall Church* of the *Land* of *Canaan*.

<small>The nationall Church of the Jewes.</small>

<small>1 Sam. 13.</small>

CHAP. LXXII.

Peace. **B**Rentius (whom you next quote, ſaith he) ſpeaketh not to your cauſe. Wee willingly grant you, that man hath no *power* to make *Lawes* to binde *conſcience*, but this hinders not, but men may ſee the *Lawes* of God obſerved which doe binde *conſcience*.

<small>Man hath no power to make lawes to binde conſcience.</small>

Truth. I anfwer, In granting with *Brentius* that man hath not power to make *Lawes* to binde *confcience*, hee overthrowes fuch his *tenent* and *practice* as *reftraine* men from their *Worfhip*, according to their Confcience and beleefe, and conftraine them to fuch *worfhips* (though it bee out of a pretence that they are convinced) which their owne *foules* tell them they have no *fatisfaction* nor *faith* in.

Secondly, whereas he affirmeth that men may make *Lawes* to fee the *Lawes* of *God* obferved.

I anfwer, as *God* needeth not the helpe of a materiall *fword* of *fteele* to affift the *fword* of the *Spirit* in the affaires of *confcience*, fo thofe men, thofe *Magiftrates*, yea that *Commonwealth* which makes fuch *Magiftrates*, muft needs have power and authority from *Chrift Jefus* to fit *Judge* and to determine in all the great controverfies concerning *doctrine, difcipline, government, &c.*

And then I aske, whether upon this ground it muft not evidently follow, that Defperate confequences unavoidable.

Either there is no lawfull *Commonwealth* nor *civill State* of men in the world, which is not qualified with this fpirituall *difcerning:* (and then alfo that the very *Commonweale* hath more *light* concerning the *Church* of *Chrift*, then the *Church* it felfe.)

Or, that the *Commonweale* and *Magiftrates* thereof muft judge and punifh as they are perfwaded in their owne *beleefe* and *confcience*, (be their *confcience Paganifh, Turkifh*, or *Antichriftian*) what is this but to confound *Heaven* and *Earth* together, and not onely to take away the *being* of *Chriftianity* out of the World, but to take away all *civility*, and the *world* out of the *world*, and to lay all upon heapes of *confufion?*

106]   CHAP. LXXIII.

Luthers testimony in this cafe difcuffed.

Peace. THe like anfwer (faith he) may bee returned to *Luther*, whom you next alledge.

Firſt, that the *government* of the *civill Magiſtrate* extendeth no further then over the *bodies* and *goods* of their *ſubjects*, not over their *ſoules*, and therefore they may not undertake to give *Lawes* unto the *ſoules* and *conſciences* of men.

Secondly, that the *Church* of *Chriſt* doth not uſe the Arme of *ſecular* power to compell men to the true profeſſion of the *truth*, for this is to be done with *ſpirituall weapons*, whereby *Chriſtians* are to be exhorted, not compelled. " But this (faith hee) hin-
" dreth not that *Chriſtians* ſinning againſt *light* of
" *faith* and *conſcience*, may juſtly be cenſured by the
" *Church* with *excommunication*, and by the *civill ſword*
" alſo, in caſe they ſhall corrupt others to the perdi-
" tion of their ſoules.

Truth. I anſwer, in this joynt *confeſſion* of the *Anſwerer* with *Luther*, to wit, that the *government* of the *civill Magiſtrate* extendeth no further then over the *bodies* and *goods* of their *ſubjects*, not over their *ſoules* : who ſees not what a cleare *teſtimony* from his own mouth and pen is given, to wit, that either the *Spirituall* and *Church* eſtate, the preaching of the *Word*, and the gathering of the *Church*, the *Baptiſme* of it, the *Miniſtry, Government* and *Adminiſtrations* thereof belong to the *civill body* of the *Commonweale?* that is, to the *bodies* and *goods* of men, which ſeemes monſtrous to imagine : Or elſe that the *civill Magiſtrate* cannot (without exceeding the bounds of his office) meddle with thoſe ſpirituall affaires.

Againe, neceſſarily muſt it follow, that theſe two are contradictory to themſelves: to wit,

The *Magiſtrates* power extends no further then the *bodies* and *goods* of the ſubject, and yet

The *Magiſtrate* muſt puniſh *Chriſtians* for ſinning againſt the *light* of *faith* and *conſcience*, and for *corrupting* the *ſoules* of men.

<small>Mr. Cottons poſitions evidently proved contradictory to themſelves.</small>

The Father of *Lights* make this worthy *Anſwerer* and all that feare him to ſee their wandring in this caſe, not only from his *feare*, but alſo from the light of *Reaſon* it ſelfe, their owne *convictions* and *confeſſions*.

Secondly, in his joint confeſſion with *Luther*, that the *Church* [107] doth not uſe the ſecular power to compell men to the Faith and Profeſſion of the *truth*, he condemneth (as before I have obſerved)

Firſt, his former *Implication, viz.* that they may bee compelled when they are convinced of the *truth* of it.

Secondly, their owne practice, who ſuffer no man of any different *conſcience* and *worſhip* to live in their juriſdiction, except that he depart from his owne *exerciſe* of *Religion* and *Worſhip* differing from the *worſhip* allowed of in the *civill State*, yea and alſo actually ſubmit to come to their *Church*.

Which howſoever it is coloured over with this varniſh, *viz.* that men are *compelled* no further then unto the hearing of the *Word*, unto which all men are bound: yet it will appeare that *teaching* and being taught in a *Church* eſtate is a *Church* worſhip, as true and proper a *Church worſhip* as the Supper of the Lord, *Act.* 2. 46.

<small>Hearing of the Word of God in a Church eſtate a part of Gods worſhip.</small>

Secondly, all persons (*Papist* and *Protestant*) that are conscientious, have alwayes suffered upon this ground especially, that they have refused to come to each *others* Church or Meeting.

CHAP. LXXIV.

<small>Papists plea for toleration of conscience.</small>

Peace. THe next passage in the *Author* which the *Answerer* descends unto, is the *testimony* of the *Papists* themselves, a lively and shining testimony from Scriptures alledged both against themselves and all that associate with them (as *power* is in their hand) in such *unchristian* and bloody both *tenents* and *practices*.

" As for the *testimony* of the *Popish* booke (saith he)
" we weigh it not, as knowing what ever they speake
" for *toleration* of *Religion*, where themselves are under
" *Hatches*, when they come to sit at *Stern* they judge
" and *practise* quite contrary, as both their *writings*
" and *judiciall proceedings* have testified to the *world*
" these many yeares.

Truth. I answer, although both *writings* and *practices* have been such, yet the *Scriptures* and *expressions* of *truth* alledged and uttered by them, speake loud and fully for them when they are under the *Hatches*, that for their *conscience* and *religion* they should not there be choaked and smothered, but suffered to breathe and walke upon the *Deckes* in the ayre of *civill liberty* and *conversation* in the Ship of the *commonwealth*, upon good assurance given of *civill obedience* to the *civill State*.

108] Againe, if this practice bee so abominable in his eyes from the *Papists*, *viz.* that they are so partiall as to persecute when they sit at *Helme*, and yet cry out against *persecution* when they are under the *Hatches*, I shall beseech the Righteous Judge of the whole *world* to present as in a Water or Glasse (where face answereth to face) the faces of the *Papist* to the *Protestant*, answering to each other in the *samenesse* of *partiality*, both of this doctrine and practice.

The Protestants partiall in the case of persecution.

When Mr. *Cotton* and others have formerly been under *hatches*, what sad and true complaints have they abundantly powred forth against *persecution?* How have they opened that heavenly Scripture, *Cant.* 4. 8. Where *Christ Jesus* calls his tender *Wife* and Spouse from the fellowship with *persecutors* in their *dens* of *Lions*, and mountaines of *Leopards?*

But comming to the Helme (as he speaks of the *Papists*) how, both by *preaching*, *writing*, *Printing*, *practice*, doe they themselves (I hope in their persons *Lambes*) unnaturally and partially expresse toward others, the cruell nature of such *Lions* and *Leopards?*

O that the *God* of Heaven might please to tell them how abominable in his eyes are a *waight* and a *waight*, a *stone* and a *stone* in the bag of *waights!* one waight for themselves when they are under Hatches, and another for others when they come to *Helme*.

A false ballance in Gods matters abominable to God.

Nor shall their confidence of their being in the *truth* (which they judge the *Papists* and *others* are not in) no nor the *Truth* it selfe priviledge them to *persecute* others, and to exempt themselves from *persecution*, because (as formerly.)

Sheep cannot hunt, no not the wolves.

First, it is against the nature of true *Sheep* to persecute or hunt the *Beasts* of the *Forrest*, no not the same *Wolves* who formerly have persecuted themselves.

Secondly, if it be a duty and charge upon all *Magistrates* in all parts of the *World* to judge and persecute in and for spirituall causes, then either they are no *Magistrates* who are not able to judge in such cases, or else they must judge according to their *Consciences*, whether *Pagan*, *Turkish* or *Antichristian*.

Pills to purge out the spirit of persecution.

Lastly, notwithstanding their confidence of the *truth* of their owne way, yet the experience of our *Fathers errours*, our owne *mistakes* and *ignorance*, the sense of our own *weaknesses* and *blindnesse* in the depths of the *prophesies* & *mysteries* of the Kingdom of *Christ*, and the great professed *expectation* of *light* to come which we are not now able to comprehend, may abate the *edge*, yea sheath up the [109] *sword* of persecution toward any, especially such as differ not from them in *doctrines* of *repentance*, or *faith*, or *holinesse* of *heart* and *life*, and hope of glorious and *eternall union* to come, but only in the way and manner of the *administrations* of *Jesus Christ*.

CHAP. LXXV.

Peace. TO close this head of the testimony of *Writers*, it pleaseth the *Answerer* to produce a contrary testimony of *Austin*, *Optatus*, &c.

Superstition & persecution have had

Truth. I readily acknowledge (as formerly I did concerning the testimony of *Princes*) that *Antichrist* is too hard for *Christ* at *votes* and *numbers*; yea and beleeve that in many points (wherein the servants of God these many hundred yeares have beene fast asleep) *superstition* and *persecution* have had more suffrages and votes from *Gods* owne people then hath either been honourable to the *Lord,* or *peaceable* to their owne or the soules of others: Therefore (not to derogate from the pretious *memory* of any of them) let us briefly consider what they have in this point affirmed. ^{many votes from Gods owne people.}

To begin with *Austin:* " They murther (saith he) " soules, and themselves are afflicted in body, and " they put men to everlasting death, and yet they " complaine when themselves are put to temporall " death.

I answer, This *Rhetoricall perswasion of humane wisdome* seems very reasonable in the eye of *flesh* and *blood,* but one *Scripture* more prevailes with faithfull and obedient soules then thousands of plausible and eloquent speeches: in particular, ^{Austins saying for persecution examined.}

First, the *Scripture* useth *soule-killing* in a large sense, not only for the *teaching* of *false prophets* and *seducers,* but even for the *offensive walking of Christians,* in which respect (1 Cor. 8.) a true *Christian* may be guilty of destroying a soule for whom *Christ* died, and therefore by this rule ought to be hanged, burned, &c. ^{Soul-killing.}

Secondly, That plausible similitude will not prove that every false *teaching* or false practice actually kills the *soule,* as the *body* is slaine, and slaine but once, for *soules* infected or bewitched may againe *recover,* 1 Cor. 5. Gal. 5. 2 Tim. 2. &c.

Thirdly, for *soule-killings,* yea also for *soule-woundings* and grievings, *Christ Jesus* hath appointed *reme-*

dies fufficient in his *Church*. There comes forth a *two edged fword* out of his *mouth* (Rev. 1. and [110] Rev. 2.) able to cut downe *Herefie* (as is confeft) yea and to kill the *Hereticke*, yea and to punifh his *foule* everlaftingly, which no *fword* of *fteele* can reach unto in any punifhment comparable or imaginable; and therefore in this cafe we may fay of this *fpirituall foule-killing* by the *fword* of *Chrifts* mouth, as *Paul* concerning the inceftuous perfon, 2 Cor. 2. *Sufficient* is this *punifhment*, &c.

<small>Punifhments provided by Chrift Jefus againft Soule-killers and Soule-wounders.</small>

Fourthly, Although no *Soule-killers*, nor *Soule-grievers* may be fuffred in the *Spirituall* State or Kingdome of *Chrift*, the *Church*; yet he hath commanded that fuch fhould be fuffered and permitted to be and live in the *World*, as I have proved on *Matth*. 13. otherwife thoufands and millions of *foules* and bodies both, muft be murthered and cut off by *civill combuftions* and bloody warres about *Religion*.

Fifthly, I argue thus: The Soules of all men in the World are either naturally *dead in Sin*, or alive in *Chrift*. If dead in finne, no man can kill them, no more then he can kill a *dead man*: Nor is it a falfe Teacher or falfe Religion that can fo much *prevent* the means of *Spirituall life*, as one of thefe two; Either the *force* of a *materiall fword*, imprifoning the Soules of men in a *State* or *Nationall Religion*, *Miniftery* or *Worfhip*; Or fecondly, *Civill warres* and *combuftions* for *Religion* fake, whereby men are immediately cut off without any longer *meanes* of *Repentance*.

<small>Men dead in Sin, cannot be Soule kill'd. A Nationall enforced Religion or a Civill War for Religion the two great preventers of foule converfion and life.</small>

Now againe, for the Soules that are alive in *Chrift*, he hath gracioufly appointed *Ordinances* powerfully *sufficient* to maintaine and cherish that *life, Armour of proofe* able to defend them against *men* and *devils.*

Secondly, the Soule once alive in Christ, is like Christ himselfe, (*Revel.* 1.) alive for ever, (*Rom.* 6.) and cannot die a *spirituall death.*

Lastly, Grant a man to be a *false Teacher,* an *Heretick,* a *Balaam,* a *Spirituall Witch,* a *Wolfe,* a *Persecuter,* breathing out *blasphemies* against *Christ,* and *slaughters* against his *followers,* as *Paul* did, *Act.* 9. I say, these who appear *Soule-killers* to day, by the grace of *Christ* may prove (as *Paul*) *Soule-savers* to morrow: and saith *Paul* to *Timothy* (1 *Tim.* 4.) thou shalt save thy selfe and them that heare thee: which all must necessarily be prevented, if all that comes within the sense of these *Soule-killers,* must (as guilty of blood) be corporally kill'd and put to *death.* [Soule killers prove (by the grace of Christ) soule savers.]

[111]   CHAP. LXVI. [LXXVI.]

Peace. DEare *Truth,* your *Answers* are so satisfactorie to *Austins* speech, that if *Austin* himselfe were now living, me thinkes he should be of your mind. I pray descend to *Optatus,* who "(saith " the Answerer) justifies *Macharius* for putting some " *Hereticks* to death, affirming that he had done no " more herein then what *Moses, Phineas* and *Elias* " had done before him. [Optatus examined.]

Truth. These are *shafts* usually drawne from the *Quiver* of the *Ceremoniall* and *typicall* state of the *Nationall Church* of the *Jewes,* whose *shadowish* and *figurative* state vanished at the appearing of the Body and *substance,* the *Sun* of *Righteousnesse,* who set up [Persecuters leave Christ, & flie to Moses for their practice.]

another *Kingdome* or *Church* (Heb. 12.) *Miniſtrie* and *Worſhip*: in which we finde no ſuch *Ordinance*, *precept* or *preſident* of killing men by Materiall Swords for *Religions* ſake.

More particularly concerning *Moſes*, I quærie what *commandement* or *practice* of *Moſes* either *Optatus* or the *Anſwerer* here intend? Probably that paſſage of *Deut.* 13. wherein *Moſes* appointed a ſlaughter either of a *perſon* or a *city* that ſhould depart from the *God* of *Iſrael*, with whom that *Nationall Church* was in Covenant. And if ſo, I ſhall particularly reply to that place in my Anſwer to the Reaſons hereunder mentioned.

Concerning *Phineas* his zealous Act:

<small>Phineas his act diſcuſſed.</small> Firſt, his ſlaying of the *Iſraelitiſh* man, and woman of *Midian*, was not for *ſpirituall*, but *corporall* filthines.

Secondly, no man will produce his *fact* as preſidentiall to any *Miniſter* of the *Goſpel* ſo to act in any *Civill ſtate* or *Commonweale*; although I believe in the *Church of God* it is *preſidentiall* for either *Miniſter* or *people* to kill and ſlay with the *two-edged ſword* of the *Spirit* of *God* any ſuch bold and open preſumptuous ſinners as theſe were.

Laſtly, concerning *Eliah*: There were two famous *acts* of *Eliah* of a killing nature:

Firſt, that of ſlaying 850 [450] of *Baals* Prophets, 1 *Kings* 18.

Secondly of the two *Captaines* and their Fifties, by fire, &c.

<small>Eliahs ſlaughters examined.</small> For the firſt of theſe, it cannot figure or type out any *materiall ſlaughter* of the many thouſands of *falſe Prophets* in the World by any *materiall ſword* of Iron

or Steele: for as that passage was [112] *miraculous,* so finde we not any such *commission* given by the *Lord Jesus* to the Ministers of the *Gospel.* And lastly, such a slaughter must not only extend to all the false *prophets* in the World, but (according to the *Answerers* grounds) to the many thousands of thousands of *Idolaters* and false *worshippers* in the *Kingdomes* and *Nations* of the *World.*

For the second Act of *Eliah,* as it was also of a *miraculous* nature: So secondly, when the *followers* of the *Lord Jesus* (Luc. 9.) proposed such a practice to the *Lord Jesus,* for injury offered to his owne person, he disclaimed it with a *milde checke* to their *angry spirits,* telling them plainly they knew not what *spirits* they were of; and addeth that gentle and mercifull *conclusion,* That he came not to destroy the *bodies* of men, as contrarily *Antichrist* doth, alledging these instances from the *Old Testament,* as also *Peters* killing *Ananias,* Acts 5. and *Peters* vision and voice, Arise *Peter,* kill and eat, Acts. 10.

Eliahs consuming the 2 Captaines and their companies by fire, discussed.

CHAP. LXXVII.

Peace. YOu have so satisfied these instances brought by *Optatus,* that me thinks *Optatus* and the Answerer himself might rest satisfied.

I will not trouble you with *Bernards* argument from Rom. 13. which you have already on that Scripture so largely answered.

But what thinke you (lastly) of *Calvin, Beza,* and *Aretius?*

Truth. Ans. Since matters of fact and opinion are barely related by the Anfwerer without their grounds, whofe grounds notwithftanding in this Difcourfe are anfwered. I anfwer, if *Paul* himfelf were joyned with them, yea or an Angel from Heaven bringing any other rule then what the Lord Jefus hath once delivered, we have *Pauls* conclufion and refolution, peremptory and dreadfull, Gal. 1. 8.

Peace. This paffage finifhed, let me finifh the whole by propofing one conclufion of the Author of the arguments, viz. "It is no prejudice to the Common-
" wealth if Liberty of Confcience were fuffered to
" fuch as feare God indeed: *Abraham* abode a long
" time amongft the Cananites, yet contrary to them
" in Religion, Gen. 13. 7. & 16. 13. Againe, he
" fojourned in Gerar, and King *Abimelech* gave him
" leave to abide in his Land, Gen. 20. 21. 23. 24.
113] " *Ifaack* alfo dwelt in the fame Land, yet con-
" trary in Religion, *Gen.* 26.

" *Jacob* lived 20 yeares in one houfe with his Unkle
" *Laban,* yet differed in Religion, *Gen.* 31.

" The people of Ifrael were about 430 yeares in
" that infamous land of Egypt, and afterwards 70
" yeares in Babylon: all which times they differed
" in Religion from the States, *Exod.* 12. & 2. *Chron.*
" 36.

" Come to the time of Chrift, where Ifrael was
" under the Romanes, where lived divers Sects of
" Religion, as Herodians, Scribes and Pharifes, Sad-
" uces and Libertines, Theudæans and Samaritanes,
" befide the Common Religion of the Jews, & Chrift
" and his Apoftles. All which differed from the

" Common Religion of the State, which was like the
" Worſhip of *Diana*, which almoſt the whole World
" then worſhipped, *Acts* 19. 20.

" All theſe lived under the Government of *Cæſar*,
" being nothing hurtfull unto the Commonwealth,
" giving unto *Cæſar* that which was his. And for
" their Religion and Conſciences towards God, he
" left them to themſelves, as having no dominion
" over their Soules and Conſciences: And when the
" Enemies of the Truth raiſed up any tumults, the
" wiſedome of the Magiſtrate moſt wiſely appeaſed
" them, *Acts* 18 14. & 19. 35.

" Unto this the Anſwerer returnes thus much:

" It is true, that without prejudice to the Com-
" mon-wealth, Libertie of Conſcience may be ſuf-
" fered to ſuch as feare God indeed, as knowing they
" will not perſiſt in Hereſie or turbulent Schiſme,
" when they are convinced in Conſcience of the ſin-
" fulnes thereof. But the queſtion is, whether an
" Heretick after once or twice Admonition, (and ſo
" after Conviction) and any other ſcandalous and
" heynous offender, may be tolerated either in the
" Church without Excommunication, or in the Com-
" mon-weale without ſuch puniſhment as may pre-
" ſerve others from dangerous and damnable infection.

CHAP. LXXIX. [LXXVIII.]

Truth. I Here obſerve the *Anſwerers partiality*, that
none but ſuch as truly feare God ſhould
enjoy *Libertie* of *Conſcience*, whence the *Inhabitants
of the World* muſt either come into [114] the eſtate

of men fearing *God*, or elſe *diſſemble* a *Religion* in hypocriſie, or elſe be driven out of the *World*: One muſt follow. The firſt is only the gift of *God*, the ſecond and third are too commonly practiſed upon this ground.

Againe, ſince there is ſo much controverſie in the World, where the name of *Chriſt* is taken up, concerning the true *Church*, the *Miniſtrie* and *Worſhip*, and who are thoſe that truly feare *God*; I aske who ſhall judge in this caſe, who be they that feare God?

<small>Dangerous conſequences flowing from the Civill Magiſtrates judging in Spirituall cauſes.</small>

It muſt needs be granted, that ſuch as have the power of *ſuffring* or not *ſuffring*,[1] ſuch *Conſciences*, muſt judge: and then muſt it follow (as before I intimated) that the *Civill State* muſt judge of the truth of the *Spirituall*; and then *Magiſtrates* fearing or not fearing *God*, muſt judge of the feare of *God*: alſo that their *judgement* or ſentence muſt be according to their *conſcience*, of what *Religion* ſoever: Or that there is no lawfull *Magiſtrate*, who is not able to judge in ſuch caſes. And laſtly, that ſince the *Soveraigne power* of all *Civill Authority* is founded in the *conſent* of the People, that every *Common-weale* hath radically and fundamentally in it a power of

<small>The World turned upſide down.</small>

true diſcerning the true feare of God, which they transfer to their *Magiſtrates* and Officers: Or elſe that there are no lawfull *Kingdomes*, *Cities*, or *Townes* in the *World*, in which a man may live, and unto whoſe Civill Government he may ſubmit: and then (as I ſaid before) there muſt be no *World*, nor is it lawfull to live in it, becauſe it hath not a true diſcerning Spirit to judge them that feare or not feare God.

[1] *Dele* the comma.

The Bloudy Tenent. 215

Laftly, although this worthy *Anfwerer* fo readily grants, that *Libertie* of *Confcience* fhould be fuffred to them that feare *God* indeed: yet we know what the *Minifters* of the *Churches* of *New-England* wrote in anfwer to the 3 [32] Queftion[s] fent to them by fome *Minifters* of *Old England*,[1] viz. that although

<small>The wonderfull anfwer of the Minifters of the Church of New-England to the</small>

---

[1] Church-Government and Church-Covenant difcuffed, In an Anfwer of the Elders of the feverall Churches in New-England To two and thirty Queftions, fent over to them by divers Minifters in *England*, to declare their judgements therein. London. 1643.

The Preface to this book is by Hugh Peter, Williams's fucceffor in the Church at Salem, who had returned to England in 1641, but the work was prepared by the Rev. Richard Mather, of Dorchefter. Cotton's *Anfwer, Pub. Narr. Club*, ii: 103. Mather's *Magnalia*, i: 409.

The thirty-firft queftion is, "Whether would you permit any Companie of Minifters and People (being otherwife in fome meafure approvable) to fit downe by you, and fet up and practife another forme of Difcipline, enjoying like libertie with yourfelves in the Commonwealth, and accepted as a fifter Church by the reft of your Churches?" p. 6.

The anfwer is in part, "Who muft have libertie to fit downe in this Commonwealth and enjoy the liberties hereof is not our place to determine, but the Magiftrates who are the rulers and governours of the Commonwealth, and of all perfons within the fame. And as for acknowledging a company to be a fifter Church, that fhall fet up and practife another forme of Church Difcipline, being otherwife in fome meafure, as you fay, approveable, we conceive the companie that fhall fo doe, fhall not be approveable therein. * * * And if that Difcipline which we here practife, be (as we are perfwaded of it) the fame which Chrift hath appointed, and therefore unalterable, we fee not how another can be lawful; and therefore if a company of people fhall come hither, and here fet up and practife another, we pray you thinke not much, if we cannot promife to approve of them in fo doing, efpecially untill we fee how approvable the men may be, and what Difcipline it is they would fet up." pp. 82, 83.

This language, and that of the remainder of the Anfwer, certainly feems to carry all that Williams has put upon it in the text, "that they could not approve their civil cohabitation with them." It is a decided negative to the queftion. It was not ftrange that with his experiences Williams fhould interpretet it fo, even if the language had been lefs explicit. The queftioners were Prefbyterians, and however it might be with individual diffidents, it is clear the New England Minifters did not mean to allow churches of different conftitution from theirs to have any place here. From a letter of Hooker's it appears that the publication of the Anfwer to the Thirty-Two Queftions in England was unexpected, if not unwelcome, to the writers, as liable to "leave a taint of difparagement upon the caufe." Palfrey's *Hiftory*

<small>Ministers of the Church of Old England.</small> they confeſt them to be ſuch perſons whom they approved of far above themſelves, yea who were in their hearts to live and die together; yet if they and other godly people with them, comming over to them, ſhould differ in *Church conſtitution*, they then could not approve their *Civill cohabitation* with them, and conſequently could not adviſe the *Magiſtrates* to ſuffer them to enjoy a Civill being within their *Juriſdiction*.

Heare O *Heavens*, and give eare O *Earth*, yea let the Heavens be aſtoniſhed, and the Earth tremble at ſuch an *Anſwer* as this from [115] ſuch excellent men to ſuch whom they eſteeme for *godlineſſe* above themſelves.

CHAP. LXXIX.

Peace. YEa, but they ſay, they doubt not if they were there but they ſhould agree; for, ſay they, either you will come to us, or you may ſhew us light to come to you, for we are but weak men, and dreame not of *perfection* in this life.

---

of New England, ii: 173.

Cotton denies with conſiderable aſperity the inference which Williams has drawn from this Anſwer. "Now ſure, if there were any ſuch Anſwer to be found in the Booke ſounding to ſuch a purpoſe, I myſelfe ſhould joyne with him in the like exclamation, and wonderment. But when I came to ſearch for that ſpeech, and neither finde in the Anſwer which he quoteth to the third Queſtion, nor in that, which I rather think he meant, the 31. I cannot but admire and adore the righteous Judgement of God, who having left the *Diſcuſſer* (in this Booke, and ſome other) to write againſt the Truth in point of Doctrine, hath herein left him to breake forth in his own hand-writing, into notorious impudent falſhood in matter of fact." *Bloody Tenent Waſhed*, pp. 184, 185. Williams makes ſimilar uſe of this paſſage in *Mr. Cotton's Letter examined*, &c., p. 19. *Publications of the Narraganſett Club*, i: 65. Cotton makes a ſimilar rejoinder, *Anſwer*, pp. 63, 64. *Publications of the Narraganſett Club*, ii: 104.

Truth. Alas, who knowes not what lamentable *differences* have beene betweene the fame *Minifters* of the *Church of England,* fome conforming, others leaving their *livings, friends, country, life,* rather then conforme; when others againe (of whofe perfonall *godlineffe* it is not queftioned) have fucceeded by *conformity* into fuch forfaken (fo called) *Livings?* How great the prefent *differences* even amongft them that feare *God,* concerning *Faith, Juftification,* and the evidence of it? concerning *Repentance* and *godly forrow,* as alfo and mainly concerning the *Church,* the *Matter, Forme, Adminiftrations* and *Government* of it?

<small>Lamentable differences even amongft them that fear God. Betweene the Prefbyterians and Independants, Covenanters and Non-covenanters, of both which many are truly godly in their perfons.</small>

Let none now thinke that the paffage to *New England* by Sea, or the nature of the *Countrey* can doe what onely the Key of *David* can doe, to wit, open and fhut the Confciences of men.

Befide, how can this bee a faithfull and upright acknowledgement of their *weakneffe* and imperfection, when they *preach, print,* and *practife* fuch violence to the *foules* and *bodies* of others, and by their *Rules* and *Grounds* ought to proceed even to the killing of thofe whom they judge fo deare unto them, and in refpect of *godlineffe* far above themfelves?

CHAP. LXXX.

Peace. YEa but (fay they) the *godly* will not perfift in *Herefie* or turbulent *Schifme,* when they are convinced in *Confcience, &c.*

Truth. Sweet *Truth,* if the Civill Court and *Magiftracy* muft judge (as before I have written) and thofe Civill Courts are as lawfull, confifting of *naturall men*

<small>The doctrine of perfecution neceffarily and moft commonly falls heavieft</small>

upon the most godly persons. as of *godly* persons, then what *consequences* necessarily will follow, I have before mentioned. And I adde, according to this *conclusion* it must follow, that, if the most [116] *godly* persons yeeld not to once or twice *Admonition* (as is maintained by the *Answerer*) they must necessarily be esteemed *obstinate* persons, for if they were *godly* (faith he) they would yeeld. Must it not then be said (as it was by one, passing sentence of *Banishment* upon some, whose godlinesse was acknowledged) that he that commanded the *Judge* not to respect the poore in the cause of *judgement*, commands him not to respect the holy or the godly person?

The doctrine of persecution drives the most godly persons out of the world. Hence I could name the place and time when a *godly* man, a most desirable person for his trade, &c. (yet something different in *conscience*) propounded his willingnesse and desire to come to dwell in a certaine *Towne* in *New England*; it was answered by the Chiefe of the place, This man differs from us, and wee desire not to be troubled. So that in conclusion (for no other reason in the world) the poore man, though godly, usefull and peaceable, could not be admitted to a Civill Being and Habitation on the Common Earth in that Wildernesse amongst them.

The latter part of the Answer concerning the *Hereticke* or obstinate person to be excommunicated, and the *scandalous offender* to be punished in the *Common-weale*, which neither of both come neere our *Question:* I have spoken [of] I feare too largely already.

Peace. Mr. *Cotton* concludes with a confident perswasion of having removed the grounds of that great *errour, viz.* that persons are not to be persecuted for cause of *conscience*.

Truth. And I beleeve (deare *Peace*) it shall appear to them that (with feare and trembling at the word of the Lord) examine these passages, that the charge of *errour* reboundeth backe[,] even such an *errour*, as may well bee called the *bloody tenent*, so directly contradicting the *spirit* and *minde* and *practice* of the *Prince* of *Peace*; so deeply guilty of the *blood* of soules compelled and forced to *Hypocrisie* in a *spirituall* and *soule rape*; so deeply guilty of the *blood* of the *Soules* under the *Altar*, persecuted in all *ages* for the *cause* of *Conscience*, and so destructive to the *civill peace* and *welfare* of all *Kingdomes, Countries*, and *Commonwealths*.

The bloody Tenent.

CHAP. LXXXI.

Peace. TO this Conclusion (*deare Truth*) I heartily subscribe, and know the¹ *God*, the *Spirit*, the *Prince*, the *Angels*, and all the true awaked Sons of Peace will call thee blessed.

117] *Truth.* How sweet and precious are these *contemplations*, but oh how sweet the *actions* and *fruitions*?

Peace. Thy lips drop as the *Honey-combe*, *Honey* and *Milke* are under thy *Tongue*; oh that these *drops*, these *streames* might flow without a *stop* or *interruption*!

Truth. The glorious white *Troopers* (*Rev.* 19.) shall in time be mounted, and he that is the most *High Prince* of *Princes*, and *Lord Generall* of *Generalls* mounted upon the Word of Truth and Meeknesse

¹ Substitute "that."

(*Pſal.* 45.) ſhall triumph glorioufly, and renew our meetings. But harke, what noiſe is this?

Peace. Theſe are the dolefull *drums*, and ſhrill ſounding *trumpets*, the roaring murthering *Canons*, the *ſhouts* of *Conquerours*, the *grones* of *wounded, dying, ſlaughtered, righteous* with the *wicked*. Deare Truth how long? how long theſe dreadfull *ſounds* and direfull *ſights*? how long before my glad *returne* and *reſtitution*?

<small>Warres for Conſcience.</small>

Truth. Sweet Peace, who will beleeve my true *report*? yet true it is, if I were once beleev'd, bleſt Truth and Peace ſhould not ſo ſoone be parted.

Peace. Deare Truth, what welcome haſt thou found of late beyond thy former times or preſent expectations?

Truth. Alas, my *welcome* changes as the *times*, and ſtrongeſt *ſwords* and *armes* prevaile: were I beleeved in this, that *Chriſt* is not delighted with the *blood* of men (but ſhed his owne for his bloodieſt *enemies*) that by the word of *Chriſt* no man for gainſaying *Chriſt*, or joyning with his enemy *Antichriſt*, ſhould bee moleſted with the *civill ſword:* Were this *foundation* laid as the *Magna Charta* of higheſt *liberties*, and good *ſecurity* given on all hands for the preſervation of it, how ſoone ſhould every brow and houſe be ſtucke with *Olive Branches*?

<small>The bleſſed Magna Charta.</small>

Peace. This heavenly *invitation* makes mee bold once more to crave thy patient *eare* and holy *tongue*. *Errour's* impatient and ſoon tyred, but thou art *Light*, and like the *Father* of *Lights*, unwearied in thy ſhinings. Loe here what once againe I preſent to thy impartiall *cenſure*.

A Model of Church and Civil Power.

Compoſed by Mr. Cotton *and the* Ministers of New-England,

And ſent to the Church at Salem, as a further Confirmation of the bloody Doctrine of Persecution for cauſe of Conscience.

Examined and Anſwered.

CHAP. LXXXII.

Truth. What haſt thou there?

Peace. Here is a *combination* of thine owne *Children* againſt thy very *life* and mine: Here is a *Modell* (framed by many able learned and godly hands) of ſuch a *Church* and *Commonweale* as wakens *Moſes* from his unknown Grave, and denies *Jeſus* yet to have ſeene the Earth.

Truth. Begin (ſweet *Peace*) read and propound. My hand ſhall not be tyred with holding the *ballances* of the *Sanctuarie:* doe thou put in, and I ſhall weigh as in the preſence of Him whoſe pure eyes cannot behold *iniquitie*.

A ſtrange Modell of a Church and Commonweale after the Moſaicall and Jewiſh pattern.

Mat. 16.
19. with
John 20.
23. Rom.
13. 1. Mat
10. 18.
Tit. 3. 1.
Acts 15.
20. Ifa.
49. 23.
Gal. 3.28.

Peace. "Thus then fpeakes the *Preface* or Entrance. "Seeing *God* hath given a diftinct power to *Church* "and *Common-weale*, the one *Spirituall* (called the "Power of the *Keyes*) the other *Civill* (called the "Power of the *Sword*) and hath made the members "of both *Societies* fubject to both Authorities, fo that "every [119] foule in the Church is fubject to the "higher powers in the Commonweale, and every "member of the Commonweale (being a member of "the Church) is fubject to the Lawes of Chrifts "Kingdome, and in him to the cenfures of the "Church; the Queftion is, how the Civill State and "the Church may difpence their feverall Govern-"ments without infringement and impeachment of "the power and honour of the One or of the Other, "and what bounds and limits the Lord hath fet "betweene both the Adminiftrations.

Chrifts
power in
hisChurch
confeft to
be above
all Magif-
trates in
fpirituall
things.

Truth. "From that conclufion (deare *Peace*) that "every mem- of the Commonweale, being a mem-"ber of the Church, is fubject to the Lawes of "Chrifts Kingdome, and in Him to the cenfure of "the Church; I obferve that they grant the *Church* of *Chrift* in *Spirituall caufes* to be fuperiour and over the higheft *Magiftrates* in the World, if members of the Church.

Hence therefore I infer, may fhe refufe to receive, and may alfo caft forth any, yea even the higheft (if obftinate in Sin) out of her *Spirituall fociety*.

Hence in this *Spirituall fociety*, that foule who hath moft of *Chrift*, moft of His *Spirit*, is moft (fpiritually) honourable, according to the *Scriptures*, quoted *Acts* 15. 20. *Ifa.* 49. 23. *Gal.* 3. 28.

And if so, how can this stand with their common *tenent*, that the Civill *Magistrate* must keep the first Table[,] set up, reforme the *Church*, and be *Judge* and *Governour* in all *Ecclesiasticall* as well as *Civil causes*?

Secondly, I observe the lamentable wresting of this one Scripture, *Isa.* 49. 23. Sometimes this Scripture must prove the *Power* of the *Civill Magistrates, Kings* and *Governours*, over the *Church* in *Spirituall causes*, &c. Yet here this Scripture is produced to prove *Kings* and *Magistrates* (in *Spirituall causes*) to be censured and corrected by the same *Church*. 'Tis true in *severall respects*, he that is a *Governour* may be a *subject*[;] but in *one* and the same *spirituall respect* to *judge* and to be *judged:* to sit on the *Bench*, and stand at the *Bar* of *Christ Jesus*, is as impossible as to reconcile the East and West together.

*Isa.*49. 23. lamentably wrested.

CHAP. LXXXII. [LXXXIII.]

The first head, That both Iurisdictions may stand together.

Peace. "WHereas divers affecting transcending "power to themselves over the "Church have perswaded the Princes of the World, "that the Kingdome of Christ in His Church can- "not rise or stand, without the falls of those Com- "monweales wherein it is set up, we do beleeve and "professe the contrary to this suggestion; the gov- "ernment of the one being of this World, the other "not; the Church helping forward the prosperity of "the Commonweale by meanes only *Ecclesiasticall*

The first head examined.

John 18. 36.

Jer. 29. 7.

<small>Ezra 7.23.
Rom. 1.
2. 3.
1 Tim. 2.
2.</small>
"and *Spirituall*; The Commonweale helping for-
"ward her owne and the Churches felicity by meanes
"politicall or temporall; the falls of Commonweales
"being knowne to arife from their fcattering and
"diminifhing the power of the Church, and the
"flourifhing of Commonweales with the well order-
"ing of the people (even in morall and civill virtues)
"being obferved to arife from the vigilant adminif-
"tration of the holy Difcipline of the Church, as
"*Bodin*,[1] (a man not partiall to Church Difcipline)
"plainely teftifieth. The vices in the free eftate of
"Geneva, *quæ legibus nufquam vindicantur*, by meanes
"of Church Difcipline, *fine vi & tumultu coercentur*;
"the Chriftian liberty not freeing us from fubjection
"to Authority, but from inthrallment and bondage
"unto finne.

<small>TheCivill Common- weal and the Spirit- uall Com- mon weale the Church, not incon-</small> *Truth. Anf.* From this *confeffion*, that the *Church* or *Kingdome* of *Chrift* may be fet up without preju- dice of the *Commonweale*, according to *John* 18. 36. My *Kingdome* is not of this *World*, &c. I obferve that although the *Kingdome* of *Chrift*, the *Church* and the *Civill Kingdome* or *Government* be not *inconfiftent*, but that both may ftand together; yet that they are *inde-*

<small>[1] Jean Bodin (1530–1596) was inclined to Judaifm. *Bayle*, ii: 43–53. An abftract of his great work, *De la Republique*, Paris, 1577, is given by Hallam, *Introduction to Lit. of Europe*, ii: 205–230.

The feverity of the civil code in Ge- neva was clofely blended with the eccle- fiaftical fyftem, and under the predomi- nant influence of Calvin the government became a ftern theocracy. "The feverity of the legiflation thus eftablifhed is evinced in fome of the minute points of difcipline. Brides, for example, were not permitted to wear wreaths in their bonnets, unlefs of unblemifhed character. Gamblers were fet in the pillory with their cards about their neck; even in 1506 the council had forbidden playing with dice, ninepins, or cards in the pub- lic ftreets. In the years 1546 and 1556 laws were paffed prohibiting the manu- facture of cards." Henry, *Life of Calvin*, i: 362, alfo Part 2, Chaps. iii., iv., v.</small>

pendent according to that *Scripture*, and that therefore there may be (as formerly I have proved) flourishing *Commonweales* and *Societies* of men where no *Church* of *Chrift* abideth; and fecondly, the *Commonweale* may be in perfect peace and quiet, notwithftanding the *Church*, the *Commonweale* of *Chrift* be in *diftractions*, and fpirituall *oppofitions* both againft their *Religions*, and fometimes amongft themfelves, as the *Church* of [121] *Chrift* in *Corinth* troubled with *divifions*, *contentions*, &c.

fiftent, though independent the one on the other.

Secondly, I obferve it is true the Church helpeth forward the profperity of the *Commonweale* by fpirituall meanes, *Jer.* 29. 7. The prayers of Gods people procure the *peace* of the *City*, where they abide, yet that *Chrifts Ordinances* and *adminiftrations* of *Worfhip* are appointed and given by *Chrift* to any *Civill State*, *Towne* or *City* as is implied by the inftance of *Geneva*, that I confidently deny.

The *Ordinances* and *Difcipline* of *Chrift Jefus*, though wrongfully and prophanely applied to naturall and unregenerate men may caft a blufh of *civility* and *morality* upon them as in *Geneva* and other places (for the fhining brightneffe of the very *fhadow* of *Chrifts Ordinances* cafts a fhame upon *barbarifme* and *incivility*) yet withall I affirme that the mifapplication of *Ordinances* to unregenerate and unrepentant perfons hardens up their foules in a dreadfull fleep and dreame of their owne bleffed eftate, and fends *millions* of *foules* to hell in a fecure expectation of a falfe *falvation*.

Chrifts Ordinances put upon a whole City or Nation, may more civilize and mortalize, but never Chriftianize them.

CHAP. LXXXIV.

The second head, concerning Superiority of each Power.

<small>The second head concerning superiority of each power.
Rom. 13. 1. 5. 6.
Isa. 49. 23.
Isa. 49. 23.
Luc. 12. 14
Joh. 8. 11.
And that *judicium* of the Church in law suits, 1 Cor. 6. 2. is only *arbitrarium* not *coactivum*.</small>

Peace. "BEcause contention may arise in future "times which of these Powers under "Christ is the greatest as it hath been under Anti-"christ, we conceive first, That the power of the "*Civill Magistrate* is superiour to the *Church policie* in "*place, honours, dignity, earthly power* in the *World*; "and the *Church* superiour to him (being a member "of the *Church*) *Ecclesiastically*, that is, in a *Church* "way ruling and ordering him by *Spirituall Ordi-*"*nances* according to *God* for his *soules* health, as any "other member, so that all the *power* the *Magistrate* "hath over the *Church* is *temporall* not *spirituall*, and "all the *power* the *Church* hath over the *Magistrate* "is *spirituall* not *temporall:* And as the *Church* hath "no *temporall power* over the *Magistrate, in ordine ad* "*bonum spirituale:* So the *Magistrate* hath no Spirit-"uall power over the Church *in ordine ad bonum tem-*"*porale.*

"Secondly, the delinquencie of either party calleth "for the exercise of the power of terrour from the "other part; for no Rulers ordained of God are a "terrour to good works, but to evill, *Rom.* [122] 13. "3. So that if the Church offend, the offence of "the Church calleth upon the Civill Magistrate, "either to seeke the healing thereof as a nursing "father by his owne grave advice, and the advice of "other Churches; or else if he cannot so prevaile[,]

"to put forth and exercife the fuperiority of his power
"in redreffing what is amiffe according to the quality
"of the offence by the courfe of civill Juftice.

"On the other fide, if the Magiftrate being a mem-
"ber of the *Church* fhall offend, the *offence* calleth
"upon the *Church* either to feek the healing thereof
"in a brotherly way by *conviction* of his finne; or elfe
"if they cannot prevaile, then to exercife the *fupe-*
"*riority* of their power in removing of the offence
"and recovering of the *offendour* by Church cenfures.

If the end of *Spirituall* or *Church* power is *bonum* *Anf.*
fpirituale, a fpirituall good; and the end of *Civill* or *Truth*.
State power is *bonum temporale*, a temporall good:
And fecondly, if the *Magiftrate* have no fpirituall
power to attaine to his temporall end, no more then
a *Church* hath any temporall power to attaine to her A contra-
Spirituall end, as is confeft: I demand if this be not diction to
a *contradiction* againft their owne *difputes*, *tenents*, and Magiftrate
practices touching that queftion of *perfecution* for fupreme
caufe of *confcience*: For if the *Magiftrate* be fupreme fpirituall
Judge (and fo confequently give fupreme *judgement*, caufes, and
fentence and *determination*) in matters of the firft yet to have
Table, and of the *Church*, and be *cuftos utriufq*₃ *Tabulæ*, all power.
keepers of both Tables (as they fpeake) and yet have
no Spirituall power as is affirmed, how can he determine what the true *Church* and *Ordinances* are, and
then fet them up with the power of the Sword? How
can he give *judgement* of a falfe *Church*, a falfe *Min-*
iftery, a falfe *Doctrine*, falfe *Ordinances*, and with a
Civil *Sword* pull them down, if he have no Spiritual
power, authority or *commiffion* from *Chrift Jefus* for
thefe ends and purpofes?

Further I argue thus: If the *civill officers* of *State* must determine, judge and punish in Spirituall *causes*, his *power, authority* and *commission* must be either *Spirituall* or *Civill,* or else he hath none at all, and so acts without a *commission* and warrant from the Lord *Jesus*, and so consequently stands guilty at the Bar of *Christ Jesus* to answer for such his practice as a transcendent *Delinquent*.

The Civill Magistrate confest to have no Civill power over the soules of men.

Now for *civill power*, these worthy *Authors* confesse that the *Government* of the *civill Magistrate* extendeth no further then over the *bodies* and *goods* of the *Subject*, and therefore hath no *civill* [123] *power* over the *Soule*, and therefore (say I) not in *Soule-causes*.

Nor spirituall.

Secondly, It is here confest in this passage, that to attaine his Civill end or *Bonum temporale*, he hath no *Spirituall power*, and therefore of necessitie out of their own mouths must they be judged for provoking the *Magistrate*, without either *Civill* or *Spirituall power*, to judge, punish and persecute in *Spirituall causes*; and to feare and tremble, lest they come neere those *frogs* which proceed out of the mouth of the *Dragon* and *Beast* and *false Prophet*, who by the same *Arguments* which the *Authours* here use stirre up the *Kings* of the Earth to make warre against the *Lambe Christ Jesus*, and his Followers, *Revel.* 17.

CHAP. LXXXV.

IN the next place I observe upon the point of *Delinquencie*, such a *confusion*, as *Heaven* and *Earth* may stand amazed at: If the *Church* offend (say they) after advice refused, in conclusion the *Magistrate* must redresse, that is, punish the *Church* (that is, in *Church offences* and cases) by a course of *Civill justice*.

On the other side, if the *Civill Magistrate* offend after *Admonition* used, and not prevailing, in conclusion the *Church* proceeds to *censure*, that is, to Excommunication, as is afterward more largely proved by them.

Now I demand, if the *Church* be a *Delinquent*, who shall judge? It is answered, the *Magistrate*. Againe, if the *Magistrate* be a *Delinquent*, I aske who shall judge? It is answered, the *Church*. Whence I observe, (which is monstrous in all cases in the *World*) that one person, to wit, the *Church* or *Magistrate*, shall be at one time the *Delinquent* at the *Bar*, and the *Judge* upon the *Bench*. This is cleere thus: The *Church* must judge when the *Magistrate* offends; and yet the *Magistrate* must judge when the *Church* offends; and so consequently in this case must judge whether she contemne *Civill Authority* in the Second *Table*, for thus dealing with him: Or whether she have broken the rules of the first Table, of which (say they) God hath made him *Keeper* and *Conserver*. And therefore, though the *Church* make him a *Delinquent* at the *Bar*, yet by their confession God hath made him a *Iudge* on the *Bench*. What *blood*, what *tumults* hath been, and must be spilt upon these grounds?

The Magistrate and the Church, by the Authors grounds, at one and the same time, in one and the same cause, made the Judges on the Bench, and Delinquents at the Barre.

124] *Peace*. Deare *Truth*, No question but the *Church* may punish the *Magistrate* spiritually in *spirituall* cases; and the *Magistrate* may punish the *Church*, *civilly*, in *civill* cases: But that for one and the same *cause* the *Church* must punish the *Magistrate*, and the *Magistrate* the *Church*, this seemes monstrous, and needs explication.

Truth. Sweet *Peace*, I illustrate with this *Instance*: A true *Church* of *Christ* (of which, according to the *Authors* supposition, the *Magistrate* is a member) chooseth and calls one of her *members* to office: The *Magistrate* opposeth: The *Church* perswaded that the *Magistrates* exceptions are insufficient (according to her *priviledge*, which these Authours maintaine against the *Magistrates* prohibition) proceeds to Ordaine her officer: The *Magistrate* chargeth the *Church* to have made an unfit and unworthy choice, and therefore according to his *place* and *power*, and according to his *conscience* and *judgement* he suppresseth such an *officer*, and makes void the *Churches* choice: Upon this the *Church* complaines against the *Magistrates* violation of her *priviledges* given her by *Christ Iesus*, aud cries out that the *Magistrate* is turned *Persecuter*; and not prevailing with *admonition*, she proceeds to *Excommunication* against him: The *Magistrate* according to his *conscience*, endures not such *profanation* of *Ordinances* as he conceives; and therefore if no *advice* and *admonition* prevaile, he proceeds against such obstinate *abusers* of *Christs* holy Ordinances, (as the *Authors* grant he may) in Civill Court of *justice*, yea and (I adde according to the *patterne* of *Israel*) cuts them off by the *sword*, as obstinate *usurpers* and *prophaners* of the holy things of *Christ*.

I demand what helpe hath any poore *Church* of *Christ* in this case, by maintaining this power of the *Magistrate* to punish the *Church* of *Christ*, I meane

An illustration demonstrating that the Civill Magistrate cannot have power over the Church in spirituall or Church causes.

The punishments Civill which the

in *spirituall* and *Soule-cafes*, for otherwife I queftion not but he may put all the *members* of the *Church* to *death* juftly, if they commit crimes worthy thereof, as *Paul* fpake, *Acts* 23. [xxv: ii.]

{*Magiftrate inflicts upon the Church for Civill crimes, lawfull and neceffary.*}

Shall the *Church* here flie to the *Popes* Sanctuarie againft *Emperours* and *Princes* excommunicate, to wit, give away their *crowns*, *kingdomes* or *dominions*, and invite forraigne *Princes* to make War upon them and their *Territories*? The *Authors* furely will difclaime this; and yet I fhall prove their *Tenents* tend directly unto fuch a practife.

125] Or fecondly, fhall fhe fay the *Magiftrate* is not a true *Magiftrate*, becaufe not able to judge and determine in fuch cafes? This, their *confeffion* will not give them leave to fay, becaufe they cannot deny *unbelievers* to be *lawfull Magiftrates*: and yet it fhall appeare (notwithftanding their *confeffion* to the contrary) their Tenents imply, that none but a *Magiftrate* after their own *confcience*, is a lawfull *Magiftrate*.

Therefore, thirdly, they muft ingenuoufly and honeftly confeffe, that if it be the duty of the *Magiftrate* to punifh the *Church* in *fpirituall cafes*, he muft then judge according to his *confcience* and *perfwafion*, whatever his *confcience* be: and then let all men judge into what a wofull ftate they bring both the *civill Magiftrate* and *Church* of *Chrift*, by fuch a *Church*-deftroying and *State*-deftroying Doctrine.

Peace. Some will here fay, in fuch a cafe either the *Magiftrate* or the *Church* muft judge; either the the *Spirituall* or *Civill* State muft be fupreme.

[*Truth.*] I anfwer, if the *Magiftrate* be of another Religion.

The true way of the God of Peace in differences between the Church & the Magistrate.

First, What hath the *Church* to judge him being without? 1 Cor. 5.

Secondly, If he be a *member* of the *Church*, doubtles the *Church* hath power to judge (in *spirituall* and *Soule-cases*) with *spirituall* and *Church* censures all that are within, 1 Cor. 5.

Thirdly, If the *Church* offend against the *civill* peace of the *State*, by wronging the *bodies* or *goods* of any, the *Magistrate* bears not the sword in vaine, Rom. 13. to correct any or all the members of the *Church*. And this I conceive to be the onely way of the God of Peace.

CHAP. LXXXVI.

The third head concerns the End of both these Powers.

[*Peace.*] "First the common and last end of both is
  " Gods glory, and Mans eternall felicitie.
  " Secondly, the proper ends:
  " First of Commonwealth, is the procuring, pre-
  " serving, increasing of externall and temporall peace
  " and felicitie of the State in all Godlines and Hon-
  " estie, 1 *Tim.* 2. 1, 2.
126] " Secondly, of the Church, a begetting, preserv-
  " ing, increasing of internall and spirituall peace and
  " felicity of the Church, in all godlinesse and honesty,
  " *Esay* 2. 3, 4. and 9. 7. So that Magistrates have
  " power given them from Christ in matters of Relig-
  " ion, because they are bound to see that outward
  " peace be preserved, not in all ungodlinesse and dis-
  " honesty (for such peace is Satanicall) but in all god-

"lineffe and honefty, for fuch peace God aymes at.
"And hence the Magiftrate is *cuftos* of both the
"Tables of godlineffe, in the firft of Honefty, in the
"fecond for Peace fake. Hee muft fee that honefty
"be preferved within his jurifdiction, or elfe the fub-
"ject will not be *bonus Cives*. Hee muft fee that
"godlineffe as well as honefty be preferved, elfe the
"fubject will not be *bonus vir*, who is the beft *bonus*
"*cives*. Hee muft fee that godlineffe and honefty
"be preferved, or elfe himfelfe will not bee *bonus*
"*Magiftratus*.

<small>Chamer. de Ecclef. p. 376. Park. part. polit. lib. 1. cap. 1.</small>

Truth. In this paffage here are divers particulars affirmed marvellous deftructive both to *godlineffe* and *honefty*, though under a faire maske and colour of both.

Firft, it will appeare that in fpirituall things they make the *Garden* and the *Wilderneffe* (as often I have intimated) I fay the *Garden* and the *Wilderneffe*, the *Church* and the *World* are all one: for thus,

<small>The Garden of the Church and the Wilderneffe of the World made all one.</small>

If the *Powers* of the *World* or *Civill State*, are bound to propofe *externall* Peace in all *godlineffe* for their end, and the end of the *Church* be to preferve internall Peace in all *godlineffe*, I demand if their end (*godlineffe*) bee the fame, is not their *power* and *ftate* the fame alfo, unleffe they make the *Church fubordinate* to the *Commonwealths* end, or the *Commonweale fubordinate* to the *Churches* end, which (being the *governour* and fetter up of it, and fo confequently the *Judges* of it) it cannot be?

Now if *godlineffe* bee the *worfhipping* and walking with *God* in *Chrift*, is not the Magiftrate and Com-

<small>The Commonweale more</small>

monweale charged more by this *tenent* with the *worship* and *Ordinances* of *God*, then the *Church*,[?] for the *Magistrate* they charge with the externall peace in *godlinesse*, and the *Church* but with the *internall*.

<small>charged by these Authors with the Worship and Ordinances, then the Church.</small>

I aske further, what is this internall peace in all *godlinesse*? whether intend they internall within the *Soule*, which onely the eye of *God* can see, opposed to *externall* or *visible*, which man also can discerne? or else whether they meane internall, that is spirituall *soule* matters, matters of *Gods Worship*, and then I say that peace (to [127] wit, of *godlinesse* or *Gods worship*) they had before granted to the *civill State*?

Peace. The Truth is, (as I now perceive) the best and most *godly* of that *judgement* declare themselves never to have seene a true *difference* betweene the *Church* and the *World*, and the *Spirituall* and *Civill State*; and howsoever these worthy *Authours* seeme to make a kinde of *separation* from the *World*, and professe that the *Church* must consist of spirituall and *living Stones, Saints, Regenerate* persons, and so make some peculiar inclosed *Ordinances*, as the Supper of the *Lord*, (which none, say they, but *godly* persons must taste of) yet by compelling all within their *Jurisdiction* to an outward *conformity* of the *Church worship*, of the *Word* and *Prayer*, and *maintenance* of the *Ministry* thereof, they evidently declare that they still lodge and dwell in the confused mixtures of the *uncleane* and *cleane*, of the *flock* of *Christ*, and *Herds* of the *World* together, I meane in *spirituall* and *religious* worship.

<small>The authors of these Positions never yet saw a true difference betweene the Church of Christ and the world, in point of worship.</small>

Truth. For a more ful and clear difcuffion of this Scripture, 1 *Tim.* 2. 1. 2. (on which is weakly built fuch a mighty building) I fhall propofe and refolve thefe foure *Quæries.*

CHAP. LXXXVII.

First, what is meant by *godlineffe* and *honefty* in this place. _{1 Tim. 2. 1. difcuffed.}

Secondly, what may the *fcope* of the holy *Spirit* of *God* be in this place.

Thirdly, whether the *civill Magiftrate* was then *cuftos utriufque Tabulæ,* keeper of both *Tables, &c.*

Fourthly, whether a *Church* or *Congregation* of *Chriftians* may not live in *godlineffe* and *honefty,* although the *civill Magiftrate* be of another *confcience* and *worfhip,* and the whole *State* and *Country* with him.

To the firft, What is here meant by *godlineffe* and *honefty?*

Anfw. I finde not that the *Spirit* of *God* here intendeth the firft and fecond Table.

For, how ever the word Εὐσέβεια fignifie *godlineffe,* or the *worfhip* of *God,* yet the fecond word Σεμνότης I finde not that it fignifies fuch an *honefty* as comprifeth the *duties* of the fecond *Table,* but fuch an *honefty* as fignifies *folemnity, gravity,* and fo it is turned by the *Tranflatours,* Tit. 2. 7. ἐν τῇ διδασκαλίᾳ ἀδιαφθορίαν, σεμνότητα, that is, in [128] *doctrine, incorruptneffe, gravity:* which *doctrine* cannot there bee taken for the *doctrine* of the *civill ftate,* or fecond Table, but the *gravity, majefty,* and *folemnity* of the fpirituall

_{The word honefty in this place of Timothy cannot fignifie here the honefty or righteoufneffe of the fecond Table.}

doctrine of *Christianity*. So that according to the Tranflatours owne rendring of that word in *Titus*, this place of *Timothy* fhould be thus rendred [In all *godlineffe* (or *worfhipping* of *God*) and *gravity*] that is, a folemne or grave profeffion of the *worfhip* of *God*; and yet this miftaken and mifinterpreted *Scripture* is that great *Caftle* and ftrong *Hold* which fo many flye unto concerning the *Magiftrates charge* over the two *Tables*.

Secondly, what is the *fcope* of the *Spirit* of *God* in this place?

The fcope of Gods Spirit in this place of Timothy.

I anfwer firft *negatively*, the *fcope* is not to fpeake of the *duties* of the *firft* and fecond *Table:*

Nor fecondly is the *fcope* to charge the *Magiftrate* with forcing the people (who have chofe him) to *godlineffe* or *Gods worfhip*, according to his *confcience*, (the *Magiftrate* keeping the peace of externall *godlineffe*, and the *Church* of *internall*, as is affirmed:) but

Secondly, *pofitively*, I fay the *Spirit* of *God* by *Paul* in this place provokes *Timothy* and the *Church* at *Ephefus*, and fo confequently all the *Minifters* of *Chrifts Churches* and *Chriftians*, to pray for two things.

Gods people muft pray for and endeavour the peace of the State they live in. Although Pagan or Popifh.

Firft, for the peaceable and quiet ftate of the Countries and places of their abode,[;] that is implyed in their praying (as *Paul* directs them) for a quiet and *peaceable* condition, and fuits fweetly with the command of the *Lord* to his people, even in *Babel*, *Jer*. 29. 7. Pray for the peace of the *City*, and feeke the *good* of it, for in the *Peace* thereof it fhall goe well with you. Which *Rule* will hold in any *Pagan* or *Popifh city*, and therefore confequently are *Gods* people to pray againſt *Warres, Famines, Peſtilences,* and eſpecially to bee far from kindling *coales* of *War,* and endeavour the bringing in and advancing their *conſcience* by the *ſword.*

Secondly, they are here commanded to pray for the *ſalvation* of *all men,* that *all men,* and eſpecially *Kings* and *Magiſtrates* might be ſaved, and come to the knowledge of the *truth,* implying that the grave or ſolemne and ſhining *profeſſion* of *godlineſſe* or *Gods worſhip* according to *Chriſt Jeſus,* is a bleſſed meanes to cauſe *all* ſorts of men to be affected with the *Chriſtian profeſſion,* and to come to the ſame knowledge of that *one God* and *one Mediatour Chriſt Jeſus.* All which tends directly againſt what it is brought for, to wit, the [129] *Magiſtrates* forcing *all* men to *godlineſſe* or the *worſhipping* of *God,* which in truth cauſeth the greateſt *breach* of *peace,* and the greateſt *diſtractions* in the *World,* and the ſetting up that for *godlineſſe* or *worſhip* which is no more then *Nebuchadnezzars golden Image,* a *State worſhip,* and in ſome places the *worſhip* of the *Beaſt,* and his *Image, Dan.* 3. *Rev.* 13.

<small>Forcing of men to godlineſſe or Gods worſhip, the greateſt cauſe of breach of Civill peace.</small>

CHAP. LXXXVIII.

THirdly, I quærie whether the *Civill Magiſtrate* (which was then the *Roman Emperour*) was *keeper* or *guardian* of both Tables (as is affirmed.)

Scripture and all *Hiſtory* tell us, that thoſe *Cæſars* were not only ignorant, without *God,* without *Chriſt,* &c. but profeſſed *worſhippers* or *maintainers* of the *Roman gods* or *divells;* as alſo notorious for all ſorts

<small>The Roman Cæſars deſcribed.</small>

of *wickednesse,* and laftly, *cruell* and bloudy *Lions,* and *Tygers* toward the *Chriftians* for many hundred yeares.

<small>Not appointed by Chrift Jefus keepers and guardians of his Church.</small>

Hence I argue from the *wifdome, love* and *faithfulneffe* of the Lord *Jefus* in his *houfe,* it was impoffible that he fhould appoint fuch *ignorant,* fuch *Idolatrous,* fuch *wicked* and fuch *cruell* perfons to be his *chiefe Officers* and *Deputy Lieutenants* under himfelfe to keep the *worfhip* of *God,* to guard his *Church,* his *Wife:* No wife and loving father was ever knowne to put his *childe,* no not his beafts, *dogs* or *fwine,* but unto fitting keepers.

Men judge it matter of high complaint, that the *Records* of *Parliament,* the *Kings children,* the *Tower* of *London,* the *Great Seale* fhould be committed to unworthy *keepers!* And can it be without high *blafphemie* conceived that the Lord *Jefus* fhould commit his *Sheep,* his *Children,* yea his *Spoufe,* his thoufand fhields and bucklers in the *Tower* of his *Church!* and laftly, his Great and Glorious *Broad Seales* of *Baptifme* and his *Supper,* to be preferved pure in their *adminiftrations,* I fay that the Lord *Jefus* who is *wifdome,* and *faithfulneffe* it felfe, fhould deliver thefe to fuch *keepers.*

Peace. Some will fay, it is one thing what perfons are in *fact* and *practice*: another what they ought to be by *right* and *office.*

Truth. In fuch cafes as I have mentioned, no man doth in the common eye of *reafon* deliver fuch matters of *charge* and *truft* to fuch as declare *themfelves* and *finnes* (like *Sodome*) at the very time of this great charge and truft to be committed to them.

130] *Peace.* It will further be faid, that many of the

Kings of *Judah* who had the charge of *eſtabliſhing, reforming* (and ſo conſequently of keeping the firſt Table) the *Church, Gods worſhip,* &c. were notoriouſly *wicked, Idolatrous, &c.*

Truth. I muſt then ſay, the caſe is not alike, for when the *Lord* appointed the *government* of *Iſrael* after tbe rejection of *Saul* to eſtabliſh a Covenant of *ſucceſſion* in the type unto *Chriſt,* let it bee minded what *patterne* and *preſident* it pleaſed the *Lord* to ſet for the after *Kings* of *Iſrael* and *Judah,* in *David* the man after His owne *Heart.*

But now the *Lord Jeſus* being come Himſelfe, and having fulfilled the former types, and diſſolved the *Nationall ſtate* of the *Church,* and eſtabliſhed a more Spirituall way of *worſhip* all the *World* over, and appointed a *Spirituall government* and *governours,* it is well knowne what the *Roman Cæſars* were, under whom both *Chriſt Jeſus Himſelfe* and his *Servants* after him lived and ſuffered; ſo that if the *Lord Jeſus* had appointed any ſuch *Deputies* (as we finde not a tittle to that purpoſe, nor have a ſhadow of true reaſon ſo to thinke) he muſt I ſay in the very firſt *inſtitution,* have pitched upon ſuch perſons for theſe *Cuſtodes utriuſq₃ Tabulæ,* keepers of both Tables, as no man wiſe, or faithfull or loving, would have choſen in any of the former *Inſtances* or caſes of a more inferiour nature.

Beſide to that great *pretence* of *Iſrael,* I have largely ſpoken to.

Secondly, I aske how could the *Roman Cæſars* or any *Civill Magiſtrates* be *cuſtodes,* keepers of the *Church* and *worſhip* of *God,* when as the *Authours* of

It pleaſed not the Lord Jeſus in the firſt inſtitution of his Church to furniſh himſelfe with any ſuch Civill Governours, as unto whom hee might commit the care of his worſhip.

these *positions* acknowledge, that their *Civill power* extends but to *bodies* and *goods*.

And for *Spirituall power* they say they have none, *ad bonum temporale* (to a temporall good) which is their proper end, and then having neither *Civill* nor *Spirituall power* from the Lord *Jesus* to this purpose, how come they to be such Keepers as is pretended?

<small>The true Keepers which Christ Jesus appointed, of his Ordinances and Worship.</small>

Thirdly, If the *Roman Emperours* were Keepers, what Keepers were the *Apostles*, unto whom the Lord *Jesus* gave the care and charge of the *Churches*, and by whom the Lord *Iesus* charged *Timothy*, 1 *Tim*. 6. to keep those *commands* of the Lord *Iesus* without spot untill his *comming*.

These Keepers were called the foundation of the *Church*, *Ephes*. 2. 20. and made up the *Crowne* of 12 Stars about the head of the [131] *Woman*, *Rev*. 12. whose names were also written in the 12 *foundations* of *New Ierusalem*, *Rev*. 21.

Yea what Keepers then are the ordinary Officers of the *Church* appointed to be the Shepherds or Keepers of the Flocke of *Christ*, appointed to be the Porters or Dore-keepers and to watch in the absence of *Christ*, *Mark* 13. 34. *Acts* 20.

Yea what charge hath the whole *Church* it selfe, which is the pillar and ground of *Truth*, 2 *Tim*. 2. in the midst of which *Christ* is present with his Power, 1 *Cor*. 5. to keep out or cast out the impenitent and obstinate, even *Kings* and *Emperours* themselves from their Spirituall society, 1 *Cor*. 5. *Jam*. 3. 1. *Gal*. 3. 28.

<small>The Kings of the As-</small>

4. I aske whether in the time of the *Kings* of *Israel* and *Iudah* (whom I confesse in the typicall and

Nationall state to be charged with both Tables) *I* aske whether the *Kings* of the *Assyrians,* the *Kings* of the *Ammonites, Moabites, Philistims,* were also constituted and ordained Keepers of the *worship* of *God* as the *Kings* of *Iudah* were (for they were also lawfull *Magistrates* in their *Dominions?*) or whether the *Roman Emperours* were *custodes,* or keepers more then they? or more then the *King* of *Babylon Nebuchadnezzar,* under whose Civill government *Gods* people lived, and in his owne Land and City, *Ier.* 29.

Assyrians&c. not charged with Gods worship as the Kings of Judah in that Nationall and typicall church.

CHAP. LXXXIX.

Peace. YOu remember (deare *Truth*) that *Constantine, Theodosius,* and others were made to beleeve that they were the *Antitypes* of the *Kings* of *Iudah,* the Church of *God*; and *Henry* the 8 was told that that Title *Defensor Fidei,* Defendour of the *Faith* (though sent him by the *Pope* for writing against *Luther*) was his owne *Diadem* due unto him from *Heaven.* So likewise since, the *Kings* and *Queens* of *England* have been instructed.

Constantine, Theodosius. &c. misinformed.

Truth. But it was not so from the beginning, as that very difference between that Nationall state of the *Church* of *God* then, and other *Kings* and *Magistrates* of the *World* (not so charged) doth clearly evince and leadeth us to the *Spirituall King* of the *Church, Christ Iesus* the *King* of *Israel,* and his *Spirituall Government* and *Governours* therein.

Fifthly, I aske whether had the *Roman Cæsars* more charge to see all their Subjects observe and submit to the *worship* of *God* in [132] their dominion

Masters of families under the Gospel not

charged to of the World, then a *master, father* or *husband* now
*force all
under him* under the *Gospel* in his *Familie?*
from their   *Families* are the *foundations* of *government,* for what
owne con- is a *Commonweale,* but a *Commonweale* of *Families*
*sciences to
his.* agreeing to live together for common good?

    Now in *families,* suppose a beleeving *Christian Husband* hath an unbeleeving *Antichristian wife,* what other charge in this respect is given to an *husband,* 1 *Cor.* 7. but to dwell with her as an husband if she be pleased to dwell with him: but, to bee so farre from forcing her from her conscience unto his, as that if for his conscience sake she would depart, he was not to force her to tarry with him, 1 *Cor.* 7. Consequently the *Father* or *Husband* of the State differing from the *Commonweale* in *Religion,* ought not to force the *Commonweale,* nor to be forced by it: yet is he to continue a *civill husbands* care, if the *Commonweale* will live with him, and abide in *civill covenant.*

    Now as a *husband* by his *love* to the *truth* and holy *conversation* in it, and seasonable *exhortations,* ought to indeavour to save his wife, yet abhorring to use *corporall compulsion* (yea, in this case to *childe* or *servant*) so ought the *Father, Husband, Governor* of the *Commonweale* endeavour to win and save whom possibly he may, yet farre from the appearance of *civill violence.*

If the   Sixthly, if the *Romane Emperours* were charged by
charge of Christ with his *Worship* in their dominion, and their
Gods wor- dominion was over the *world* (as was the *dominion* of
*ship was
left with* the *Grecian, Persian,* and *Babylonian Monarchy* before
the Ro- them) who sees not if the whole world bee forced

to turne *Chriſtian* (as afterward and ſince it hath pre-tended to doe) who ſees not then that the world (for whom Chriſt Jeſus would not pray) and the *God* of it, are reconciled to *Jeſus Chriſt,* and the whole *field* of the *world* become his incloſed *garden?*

mane Emperour, then was he bound to turne the whole world into the Garden, Flock and Spouſe of Chriſt. Millions put to death.

Seventhly, if the *Romane Emperors* ought to have been by *Chriſts* appointment *Keepers* of both *Tables, Antitypes* of *Iſrael* and *Judahs Kings,* how many *millions* of *Idolaters* and *Blaſphemers* againſt *Chriſt Jeſus* and his worſhip ought they to have put to death according to Iſraels patterne?

Laſtly, I aske (if the *Lord Jeſus* had delivered his *Sheepe* and *Children* to theſe *Wolves,* his *Wife* and *Spouſe* to ſuch *Adulterers,* his precious *Jewels* to ſuch great *Theeves* and *Robbers* of the *world* as the *Romane Emperours* were, what is the *reaſon* that he was never pleaſed [133] to ſend any of his *ſervants* to their *gates* to crave their *helpe* & *aſſiſtance* in this his worke, to put them in minde of their office, to chalenge and claime ſuch a ſervice from them according to their office, as it pleaſed God alwayes to ſend to the Kings of Iſrael and Judah in the like caſe?

Chriſt never ſent any of his Miniſters or Servants to the Civill Magiſtrate for help in ſpirituall matters.

Peace. Some will here object *Pauls* appealing to *Cæſar.*

Truth. And I muſt refer them to what I formerly anſwered to that Objection. *Paul* never appealed to *Cæſar* as a Judge appointed by Chriſt Jeſus to give definitive ſentence in any ſpirituall or Church controverſie, but againſt that civill *violence* and *murther* which the *Jewes* intended againſt him, *Paul* juſtly appealed: For otherwiſe if in a *ſpirituall cauſe* he ſhould have appealed, he ſhould have overthrowne his owne *Apoſtleſhip* and *Power* given him by *Chriſt Jeſus* in *ſpirituall* things, above the higheſt *Kings* or *Emperors* of the world beſide.

CHAP. XC.

Peace. BLeſſed *Truth*, I ſhall now remember you of the fourth Quærie upon this place of *Timothy*, to wit, whether a Church of *Chriſt Ieſus* may not live in *Gods worſhip* and comelineſſe, notwithſtanding that the *civill Magiſtrate* profeſſe not the ſame but a contrary *Religion* and *Worſhip* in his owne perſon and the Country with him.

<small>Chriſt Jeſus hath left power in his Church to preſerve her ſelfe pure, though in an idolatrous Countrey.</small> *Truth.* I anſwer the Churches of *Chriſt* under the *Roman Emperours* did live in all *godlineſſe* and *chriſtian* gravity, as appeares by all their holy and glorious practices, which the Scripture abundantly teſtifies.

Secondly, this flowes from an *inſtitution* or *appointment* of ſuch a *power* and *authority*, left by the Lord *Ieſus* to his *Apoſtles* and *Churches*, that no ungodlineſſe or diſhoneſty in the firſt appearance of it was to be ſuffered, but ſuppreſt and caſt out from the *Churches of Chriſt*, even the little Leaven of doctrine or practice, 1 *Corinth.* 5. *Gal.* 5.

Laſtly, I adde, that although ſometimes it pleaſeth the *Lord* to vouchſafe his *ſervants peace* and *quietneſſe*, and to command them here in *Timothy* to pray for it, for thoſe good ends and purpoſes for which *God* hath appointed *civill Magiſtracy* in the *world*, to keepe the *world* in *peace* and *quietneſſe*.[;] Yet *Gods* <small>Gods people have</small> people have uſed moſt to [134] abound with *godlineſſe* and *honeſty*, when they have enjoyed leaſt *peace* and *quietneſſe*. Then like thoſe *ſpices*, Cant. 4. *Myrrhe*, *Frankincenſe*, *Saffron*, *Calamus*, &c. they have yeelded the ſweeteſt favour to *God* and man, when they were pounded and burnt in cruell *perſecution* of the *Romane Cenſors*: then are they (as *Gods Veniſon*) moſt ſweet when moſt hunted: *Gods* Stars ſhining brighteſt in the darkeſt night: more heavenly in *converſation*, more *mortified*: more abounding in *love* each to other, more longing to be with *God*: when the *inhoſpitable* and *ſalvage World* have uſed them like *ſtrangers*, and forced them to haſten home to another Country which they profeſſe to ſeeke.

uſed to ſhine in brighteſt godlineſſe when they have enjoyed leaſt quietnes.

CHAP. XCI.

Peace. Deare *Truth*, it ſeemes not to be unſeaſonable to cloſe up this *paſſage* with a ſhort deſcant upon that *Aſſertion*, viz. "A *ſubject* without "*godlineſſe* will not be *bonus vir*, a good man, nor a "*Magiſtrate* except he ſee *godlineſſe* preſerved, will "not be *bonus Magiſtratus*.

Truth. I confeſſe that without *godlineſſe* or a true *worſhipping* of God with an upright heart according to *Gods Ordinances*, neither *Subjects* nor *Magiſtrates* can pleaſe *God* in *Chriſt Ieſus*, and ſo be ſpiritually or *chriſtianly good*, which few *Magiſtrates* and few men either come to, or are ordained unto: *God* having choſen a little *flock* out of the world, and thoſe generally poore and meane, 1 *Cor.* 1. *Iam.* 2. Yet this I muſt remember you of, that when the moſt *High God* created *all things* of *nothing*, he ſaw and acknowledged divers ſorts of *goodneſſe*, which muſt ſtill be

Few Magiſtrates, few men ſpiritually and chriſtianly good.

Yet divers sorts of goodnesse naturall, artificiall, civill, &c.

acknowledged in their diſtinct kindes: a good *Ayre*, a good *Ground*, a good *Tree*, a good *Sheepe*, &c.

I ſay the ſame in Artificialls, a good *Garment*, a good *Houſe*, a good *Sword*, a good *Ship*.

I alſo adde a good *City*, a good *Company* or *Corporation*, a good *Huſband, Father, Maſter*.

Hence alſo we ſay, a good *Phyſitian*, a good *Lawyer*, a good *Sea-man*, a good *Merchant*, a good *Pilot*, for ſuch or ſuch a *ſhoare* or *Harbour*, that is, Morally, Civilly good in their ſeverall *Civill reſpects* and imployments.

Hence (*Pſal.* 133.[122]) the *Church* or Citie of *God* is compared to [135] a *Citie* compact within it ſelfe; which compactnes may be found in many *Townes* and *Cities* of the *World*, where yet hath not ſhined any ſpirituall or ſupernaturall *goodneſſe*. Hence the Lord *Jeſus* (*Matth.* 12.) deſcribes an ill ſtate of an *houſe* or *kingdome*, viz. to be divided againſt it ſelfe, which cannot ſtand.

The Civill Goodnes of Cities, Kingdomes, Subjects, Magiſtrates, muſt be owned, although Spirituall goodnes (proper to the Chriſtian State or Church) be wanting.

Theſe I obſerve to prove, that a *Subject*, a *Magiſtrate*, may be a good *Subject*, a good *Magiſtrate*, in reſpect of *civill* or *morall goodnes*, which thouſands want, and where it is, it is commendable and beautifull, though *Godlines* which is infinitely more beautifull, be wanting, and which is onely proper to the *Chriſtian ſtate*, the *Commonweale* of *Iſrael*, the true *Church*, the holy *Nation*, Epheſ. 2. 1 Pet. 2.

Laſtly, however the *Authors* deny that there can be *Bonus Magiſtratus*, a good Magiſtrate, except he ſee all *Godlines* preſerved; yet themſelves confeſſe that *civill honeſty* is ſufficient to make a good *Subject*, in theſe words, viz. He muſt ſee that *Honeſtie* be preserved within his *jurisdiction*, else the *Subject* will not be *Bonus cives*, a good *citizen* : and doubtlesse (if the *Law* of *Relations* hold true) that *civill* honestie which makes a good *citizen*, must also (together with qualifications fit for a Commander) make also a good *Magistrate*.

CHAP. XCII.

Peace. THe 4. head is, The proper meanes of both these Powers to attaine their ends.

" First, the proper meanes whereby the Civill
" Power may and should attaine its end, are onely
" Politicall, and principally these Five.

" First the erecting and establishing what forme of
" Civill Government may seeme in wisedome most
" meet, according to generall rules of the Word, and
" state of the people.

" Secondly, the making, publishing, and establish-
" ing of wholesome Civill Lawes, not onely such as
" concerne Civill Justice, but also the free passage of
" true Religion: for, outward Civill Peace ariseth
" and is maintained from them both, from the latter
" as well as from the former:

" Civill peace cannot stand intire, where Religion
" is corrupted, 2 *Chron.* 15. 3. 5. 6. *Judg.* 8. And yet
" such Lawes, though conversant [136] about Relig-
" ion, may still be counted Civill Lawes, as on the
" contrary, an Oath doth still remaine Religious,
" though conversant about Civill matters.

" Thirdly, Election and appointment of Civill offi-
" cers, to see execution of those Lawes.

"Fourthly, Civill Punifhments and Rewards, of
"Tranfgreffors and Obfervers of thefe Lawes.
"Fifthly, taking up Armes againft the Enemies of
"Civill Peace.

"Secondly, the meanes whereby the Church may
"and fhould attaine her ends, are only ecclefiafticall,
"which are chiefly five.
"Firft, fetting up that forme of Church Govern-
"ment only, of which Chrift hath given them a pat-
"tern in his Word.
"Secondly, acknowledging and admitting of no
"Lawgiver in the Church, but Chrift, and the pub-
"lifhing of his Lawes.
"Thirdly, Electing and ordaining of fuch officers
"onely, as Chrift hath appointed in his Word.
"Fourthly, to receive into their fellowfhip them
"that are approved, and inflicting Spirituall cenfures
"againft them that offend.
"Fifthly, Prayer and patience in fuffering any evill
"from them that be without, who difturbe their
"peace.
"So that Magiftrates, as Magiftrates, have no power
"of fetting up the Forme of Church Government,
"electing Church officers, punifhing with Church
"cenfures, but to fee that the Church doth her duty
"herein. And on the other fide, the Churches as
"Churches, have no power (though as members of
"the Commonweale they may have power) of erect-
"ing or altering formes of Civill Government, elect-
"ing of Civill officers, inflicting Civill punifhments
"(no not on perfons excommunicate) as by depofing

" Magiſtrates from their Civill Authoritie, or with-
" drawing the hearts of the people againſt them, to
" their Lawes, no more then to diſcharge wives, or
" children, or ſervants, from due obedience to their
" husbands, parents, or maſters: or by taking up
" armes againſt their Magiſtrates, though he perſe-
" cute them for Conſcience: for though members of
" Churches who are publique officers alſo of the Civill
" State, may ſuppreſſe by force the violence of Uſur-
" pers, as *Iehoiada* did *Athaliah*, yet this they doe not
" as members of the Church, but as officers of the
" Civill State.

137] *Truth.* Here are divers conſiderable *paſſages* which I ſhall briefly examine, ſo far as concernes our *controverſie.*

Firſt, whereas they ſay, that the *Civill Power* may erect and eſtabliſh what *forme* of *civill Government* may ſeeme in *wiſedome* moſt meet, I acknowledge the *propoſition* to be moſt true, both in it ſelf, and alſo conſidered with the end of it, that a *civill Government* is an *Ordinance* of *God*, to conſerve the *civill peace* of people, ſo farre as concernes their *Bodies* and *Goods*, as formerly hath beene ſaid.

But from this *Grant* I infer, (as before hath been touched) that the *Soveraigne, originall,* and *foundation* of *civill power* lies in the *people*, (whom they muſt needs meane by the *civill power* diſtinct from the Government ſet up.) And if ſo, that a People may erect and eſtabliſh what *forme* of *Government* ſeemes to them moſt meete for their *civill condition:* It is evident that ſuch *Governments* as are by them erected and eſtabliſhed, have no more *power,* nor for no longer

Civill power originally and fundamentally in the people.

time, then the *civill power* or people confenting and agreeing fhall betruft them with. This is cleere not only in *Reafon,* but in the experience of all *common-weales,* where the people are not deprived of their *naturall freedome* by the power of *Tyrants.*

<small>Mr. Cotton and the New-Englifh Minifters give the Government of Chrifts Church or Spoufe into the hands of the people or Commonweale.</small>

And if fo, that the Magiftrates receive their power of governing the Church, from the People; undeniably it followes, that a *people,* as a *people,* naturally confidered (of what *Nature* or *Nation* foever in *Europe, Afia, Africa* or *America*) have fundamentally and originally, as men, a power to governe the *Church,* to fee her doe her *duty,* to correct her, to redreffe, reforme, eftablifh, &c. And if this be not to pull *God* and *Chrift,* and *Spirit* out of *Heaven,* and fubject them unto *naturall,* finfull, inconftant men, and fo confequently to *Sathan* himfelfe, by whom all *peoples* naturally are guided, let *Heaven* and *Earth* judge.

<small>The very Indian Americans made Governours of the Church by the Authors of thefe Pofitions.</small>

Peace. It cannot by their owne *Grant* be denied, but that the *wildeft Indians* in *America* ought (and in their kind and feverall degrees doe) to agree upon fome *formes* of *Government,* fome more *civill,* compact in Townes, &c. fome leffe. As alfo that their *civill* and *earthly Governments* be as lawfull and true as any *Governments* in the *World,* and therefore confequently their *Governors* are *Keepers* of the *Church* or both *Tables,* (if any Church of Chrift fhould arife or be amongft them :) and therefore laftly, (if *Chrift* have betrufted and charged the *civill* Power with his *Church*) they muft [138] judge according to their *Indian* or *American confciences,* for other *confciences* it cannot be fuppofed they fhould have.

CHAP. XCIII.

Truth. Againe, whereas they say that outward Civill peace cannot stand where *Religion* is corrupted; and quote for it, 2 *Chron.* 15. 3. 5. 6. & *Judges* 8.

I answer with *admiration* how such excellent *spirits* (as these *Authors* are furnished with, not only in heavenly but earthly affaires) should so forget, and be so fast asleep in things so palpably evident, as to say that outward *civill* peace cannot stand, where *Religion* is corrupt. When so many stately *Kingdomes* and *Governments* in the *World* have long and long enjoyed *civill* peace and quiet, notwithstanding their *Religion* is so corrupt, as that there is not the very Name of *Jesus Christ* amongst them: And this every *Historian, Merchant, Traveller,* in *Europe, Asia, Africa, America,* can testifie: for so spake the *Lord Jesus* himselfe, *Joh.* 16. The *world* shall sing and rejoyce.

Many Civill States in flourishing peace and quiet, where the Lord Jesus is not founded.

Secondly, for that Scripture 2 *Chron.* 15. 3. &c. relating the miseries of *Israel* and *Judah,* and *Gods* plagues upon that people for corruption of their *Religion,* it must still have reference to that peculiar state unto which *God* called the seed of one man, *Abraham,* in a *figure,* dealing so with them as he dealt not with any Nation in the World, *Psal.* 146. *Rom.* 9.

The *Antitype* to this State I have proved to be the *Christian Church,* which consequently hath been and is afflicted with spirituall *plagues, desolations* and *captivities,* for corrupting of that *Religion* which hath been revealed unto them. This appeares by the 7

Churches, and the people of *God*, now so many hundred yeares in wofull *bondage* and slaverie to the mysticall *Babel*, untill the time of their joyfull *deliverance*.

Peace. Yea but they say that such *Lawes* as are conversant about *Religion*, may still be accounted *Civill Lawes*, as on the contrary an Oath doth still remaine *Religious*, though conversant about *Civill* matters.

Truth. Lawes respecting *Religion* are two-fold:

First, such as concerne the *acts* of *Worship* and the *Worship* it self, the *Ministers* of it, their *fitnes* or *unfitnes*, to be suppressed or [139] established: and for such Lawes we find no footing in the New *Testament* of Jesus Christ.

Secondly, *Lawes* respecting *Religion* may be such as meerly concerne the *Civill State*, *Bodies* and *Goods* of such and such persons, professing these and these *Religions*, viz. that such and such persons, notorious for *Mutinies*, *Treasons*, *Rebellions*, *Massacres*, be disarmed: Againe, that no persons *Papists*, *Jewes*, *Turkes*, or *Indians* be disturbed at their *worship*, (a thing which the very *Indians* abhor to practice toward any.) Also that *imanitie* and *freedome* from *Tax* and *Toll* may be granted unto the people of such or such a *Religion*, as the *Magistrate* pleaseth, *Ezra* 7.

These and such as are of this nature, concerning only the *bodies* and *goods* of such and such *Religious persons*, I confesse are meerely Civill.

But now on the other hand, that *Lawes* restraining persons from such and such a *Worship*, because the *Civill state* judgeth it to be false:

That *Laws* constraining to such & such a *worship*,

<small>Lawes concerning Religion, either Religious,

or Civill.

The very Indians abhor to disturbe any Conscience at Worship.</small>

because the *Civill State* judgeth this to be the only true way of worshipping *God*:

That such and such a *Reformation* of *Worship* be submitted unto by all Subjects in such a *Iurisdiction*: *Canons and Constitutions*

That such and such *Churches, Ministers, Ministries* be pull'd downe, and such and such *Churches, Ministries*, and *Ministrations* set up: *pretended Civill, but indeed Ecclesiasticall.*

That such *Lawes* properly concerning *Religion, God*, the *Soules* of men, should be *Civill Lawes* and *Constitutions*; is as far from *Reason*, as that the *Commandements* of *Paul*, which he gave the *Churches* concerning *Chrifts worship* (1 *Cor.* 11 & 1 *Cor.* 14.) were *Civill* and *Earthly constitutions*: Or that the *Canons* and *Constitutions* of either *œcumenicall* or *Nationall* Synods concerning *Religion*, should be *Civill* and *State-conclusions* and agreements.

To that instance of an *Oath* remaining *religious* though conversant about *civill things*; I answer and acknowledge, an *Oath* may be spirituall, though taken about earthly *businesse*, and accordingly it will prove, and onely prove what before I have said, that a *Law* may be civill though it concerne persons of this and of that *religion*, that is as the *persons* professing it are concerned in *civill respects* of *bodies* or *goods*, as I have opened; whereas if it concerne the soules and religions of men simply so considered in reference to *God*, it [140] must of necessity put on the nature of a *religious* or *spirituall ordinance* or *constitution*. *Laws meerely concerning spirituall things must needs be spirituall.*

Beside, it is a most improper and fallacious instance[;] for an *oath*, being an *invocation* of a true or false *God* to judge in a case, is an action of a *spirituall* and *religious nature*, what ever the *subject* matter be about which it is taken, whether *civill* or *religious*: but a *law* or *constitution* may be *civill* or *religious*, as the *subject* about which it is *conversant* is, either *civill* (meerly concerning *bodies* or *goods*) or *religious* concerning *soule* and *worship*.

CHAP. XCIV.

Peace. THeir fifth Head is concerning the Magistrates power in making of Lawes.

" First, they have power to publish and apply such
" Civill Lawes in a State as either are exprest in the
" Word of God in *Moses* Judicialls (to wit, so far as
" they are of generall and morall equity, and so bind-
" ing all Nations in all Ages) to bee deducted by way
" of generall consequence and proportion from the
" word of God.

" For in a free State no Magistrate hath power
" over the bodies, goods, lands, liberties of a free peo-
" ple, but by their free consents. And because free
" men are not free Lords of their owne estates, but
" are onely stewards under God, therefore they may
" not give their free consents to any Magistrate to
" dispose of their bodies, goods, lands, liberties at
" large as themselves please, but as God (the sove-
" raigne Lord of all) alone. And because the Word
" is a perfect rule as wel of righteousnes as of holines,
" it will be therfore necessary that neither the people
" give consent, nor that the Magistrate take power to
" dispose of the bodies, goods, lands, liberties of the
" people, but according to the Lawes and Rules of
" the Word of God.

"Secondly, in making Lawes about civill and indif-
"ferent things about the Commonweale.

"Firſt, he hath no power given him of God to
"make what laws he pleaſe, either in reſtraining
"from, or conſtraining to the uſe of indifferent things,
"becauſe that which is indifferent in its nature, may
"may ſometimes bee inexpedient in its uſe, and con-
"ſequently unlawfull, 1 *Cor.* 2. 5. it having been long
"ſince defended upon good ground, *Quicquid non
"expedit, quatenus non expedit, non licet*.

141] "Secondly, he hath no power to make any ſuch
"Lawes about indifferent things, wherein nothing
"good or evill is ſhewne to the people, but onely or
"principally the meere authority or wil of the impo-
"ſer for the obſervance of them, *Coloſ.* 2. 21, 22. 1
"*Cor.* 7. 23, compared with *Epheſ.* 6. 6.

"It is a prerogative proper to God to require obe-
"dience of the ſonnes of men, becauſe of his author-
"ity and will.

"The will of no man is *Regula recti*, unleſſe firſt
"it bee *Regula recta*.

"It is an evill ſpeech of ſome, that in ſome things
"the will of the Law, not the *ratio* of it, muſt be the
"Rule of Conſcience to walke by ; and that Princes
"may forbid men to ſeeke any other reaſon but their
"authority, yea when they command *frivola & dura*.
"And therefore it is the duty of the Magiſtrate in
"all lawes about indifferent things, to ſhew the Rea-
"ſons, not onely the Will, to ſhew the expediency,
"as well as the indifferency of things of that nature.

"For we conceive in Lawes of this nature, it is
"not the will of the Lawgiver onely, but the Reaſon

"of the Law which bindes. *Ratio est Rex Legis, &*
"*Lex est Rex Regis.*

"Thirdly, becaufe the judgement of expedient and
"inexpedient things is often difficult and diverfe, it
"is meet that fuch Lawes fhould not proceed with-
"out due confideration of the Rules of Expediency
"fet downe in the Word, which are thefe three:

"Firft, the rule of Piety, that they may make for
"the glory of God, 1 *Cor.* 10. 31.

"Secondly, the rule of Charity, that no fcandall
"come hereby to any weake brother, 1 *Cor.* 8. 13.

"Thirdly, the Rule of Charity, that no man be
"forced to fubmit againft his *confcience, Rom.* 14. 14.
"23. nor be judged of contempt of lawfull *Authority*,
"becaufe he is not fuddenly perfwaded of the *expedi-*
"*ency* of indifferent things; for if the people be bound
"by *God* to receive fuch Lawes about fuch things,
"without any triall or fatisfaction to the *confcience*,
"but muft judge them *expedient*, becaufe the *Magif-*
"*trate* thinkes them fo, then the one cannot be pun-
"ifhed in following the other, in cafe he fhall finne
"in calling *Inexpedient Expedient*; but *Chrift* faith
"the contrary, If the *blinde* lead the *blinde*, they fhall
"both fall.

142] *Truth.* In this paffage thefe worthy Men lay downe fuch a *ground*, as the *gates* of *Hell* are not able to fhake concerning the *Magiftrates* walking in indifferent things: And upon which *ground* that *Towre* of *Lebanon* may be raifed whereon there hang a thoufand *fhields* and *bucklars, Cant.* 4. to wit, that invincible *Truth*, That no man is to be *perfecuted* for caufe of *confcience:* The ground is this: The *Mag-*

<small>The Authors large confeffion of the liberty of confcience from the Laws of</small>

iſtrate hath not *power* to make what *Lawes* he pleaſe, either in *reſtraining* or *conſtraining* to the uſe of indifferent things: And further he confeſſeth that the *reaſon* of the *Law*, not the *will* of it muſt be the rule of conſcience. And they adde this impregnable reaſon: viz. " If the people be bound to receive ſuch " Lawes without ſatisfaction to conſcience, then one " cannot be puniſhed for following the other, in caſe " he ſhall ſinne contrary to Chriſt Jeſus, who ſaith, " If the blinde lead the blinde, they ſhall both fall.

<small>Civill authority in ſpirituall caſes.</small>

Hence I argue, If the *Civill Magiſtrate* have no power to *reſtraine* or *conſtraine* their *ſubjects* in things in their owne nature indifferent, as in eating of *meats*, wearing this or that *garment*, uſing this or that *geſture*, but that they are bound to try and examine his *commands*, and ſatisfie their owne *reaſon*, *conſcience* and *judgement* before the *Lord*, and that they ſhall ſinne, if they follow the *Magiſtrates* command, not being perſwaded in their owne ſoule and conſcience that his commands are according to *God!*[:] It will be much more unlawfull and heynous in the *Magiſtrate* to compell the ſubjects unto that which (according to their *conſciences* perſwaſion) is ſimply unlawfull as unto a falſely conſtituted *Church*, *Miniſtry*, *Worſhip*, *Adminiſtration*, and they ſhall not eſcape the Ditch, by being led blindefold by the Magiſtrate, but though hee fall in firſt, yet they ſhall [fall] in after him, and upon him, to his greater and more dreadfull judgement.

<small>Civill Magiſtrates confeſſed not to have power to urge the conſcience in indifferent things.</small>

In particular thus, If the Magiſtrate may reſtraine me from that geſture in the Supper of the Lord, which I am perſwaded I ought to practice, he may alſo reſtraine me by his commands from that Supper of the Lord it felfe in fuch or fuch a Church according to my confcience.

If he cannot (as they grant) conftraine me to fuch or fuch a garment in the worfhip of God, can he conftraine me to worfhip God by fuch a Miniftry, and with fuch worfhip, which my foule and confcience cannot be perfwaded is of God?

143] If he cannot command me in that circumftance of time to worfhip God this or that day, can he command mee to the worfhip it felfe?

<small>A threefold guilt lying upon Civill powers commanding the fubjects foule in worfhip.</small>

Peace. Me thinkes I difcerne a threefold guilt to lye upon fuch Civill powers as impofe upon and inforce the confcience, though not unto the miniftration and participation of the Seales,[1] yet either to depart from that worfhip which it is perfwaded of, or to any exercife or worfhip which it hath not faith in.

Firft, of an appearance of that Arminian Popifh doctrine of Freewill, as if it lay in their owne power and ability to beleeve upon the Magiftrates command fince it is confeffed that what is fubmitted to by any without faith it is finne, be it never fo true and holy, *Rom.* 14.

Secondly, fince God only openeth the heart and worketh the will, *Phil.* 2. it feemes to be an high prefumption to fuppofe that together with a command reftraining from, or conftraining to worfhip, that God is alfo to be forced or commanded to give faith to open the heart to incline the will, &c.

Thirdly, A guilt of the hypocrifie of their fubjects and people in forcing them to act and practice in matters of Religion and Worfhip againft the doubts and checks of their confciences, caufing their bodies

[1] Sacraments.

to worship, when their soules are far off, to draw near with their lips, their hearts being far off, &c.

With lesse sinne ten thousand fold may a naturall Father force his daughter, or the Father of the Commonweale force all the maydens in a Country to the marriage beds of such and such men whom they cannot love, then the soules of these and other subjects to such worship or Ministry, which is either a true or false, because *Cant.* 1. 16.

Truth. Sweet *Peace*, your conclusions are undeniable, and O that they might sinke deep into those Noble and Honourable Bosomes it so deeply concernes! but proceed.

Persons may with lesse sin be forced to marry whom they cannot love, then to worship where they cannot beleeve.

CHAP. XCV.

Peace. IN that fifth head they further say thus:
" "Thirdly, in matters Ecclesiasticall we
" beleeve, first, That Civill Magistrates have no power
" to make or constitute Lawes about Church affaires
" which the Lord Jesus hath not [144] ordained in
" his Word for the well ordering of the Church; for
" the Apostle solemnely chargeth *Timothy*, and in
" him all Goverours of the Church, before God and
" and the Lord Jesus Christ (who is the only Poten-
" tate, the King of Kings, and Lord of Lords) that
" the Commandement given by him for the ordering
" of the Church be kept without spot unrebukeable
" to the appearing of the Lord Jesus Christ, 1 *Tim.*
" 6. 14. 15. And this Commandement given in the
" Word, the Apostle saith is able to make the man
" of God perfect in all Righteousnesse, 2 *Tim.* 3. 17.

"And indeed the adminiſtration of all Chriſts affaires
"doth immediately aime at ſpirituall and divine ends
"(as the worſhip of God and the ſalvation of mens
"ſoules:) and therefore no Law nor meanes can be
"deviſed by the wiſdome or wit of man that can be
"fit or able to reach ſuch ends, but uſe muſt be made
"of ſuch onely as the divine Wiſdome and holy Will
"of God hath ordained.

"Secondly, We beleeve the Magiſtrates power in
"making Lawes about Church affaires, is not only
"thus limited and reſtrained by Chriſt to matters
"which concerne the ſubſtance of Gods worſhip and
"of Church government, but alſo ſuch as concerne
"outward order, as in Rites and Ceremonies for uni-
"formities ſake: For we finde not in the Goſpell
"that Chriſt hath any where provided for the uni-
"formity of Churches, but onely for their unity.

"*Paul* in matters of Chriſtian libertie commendeth
"the unity of their Faith in the holy Spirit, giving
"order that wee ſhould not judge nor condemne one
"another in difference of judgement and practice of
"ſuch things where men live to God on both ſides,
"even though there were ſome errour on one ſide,
"*Rom.* 14. to the 6. How much leſſe in things indif-
"ferent, where there may be no errour on either ſide.

"When the Apoſtle directeth the Church of
"Corinth that all things be done decently and in
"order, he meant not to give power to Church Offi-
"cers, or to Civill Magiſtrates to order what ever
"they ſhould thinke meet for decencie and order;
"but only to provide that all the Ordinances of God
"be adminiſtred in the Church decently without

"unnaturall or uncivill uncomelinesse (as that of long
"haire, or womens prophesying, or the like) and
"orderly without confusion or disturbance of edifi-
"cation, as the speaking of many at once in the
"Church.

145] "Thirdly, we doe neverthelesse willingly grant
"that Magistrates upon due and diligent search what
"is the counsell and will of God in his Word con-
"cerning the right ordering of the Church, may and
"ought to publish and declare, establish and ratifie
"such Lawes and Ordinances as Christ hath appointed
"in his Word for the well ordering of Church
"affaires, both for the gathering of the Church, and
"the right admistration of all the Ordinances of God
"amongst them in such a manner as the Lord hath
"appointed to edification. The Law of *Artaxerxes*,
"*Ezra* 7. 23. was not usurpation over the Churches
"liberty, but a Royall and just confirmation of them:
"Whatsoever is commanded by the God of Heaven:
"For why should there be wrath against the King
"and his Sonnes?

Truth. Deare *Peace*, me thinkes I see before mine eyes a *wall* daubed up (of which *Ezekiel* speakes) with untempered *morter:* Here they restraine the *Magistrate* from making *Lawes* either concerning the substance or *ceremony* of *Religion,* but such only as *Christ* hath commanded, and those, say they, they must publish and declare after the example of *Arta-xerxes.*

I shall herein performe two things: First, examine this *Magistrates* duty to publish, declare, &c. such Laws and Ordinances as *Christ* hath appointed.

262   *The Bloudy Tenent.*

Secondly, I shall examine that proofe from *Artaxerxes, Ezra* 7. 23.

<small>Gods Israel desirous of Sauls arme of flesh.</small>

In the first, me thinks I heare the voice of the people of *Israel*, 1 *Sam.* 8. 5. Make us a *King* that may rule over us after the manner of the *Nations*, rejecting the *Lord* ruling over them by his holy Word in the mouth of his *Prophets*, and sheltring themselves under an Arme of *Flesh*; which Arme of *Flesh God* gave them in His *Anger*, and cut off againe in His *Wrath*, after he had persecuted *David* the figure of *Christ Jesus* who hath given his people the *Scepter* and *Sword* of his *Word* and *Spirit*, and refused a temporall *Crowne* or *Weapons* in the dispensation of his *Kingdome*.

Where did the Lord Jesus or his Messengers charge the Civill Magistrate, or direct Christians to petition him, to publish, declare or establish by his Arme of Flesh and Earthly weapons the Religion and worship of Christ Jesus?

I finde the Beast and false Prophet (whose rise and doctrine is not from Heaven, but from the Sea and Earth) dreadfull and terrible [146] by a Civill Sword and dignitie, *Rev.* 13. 2.

<small>The 7 headed Beast, and the Lambe differ in their weapons.</small>

I find the Beast hath gotten the power and might of the Kings of the Earth, *Revel.* 17. 13.

But the Lambes weapons are Spiritually mighty, 2 *Cor.* 10. &c. his Sword is two-edged comming out of his *mouth*, Revel. 1. His *preparations* for *War* are *white Horses* and *white Harnesse*, which are confest by all to be of a *spirituall nature*, Revel. 19.

<small>Naboths case typicall.</small>

When that *whore Jesabel* stabbed *Naboth* with her Pen, in stirring up the people to stone him as a *Blas-*

phemer of *God* and the *King,* what a glorious maske or vaile of *Holines* put fhe on? Proclaime a *Faſt,* fet a day apart for *humiliation*; and for *confirmation,* let all be ratified with the *Kings* Authoritie, Name, and Seale, 1 *Kings,* 21. 8.

Was not this recorded for all *Gods Naboths,* ſtanding for their Spirituall interefts in heavenly things (typed out by the typicall earth and ground of *Canaans* land) that they through patience and Comfort of the Scriptures might have hope, *Rom.* 15. 4.?

Againe, I demand who fhall here fit Judge, whether the Magiſtrate command any other Subſtance or Ceremonie but what is Chriſts?

By their former Concluſions, every Soule muſt judge what the Magiſtrate commandeth, and is not bound, even in indifferent things, to the Magiſtrates Law, further then his own Soule, Confcience and judgement afcends to the Reafon of it: Here the Magiſtrate muſt make Lawes for that Subſtance and Ceremony which Chriſt appointed: But yet he muſt not doe this with his eyes open, but blindfold and hoodwinkt; for if he judge that to be the *Religion* of *Chriſt,* and fuch to be the order there in which their *Confciences* judge otherwife, and aſſent not to, they profeſſe they muſt fubmit only to *Chriſts lawes,* and therefore they are not bound to obey him.

Oh what is this but to make ufe of the *Civill Powers* and *Governours* of the *World,* as a *Guard* about the Spirituall *Bed* of Soule-whoredomes, in which the *Kings* of the *Earth* commit Spirituall *fornication* with the great *Whore,* Rev. 17. 2.? as a Guard while the Inhabitants of the Earth are drink-

[margin:] Civill Powers abufed as a Guard about the Bed of Spirituall

whore-domes. ing themselves drunke with the wine of her fornication.

But oh what terrifyings, what allurings are in *Jeremies* Curse and Blessing! *Jer.* 17. Cursed is the man that trusteth in man, that maketh [147] Flesh his Arme (too too common in spirituall matters) and whose heart departeth from Jehovah: He shall be as an Heath in the Wildernes (even in the spirituall and mysticall wildernes) and shall not see when comfort comes) but shall abide in drouth in the wildernesse in a barren land, &c.

CHAP. XCVI.

Peace. O What mysteries are these to Flesh and Blood! how hard for flesh to forsake the Arme thereof! But passe on (deare *Truth*) to their proofe propounded, *Ezra* 7. 23. wherein *Artaxerxes* confirmed by Law what ever was commanded by the *God* of Heaven.

Ezra 7.23. discussed. *Truth.* In this Scripture I mind first the people of God captivated under the *dominion* and government of the *Kings* of *Babel* and *Persia*.

Secondly, *Artaxerxes* his favour to these Captives,
1. Of *freedome* to their *Consciences*.
2. Of *bountie* towards them.
3. Of exempting of some of them from common charges.

Thirdly, *Punishments* on offenders.

Fourthly, the *ground* that caries him on to all this.

Fifthly, *Ezra* praising of *God* for putting this into the heart of the *King*.

Concerning the people of *God* the *Jewes*, they were as *Lambes* and *Sheep* in the jawes of the *Lyon*, the dearely beloved of his Soule under the devouring *Tyrants* of the World, both the *Babylonian* and the *Persian*, farre from their owne *Nation*, and the Government of their own anointed *Kings*, the *figures* of the true *King* of the *Jewes* the Lord *Jesus Christ*.

_{Gods people not subject to the Kings of Babell of Persia in Spirituals.}

In this respect it is cleere, that the *Iewes* were no more subject to the *Kings* of *Babylon* and *Persia* in Spirituall things, then the *Vessels* of the *Sanctuary* were subject to the *King* of *Babels* use, *Dan.* 5.

Concerning this *King* I consider, first his person, a *Gentile Idolater*, an oppressing *Tyrant*, one of those devouring *Beasts*, Dan. 7. & 8. An hand of bloody *Conquest* set the Crown upon the head of these *Monarchs*; and although in *Civill* things they might challenge subjection, yet why should they now sit down in the throne [148] of *Israel*, and governe the people and *Church* of *God* in Spirituall things?

Secondly, consider his acts of Favour, and they will not amount to a positive Command, that any of the *Iewes* should goe up to build the *Temple*, nor that any of them should practice his own *worship*, which he kept and judged the best for his owne Soule and People.

_{Tyrants hearts sometimes wonderfully mollified towards Gods people.}

'Tis true, he freely permits them, and exerciseth a bounteous *assistance* to them: All which argues no more, but that sometimes it pleaseth *God* to open the hearts of *Tyrants* greatly to favour and further his people. Such favour found *Nehemiah*, and *Daniel*, and others of *Gods* people have and shall finde, so often as it pleaseth Him to honour them that honour Him, before the Sonnes of Men.

Peace. Who sees not how little this Scripture contributes to their *Tenent?* but why (say some) should this *King* confirme all with such severe punishments? and why for all this should *Ezra* give thankes to *God,* if it were not imitable for aftertimes?

Truth. The Law of *God* which he confirmed, he knew not, and therefore neither was, nor could he be a Judge in the Case.

And for his Ground, what was it but the common *terrours* and *convictions* of an affrighted Conscience?

<small>Nabuchadnezzar, Darius, and Artaxerxes their decrees examined.</small>
In such fits and *pangs,* what have not *Pharaohs, Sauls, Ahabs, Herods, Agrippa's* spoken? and what wonderfull decrees have *Nabuchadnezzar, Cyrus, Darius, Artaxerxes* put forth concerning the *God* of *Israel,* Dan. 3. & 6. & Ezra 1. & 7. &c. and yet as farre from being charged with (as they were from being affected to) the Spirituall Crown of Governing the Worship of God, and the Conscience of his people.

Tis true, *Ezra* most piously and justly gave thankes to God for putting such a thing into the heart of the King: But what makes this pattern for the Laws of Civill Governours now under the Gospell? It suited well with that Nationall state of Gods Church, that the Gentile King should release them, permit them to returne to their own Land, assist them with other favours, and enable them to execute punishments upon offenders according to their Nationall State.

<small>Ezra's thanksgiving for the Kings decree examined.</small>

149] But did God put such a thing as this into the heart of the King, viz. to restraine upon paine of Death all the millions of men under his Dominion from the Idolatries of their severall and respective

Countries? to conſtraine them all upon the like pen-
altie to conforme to the Worſhip of the God of Iſrael,
to build him a Temple, erect an Altar, ordaine Prieſts,
offer ſacrifice, obſerve the Faſts and Feaſts of Iſrael?
yea did God put it into the Kings heart to ſend
Levites into all the parts of his Dominion, compelling them to heare; which is but a naturall thing
(as ſome unſoundly ſpeake) unto which all are bound
to ſubmit?

Well however, *Ezra* gives thankes to God for the
King; and ſo ſhould all that feare God in all Coun- The duty of all Civill States to-ward the Conſciences of their Subjects.
tries, if he would pleaſe to put it into the hearts of
the Kings, States and Parliaments, to take off the
yoakes of Violence, and permit (at leaſt) the Conſciences of their Subjects, and eſpecially ſuch as in
truth make Conſcience of their Worſhips to the God
of Iſrael: and yet no cauſe for *Ezra* then, or Gods
Ezra's and Iſraelites now, to acknowledge the care
and charge of Gods worſhip, Church and Ordinances,
to lie upon the ſhoulders of *Artaxerxes*, or any other
Civill Prince or Ruler.

Laſtly for the Confirmation or Ratification which
they ſuppoſe Magiſtrates are bound to give to the Chriſt needs no humane confirmations.
Lawes of Chriſt, I anſwer, Gods cauſe, Chriſts Truth,
and the two-edged ſword of his Word, never ſtood
in need of a temporall Sword, or an humane Witnes
to confirme and ratifie them. If we receive the witneſſe of an honeſt man, the witneſſe of the moſt holy
God is greater, 1 *Iohn* 5.

The reſult and ſumme of the whole matter is this: 1. The ſum of the Ex-amples of Gentile
It may pleaſe *God* ſometimes to ſtir up the *Rulers* of
the Earth to permit and tolerate, to favour and coun-

Kings decreeing for Gods worship in Scripture. tenance *Gods* people in their *worſhips*, though only out of ſome ſtrong conviction of *conſcience* or *feare* of *wrath*, &c. and yet themſelves neither underſtand *Gods* worſhip, nor leave their owne ſtate, Idolatry or Country worſhip.

For this *Gods* people ought to give thankes unto *God*; yea and all men from this example may learne not to charge upon the *Magiſtrates* conſcience (beſides the care of the *Civill peace*, the bodies and goods of men) the Spirituall peace in the worſhip of *God* and *ſoules* of men: but hence are *Magiſtrates* inſtructed favourably to permit their ſubjects in their *worſhips*, although themſelves bee [150] not perſwaded to ſubmit to them, as *Nebuchadnezzar, Cyrus, Darius* and *Artaxerxes* did.

CHAP. XCVII.

Peace. THe ſixt queſtion is this: How far the *Church* is ſubject to their Lawes?

" All thoſe (ſay they) who are members of the
" Commonweale are bound to be ſubject to all the
" juſt and righteous Laws thereof, and therefore
" (memberſhip in Churches not cutting men off from
" memberſhip in commonweales) they are bound to
" be ſubject, even every ſoule, *Rom.* 13. 1. as Chriſt
" himſelfe and the Apoſtles were in their places
" wherein they lived, and therefore to exempt the
" Clergy (as the Papiſts do) from Civill ſubjection,
" and to ſay that *generatio Clerici*, is *corruptio ſubditi*,
" is both ſinfull and ſcandalous to the Goſpel of God;
" and though all are equally ſubject, yet Church

"members are more especially bound to yeeld subjec-
"tion, and the most eminent most especially bound,
"not only because conscience doth more strongly
"binde, but also because their ill examples are more
"infectious to others, pernicious to the State, and pro-
"voke Gods wrath to bring vengeance on the State.

"Hence if the whole Church or officers of the
"Church shall sin against the State or any person by
"sedition, contempt of Authority, heresie, blasphemy,
"oppression, slander, or shall withdraw any of their
"members from the service of the State without the
"consent thereof, their persons and estates are liable
"to Civill punishments of Magistrates according to
"their righteous and wholsome Lawes, *Exod.* 22. 20.
"*Levit.* 24. 16. *Deut.* 13. 5. & 18. 10.

Truth. What concernes this head in civill things, I gladly subscribe unto : what concernes heresie, blasphemy, &c. I have plentifully before spoken to, and shall here only say 2 things:

First, those Scriptures produced concerne only the people of God in a Church estate, and must have reference onely to the Church of Christ Jesus, which (as Mr. *Cotton* confesseth)[1] is not Nationall but Con-

---

[1] "The Church which Christ in his Gospell hath instituted, and to which he hath committed the keyes of his kingdom, the power of binding and loosing, the tables and seals of the Covenant, the Officers and censures of his Church, the administration of all his public Worship and Ordinances, is, *Cœtus fidelium*, a Communion of Saints, a Combination of faithfull godly men, meeting for that end, by common and joynt consent, into one Congregation; which is commonly called *a particular visible Church.* * * *

The Church of *Corinth,* even the whole Church, did meet together every Lords day, in one place, for the Administration of the holy Ordinances of God, to publick Edification, 1 *Cor.* 14. 23. & 16. 1, 2. Which frequent meeting every Lords day in one place, to such ends, cannot possibly be compatible to any Diocesan, Provinciall, or Nationall Assembly." *The Way of the Churches,* Chap. I. Prop. 1.

gregationall of so many as may meet in one place, 1 *Cor.* 14. & therefore no Civill State can be the antitype and parallell; to which purpose upon the 11 Question I shall at large [151] shew the difference betweene that Nationall Church and State of Israel, and all other States and Nations in the World.

<small>The Law of putting to death blasphemers of Christ cuts off al hopes from the Jews of partaking in his bloud.</small>

Secondly, If the Rulers of the Earth are bound to put to death all that worship other gods then the true God, or that blaspheme (that is speake evill of in a lesser or higher degree) that one true God; it must unavoidably follow that (the beloved for the Fathers sake) the Jewes whose very Religion blasphemeth Christ in the highest degree, I say they are actually sonnes of death, and all to be immediately executed according to those quoted Scriptures: And

<small>The direfull effects of fighting for conscience.</small>

Secondly, the Townes, Cities, Nations and Kingdomes of the World must generally be put to the sword, if they speedily renounce not their Gods and Worships, and so cease to blaspheme the true God by their Idolatries: This bloody consequence cannot be avoided by any Scripture rule, for if that rule be of force Deut. 13. & 18. not to spare, or shew mercy upon person or City falling to Idolatry, that bars out all favour or partiality; and then what heapes upon heapes in the slaugher houses and shambles of Civill Warres must the world come to, as I have formerly noted, and that unnecessarily, it being not required by the Lord Jesus for his sake, and the Magistrates power and weapons being essentially Civill, and so not reaching to the impiety or ungodlinesse, but the incivility and unrighteousnesse of tongue or hand?

CHAP. XCVIII.

Peace. DEare *Truth*, thefe are the poyfoned daggers ftabbing at my tender heart! Oh when fhall the Prince of peace appeare and reconcile the bloudy fons of men? but let me now propofe their 7 head: viz.

"In what order may the Magiftrate execute pun-
"ifhment on a Church or Church-member that
"offendeth his Lawes.

"Firft, groffe and publicke notorious finnes which
"are againft the light of confcience as Herefie, &c.
"there the Magiftrate keeping him under fafe ward
"fhould fend the offendour firft to the Church to
"heale his confcience, ftill provided that the Church
"be both able and willing thereunto: By which
"meanes the Magiftrate fhall convince fuch an ones
"confcience that he feeketh his healing, rather then
"his hurt.

152] "The cenfure alfo againft him fhall proceed
"with more power and bleffing, and none fhall have
"caufe to fay that the Magiftrate perfecutes men for
"their confciences, but that he juftly punifheth fuch
"an one for finning rather againft his confcience,
"*Tit.* 3. 10.

"Secondly, in private offences how the Magiftrate
"may proceed, fee Chap. 12. It is not materiall
"whether the Church or Magiftrate take it firft in
"hand. Only with this caution, that if the State take
"it firft in hand, they are not to proceed to death or
"banifhment, untill the Church hath taken their
"courfe with him, to bring him to Repentance, pro-

"vided that the Church be willing and ready there-
"unto.

Secondly, in such sinnes wherein men plead Conscience, as Heresie, &c.

Truth. Here I have many just exceptions and considerations to present.

First, they propose a distinction of some sinnes: some are against the light of conscience, &c. and they instance in Heresie.

Ans. I have before discust this point of an Heretick sinning against light of conscience: And I shall adde that howsoever they lay this down as an infallible conclusion that all Heresie is against light of Conscience; yet (to passe by the discussion of the nature of Heresie, in which respect it may so be that even themselves may be found hereticall, yea and that in fundamentalls) how doe all Idolaters after light presented, and exhortations powerfully pressed, either Turkes or Pagans, Jewes or Antichristians, strongly even to the death hold fast (or rather are held fast by) their delusions.

Errour is confident as well as Truth.

Yea Gods people themselves, being deluded and captivated are strongly confident even against some fundamentalls, especially of worship, and yet not against the light, but according to the light or eye of a deceived conscience.

God people as well as others will be found obstinate in fundamentall errors in which sufferings and persecution doth harden.

Now all these consciences walke on confidently and constantly even to the suffering of death and torments, and are more strongly confirmed in their beleefe and conscience, because such bloudy and cruell courses of persecution are used toward them.

Secondly, speakes not the Scripture expresly of the

Jew, *Isa.* 6. *Mat.* 13. *Acts* 28. that God hath given them the spirit of slumber, eyes that they should not see, &c. all which must be spoken of the very conscience, which he that hath the golden key of *David* can [153] only shut and open, and all the Picklocks or Swords in all the *Smiths* shops in the *World* can neither by *force* or *fraud* prevent his time.

Is it not said of *Antichristians*, 2 Thessal. 2. that God hath sent them strong *delusions*, so strong and efficacious, that they beleeve a Lie and that so Confidently, and some so Conscientiously, that Death it selfe cannot part betweene the *Delusion* and their Conscience. Strong delusions.

" Againe, the *Magistrate* (say they) keeping him
" in safe ward: that is, the Heretick, the Blasphemer,
" Idolater, &c.

Peace. I here aske all men that love even the Civill Peace, where the Lord Jesus hath spoken a tittle of a Prison or safe ward to this purpose.

Truth. We find indeed a prison threatned by God to his irreconciled enemies, neglecting to account with him, *Matth.* 5.

We finde a prison into which persecuters cast the Saints: So *John*, so *Paul*, and the Apostles, *Matth.* 14. 10. &c. were cast, and the great Commander of, and caster into prison, is the Devill, *Revel.* 2. Spirituall prisons.

Wee finde a Spirituall prison indeed, a prison for Spirits, 1 *Pet.* 3. 19. the Spirits formerly rebellious against Christ Jesus speaking by *Noah* unto them, now kept in safe ward against the judgement of the great day.

In Excommunication, a Soule obstinate in sinne is

delivered to Sathan his Jaylour, aud he keeps him in safe ward, untill it pleaseth God to release him.

There is a prison for the Devill himselfe a thousand yeares, *Rev.* 20. And a Lake of eternall fire and brimstone, into which the Beast and False Prophet, and all not written in the Lambes booke, and the Devill that deceived them, shall eternally be there secured and tormented.

<small>Christ Jesus appointed no materiall prisons for Blasphemers of him, &c.</small>

But neither amongst these, nor in any other passage of the New Testament, doe we finde a prison appointed by Christ Jesus for the Heretick, Blasphemer, Idolater, &c. being not otherwise guilty against the Civill State.

'Tis true, Antichrist (by the helpe of Civill Powers) hath his prisons, to keep Christ Iesus and his members fast: such prisons may well be called the Bishops prisons, the Popes, the Devils prisons: These inquisition houses have ever been more terrible then the Magistrates.

<small>The Bishops prisons.</small>

154] At first, persecuting Bishops borrowed prisons of the Civill Magistrate (as now their successors doe still in the world) but afterward they wrung the keyes out of the Magistrates hands, and hung them at their own Girdles, and would have prisons of their owne, as doubtlesse will that Generation still doe, if God prevent them not.

CHAP. XCIX.

Peace. Gaine (say they) the *Magistrate* should send him first to the *Church* to heale his *Conscience.*

Truth. Is not this as the Prophet speakes, *Like mother,* like *daughter?* So the *mother* of *whoredomes* the *Church* of *Rome* teacheth and practiseth with all her *Hereticks:* First let the holy *Church* convince them, and then deliver them to the Secular power to receive the punishment of *Hereticks*.

> Like mother like daughter.

Peace. Me thinks also they approach neere that Popish Tenent, *Ex opere operato:* for their Exhortations and Admonitions must necessarily be so operative and prevalent, that if the *Heretick* repent not, he now sins against his *Conscience*: not remembring that *Peradventure,* 2 Tim. 2. If *peradventure,* God will give them *repentance:* and how strong *delusions* are, and *believing* of *lies,* and how hard it is to be undeceived, especially in *Spirituals?*

> Conscience not so easily healed and cured.

Truth. And as it may so prove, when an *Heretick* indeed is brought to this *Colledge* of *Physitians* to have his conscience healed, and one *Heretick* is to cure another: So also when any of *Chrifts Witnesses* (supposed *Hereticks*) are brought before them, how doth the *Lord Jesus* suffer whippings and stabs, when his *Name,* and *Truths,* and *Witnesses,* and *Ordinances* are all prophaned and blasphemed?

Besides, suppose a Man to be an *Heretick,* and yet suppose him brought as the *Magistrates* Prisoner, though to a true *Church,* to heale his *Conscience:* What promise of *Presence* and *Blessing* hath the *Lord Iesus* made to his *Church* and *Spouse* in such a way? and how common is it for *Hereticks* either to be desperately hardned by such cruell courses (yet pretending Soule-healing) or else through *feare* and *terrour* to practice grosse hypocrisie even against their

> Wounding instead of healing of Consciences.

consciences? So that these *Chirurgions* and *Physitians* pretending to heale *Consciences*, by such a course wound them deeper, and declare [155] themselves *Chirurgions* and *Physitians* of no value.

Peace. But what thinke you of the Proviso added to their Proposition, viz. Provided, the Church bee able and willing?

Truth. Doubtles this proviso derogates not a little from the nature of the Spouse of Christ. For she, like that gracious woman, *Prov.* 31. 26. openeth her mouth with wisedome, and in her tongue is the Law of Grace: she is the pillar and ground of Truth, 2 *Tim.* 2. The golden candlestick from whence true light shineth: the Angels or Ministers thereof able to try false Apostles (*Rev.* 2.) and convince the Gain-sayers, *Tit.* 1.

<small>Chrifts Spoufe able and willing to heale wounded confcien-ces.</small>

Againe (according to their principles of suppressing persons and Churches falsely worshipping) how can they permit such a blind and dead Church not able and willing to heale a wounded Conscience?

Peace. What should be the reason of this their expression?

Truth. Doubtles their *Consciences* tell them how few of those *Churches* (which they yet acknowledge *Churches*) are able and willing to hold forth *Christ Iesus* the *Sun* of *Righteousnes*, healing with his wings the doubting and afflicted *conscience*.

Lastly, their *conscience* tells them, that a Servant of *Christ Iesus* may possibly be sent as an *Heretick* to be healed by a *false Church*, which *Church* will never be willing to deale with him, or never be able to convince him.

Peace. "Yea, but they say, by such a course the "*Magistrate* shall convince such an ones *conscience*; "that hee seekes his good, &c.

Truth. If a man thus bound be sent to a *Church* to be healed in his *conscience,* either he is an *Heretick,* or he is not.

Admit he be: yet he disputes in *feare*, as the poor theefe:[1] the *Mouse* disputes with a terrible persecuting *Cat:* who while she seemes to play and gently tosse, yet the conclusion is a proud insulting and devouring crueltie.

If no Heretick but an innocent and faithfull witnes of any Truth of Jesus; disputes he not as a *Lambe* in the *Lyons* paw, being sure in the end to be torne in pieces?

Peace. They adde: The *censure* this way proceeds with more *power* and blessing.

Truth. All power and blessing is from that blessed Son of God, [156] unto whom all power is given from the *Father*, in Heaven and Earth. He hath promised his *presence* with his *Messengers*, preaching and baptizing to the worlds end, ratifying in Heaven what they binde or loose on Earth.

But let any man shew me such a *commission, instruction* and *promise* given by the *Son* of *God* to *Civill powers* in these spirituall affaires of his *Christian Kingdome* and *Worship*?

Peace. Lastly they conclude, "This course of first "sending the Heretick to be healed by the Church, "takes away all excuse; for none can say that he is "persecuted for his Conscience, but for sinning against "his Conscience.

A persecuting Church disputes with an Heretick as a Cat with the Mouse; and with a true Witnes as a Lyon with a Lambe in his paw.

[1] Insert comma for colon.

Truth. *Jesabel* placing poore *Naboth* before the *Elders* as a blasphemer of *God* and the *King*, and sanctifying the plotted and intended murther with a day of *humiliation*, may seeme to take away all excuse, and to conclude the *Blasphemer* worthy to be stoned: But *Jehovah* the *God* of *Recompences* (*Ier.* 51.) when he makes *Inquisition* for *blood*, will find both *Iesabel* and *Ahab* guilty, and make the *Dogs* a feast with the flesh of *Iesabel*, and leave not to *Ahab* a man to pisse against the wall; for (as *Paul* in his owne plea) there was nothing committed worthy of *death*: and against thee, O *King*, saith *Daniel*, I have not sinned (*Dan.* 6.) in any Civill fact against the State.

margin: Persecutours endure not so to be called.

CHAP. C.

Peace. Their eighth question is this: viz. What power Magistrates have about the gathering of Churches?

"First, the Magistrate hath power, and it is his "duty to incourage and countenance such persons, as "voluntarily joyn themselves in holy Covenant, both "by his presence (if it may be) and promise of pro-"tection, they accepting the right hand of fellow-"ship from other neighbour Churches.

"Secondly, he hath power to forbid all Idolatrous "and corrupt Assemblies, who offer to put them-"selves under their patronage, and shall attempt to "joyne themselves into a Church-estate, and if they "shall not hearken, to force them therefrom by the "power of the Sword, *Psal.* 101. 8.[1] For our toler-

---

[1] "Idolatry, Blasphemy, Heresy, venting corrupt & pernicious opinions, that destroy the foundation, open contempt of the word preached, prophana-

" ating many Religions in a State in severall Churches,
" beside the provoking of God, may in time not only
" corrupt, leaven, divide, and so destroy the peace
157] " of the Churches, but also dissolve the contin-
" uity of the State, especially ours whose wals are
" made of the stones of the Churches; it being also
" contrary to the end of our planting in this part of
" the World, which was not only to enjoy the pure
" Ordinances, but to enjoy them all in purity.[1]

"Thirdly, He hath power to compell all men
" within his grant, to heare the Word,[2] for hearing
" the Word of God is a duty which the light of
" Nature leadeth even Heathens to: The Ninivites
" heard *Jonah*, though a stranger, and unknowne
" unto them, to be an extraordinary Prophet, *Jonah*
" 3. And *Eglon* the King of *Moab* hearing that *Ehud*
" had a message from God, he rose out of his seat for
" more reverent attention, *Judg.* 3. 20.

"Yet he hath no power to compell all men to
" become members of Churches, because he hath not
" power to make them fit members for the Church,
" which is not wrought by the power of the Sword,
" but by the power of the Word: Nor may he force
" the Churches to accept of any for members, but
" those whom the Churches themselves can freely
" approve of.[3]

tion of the Lords day, disturbing the peaceable administration & exercise of the worship & holy things of God, & the like, are to be restrayned, & punished by civil authority." *A Platforme of Church Discipline gathered out of the Word of God: and agreed upon by the Elders: and Messengers of the Churches assembled in the Synod at Cambridge,* &c. Chap. xvii. 8. p. 29. Printed at *Cambridge*, by S G in *New England*, 1649.

[1] See note, p. 215 *supra*.
[2] See note, p. 194 *supra*.
[3] "It is not in the power of Magistrates to compell their subjects to become church-members, & to partake at the

Truth. To the first branch of this *head*, I answer, That the *Magistrate* should encourage and countenance the *Church*, yea and protect the persons of the *Church* from violence, disturbance, &c. it being truly noble and glorious, by how much the *Spouse* and *Queene* of the *Lord Jesus* transcends the *Ladies, Queens,* and *Empresses* of the *World*, in *glory, beauty, chastity* and *innocency*.

'Tis true, all *Magistrates* in the *world* do this: viz. Incourage and protect that *Church* or *Assembly* of *worshippers*, which they judge to be true and approve of; but not permitting other consciences then their owne:[1] It hath come to passe in all ages, and yet doubtlesse will, that the Lord *Jesus* and His *Queene* are driven and persecuted out of the World.

To the second, That the Magistrate ought to suppresse all Churches which he judgeth false, he quoteth *Psal.* 101. 8. " Betimes I will cut off the wicked " of the Land, that I may cut off all evill doers from " the City of Jehovah: unto which, he addeth foure Reasons.

Peace. Deare *Truth*, first, a word to that Scripture, so often quoted, and so much boasted of.

Truth. Concerning that holy Land of *Canaan*, concerning the *City* of *Jehovah*, *Jerusalem*, out of which King *David* here resolves [158] to cut off all the wicked and evill doers.[2] I shall speake more largely on the 11 *Head* or *Question* in the *differences* between that and all other Lands.

Psal. 101. 8. concerning the cutting off the wicked, examined.

Lords table. * * * Those whom the church is to cast out if they were in, the Magistrate ought not thrust into the church, nor to hold them therein."

Cambridge Platform, xvii: 4. p. 28.
[1] Comma for colon.
[2] *Dele* period.

At present I answer, There is no holy Land or *City* of the *Lord,* or *King* of *Sion,* &c. but the *Church* of *Jesus Christ,* and the King thereof, according to 1 *Pet.* 2. 9. Ye are a holy *Nation,* and *Jerusalem* is the holy people of God in the true profession of *Christianity, Heb.* 12. *Gal.* 4. & *Rev.* 21. Out of which the *Lord Jesus* by his holy Ordinances, in such a *government,* and by such *governours* as he hath appointed, he cuts off every wicked person and evill doer. *No Land of Canaan, nor holy City now.*

If *Christ Jesus* had intended any difference of *place, Cities* or *Countries,* doubtlesse *Jerusalem* and *Samaria* had been thought of, or the Cities of *Asia,* wherein the *Christian Religion* was so gloriously planted.

But the *Lord Jesus* disclaimes *Jerusalem* and *Samaria* from having any respect of *holinesse* more then other *Cities, John* 4.

And the Spirit of God evidently testifieth that the *Churches* were in the *Cities* and *Countries,* not that the whole *Cities* or *Countries* were *Gods* holy Land, and *Cities* out of which all *false worshippers* and *wicked persons* were to be cut, *Rev.* 2. & 3. *No difference of Lands and Cities since the comming as was before the comming of the Lord Jesus.*

The *Divells* throne was in the City of *Pergamus,* in respect of the state and persecution of it, and yet there was also the *Throne* of the *Lord Jesus* set up in His *Church* of *worshippers* in *Pergamus,* out of which the *Balaamites,* and *Nicholaitans* and every false *worshipper* was to be cast, though not out of the City of *Pergamus,* for then *Pergamus* must have beene throwne out of *Pergamus,* and the *World* out of the *World.*

CHAP. CI.

Peace. OH that my head were a *fountaine*, and mine eyes *Rivers* of *teares* to lament my *children*, the *children* of *peace* and *light*, thus darkniug that, and other lightfome Scriptures with fuch darke and direfull clouds of *bloud*.

Truth. Sweet *Peace*, thy teares are feafonable and precious, and botled up in the *Heavens:* but let me adde a fecond confideration from that Scripture: If that Scripture may now literally be applied to Nations and Cities in a parallel to *Canaan* and *Ierufalem* fince 159] the *Gofpel*, and this Pfal. 101. be literally to be applied to *Cities*, *Townes*, and *Countries* in *Europe* and *America*, not only fuch as affay to joyne themfelves (as they here fpeake) in a corrupt *Church* eftate, but fuch as know no *Church* eftate, nor *God*, nor *Chrift*, yea every wicked perfon and evill doer, muft be hanged or ftoned, &c. as it was in *Ifrael*, and if fo, how many *thoufands* and *millions* of men and women in the feverall *Kingdomes* and *governments* of the *World* muft be cut off from their *Lands*, and deftroyed from their *Cities*, as this Scripture fpeakes?

Thirdly, fince thofe perfons in the *New Englifh* plantations accounted unfit for *Church* eftate, yet remaine all members of the *Church* of *England*, from which *New England* dares not feparate, no not in their *Sacraments* (as fome of the *Independents* have publifhed[1]) what *riddle* or *myfterie*, or rather *fallacie* of Sathan is this?

Sidenote: The bloudy interpretation of Pfal. 101.

[1] The views of the Independents were given in "An Apologetical Narration, humbly fubmitted to the Honourable Houfes of Parliament, &c.," publifhed in 1643, concerning which Williams publifhed his "Queries of Higheft Con-

Peace. It will not be offence to *charity* to make conjecture: First, herein *New England Churches* secretly call their *Mother Whore*, not daring in *America* to joyne with their owne *Mothers* children, though unexcommunicate, no nor permit them to worship *God* after their consciences, and as their Mother hath taught them this secretly and silently, they have a minde to doe, which publickly they would seem to *disclaime*, and professe against.

The New English separate in America, but not in Europe.

Secondly, If such members of *Old England* should be suffered to enjoy their *consciences* in *New*, (however it is pretended they would profane *Ordinances* for which they are unfit (as true it is in that *naturall persons* are not fit for *Spirituall worship*) yet this appears not to be the bottome, for in *Old England* the *New English* joyne with *Old* in the *ministrations* of the *Word, Prayer, singing, contribution, maintenance* of the *Ministrie, &c.*) if I say, they should set up Churches after their *conscience*, the *greatnesse* and *multitudes* of their owne Assemblies would decay, and with all the contributions and *maintenance* of their *Ministers*, unto which all or most have beene forced.

The New English permit not their brethren of Old England to enjoy their consciences lest their owne numbers might exceed their owne, or at least the greatnesse of their owne Assemblies &

Truth. Deare *Peace*, These are more then conjectures, thousands now espie, and all that love the

---

sideration," in 1644, and at about the same time with the "Bloudy Tenent." They say, "As to the Church of England, we professe before God and the world, that we do apprehend a great deal of defilement in their way of worship, and a great deal of unwarranted power exercised by their church governors, yet we allow multitudes of their parochial churches to be true churches, and their ministers true ministers. In the late times, when we had no hopes of returning to our own country, we held communion with them, and offered to receive to the Lords Supper some that came to visit us in our exile, whom we knew to be godly, upon that relation and membership they held in their parish churches in England, they professing themselves to be members thereof, and belonging thereto." p. 78. Neal's *Puritans*, 1: 491.

maintenances decrease. purity of the worſhip of the living God ſhould lament ſuch halting: I ſhall adde this, not only doe they partially neglect to cut off the wicked of the Land, but ſuch as themſelves eſteemed beloved and godly have they driven forth, and keep out others which would come unto them, eminently godly by their owne confeſſion, becauſe differing in conſcience 160] and worſhip from them, and conſequently not to be ſuffered in their holy Land of *Canaan*.[1]

But having examined that Scripture alledged, let us now weigh their Reaſons.

Firſt (ſay they) the not cutting off by the ſword, but tolerating many *Religions* in a State would provoke God: unto which

Chriſt Jeſus never appointed all Religions but his owne to be cut off by the Civill Sword. I anſwer, firſt (and here being no Scripture produced to theſe *Reaſons*, ſhall the ſooner anſwer) that no proofe can be made from the *Inſtitutions* of the *Lord Ieſus* that all Religions but one are to be cut off by the *Civill Sword*; that Nationall *Church* in that typicall Land of *Canaan* being aboliſhed, and the *Chriſtian Commonweale* or *Church* inſtituted.

A bloudy mother. Secondly, I affirme that the cutting off by the Sword other *Conſciences* and *Religions* is (contrarily)

---

[1] The reference to his own baniſhment and to their refuſal to allow the Preſbyterians to come to New England and ſet up another form of Church-government (p. 215) is obvious. In the previous ſentences where alluſion is made to members of the Church of England being "ſuffered to enjoy their own conſciences in New England" and "to ſet up churches after their conſcience," Williams may poſſibly have had in mind the caſe of John and Samuel Browne, who had been ſent home to England from Salem in 1629 for ſetting up ſeparate worſhip according to the Book of Common Prayer. *Morton's Memorial*, p. 148. Williams arriving in Salem but little over a year afterward muſt have heard of it, and his mind, with the opinions about religious liberty then growing in it, muſt have been prepared to be impreſſed by ſuch a tranſaction, in which men of ſtanding received treatment ſo ſimilar to his own.

moſt provoking unto God, expreſſely againſt his will concerning the Tares *Matth.* 13. as I have before proved;[1] as alſo the bloudy *mother* of all thoſe monſtrous miſchiefes (where ſuch cutting off is uſed) both to the *ſoules* and *bodies* of men.

Thirdly, let *conſcience* and *experience* ſpeake how in the not cutting off their many *Religions*, it hath pleaſed God not only not to be provoked, but to proſper the ſtate of the united Provinces our next neighbours, and that to admiration.[2]

Peace. The ſecond reaſon is, ſuch tolerating would leaven, divide and deſtroy the peace of the Churches.

Truth. This muſt alſo be denied upon ſo many former *Scriptures* & *Reaſons* produced, proving the power of the *Lord Ieſus*, and the ſufficiencie of his *Spirituall* power in his *Church*, for the purging forth and conquering of the leaſt *evill*, yea and for the bringing every thought in ſubjection unto *Chriſt Ieſu*, 2 Cor. 10. *Chriſts Spirituall power, moſt powerfull.*

I adde, they have not produced one Scripture, nor can, to prove that the permitting of *leaven* of falſe *doctrine* in the *World* or *Civill State*, will leaven the *Churches* : only we finde that the permiſſion of *leaven* in *perſons, doctrines* or *practices* in the *Church*, that indeed will corrupt and ſpread, 1 *Cor.* 5. & *Gal.* 5. but this *Reaſon* ſhould never have been alledged, were not the particular *Churches* in *New England*, but as ſo many implicite *Pariſh Churches* in one implicite *Nationall Church*. *Chriſt forbidding his followers to permit leaven in the Church, doth not forbid to permit leaven in the World.*

[1] See Chapter 27.
[2] "In that age (17th century) the immenſe proſperity of Holland was everywhere regarded with admiration. In all that related to trade, her ſtateſmen were conſidered as oracles, and her inſtitutions as models." Macaulay, *Hiſt. of England*, iv. p. 111.

Peace. Their third *Reason* is, it will diffolve the *continuity* of the State, efpecially theirs, where the *walls* are made of the ftones of the *Churches.*

161] *Truth.* I anfwer briefly to this bare *affirmation* thus, that the true *Church* is a *wall* fpirituall and myfticall, *Cant.* 8. 9.

Then confequently a falfe Church or Company is a falfe or pretended *wall*, and none of *Chrifts.*

The *civill State, Power* and *Government* is a *civill wall, &c.* and

Laftly, the *walls* of *Earth* or ftone about a City are the naturall or artificiall wall or defence of it.

The Wall, *Cant.* 8. 9. difcuffed. Now in confideration of thefe foure wals I defire it may be proved from the Scriptures of *Truth*, how the falfe *fpirituall wall* or company of falfe *worfhippers* fuffred in a *City* can be able to deftroy the true *Chriftian wall* or company of *beleevers.*

A fpirituall wall cannot properly impaire the civil. Againe, how this falfe *fpirituall wall* or falfe *Church* permitted, can deftroy the *civill wall*, the *State* and *Government* of the *City* and *Citizens*, any more then it can deftroy the *naturall* or *artificiall wall* of earth or ftone.

Spirituall may deftroy *fpirituall*, if a ftronger and victorious, but *fpirituall* cannot reach to *artificiall* or *civill.*

Peace. Yea but they feare the falfe *fpirituall wall* may deftroy their *civill*, becaufe it is made of the ftones of *Churches.*

Truth. If this have reference to that practice amongft them, *viz.* that none but members of *Churches* enjoy *civill* freedome amongft them (ordinarily) in imitation of that *Nationall Church* and *State* of the *Jewes*, then I anfwer, they that follow

Moses Church constitution) which the *New English* by such a practice implicitely doe) must cease to pretend to the Lord *Jesus Christ* and his *institutions*.

Secondly, we shall finde lawfull *civill States* both before and since *Christ Iesus*, in which we finde not any tidings of the true *God* our [or] *Christ*. {Many flourishing Civill States where true Churches are not found.}

Lastly, their *civill New English State* framed out of their *Churches* may yet stand, subsist and flourish, although they did (as by the word of the *Lord* they ought) permit either *Jewes* or *Turkes* or *Antichristians* to live amongst them subject unto *their Civill Government*.

CHAP. CII.

Peace. ONe branch more, *viz.* the third remaines of this Head, and it concerns the hearing of the Word, " unto which (say they) all men are " to be compelled, because hearing of the [162] word " is a duty which even Nature leadeth Heathens to : " for this they quote the practice of the Ninevites " hearing *Ionah*, and *Eglon* (King of Moab) his rising " up to *Ehuds* pretended message from God, *Judg.* 3.

Truth. I must deny that position : for light of Nature leadeth men to heare that onely which Nature conceiveth to be good for it, and therefore not to heare a Messenger, Minister or Preacher, whom *conscience* perswades is a false *messenger* or *deceiver*, and comes to deceive my soule, as Millions of men and women in their severall respective *religions* and *consciences* are so perswaded, conceiving their owne to be true. {Hearing discussed. Every Religion prefers its owne Priests and Ministers before all other.}

Secondly, as concerning the *instances*, *Ionah* did not compell the Ninevites to heare that *message* which he brought unto them.

Jonahs preaching to the Ninevites, and their hearing of his message examined.

Besides the matter of *compulsion* to a constant *worship* of the *word* in *Church estate* (which is the *Question*) comes not neare *Ionahs* case.

Nor did *Christ Jesus* or any of his *Embassadours* so practice: but if persons refused to heare the command of the *Lord Iesus* to his Messengers was onely to depart from them, shaking off the dust of their *feet* with a denunciation of *Gods wrath* against them, *Math.* 10. *Act.* 14.

Eglon his rising up to Ehuds message, examined.

Concerning *Eglon* his rising up: First, *Ehud* compelled not that King either to heare or reverence, and all that can bee imitable in *Eglon*, is a voluntary and willing *reverence* which persons ought to expresse to what they are perswaded comes from *God*.

But how doe both these instances mightily convince and condemne themselves, who not onely professe to turne away from, but also persecute or hunt all such as shall dare to professe a *Ministry* or *Church* estate differing from their owne, though for personall *godlinesse* and excellency of gifts reverenced by themselves.

Thirdly, to the point of *compulsion*: It hath pleased the *Lord Iesus* to appoint a twofold Ministry of his Word.

A twofold Ministry of Christ, converting and feeding.

First, for *unbeleevers* and their *conversion*, according to *Math.* 28. 19. *Marc.* 16. 15, 16. and the constant practice of the Apostles in the first preaching of the *Gospel*.

Secondly, a Ministry of *feeding* and *nourishing* up

such as are *converted* and brought into *Church estate*, according to *Ephes.* 4. *&c.* Now to neither of these doe we finde any compulsion appointed by the *Lord Iesus*, or practised by any of his.

163] The compulsion preached and practised in *New England*, is not to the hearing of that *Ministry* sent forth to convert unbeleevers, and to constitute *Churches*: for such a *Ministry* they practise not but to the hearing of the word of *edification, exhortation, consolation,* dispenced onely in the *Churches* of *worshippers:* I apply,

When *Paul* came first to *Corinth* to preach *Christ Iesus*, by their Rule the Magistrates of *Corinth* ought by the Sword to have compelled all the people of *Corinth* to heare *Paul*.

Secondly, after a Church of *Christ* was gathered (by their rule) the *Magistrates* of *Corinth* ought to have compelled the people still (even those who had refused his Doctrine, for the few onely of the Church embraced it) to have heard the Word still, and to have kept one day in seven to the *Christians God*, and to have come to the *Christians Church* all their dayes. And what is this but a setled formality of *Religion* and *Worship*, unto which a people are brought by the power of the sword? Paul never used any civill compulsion.

And however they affirme that persons are not to be compelled to be *members* of *Churches*, nor the Church compelled to receive any: Yet if persons be compelled to forsake their Religion which their hearts cleave to, and to come to *Church*, to the worship of the *Word, Prayers, Psalmes*, and *Contributions*, and this all their dayes: I aske whether this be not this peoples Religion, unto which submitting, The New English forcing their subjects to church all their daies and yet forcing them not to any Re-

ligion (as they say) they force the people then to be of no religion all their dayes they fhall be quiet all their dayes, without the inforcing them to the practice of any other Religion? And if this bee not fo, then I aske, Will it not inevitably follow, that they (not onely permit, but) enforce people to bee of no Religion at all, all their dayes?

This toleration of Religion, or rather irreligious *compulfion*, is above all *tolerations* monftrous, to wit, to compell men to bee of no *Religion* all their dayes. I defire all men and thefe worthy *Authors* of this Modell, to lay their hands upon their heart, and to confider whether this *compulfion* of men to heare the *Word*, (as they fay) whether it carries men, to wit, to be of no *Religion* all their dayes, worfe then the very *Indians*, who dare not live without *Religion* according as they are perfwaded.

Laftly, I adde, from the *Ordinance* of the Lord *Jefus*, and practice of the Apoftles (Acts 2. 42.) where the Word and Prayer is joyned with the exercife of their *fellowfhip*, and breaking of Bread; in which Exercifes the *Church* continued conftantly: *The Civill State can no more lawfully compell the Confciences of men to Church to heare the Word, then to receive the Sacraments.* that it is apparent [164] that a *Civill State* may as lawfully compell men by the *civill fword* to the breaking of *bread*, or Lords Supper, as to the *Word* or *Prayer*, or *Fellowfhip*.

For firft, they are all of the fame *nature*, *Ordinances* in the *Church* (I fpeake of the *feeding Miniftrie* in the *Church*, unto which perfons are compell'd) and *Church Worfhip*. Secondly, every *confcience* in the *World* is fearfull, at leaft fhie of the *Priefts* and *Minifters* of other *Gods* and *Worfhips*, and of holding Spirituall fellowfhip in any of their Services. Which is the cafe of many a Soule, viz. to queftion the Minifters themfelves, as well as the Supper it felfe.

CHAP. CIII.

Peace. Deare *Truth*, This preſſing of men to the Spirituall Battels of Chriſt Jeſus, is the cauſe why (as it is commonly with preſt Souldiers) that ſo many thouſands flie in the day of Battell. But I preſent you with the 9. Queſtion, *viz.*

What power the Magiſtrate hath in providing of Church-Officers?

" Firſt (ſay they) the Election of Church officers " being the proper Act of the Church, therefore the " Magiſtrate hath no power (either as Prince or " Patron) to aſſume ſuch power unto himſelfe. When " Chriſt ſends to preach by his ſupreme power, the " Magiſtrate may ſend forth by his power ſubordinate, " to gather Churches, and may force people to heare " them, but not inveſt them with office amongſt them.

" Secondly, the Maintenance of Church-officers " being to ariſe from all thoſe who are ordinarily " taught thereby (*Gal.* 6. 6.) hence it is the dutie of " the Civill Magiſtrate to contend with the people, " as *Nehemiah* did,[1] *chap.* 13. *ver.* 10. 11. who doe " neglect and forſake the due maintenance of the

---

[1] "Not only Members of Churches, but *all that are taught in the Word*, are to contribute unto him that teacheth in all good things. In caſe that Congregations are defective in their contributions, the Deacons are to call upon them to do their duty: if their call ſufficeth not, the church by her powr is to require it of their Members, & where church- powr through the corruption of men, doth not, or cañot attaine the end, the Magiſtrate is to ſee miniſtry be duely provided for, as appeares from the commended example of Nehemiah. The Magiſtrates are nurſing fathers & nurſing mothers, & ſtand charged with the cuſtody of both Tables &c." *Cambridge Platform*, xi: 4. p. 16.

"Church of God, and to command them to give such
"portions for the maintenance of Church officers, as
"the Gospell commandeth to be offered to them
"freely and bountifully, 2 *Cor.* 9. 5, 6, 7. According
"as *Hezekiah* commanded the people to give to the
"Priests and Levites the portions appointed by the
"Law, that they might be incouraged in the Law of
"the Lord, 2 *Chron.* 31. 4.

"Thirdly, the furnishing the Church with set offi-
"cers, depending much upon erecting and main-
"tenance of Schooles, and [165] good education of
"youth: and it lying chiefly in the hand of the
"Magistrate to provide for the furthering thereof,
"they may therefore and should so farre provide for
"the Churches, as to erect Schooles, take care for
"fit Governours and Tutours, and commend it to all
"the Churches, if they see it meet, that in all the
"Churches within the Jurisdiction once in a yeare,
"and if it may be, the Sabbath before the Generall
"Court of Election, there be a Free-will offering of
"all people for the maintenance of such Schooles:
"And the monies of every Towne so given, to be
"brought on the day of Election to the Treasurie of
"the Colledge, and the monies to be disposed by such
"who are so chosen for the disposing thereof.

Truth. In the choice of officers, it is very obscure what they mean by this supreme power of Christ Jesus sending to preach.

We know the Commission of the Lord Jesus to his first Messengers to goe into all Nations to preach and gather Churches, and they were immediately sent forth by him: but Mr. *Cotton* elswhere holdeth, that there is now extant no immediate *Ministry* from *Christ*, but *mediate*, that is, from the *Church*.[1]

Let us first see how they agree with themselves, and secondly how they agree with the *Magistrate* in this busines.

First, if they hold a sending forth to preach by Christs supreme power, according to *Math.* 28. *Mark* 16. *Rom.* 10. they must necessarily grant a time, when the *Church* is not, but is to be constituted out of the *Nations* and *Peoples* now converted by this *preaching*: whence according to the *course* of *Scripture*, the nature of the *Worke*, and their own *Grant* in this place, it is apparent that there is a *Ministery* before the *Church*, gathering and espousing the Church to *Christ*: and therefore their other *Tenent* must needs be too light, viz. that there is no *Ministry* but that which is *mediate* from the *Church*. *In the first patterne there is a converting Ministrie, to gather the Church or Flock of Christ.*

Peace. Blessed *Truth*, this doctrine of a *Ministry* before the *Church*, is *harsh* and *deep*, yet most *true*, most *sweet*: Yet you know their *Ground*, that two or three Godly *persons* may joyne themselves together, become a *Church*, make officers, send them forth to preach, to convert, baptize, and gather New *Churches*.

Truth. I answer, first we find not in the first *institution* and *patterne*, that ever any such two, or three,

---

[1] We have failed to discover any precise expression of this sentiment in any of Cotton's works published before this. In his *Answer*, p. 82, *Pub. Narr. Club*, ii: 135, he says, "The Power of the Ministeriall Calling is derived chiefly from Christ, furnishing his servants with Gifts fit for the Calling; and nextly, from the Church, (or Congregation) who observing such whom the Lord hath gifted, doe elect and call them forth to come and helpe them." In *The Way of the Churches*, p. 39, he says, "The Church hath not *absolute* power to choose whom they list, but *ministeriall* power onely, to choose whom Christ hath chosen, hath gifted and fitted for them."

or more, did gather and conſtitute themſelves a *Church* of *Chriſt*, without a *Miniſtrie* ſent [166] from *God* to invite and call them by the *Word*, and to receive them unto *fellowſhip* with *God* upon the receiving of that *Word* and *Meſſage*: And therefore it may very well be quæried how without ſuch a Miniſtry two or three become a Church? and how the power of Chriſt is conveyed unto them; Who eſpouſed this people unto *Jeſus Chriſt*, as the *Church* at *Corinth* was eſpouſed by *Paul*, 2 Cor. 11.? If it be ſaid themſelves, or if it be ſaid the Scriptures, let one inſtance be produced in the firſt *patternes* and *practices* of ſuch a Practice.

<small>No preſident of any people in the Goſpell converting & gathering themſelves without ſome Meſſenger ſent from the Lord to effect thoſe ends.</small>

It hath been generally confeſt, that there is no comming to the *Mariage feaſt* without a *Meſſenger* inviting, ſent from *God* to the *Soules* of men, *Matth*. 22. *Luc*. 14. *Rom*. 10.

We finde when the *Theſſalonians* turned to *God* from their *Idolls* to ſerve the living and true *God*, 1 *Theſſal*. 1. 9. it pleaſed *God* to bring a *Word* of *Power* unto them by the mouth of *Paul* in the ſame place.

Peace. You know (deare *Truth*) it is a common plea, that Gods people now are converted already, and therefore may congregate themſelves, &c.

Truth. Two things muſt here be cleered:

<small>Profeſſed publique converſion is not onely from ſinnes againſt the ſecond Table in</small>

Firſt, doth their *converſion* amount to externall turning from *Idolls*, 1 Theſſ. 1. 9. beſide their internall *Repentance*, *Faith*, *Love*, *&c*. Secondly, who wrought this *converſion*, who begot theſe Children? (for though the *Corinthians* might have ten thouſand *Teachers*, yet *Paul* had begotten them by the *Word*.

'Tis true (as Mr. *Cotton* himſelfe elſewhere acknowledgeth) *God* sendeth many *Preachers* in the way of his *providence* (even in *Babel* mysticall) though not according to his *Ordinance* and *Institution:* So even in the *wildernesse* (*Rev.* 12.) *God* provideth for the sustentation of the woman, *Rev.* 12. by which *provision* even in the most *Popish times* and *places*, yea and by most false and *Popish callings* (now in this lightsome Age confest so to be) *God* hath done great things to the personall *conversion, consolation,* and *salvation* of his people. personall Repentance, but from false worship also.

But as there seems yet to be desired such *constitution* of the *Christian Church*, as the first *institution* and *patterne* calls for : So also such a *calling* and *converting* of *Gods people* from *Antichristian Idols* to the *Christian Worship* : And therefore such a *Ministry* (according to the first patterne) sent from *Christ Jesus* to renew and restore [167] the *Worship* and *Ordinances* of God in *Christ*. A true Ministery necessary before conversion, and therefore before the Church in the first patterne.

Lastly, if it should be granted that without a *Ministry* sent from *Christ* to gather *Churches*, that *Gods people* in this Country may be *called, converted* from *Antichristian Idolls*, to the true *worship* of God in the true *Church* estate and *Ordinances*, will it not follow that in all other Countries of the World *Gods* Elect must or may be so converted from their severall respective false *worships* and *Idolatries*, and brought into the true *Christian Church* estate without such a *Ministry* sent unto them? Or are there two *wayes* appointed by the Lord *Jesus*, one for this Country, and another for the rest of the *World?* Or lastly, if two or three more (without a *Ministry*) shall arise up, become a *Church*, make *Ministers, &c.* I ask The true way of the Ministry sent with that commission Matth.28. discussed.

whether thofe two or three, or more[,] muft not be accounted immediately and extraordinarily ftirred up by *God,* and whether this be that fupreme power of C*hrift Jefus* (which they fpeake of) fending forth two or three private perfons to make a C*hurch* and *Minifters,* without a true *Miniftry* of C*hrift Iefus* firft fent unto themfelves? Is this that *commiffion* (which all Minifters pretend unto) *Mat.* 28. 19. *&c.* firft, in the hands of two or three private perfons becomming a C*hurch,* without a mediat call from which C*hurch* (fay they) there can be no true *Miniftry,* and yet alfo confeffe that C*hrift* fendeth forth to preach by his *fupreme power;* and the *Magiftrate* by his power fubordinate to gather Churches?

CHAP. CIV.

Peace. YOu have taken great paines to fhew the irreconciliableneffe of thofe their two affertions, *viz.* Firft, there is now no Miniftry (as they fay) but what is mediat from the Church, and yet fecondly, Chrift Jefus fends Preachers forth by his fupreme power to gather the Church: I now wait to heare, how, as they " fay, the Magiftrate may fend " forth by his power fubordinate to gather Churches, " enforcing the people to heare, &c.

The Civill Magiftrate not betrufted with gathering of Churches. *Truth.* If there be a *Miniftry* fent forth by C*hrifts* fupreme *power;* and a *Miniftry* fent forth by the *Magiftrates* fubordinate power to gather Churches, I aske what is the difference between thefe two? Is there any gathering of Churches but by that *commiffion,* *Mat.* 28. *Teach and baptize?* And is the *civill* Mag-

iſtrate [168] intruſted with a power from *Chriſt* as his *Deputy* to give this *commiſſion*, and ſo to ſend out *Miniſters* to preach and baptize?

As there is nothing in the *Teſtament* of *Chriſt* concerning ſuch a *delegation* or *aſſignment* of ſuch power of Chriſt to the *civill Magiſtrate:* So I alſo ask, ſince in every free State *civill Magiſtrates* have no more power but what the peoples of thoſe *States, Lands* and *Countries* betruſt them with, whether or no (by this meanes) it muſt not follow that *Chriſt Ieſus* hath left with the Peoples and Nations of the World, his Spirituall Kingly power to grant commiſſions and ſend out Miniſters to themſelves, to preach, convert and baptize themſelves? How inevitably this followes upon their concluſion of power in Magiſtrates to ſend, &c. and what unchriſtian and unreaſonable conſequences muſt flow from hence, let all conſider in the feare of *God*. *If the Magiſtrate then much more the people of the world, from whom the Magiſtrates receive their power.*

Iehoſaphats ſending forth the *Levites* to teach in *Iudah, &c.* as they alledge it not; ſo elſewhere it ſhall more fully appeare to be a type and figure of *Chriſt Ieſus* the only King of his Church providing for the feeding of his Church and People by his true *Chriſtian Prieſts* and *Levites*, viz. The *Miniſtry* which in the *Goſpel* he hath appointed. *Iehoſaphat (2 Chron. 17.) a figure of Chriſt Jeſus in his Church not of the Civill Magiſtrate in the State.*

CHAP. CV.

Peace. WE have examined the Miniſtry, be pleaſed (deare *Truth*) to ſpeake to the ſecond branch of this head, *viz.* the maintenance of it: They affirme that the Magiſtrate may force out the Ministers maintenance from all that are taught by them, and that after the patterne of Israel, and the argument from 1 Cor. 9. Gal. 6. 6.

Truth. This theame, *viz.* concerning the maintenance of the Priests and Ministers of worship, is indeed the Apple of the Eye, the *Dianah* of the *Dianah*[1], *&c.* yet all that love Christ Jesus in sincerity, and soules in and from him will readily professe to abhorre filthy lucre (*Tit.* 1.) and the wages of *Balaam* (both more common and frequent then easily is discernable.)

<small>Gal. 6. 6. Concerning the maintenance of the Ministry examined.</small> To that Scripture *Gal.* 6. 6. Let him that is taught in the Word make him that teacheth partaker of all his goods: I answer, That teaching was of persons converted, beleevers entred into the Schoole and Family of Christ the Church, which Church being 169] rightly gathered, is also rightly invested with the *power* of the *Lord Jesus,* to force every soule therein by spirituall *weapons* and *penalties* to doe its duty.

But this forcing of the *Magistrate* is intended and practised to all sorts of *persons* without as well as within the *Church, unconverted, naturall* and dead in sinne, as well as those that live, and feeding enjoy the *benefit* of spirituall food.

<small>Christ Jesus never appointed a maintenance of his Ministers from the unconverted and unbeleeving.</small> Now for those sorts of persons to whom *Christ Iesus* sends his Word out of *Church* estate, *Iewes* or *Gentiles,* (according to the *Parable* of *Math.* 13. *highway hearers, stony ground,* and *thorny ground* hearers) wee never finde title of any *maintenance* to bee expected, least of all to bee forced and exacted from them. By *civill power* they cannot be forced, for it is no *civill payment* or businesse, no matter of *Cæsar,*

[1] Of the Ephesians. Acts xix: 28.

but concerning *God:* nor by *spirituall power*, which hath nothing to doe with those which are without, 1 *Cor.* 5.

It is reasonable to expect and demand of such as live within the *state* a *civill maintenance* of their *civill officers*, and to force it where it is denyed. It is reasonable for a *Schoole-master* to demand his recompence for his labour in his *Schoole*: but it is not reasonable to expect or force it from *stranges, enemies, rebels* to that City, from such as come not within, or else would not bee received into the *Schoole*. What is the *Church* of *Christ Jesus*, but the *City*, the *Schoole*, and *Family* of *Christ*? the *Officers* of this *City, Schoole, Family*, may reasonably expect maintenance from such [as] they minister unto, but not from strangers, enemies, &c.

Peace. It is most true that sinne goes in a *linke,* for that *tenent* that all the men of the *world* may bee compelled to heare *Christ* preach (and enjoy the *labours* of the *Teacher* as well as the *Church* it selfe) forceth on another also as evill, *viz.* that they should also be compelled to pay, as being most equall and reasonable to pay for their conversion.

Truth. Some use to urge that Text of *Luc.* 14. Compell them to come in.[1] Compell them to *Masse*

They that compell men to heare, compell men also to pay for their hearing and conversion Luc. 14. Compell

---

[1] Augustine fell into this false interpretation in advocating the coercion of heretics. "In illis ergo, qui leniter primò adducti sunt, completa est prior obedientia: in istis autem, qui coguntur, inobedientia coërcetur. Quapropter si potestate quam per religionem ac fidem regum, tempore quo debuit, divino munere accepit Ecclesia, hi qui inveniuntur in viis & in sepibus, id est in hæresibus & in schismatibus coguntur intrare." Ep. ad Bonifacium, 185. *Opera,* tom. ii: 653.

"Putas neminem debere cogi ad justitiam, cum legas patremfamilias dixisse servis, *Quocumque inveneritis cogite intrare?*" Ep. ad Vincentium, 93. *Opera,* tom. ii: 232. Cf. Ep. ad Donatum, 174. *Opera,* tom. ii: 616.

them, examined.

(say the *Papists*:) compell them to Church and Common prayer, say the *Protestants:* Compell them to the *Meeting*, say the *New English*. In all these *compulsions* they disagree amongst themselves: but in this, *viz.* Compell them to pay[;] in this they all agree.

Two sorts of compulsion.

There is a double violence which both Errour and Falshood use to the soules of men.

Morall and

170] First, morall and perswasive, such was the perswasion first used to *Ioseph* by his *Mistris:* such was the *perswasions* of *Tamar* from *Ammon*: such was the compelling of the *young man* by the Harlot, *Prov.* 7. shee caught him by her much faire *speech* and *kisses*. And thus is the whole world compelled to the worship of the Golden *Image, Dan. 3.*

Civill Compulsion.

The second Compulsion is *civill*, such as *Iosephs* Mistris began to practise upon *Ioseph* to attaine her whorish desires.

Such as *Ammon* practised on *Tamar* to satisfie his brutish lust.

And such was *Nabuchadnezzars* second compulsion, his fiery Furnace, *Dan. 3.* and mysticall *Nabuchadnezzars* killing all that receive not his marke, *Rev. 13.*

Calvin also follows Augustine and sustains the argument for persecution drawn from his passage; "Interea non improbo, quod Augustinus hoc testimonio sæpius contra Donatistas usus est, ut probaret, priorum principum edictis ad veri Dei cultum et fidei unitatum licite cogi præfractos et rebelles : quia, etsi voluntaria est fides, videmus tamen, iis mediis utiliter domari eorum pervivaciam, qui non nisi coacti parent." *Commentarii, in loco,* tom. ii: 43.

Bayle used this text for the title of his book *Contrains-les d'entrer*, in which more directly than in his Dictionary he advocates religious toleration. "At the beginning of this work Bayle disclaims any intention of entering into a critical examination of the passage that he had taken as his motto. His refutation of the persecutor's interpretation rests not on any detailed criticism, but on a broad and general principle." Lecky, *Rationalism in Europe,* ii: 66.

The firſt ſort of theſe *violences*, to wit, by power-full argument and perſwaſion, the *Miniſters* of the *Goſpel* alſo uſe. Hence all thoſe powerfull perſwaſions of Wiſedomes *Maidens, Pro.* 9. Hence (ſaith *Paul*) knowing the *terrour* of the *Lord*, we perſwade men, 2 *Cor.* 5. and pull ſome out of the fire, ſaith *Iude* : ſuch muſt that *compulſion* be, *Luc.* 14. *viz.* the powerfull perſwaſions of the *Word*, being that two-edged ſword comming out of the mouth of *Chriſt Ieſus* in his true *Miniſters* ſent forth to invite poore ſinners to partake of the *Feaſt* of the *Lambe* of God. The *civill Miniſters* of the Commonweale cannot be ſent upon this *buſineſſe* with their *civill weapons* and *compulſions*, but the *ſpirituall Miniſter* of the *Goſpel* with his ſpirituall ſword of *Chriſts* mouth, a *ſword* with two edges.

The Miniſters of Chriſt Jeſus compell with no other ſword then that of Chriſts mouth, the ſword of the Spirit with two edges.

But more particularly the *contributions* of *Chriſts Kingdome* are all holy and ſpirituall, though conſiſting of materiall earthly *ſubſtance*, (as is *Water* in *Baptiſme, Bread* and *Wine* in the *Supper*) and joyned with prayer and the *Lords Supper, Act.* 2. 42.

The maintenance of the Miniſtry ſpirituall.

Hence as Prayer is called *Gods ſacrifice*, ſo are the *contributions* and mutuall ſupplyes of the Saints, *ſacrifices, Phil.* 4.

Hence alſo as it is impoſſible for *naturall* men to bee capable of *Gods worſhip*, and to feed, be nouriſhed and edified by any ſpirituall ordinance, no more then a *dead childe* can *ſucke* the breaſt, or a *dead man feaſt* :

Naturall men can neither truly worſhip nor maintain it.

So alſo is it as impoſſible for a *dead man* yet lodged in the grave of Nature to contribute ſpiritually (I meane according to *Scriptures* rule) as for a *dead man* to pay a *reckoning*.

I queſtion not but naturall men may for the outward act *preach, pray, contribute,* &c. but neither are they worſhippers ſuitable to him [171] who is a Spirit (*Iohn* 4.) nor can they (leaſt of all) bee forced to worſhip or the maintenance of it, without a guilt of their hypocriſie.

Peace. They will ſay, what is to be done for their ſoules?

Truth. The *Apoſtles* (whom wee profeſſe to imitate) preached the *Word* of the *Lord* to unbeleevers, without mingling in *worſhip* with them, and ſuch *Preachers* and preaching, ſuch as pretend to be the true *Miniſtry* of *Chriſt*, ought to be and practiſe: Not forcing them all their dayes to come to *Church* and pay their *duties*, either ſo confeſſing that this is their *Religion* unto which they are forced: or elſe that (as before) they are forced to be of no Religion all their dayes.

<small>Rebels not ſubdued by compliance, but reſiſtance.</small> The way to ſubdue *Rebels* is not by *correſpondence* and *communion* with them, by forcing them to keepe the *City Watches*, and pay *ſeſſements*, &c. which all may be practiſed (upon compulſion) treacherouſly, the firſt work with ſuch is powerfully to ſubdue their judgments and wills, to lay downe their *weapons*, and yeeld willing ſubjection: then come they orderly into the City, and ſo to Citie priviledges.

CHAP. CVI.

Peace. Pleaſe you now (deare Truth) to diſcuſſe the Scriptures from the *Old Teſtament, Nehem.* 13. and 2 *Chron.* 31.

Truth. God gave unto that *Nationall Church* of the Jewes that excellent Land of *Canaan,* and therein *Houses* furnished, *Orchards, Gardens, Vineyards, Olive yards, Fields, Wells,* &c. they might well in this setled abundance, and the promised continuation and increase of it afford a large temporall supply to their *Priests* and *Levites,* even to the *Tenth* of all they did possesse.

<small>The nationall Church of the Jewes might well be forced to a settled maintenance of their priests but not so the the Christian Church.</small>

Gods people are now in the *Gospel* brought into a spirituall land of *Canaan,* flowing with spirituall milk and honey, and they abound with *spirituall* and heavenly *comforts,* though in a poore and *persecuted condition,* therefore an inforced setled maintenance is not sutable to the *Gospel,* as it was to the *Ministry* of *Priests* and *Levites* in the *Law.*

Secondly, in the change of the Church estate, there was also a change of the *Priesthood* and of the *Law, Heb.* 7. Nor did the *Lord Iesus* appoint that in his *Church,* and for the maintenance of his [172] *Ministrie,* the *Civill sword* of the *Magistrate,* but that the Spirituall Sword of the Ministrie should alone compell.

3. Therefore the *compulsion* used under *Hezekiah* and *Nehemiah,* was by the *civill* and *corporall* Sword, of a type (in that typicall State) not of another *materiall* and *corporall,* but of an heavenly and spirituall, even the *sword* of the *Spirit,* with which *Christ* fighteth, *Revel.* 3. which is exceeding sharpe, entring in between the *soule* and *spirit,* Heb. 4. and bringing every thought into *captivitie* to the *obedience* of *Christ Jesus:* He that submits not at the shaking of this *sword,* is cut off by it; and he that despiseth this

<small>The Civill Sword of the National Church of the Jewes could not type out a Civill, but a Spirituall Sword of the</small>

The Bloudy Tenent.

Christian Church. — *sword*, all the power in the *World* cannot make him a true *worshipper*, or by his purse a mainteiner of *Gods worship*.

No man should be bound to worship, nor maintaine a Worship against his own consent. — Lastly, If any man professing to be a *Minister* of *Christ Jesus*, shall bring men before the *Magistrate* (as the practice hath been, both in *Old* and *New England*) for not paying him his *wages* or his due: I aske (if the voluntarie consent of the party hath not obliged him) how can either the officers of the *Parish*, *Church*, or of the *Civill State* compell this or that man to pay so much (more or lesse) to maintaine such a *Worship* or *Ministrie*? I ask further, if the determining what is each mans due to pay, why may they not determine the tenth and more, as some desired (others opposing) in *New England*, and force men not only to maintenance, but to a *Jewish* maintenance.

Peace. Yea but (say they) is not the *Labourer* worthy of his hire?

Christs labourers worthy of their hire, but from them that hire them — *Truth.* Yes, from them that hire him, from the *Church*, to whom he laboureth or ministreth, not from the *Civill State*: no more then the Minister of the Civill State is worthy of his hire from the Church, but from the Civill State, (in which I grant the persons in the Church ought to be assistant in their Civill respects.)

Peace. What maintenance (say they) shall the Ministrie of the Gospell have?

What maintenance Christ hath appointed — *Truth.* We finde two wayes of maintenance for the Ministrie of the Gospell, proposed for our direction in the New Testament.

First, the free and willing contribution of the

Saints, according to 1 *Cor.* 16. *Luc.* 8. 3. &c. upon which both the Lord Jesus, and his Ministers lived. *his Ministers in the Gospell.*

Secondly, the diligent worke and labour of their owne hands, [173] as *Paul* tells the Thessalonians, and that in two cases:

1. Either in the inabilities and necessities of the Church.

2. Or for the greater advantage of Christs truth; as when *Paul* saw it would more advantage the name of Christ, he denies himselfe, and falls to worke amongst the Corinthians and Thessalonians.

Let none call these cases extraordinary: for if persecution be the portion of Christs sheep, and the *busines* or *worke* of *Christ* must be dearer to us then our right eyes or lives, such as will follow *Paul*, and follow the *Lord Jesus*, must not thinke much at, but rejoyce in *poverties, necessities, hunger, cold, nakednesse,* &c. The *Stewards* of *Christ Jesus* must be like their *Lord,* and abhorre to steale as the evill *Steward*, pretending that he shamed to beg, but peremptorily, dig he could not.

CHAP. CVII.

Peace. ONe and the last branch (deare *Truth*) remaines concerning Schooles.

"The *Churches* (say they) much depend upon the "*Schooles*, and the *Schooles* upon the *Magistrates*.

Truth. I honour *Schooles* for *Tongues* and *Arts:*[1]

---

[1] In *The Hireling Ministry none of Christs,* (London, Printed in the second Moneth, 1652.) pages 14, 15, 16, 17, Williams repeats these views on the English Universities at greater length. He expressly disclaims any prejudice against learning and education. "I heartily acknowledge that among all the *out-*

The Bloudy Tenent.

Universities of Europe a cause of universall sins & plagues, yet Schooles honourable for Tongues and Arts.

but the *institution* of *Europes Universities*, devoting persons (as is said) for *Scholars*, in a *Monasticall* way, forbidding *Mariage* and Labour to, I hold as far from the mind of Iesus Christ, as it is from propagating his Name and Worship.

We count the Universities the Fountaines, the Seminaries or Seed-plots of all Pietie: but have not those Fountaines ever sent what streames the Times have liked? and ever changed their taste and colour to the Princes eye and Palate?

For any depending of the Church of Christ upon such Schooles, I finde not a tittle in the Testament of Christ Iesus.

Christs church his

I finde the *Church* of Christ frequently compared

ward *Gifts* of God, humane learning and the *knowledge* of *Languages* and good *Arts*, are excellent and excell other outward *gifts*, as far as *light* excels *darknesse*, and therefore that *Schools* of *humane* Learning, ought to be maintained, in a due way and cherished." p. 14. "Far be it from me to derogate from that *honourable civility* of training up of *Youth* in *Languages* and other humane *Learning*. All that I bear witnesse against, is the *counterfeiting* and *sacrilegious* arrogating of the *titles* and *rights* of Gods Saints, and *Churches* which are the only *Schools* of the *Prophets*." p. 17. " Upon a due survey of their *Institutions* and continuall practices compared with the last *Will* and *Testament* of Christ Jesus, they will be found to be none of Christs, and that in many respects. First, as to the name *Schollar*, although as to *humane learning*, many wayes lawfull, yet as it is appropriated to such as practise the Ministry, have been at the *Universities* (as they say) It is a *sacrilegious* and theevish title, robbing all *beleevers* and *Saints*, who are frequently in the *Testament* of Christ, stiled Disciples or Schollars of Christ Jesus, and only they as *Beleevers*. Secondly, As to their Monkish and idle course of life. * * * Thirdly, As to their *Popish* and vaunting *Titles* so strange from the *New Testament* and *language* of *Christ Jesus*. * * * Fourthly, As to their (pretended) *Spirituall* and holy exercises proper onely to the *Churches* and *Assemblies* of the *Saints* (the onely *Schools* of the *Prophets* appointed by *Christ Jesus*: Fifthly, As to their being prepared and fitted by these means, as in a way of *Prentiship*, to set up the *Trade* and way of *Preaching*, the science or faculty of *Spirituall merchandise* (*Revel.* 18. in a deep *Mistery*) of all sorts of *Spices* and precious things, the precious and sweet *Truths* and *Promises* of holy Scripture, &c." pp. 14. 15. 16.

to a *Schoole*: All *Beleevers* are his *Disciples* or *Schol-* ars, yea *women* also, *Acts* 9. 36. There was a certaine *Disciple* or *Scholar* called *Dorcas*.

<small>Schoole, and all Believers Scholars.</small>

Have not the *Universities* sacrilegiously stole this blessed name of *Christs Scholars* from his people? Is not the very Scripture language it selfe become *absurd*, to wit, to call *Gods* people, especially Women (as *Dorcas*) *Scholars*?

174] *Peace.* Some will object, how shall the *Scriptures* be brought to *light* from out of *Popish darknesse*, except these *Schooles* of *Prophets* convey them to us?

Truth. I know no *Schooles* of *Prophets* in the *New Testament*, but the particular *Congregation* of *Christ Jesus*, 1 Cor. 14. And I question whether any thing but Sinne stopt and dried up the *current* of the *Spirit* in those rare *gifts* of *tongues* to Gods *sons* & *daughters*, serving so admirably both for the understanding of the *Originall* Scriptures, and also for the propagating of the name of *Christ*.

Who knowes but that it may please the *Lord* againe to cloath his people with a spirit of *zeale* and *courage* for the name of *Christ*, yea and powre forth those fiery streames againe of *Tongues* and *Prophecie* in the *restauration* of *Zion*?

<small>Who knowes but God may againe powre forth the gifts of Tongues?</small>

If it be not his holy pleasure so to doe, but that his people with daily study and labour must *dig* to come at the *Originall Fountaines*, *Gods people* have many wayes (besides the Universitie, *lazie* and *Monkish*) to attaine to an excellent measure of the knowledge of those *tongues*.

<small>Tongues attainable out of Oxford or Cambridge.</small>

That most despised (while living) and now much

Mr. Ains- honoured Mr. *Ainsworth*,[1] had scarce his Peere
worth. amongst a thousand *Academians* for the Scripture *Originalls*, and yet he scarce set foot within a *Colledge* walls.

CHAP. CVIII.

Peace. I Shall now present you with their 10. Head, viz. concerning the Magistrates power in matters of Doctrine.

"That which is unjustly ascribed to the Pope, is
"as unjustly ascribed to the Magistrates, viz. to have
"power of making new Articles of Faith, or Rules
"of Life, or of pressing upon the Churches to give
"such publike honour to the Apocrypha writings, or
"Homilies of men, as to read them to the people in
"the roome of the Oracles of God.

Truth. This *Position* simply considered I acknowledge a most holy truth of *God*, both against the *Pope*, and the *Civill Magistrates* challenge, both pretending to be the *Vicars* of *Christ Jesus* upon the *Earth.* Yet two things here I shall propose to *consideration.*

---

[1] Henry Ainsworth was a Separatist, and teacher of the church in Amsterdam. He wrote *Annotations of the Five Books of Moses, the Psalms, and the Song of Solomon.* A list of his works is given in Brook's *Puritans*, ii : 303.

Bishop Hall (*Apology against Brownists,* Works, x: 5–113.) treats Ainsworth with as much respect as he could feel for one of his sect, and evidently regards him as its most learned man.

Even Cotton gave him praise. "Mr. *Aynsworths* name is of best esteeme (without all exception) in that way, who refused Communion with hearing in England." *Cotton's Answer*, p. 122. "Mr. Ainsworth, a man of a more modest and humble spirit, and diligently studious of the Hebrew Text, hath not been unuseful to the Church in his Exposition of the *Pentateuch*, especially of *Moses* his Rituals, notwithstanding some uncircumcised, and ungrounded Rabbinical observations recited, but not refuted." *Way of Cong. Churches Cleared*, p. 6.

First, since the *Parliament* of *England* thrust the *Pope* out of his *chaire* in *England,* and set downe *King Henry* the 8. and his *Successours* [175] in the *Popes* roome, establishing them supreme *Governours* of the *Church* of *England,*[:] since such an absolute *government* is given by all men to them to be *Guardians* of the first *Table* and *worship* of God; to set up the true *worship,* to suppresse all *false,* and that by the power of the *Sword*; and therefore consequently they must judge and determine what the *true* is, and what the *false.*[:]

King Henry the 8. set down in the Popes chaire in England.

And since the *Magistrate* is bound (by these *Authours* principles) to see the *Church,* the *Church* officers and members doe their duty, he must therefore judge what is the *Churches* duty, and when she performes or not performes it, or when she exceeds, so likewise when the *Ministers* performe their duty, or when they exceed it.

If the Magistrate must punish in Spirituall cases he must of necessity be judge in Spirituall causes also.

And if the *Magistrate* must judge, then certainly by his owne *eye,* and not by the *eyes* of others, though assembled in a *Nationall* or *Generall Councell.*

Then also upon his judgement must the people rest, as upon the minde and judgement of Christ, or else it must be confest that he hath no such power left him by Christ to compell the soules of men in matters of Gods worship.

Secondly, concerning the *Apocrypha* writings and *Homilies* to be urged by the Magistrate to be read unto the people as the *Oracles* of *God:* I aske if the *Homilies* of *England* contain not in them much pretious and heavenly matter! Secondly, if they were not penn'd (at least many of them) by *excellent* men

Apocripha, Common Prayer and Homilies, pretious to our forefathers.

for *learning, holinesse*, and *witnesse* of *Chrifts Truth* incomparable. Thirdly, were they not authorifed by that moft rare and pious *Prince Ed.* 6. then *head* of the *Church* of *England*? With what great folemnity and rejoycing were they received of thoufands?'

Yet now behold their *children* after them fharply cenfure them for *Apocrypha* writings and *Homilies* thruft into the roome of the *Word* of *God*, and fo falling into the *confideration* of a falfe and counterfeit *Scripture*.

A cafe. I demand of thefe worthy men whether a fervant of God might then lawfully have refufed to read or heare fuch a falfe Scripture?

Secondly, if fo, whether *King Edward* might have lawfully compelled fuch a man to yeeld and fubmit,

---

[1] Bifhop Short fays (*Hiftory of Church of England*, chap. viii. §412, note,) "The hiftory of the compofition of the Homilies is buried in fo much obfcurity that a fhort note will convey to the reader all that is known concerning them. The firft volume is generally attributed to Cranmer, Ridley, Latimer, Hopkins and Becon. Burnet (Pref. to the Thirty Nine Articles, p. iii.) fays that Jewel was particularly engaged in compiling the fecond. Archbifhop Parker, however, in 1563, fpeaks of them as being "revifed and finifhed, with a fecond part by him and the other bifhops." (Strype's *Parker*, i: 253.) The homilies on Salvation, Faith, and Good Works, are with reafon attributed to Cranmer." The firft edition of the firft book was publifhed July, 1547, 1 Edward VI.

The Puritans always felt a diflike for the public ufe of the Apocrypha. It was one of the accufations of Martin Mar-prelate againft Archbifhop Whitgift, "that he commanded the Apocrypha to be bound up with the Bibles." Strype's *Life of Whitgift*, i: 590. It was one of the objections to the Book of Common Prayer in the Apology of the Lincolnfhire minifters prefented to James I. in 1604, that it made a difproportionate ufe of leffons from the Apocrypha. Neal's *Puritans*, i: 246. In the Hampton Court Conference (Jan. 16, 1603,) the Puritan minifters took exceptions efpecially to the Service book, and among other points to the reading of the Apocrypha. Strype's *Whitgift*, iii: 404. In the Savoy Conference (1661) the fame exceptions were taken by Baxter in behalf of the Nonconformifts, but only to lead to the infertion of new Apocryphal leffons, with the conceffion that they fhould not be read on Sundays. Short, *Hift. Church of England*, chap. xv. §671. Neal's *Puritans*, ii: 233.

or elfe have perfecuted him, yea (according to the Authors principles) whether he ought to have fpared him, becaufe after the *admonitions* of fuch pious and learned men, this man fhall now prove an *Hereticke*, and as an obftinate perfon finning againft the *light* of his owne *confcience?*

176] In this cafe what fhall the *confcience* of the fubject doe, awed by the *dread* of the moft *High?* What fhall the *confcience* of the *Magiftrate* do, zealous for his glorious *Reformation*, being conftantly perfwaded by his *Clergy* of his *Lieutenantfhip* received from *Chrift?*

Again, what *priviledge* have thofe worthy fervants of *God* either in *Old* or *New England*, to be exempted from the miftakes, into which thofe glorious *Worthies* in *K. Edwards* time did fall? and if fo, what bloudy *conclufions* are prefented to the World, perfwading men to plucke up by the *Roots* from the Land of the living, all fuch as feem in their eyes hereticall or obftinate? *[Reformations are fallible. Bloudy conclufions.]*

CHAP. CIX.

Peace. DEare *Truth*, What darke and difmall bloudy paths doe we walke in? How is thy name and mine in all ages cried up, yet as an Englifh Flag in a Spanifh bottome, not in truth but dangerous treachery and abufe both of *Truth* and *Peace?*

We are now come to the 11 Head which concernes the Magiftrates power in worfhip. *[11 Head.]*

"Firft, they have power (fay they) to reforme
"things in the worfhip of God in a Church cor-

"rupted, and to eſtabliſh the pure worſhip of God,
"defending the ſame by the power of the ſword
"againſt all thoſe who ſhall attempt to corrupt it.[1]

"For firſt, the reigning of Idolatry and corruption
"in Religion is imputed to the want of a King,
"*Iudges* 17. 5, 6.

"Secondly, Remiſſenes in Reforming Religion, is
"a fault imputed to them who ſuffered the High
"Places in *Iſrael*[,] and in *Gallio*, who cared not for
"ſuch things, *Acts* 18.

"Thirdly, Forwardneſſe this way is a duty not only
"for Kings in the Old Teſtament, but for Princes
"under the New, 1 *Tim.* 2. 2. *Rom.* 13. 4. *Eſay* 49.
"23. Neither did the Kings of *Iſrael* reforme things
"amiſſe as types of Chriſt, but as Civill Magiſtrates,
"and ſo exemplary to all Chriſtians. And here Ref-
"ormation in Religion is commendable in a Perſian
"King, *Ezra* 7. 23. And it is well knowne that
"remiſſenes in Princes of Chriſtendome in matters
"of Religion and Worſhip (divolving the care thereof
"only to the Clergy, and ſo ſetting the Hornes thereof
"upon the Churches head) hath been the cauſe of
"Antichriſtian inventions, uſurpations and corruptions
"in the Worſhip and Temple of God.

177] "Secondly, they have not power to preſſe upon
"the Churches, ſtinted Prayers, or ſet Liturgies,
"whether New or Old, Popiſh, or others under col-
"our of uniformity of Worſhip, or morall goodneſſe

---

[1] "If any church one or more ſhall grow ſchiſmaticall, rending itſelf from the communion of other churches, or ſhall walke incorrigibly or obſtinately in any corrupt way of their own, contrary to the rule of the word; in ſuch caſe the Magiſtrate is to put forth his coercive power as the matter ſhall require." *Cambridge Platform*, xvii: 9. p. 29.

"of them both for matter and forme, conceiving our
"arguments fent to our Brethren in *England* concern-
"ing this Queftion to evince this Truth.[1]

"Thirdly, they have no power to preffe upon the
"Churches, neither by Law (as hath been faid before)
"nor by Proclamation and command, any facred
"fignificant ceremonies, whether more or leffe, Popifh
"or Jewifh rite, or any other device of man, be it
"never fo little in the worfhip of God, under what
"colour foever of indifferencie, civility, ufing them
"without opinion of fanctity, publicke peace or obe-
"dience to righteous Authority, as Surplice, Croffe,
"kneeling at Sacrament; Salt and Spitle in Baptifme,
"Holy dayes: They having beene fo accurfed of God,
"fo abufed by man, the impofing of fome ever mak-
"ing way for the urging of more, the receiving of
"fome making the confcience bow to the burthen
"of all.

"Fourthly, they have not power to governe and
"rule the acts of worfhip in the Church of God.

---

[1] An Anfwer of the Elders of the Severall Chvrches in New England unto Nine Pofitions, fent over to them (By divers Reverend and godly Minifters in England) to declare their Judgements therein. Written in the Yeer, 1639. London, 1643.

This Book is printed and bound, having a confecutive paging, with "An Apologie for Church-Covenant, &c. Sent over in Anfwer to Mafter Bernard, in the Yeare 1639." It is alfo bound together with The Anfwer to Two and Thirty Queftions, (fee p. 215, *fupra*) and is connected with it on the title-page, although with feparate pagination. That this, as well as the other work was written by Richard Mather we have not only the evidence cited on page 215, but alfo the teftimony of his fon-in-law, Increafe Mather. "There is a book which bears the title of 'Anfwer of the Elders' &c. printed in the year 1643, of which book my father Mather was the fole author, & he wrote it in the primitive times of thofe churches (viz. in the year 1639) as himfelf affured me." *Order of the Gofpel*, p. 73.

The firft Pofition is "That a ftinted Forme of Prayer, or fet Liturgie, is unlawfull." pp. 55–60.

"It is with a Magiftrate in a State, in refpect of "the acts of thofe who worfhip in a Church, as it is "with a Prince in a Ship, wherein, though he be "governour of their perfons (elfe he fhould not be "their Prince) yet is not governour of the actions of "the Mariners (then he fhould be Pilot:) Indeed if "the Pilot fhall manifeftly erre in his action, he may "reprove him, and fo any other paffenger may: Or "if he offend againft the life and goods of any, he "may in due time and place civilly punifh him, "which no other paffenger can doe: For, it is proper "to Chrift, the Head of the Church, as to prefcribe, "fo to rule the actions of his own worfhip in the "wayes of his fervants, *Efay* 9. 6, 7. The govern-"ment of the Church is upon his fhoulder, which "no Civill officer ought to attempt: And therefore "Magiftrates have no power to limit a Minifter either "to what he fhall preach or pray, or in what manner "they fhall worfhip God, left hereby they fhall "advance themfelves above Chrift, and limit his "Spirit.

Truth. In this generall Head are propofed two things.

Firft, what the Magiftrate ought to doe pofitively concerning the worfhip of God.

178] Secondly, what he may doe in the worfhip of God.

What he ought to doe is comprifed in thefe par-ticulars.

Firft, he ought to reforme the worfhip of God when it is corrupted.

Secondly, he ought to eftablifh a pure worfhip of God.

Thirdly, he ought to defend it by the fword: he ought to reftrain Idolatry by the fword, and to cut off *offendours*, as former paffages have opened.

For the proofe of this pofitive part of his duty are propounded three forts of Scriptures.

Firft, from the practice of the *Kings* of *Ifrael* and *Judah*.

Secondly, fome from the New *Teftament*.

Thirdly, from the practice of *Kings* of other *Nations*.

Unto which I anfwer.

Firft, concerning this latter, the *Babylonian* and *Perfian Kings, Nebuchadnezzar, Cyrus, Darius, Artaxerxes*: I conceive I have fufficiently before proved,[1] that thefe *Idolatrous Princes* making fuch *Acts* concerning the *God* of *Ifrael*, whom they did not *worfhip* nor *know*, nor meant fo to doe, did onely *permit* and tolerate, and *countenance* the *Jewifh worfhip*, and out of ftrong *convictions* that this *God* of Ifrael was able to doe them good (as well as their owne *gods*) to bring wrath upon them and their *Kingdomes*, as they beleeved their owne alfo did, in which refpect all the *Kings* of the *world* may be eafily brought to the like: but are no *prefident* or *patternes* for all *Princes* and *Civill Magiftrates* in the *World*, to chalenge or affume the *power* of *ruling* or *governing* the *Church* of *Chrift*, and of wearing the fpirituall *Crowne* of the *Lord*, which he alone weareth in a *fpirituall* way by his *Officers* and *Governours* after his owne holy appointment.

The argument from the Babylonian and Perfian kings reminded.

Secondly, for thofe of the New *Teftament* I have (as I beleeve) fully and fufficiently anfwered.

[1] Chap. xcvi.

So also that prophesie of *Isa.* 49.[1]

The president of the Kings and Governours of Israel and Judah examined.
Lastly, however I have often touched those Scriptures produced from the practice of the *Kings* of *Israel* and *Judah:* yet because so great a *waight* of this controversie lyes upon this *president* of the *Old Testament*, from the duties of this *nature* enjoyned to those *Kings* and *Governours*, and their practices, *obeying* or *disobeying*, accordingly *commended* or *reproved*. I shall (with the helpe of *Christ Iesus*, the true *King* of *Israel*) declare and demonstrate how weake 179] and brittle this supposed *Pillar* of *Marble* is, to beare up and sustain such a mighty burthen and waight of so many high concernments as are laid upon it. In which I shall evidently prove that the

The state of Israel relating to spirituall matters proved typicall.
state of *Israel* as a *Nationall State* made up of *Spirituall* and *Civill power,* so farre as it attended upon the *spirituall*, was meerly figurative and typing out the *Christian Churches* consisting of both *Jewes* and *Gentiles*, enjoying the true power of the *Lord Iesus,* establishing, reforming, correcting, defending in all cases concerning his *Kingdome* and *Government.*

CHAP. CX.

Peace. Blessed be the *God* of *Truth*, the *God* of *Peace*, who hath so long preserved us in this our retired *conference* without *interruptions:* His *mercy* still shields us while you expresse and I listen to that so much *imitated,* yet most *unimitable State* of *Israel.*

The Persian Kings
Yet before you descend to *particulars* (deare Truth) let me cast one *Mite* into your great *Treasury* con-

[1] Chap. lxxxii.

cerning that Instance (just now mentioned) of the *Persian Kings*.

Me thinkes those *presidents* of *Cyrus, Darius* and *Artaxerxes* are strong against *New Englands Tenent* and *practice*. Those *Princes* professedly gave free *permission* and bountifull *incouragement* to the *Consciences* of the *Iewes*, to use and practise their *Religion*, which *Religion* was most eminently contrary to their owne *Religion* and their Countries worship.

<small>make evidently against such as produce them for maintenance of the doctrine of persecution.</small>

Truth. I shall (sweet Peace) with more delight passe on these rough wayes, from your kinde acceptance and unwearied patience in attention.

In this discovery of that vast and mighty difference betweene that State of Israel and all other States (onely to bee matched and parallel'd by the Christian Church or Israel) I shall select some maine and principall considerations concerning that State wherein the irreconciliable *differences* and disproportion may appeare.

First, I shall consider the very *Land* and *Country* of *Canaan* it selfe, and present some *considerations* proving it to be a *None-such*.

First, this *Land* was espyed out and chosen by the *Lord* out of all the *Countries* of the *World* to be the seat of his Church and people, *Ezek.* 20. 6.

But now there is no respect of *Earth*, of *Places* or *Countries* with the *Lord*: So testified the *Lord Iesus Christ* himselfe to the [180] woman of *Samaria* (*Iohn* 4.) professing that neither at that *Mountaine* nor at *Ierusalem* should men *worship* the *Father*.

<small>The Land of Canaan chosen by God to be the seat of the Church, but under the New Testament all Nations alike.</small>

While that Nationall State of the *Church* of the *Iewes* remained, the Tribes were bound to goe up to

Ierusalem to *worship*, *Psal.* 122. But now, *in every Nation* (not the whole Land or Country as it was with Canaan) he that feareth God and worketh righteousnesse is accepted with him, *Act.* 10. 35. This then appeared in that large Commission of the Lord Jesus to his first Ministers: Goe into *all Nations*, and not onely into Canaan, to carry tidings of Mercy, &c.

Secondly, the former Inhabitants thereof, seven great and mightie *Nations* (*Deuter.* 7.) were all devoted to destruction by the Lords owne mouth, which was to bee performed by the impartiall hand of the Children of Israel, without any sparing or shewing *Mercy*.

<small>The inhabitants of Canaans Land everysoule to be put to death that the Israelites might enjoy their possessions: not so now.</small>

But so now it hath not pleased the Lord to devote any people to present Destruction, commanding his people to kill and slay without *Covenant* or *Compassion*, *Deuteronomy* 7. 2.

Where have *Emperours*, *Kings*, or *Generals* an immediate call from God to destroy whole Cities, City after City, Men, women, Children, Old and Young, as *Ioshua* practised? *Ioshua* 6. and 10. Chapters, &c.

This did Israel to these seven Nations, that they themselves might succeed them in their Cities, Habitations, and Possessions.

This onely is true in a spirituall *Antitype*, when Gods people by the Sword (the two-edged Sword of *Gods Spirit*) slay the ungodly and become *Heires*, yea fellow *Heires* with *Christ Iesus*, *Romanes* 8. *Gods* meeke people inherit the earth, (*Matthew* 5.) They mystically like *Noah* (*Hebrewes* 11.) condemne the whole unbeleeving World, both by present and future sentence, 2 *Corinth*. 6. 2.

CHAP. CXI.

THirdly, the very *materials*, the *Gold* and *Silver* of the Idols of this Land were odious and abominable, and dangerous to the people of *Israel*, that they might not desire it, nor take it to themselves, 181] *Deut.* 7. 25. 26. left themselves also become a *curse*, and like unto those cursed abominable things. Whereas we finde not any such accursed *nature* in the *materials* of *Idols* or *Images* now, but that (the *Idolatrous formes* being changed) the *silver* and *gold* may be cast and coyned, and other *materialls* lawfully employed and used. *The very materiall gold & silver of the Canaans Images typically to be abhorred.*

Yet this we finde in the *Antitype*, that *gold, silver*, yea *house, land*, yea *wives, children*, yea *life* it selfe, as they allure and draw us from *God* in *Christ*, are to be abominated and hated by us, without which *hatred* and *indignation* against the most plausible and pleasing enticings from *CHRIST JESUS*, it is impossible for any man to bee a true *Christian*, Luke 14. 16.

Fourthly, this Land, this *Earth* was an *Holy land,* Zach. 2. 12. Ceremonially and typically *holy, Fields,* Gardens, Orchards, Houses, &c. which *Holines* the World knowes not now in one *Land*, or *Country,* House, Field, Garden, &c. one above another. *The Land of Canaan ceremnonially holy.*

Yet in the Spirituall *Land of Canaan* the *Christian Church*, all things are made holy and pure (in all Lands) to the pure, *Tit.* 1. meats and drinkes are sanctified, that is, dedicated to the holy use of the thankfull *Believers*, 1 Tim. 4. yea and the *unbelieving Husband, Wife*, and their Children are sanctified and made holy to *Believers*, insomuch that that golden *Greater holynesse in the Antitype under the Gospel, then in the types under the Law.*

inscription (peculiar to the *forehead* of the *High Priest*) *Holines to Jehovah*, shall be written upon the very *Bridles* of the *Horses*, as all are dedicated to the service of *Christ Jesus* in the Gospels peace and holines.

<small>The Land of Canaan Jehovahs Land.</small> Fifthly, the Lord expresly calls it his own Land, *Levit.* 25. 23. *Hos.* 9. 3. *Jehovah* his Land, a terme proper unto Spirituall *Canaan*, the *Church* of *God*, which must needs be in respect of his choice of that *Land* to be the Seate and Residence of his *Church* and *Ordinances*.

But now the partition *wall* is broken down, and in respect of the *Lords* speciall proprietie to one Country more then another, what difference between *Asia* and *Africa*, between *Europe* and *America*, between *England* and *Turkie*, *London* and *Constantinople*?

<small>Emanuels Land: so no Land or country more then another.</small> This Land (among many other glorious *Titles* given to it) was called *Emanuels* land, that is, *God with us*, *Christ* his land, or *Christian* land, *Isa.* 8. 8.

But now: *Jerusalem* from above is not materiall and Earthly, [182] but Spirituall, *Gal.* 4. *Heb.* 12. *Materiall Jerusalem* is no more the *Lords* citie then *Jericho*, *Ninivie*, or *Babell* (in respect of place or Countrey) for even at *Babell* literall was a *Church* of *Jesus Christ*, 1 *Pet.* 5.

<small>The Blasphemous titles of the Christned and Christian World.</small> It is true that *Antichrist* hath *christned* all those *Countries* whereon the *Whore* sitteth, *Revel.* 17. with the Title of *Christs land*, or *Christian land*.

And *Hundius*,[1] in his *Map* of the *Christian* World,

---

[1] Josse Hondius (1546–1611) was an engraver and one of the geographers who in the 16th century begun to give more accuracy to cosmography, although re-

makes this land to extend to all *Asia*, a great part of *Africa*, all *Europe*, and a vast part of *America*, even so farre as his *unchristian Christenings* hath gone. But as every false C*hrist* hath *false Teachers, false Christians, false Faith, Hope, Love*, &c. and in the end *false Salvation*, so doth he also counterfeit the false Name of C*hrist*, C*hristians*, C*hristian* land or Countrey.

Sixthly, this Land was to keepe her *Sabbaths* unto *God:* Sixe yeares they were to sow their *Fields*, and prune their *Vines*, but in the 7. yeare they were not to sow their *Fields*, nor prune their *Vineyards*, but to eat that which grew of it selfe or own accord. The materiall Land of Canaan was to keep her Sabboths, so no materiall land or Country now.

But such *Observations* doth not *God* now lay upon any Fields, Vineyards, &c. under the Gospell.

Yet in the Spirituall land of *Canaan*, the true *Church*, there is a Spirituall *Soule-rest* or *Sabbath*, a quiet depending upon *God*, a living by *Faith* in him, a making him our *portion*, and casting all care upon him who careth for us: yea sometimes he feedeth his by immediate gracious workes of *Providence*, when comforts arise out of the *Earth*, without secondary meanes or causes, as here, or as elsewhere *Manna* descended from *Heaven*. God feedeth his sometimes immediately.

Seventhly, such portions and possessions of *Lands, Fields, Houses, Vineyards*, were sold with *caution* or *proviso* of returning againe in the yeare of *Jubilee* to the right owners, *Levit.* 25. 23.

---

taining many of the errors of their predecessors. He published his maps at Amsterdam. He enlarged and improved the Grand Atlas of Mercator. *Biographie Universelle*, xix: 514. The text gives only an instance of the general inaccuracy which marked the maps of that period.

"The *World* divided (say our ablest *Cosmographers*) into *thirty* parts, as yet but *five* of *thirty* have heard of the sweet name of *Jesus* a *Saviour*." Hireling Ministry. p. 3.

Such *cautions*, such *provisos* are not now injoyned by *God* in the sale of *lands, fields, inheritances*, nor no such *Jubilee* or *Redemption* to be expected.

<small>The Jubilee of Canaan a type of restitution and redemption in the Gospell.</small>

Yet this also finds a fulfilling in the *spirituall Canaan*, or *Church* of *God*, unto which the *silver Trumpet* of *Jubilee*, the *Gospel*, hath sounded a spirituall *restitution* of all their spirituall *rights* and *inheritances*, which either they have lost in the fall of the first man *Adam*, or in their particular falls, when they are captive and sold unto sin, *Rom*. 7. Or lastly in the spirituall *captivitie* of *Babels bondage:* how 183] sweet then is the name of a *Saviour*, in whom is the joyfull sound of *Deliverance* and *Redemption!*

<small>Canaans land a type of the Kingdome of God on Earth and in Heaven</small>

Eightly, this Land or Country was a figure or type of the kingdome of *Heaven* above, begun here below in the *Church* and *Kingdome* of *God*, *Heb*. 4. 8. *Heb*. 11. 9. 10. Hence was a *Birthright* so pretious in *Canaans* Land: Hence *Naboth* so inexorable and resolute in refusing to part with his Inheritance to King *Ahab*, counting all *Ahabs* seeming *reasonable* offers most *unreasonable*, as soliciting him to part with a *Garden* plot of *Canaans* land, though his refusall cost him his very life.

<small>Why Naboth refused to part with a Garden plot to his King upon hazard of his life.</small>

What *Land*, what *Country* now is *Israels Parallel* and *Antitype*, but that holy *mysticall* Nation the *Church* of *God*, peculiar and called out to him out of every Nation and Country, 1 *Pet*. 2. 9. In which every true *spirituall Naboth* hath his *spirituall inheritance*, which he dares not part with, though it be to his *King* or *Soveraigne*, and though such his *refusall* cost him this present life.

CHAP. CXII.

Peace. Doubtleſſe that *Canaan* Land was not a patterne for all *Lands*: It was a *none-ſuch*, *unparalleled* and unmatchable.

Truth. Many other *conſiderations* of the ſame nature I might annex, but I picke here and there a flowre, and paſſe on to a ſecond Head concerning the people themſelves, wherein the ſtate of the people ſhall appeare unmatchable, but only by the true Church and Iſrael of God. The difference of the people of Iſrael and all other Peoples.

Firſt, the people of Iſrael were all the Seed or Offſpring of one man *Abraham*, *Pſal.* 105. 6. and ſo downward the Seed of *Iſaac* and *Jacob*, hence called the *Iſrael* of God, that is, *wraſtlers* and *prevailers* with *God*, diſtinguiſhed into twelve *Tribes* all ſprung out of *Iſraels* loynes. The people of Iſrael the ſeed of one man.

But now, few *Nations* of the World but are a mixed Seed, the people of *England* eſpecially[:] the *Britaines*, *Picts*, *Romanes*, *Saxons*, *Danes* and *Normans*, by a wonderfull providence of *God* being become one *Engliſh* people.

Only the Spirituall *Iſrael* and Seed of *God* the New-borne are but one: *Chriſt* is the Seed, *Gal.* 3. and they only that are *Chriſts* are only *Abrahams* Seed and Heires according to the promiſe. Only made good in the Spirituall ſeed, the regenerate or new-borne.

This Spirituall Seed is the only *Antitype* of the former figurative [184] and typicall: A *Seed* which all *Chriſtians* ought to propagate, yea even the *unmarried* men and women (who are not capable of *naturall offspring*) for thus is this called the Seed of *Chriſt* (who lived and died unmarried) *Iſa.* 59. 21.

Secondly, this people was selected and separated to the *Lord*, his *Covenant* and *Worship*[,] from all the *people* and *Nations* of the *World* beside to be his peculiar and onely people, *Levit*. 20. 26. &c.

<small>The people of Israel separate from all Nations in Spirituall and in some Civill things.</small>

Therefore such as returned from *Babylon* to *Jerusalem*, they separated themselves to eat the *Passeover*, *Ezra* 6. And in that solemne *humiliation* and *confession* before the *Lord*, *Nehem*. 9. the *children* of *Israel* separated themselves from all strangers.

This separation of theirs was so famous, that it extended not only to *Circumcision*, the *Passeover*, and matters of *Gods worship*, but even to *temporall* and *civill things*: Thus (*Ezra* 9.) they separated or put away their very wives, which they had taken of the strange *Nations* contrary to the Commandement of the *Lord*.

<small>No Nation so separated to God in the Gospel, but only the new-borne Israel that feare God in every Nation.</small>

But where hath the *God* of *Heaven* in the *Gospel* separated whole *Nations* or *Kingdomes* (*English*, *Scotch*, *Irish*, *French*, *Dutch*, &c.) as a peculiar people and *Antitype* of the people of *Israel?* Yea where the least footing in all the Scripture for a *Nationall Church* after *Christs* comming?

Can any people in the *world* patterne this *samplar* but the *New-borne Israel*, such as feare *God* in every *Nation* (*Acts* 10. 35.) commanded to come forth and separate from all uncleane things or persons, (2 *Cor*. 6.) and though not bound to put away strange wives as Israel did, because of that peculiar respect upon them in *Civill* things, yet to be holy or set apart to the *Lord* in all manner of *civill conversation*, 1 *Pet*. 1. Only to marry in the *Lord*, yea and to marry as if they married not 1 *Cor*. 7. yea to hate *wife* and *children, father, mother, houſe* and *land,* yea and life it ſelfe for the *Lord Jeſus, Luc.* 14.

Thirdly, this Seed of *Abraham* thus ſeparate from all people unto the *Lord* was wonderfully redeemed and brought from *Ægypts bondage* through the *Red Sea,* and the *Wilderneſſe* unto the Land of *Canaan,* by many ſtrange ſignes and wonderfull *miracles,* wrought by the outſtretched hand of the *Lord,* famous and dreadfull, and to be admired by all ſucceeding *peoples* and *generations, Deut.* 4. 32, 33, 34. Aske now from one ſide of the *Heaven* unto the other, whether there hath been ſuch a thing as this, &c? *The whole people of Iſrael miraculouſly brought forth of Egypt.*

185] And we may aske againe from one ſide of the Heaven unto the other whether the Lord hath now ſo miraculouſly redeemed and brought unto *Himſelfe* any *Nation* or people as he did this people of Iſrael. *Not ſo any whole Nation now.*

Peace. The *Engliſh, Scotch, Dutch,* &c. are apt to make themſelves the parallels, as wonderfully come forth of Popery, &c.

Truth. 1. But firſt, whole Nations are no Churches under the Goſpel.

Secondly, bring the *Nations* of *Europe* profeſſing *Proteſtaniſme* to the ballance of the *Sanctuary,* and ponder well whether the *body, bulke,* the generall or one hundreth part of ſuch peoples be truly turned to God from *Popery.* *Popery not ſo eaſily turned from as is conceived*

Who knowes not how eaſie it is to turne, and turne, and turn againe whole *Nations* from one *Religion* to another?

Who knowes not that within the compaſſe of one poore *ſpan* of 12 yeares revolution, all *England* hath become from halfe *Papiſt,* halfe *Proteſtant,* to be *Wonderfull turnings in Religion in 12 yeares compasse in England.* absolute *Protestants*; from absolute *Protestants*, to absolute *Papists*; from absolute *Papists* (changing as fashions) to absolute *Protestants?*

The Pope not unlike to recover his Monarchie over Europe before his downfall. I will not say (as some worthy witnesses of *Christ* have uttered) that all *England* and *Europe* must againe submit their faire necks to the *Popes* yoake:[1] But this, I say, many *Scriptures* concerning the destruction of the *Beast* and the *Whore* looke that way: And I adde, they that feele the pulse of the people seriously must confesse that a *victorious Sword*, and a *Spanish Inquisition* will soone make millions face about as they were in the Fore-Fathers times.

CHAP. CXIII.

Peace. O That the *Steersmen* of the *Nations* might remember this, Bee wise and kisse the Sonne, lest he goe on in this His dreadfull anger, and dash them in peeces here and eternally.

---

[1] See Chap. xxix. pp. 136, 137, *supra*, where the same thought is expressed. To this Cotton replied (*Bloudy Tenent Washed*, p. 82,) "The Prophecie of *England's* Revolt againe to Popery, wanteth Scripture Light." To this Williams rejoins (*Bloody Tenent yet more Bloody*, p. 119,) "He that loves *Christ Jesus* in sincerity, cannot but long that *Christ Jesus* would speedily be pleased with the breath of his mouth to consume that man of sin: But yet that worthy servant of *God* (according to his *conscience*) Master *Archer*, doth not barely propose his *opinion*, but also his *Scripture-grounds*, which I believe, compared with all former *experiences*, will seem to be of great & weighty *consideration*."

Henry Archer was a non-conformist preacher in London, who fled to Holland and was pastor of the English church in Arnheim in connection with Dr. Thomas Goodwin, the first of the Five Dissenting Brethren to whom Williams's "Queries" was addressed. He was a Millenarian, and wrote a work entitled "The Personal Reign of Christ upon Earth. In a Treatise wherein is fully & largely laid open & proved, that Jesus Christ, together with his Saints, shall visibly possess a monarchicall State and Kingdom in the World, 1642." Brook, *Lives of the Puritans*, ii: 455.

Truth. I therefore thirdly adde, That only such as are *Abrahams* Seed, *circumcised* in Heart, *New-borne*, *Israel* (or *wrastlers* with *God*) are the *Antitype* of the former *Israel*, these are only the holy *Nation* (1 *Pet.* 2.) wonderfully redeemed from the *Ægypt* of this *World* (*Titus* 2. 14.) brought through the *Red Sea* of *Baptisme* (1 *Cor.* 10.) through the Wildernesse of *afflictions*, and of the *peoples* (*Deut.* 8. [186] *Ezek.* 20.) into the *Kingdome* of *Heaven* begun below, even that *Christian* Land of *Promise*, where flow the ever-flowing streames and Rivers of Spirituall milke and honey.

<small>Who are now the true Seed of Abraham.</small>

Fourthly, All this people universally (in typicall and ceremoniall respect) were holy and cleane in this their *separation* and *sequestration* unto *God, Exod.* 19. 5. Hence, even in respect of their naturall birth in that Land they were an *holy Seed*, and *Ezra* makes it the matter of his great complaint, *Ezra* 9. 1. 2. The holy Seed have mingled themselves.

<small>The people of Israel all holy in a typicall holinesse.</small>

But where is now that *Nation* or *Country* upon the face of the *Earth*, thus cleane and holy unto *God*, and bound to so many ceremoniall cleansings and purgings?

Are not all the *Nations* of the *Earth* alike cleane unto *God*, or rather alike uncleane, untill it pleaseth the *Father* of *mercies* to call some out to the *Knowledge* and *Grace* of his Sonne, making them to see their *filthinesse* and strangenesse from the *Commonweale* of *Israel*, and to wash in the bloud of the Lambe of *God*.

<small>All Nations now alike since the comming of the Lord Jesus.</small>

This taking away the difference between *Nation* and *Nation*, *Country* and *Country*, is most fully and admirably declared in that great vision of all sorts of living creatures prefented unto *Peter*, *Acts* 10. whereby it pleafed the *Lord* to informe *Peter* of the abolifhing of the difference between *Jew* and *Gentile* in any holy or unholy, cleane or uncleane refpect.

Fifthly, (not only to fpeake of all, but to felect one or two more) This people of *Ifrael* in that Nationall State were a type of all the Children of God in all ages under the profeffion of the *Gofpell*, who are therefore called the Children of *Abraham*, and the *Ifrael* of God, *Gal.* 3. & *Gal.* 6. A Kingly *Priefthood* and *holy Nation* (1 *Pet.* 2. 9.) in a cleare and manifeft *Antitype* to the former *Ifrael, Exod.* 19. 6.

The children of Ifrael a figure of the Ifrael or people of God only under the Gofpel.

Hence *Chriftians* now are figuratively in this refpect called *Jewes, Rev.* 3. where lies a cleare diftinction of the *true* and *falfe* Chriftian under the confideration of the *true* and *falfe Jew*: Behold I will make them of the Synagogue of *Sathan* that fay they are Jewes and are not, but doe lie, *Rev.* 3. But fuch a typicall refpect we finde not now upon any People, *Nation* or *Country* of the whole *World*: But out of all *Nations, Tongues* and *Languages* is God pleafed to call fome and redeem them to Himfelfe (*Rev.* 5. 9.) And hath made no difference betweene the *Iewes* and *Gentiles*, [187] *Greekes* and *Scithians, Gal.* 3. who by *Regeneration* or fecond birth, become the Ifrael of God, *Gal.* 6. the *Temple* of God, 1 *Cor.* 3. and the true *Jerufalem, Heb.* 12.

The people of Ifrael different from all the world in their figu-

Laftly, all this whole *Nation* or people, as they were of one *typicall feed* of *Abraham*, & fealed with a fhamefull & painfull *Ordinance* of *cutting* off the *fore-skin*, wch differenced them from all the *World* befide: So alfo were they bound to fuch and fuch *solemnities* of *figurative worships*. Amongst many others I shall end this passage concerning the people with a famous observation out of *Numb.* 9. 13. viz. All that whole *Nation* was bound to celebrate and keepe the *Feast* of the *Passeover* in his season, or else they were to be put to *death*. But doth God require a whole *Nation, Country* or *Kingdome* now thus to celebrate the *spirituall Passeover*, the *Supper* and *Feast* of the *Lambe Christ Jesus*, at such a time once a yeare, and that whosoever shall not so doe shall bee put to death? What horrible *prophanations*, what grosse *hypocrisies*, yea what wonderfull *desolations* (sooner or later) must needs follow upon such a course? rative and ceremoniall worships.

Tis true, the people of Israel, brought into covenant with *God* in *Abraham*, and so successively borne in Covenant with *God*, might (in that state of a Nationall *Church*) solemnly covenant and sweare that whosoever would not seeke *Jehovah the God of Israel*, should be put to death, 2 *Chron.* 15. whether small or great, whether man or woman. Israel Gods only Church might well renew that Nationall Covenant and ceremoniall worship

But may whole *Nations* or *Kingdomes* now (according to any one *title* exprest by *Christ Iesus* to that purpose) follow that patterne of *Israel* and put to death all, both men and women, great and small, that according to the rules of the *Gospel* are not borne againe, penitent, humble, heavenly, patient? &c. What a world of hypocrisie from hence is practised by thousands, that for feare will stoope to give that God their bodies in a forme, whom yet in truth their hearts affect not? which other Nations cannot imitate.

Yea also what a world of prophanation of the holy Name and holy Ordinances of the Lord in prostitu- The hypocrisies, *prophana-tions, and slaughters which such imitation now in the Gospell produce.* ting the holy things of God (like the Vessels of the Sanctuary, *Dan.* 5.) to prophane, impenitent and unregenerate persons?

Lastly, what slaughters both of men and women must this necessarily bring into the world, by the Insurrections and Civill Warres about Religion and Conscience? Yea what slaughters of the innocent and faithfull witnesses of Christ Jesus, who choose to bee 188] slaine all the day long for Christ his sake, and to fight for their Lord and Master Christ, onely with spirituall and Christian weapons?

CHAP. CXIV.

Peace. IT seemes (deare *Truth*) a mighty *Gulfe* betweene that people and Nation, and the *Nations* of the *world* then extant and ever since.

Truth. As sure as the blessed substance to all those shadowes, *Christ Iesus* is come, so unmatchable and never to bee paralleld by any *Nationall* State was that *Israel* in the *Figure* or *Shadow*.

And yet the *Israel* of *God* now, the *Regenerate* or *Newborne*, the circumcised in *Heart* by *Repentance* and *Mortification*, who willingly submit unto the *Lord Iesus* as their onely *King* and *Head*, may fitly parallell and answer that *Israel* in the type, without such danger of *hypocrisie*, of such horrible *prophanations*, and of firing the *Civill State* in such bloody *combustions*, as all *Ages* have brought forth upon this compelling a whole *Nation* or *Kingdome* to be the *antitype* of *Israel*.

Peace. Were this Light entertained, some hopes would shine forth for my returne and *restauration.*

Truth. I have yet to adde a third *consideration* concerning the *Kings* and *Governours* of that Land and people.

They were to be (unlesse in their *captivities*) of their *Brethren*, members of the true *Church* of *God*, as appears in the History of *Moses*, the *Elders* of *Israel*, and the *Iudges* and *Kings* of Israel afterward.

But first, who can deny but that there may be now many lawfull *Governours, Magistrates* and *Kings* in the *Nations* of the World, where is no true *Church* of *Iesus Christ?*

Secondly, we know the many excellent *gifts* wherewith it hath pleased God to furnish many, inabling them for publike service to their *Countries* both in *Peace* and *War* (as all *Ages* and *Experience* testifies) on whose soules hee hath not yet pleased to shine in the face of *Iesus Christ*: which *Gifts* and *Talents* must all lye buried in the *Earth*, unlesse such persons may lawfully be called and chosen to, and improved in *publike service*, notwithstanding their different or contrary *Conscience* and *Worship.*

Thirdly, if none but true *Christians*, members of *Christ Iesus* might be *Civill Magistrates*, and publikely intrusted with *civill affaires*, [189] then none but *members* of *Churches, Christians* should be *Husbands* of *Wives, Fathers* of *Children, Masters* of *Servants*: But against this *doctrine* the whole *creation,* the *whole World* may justly rise up in armes, as not onely contrary to true *Piety*, but common *Humanity* it selfe. For if a *Commonweale* bee lawfull amongst

marginalia: The difference of the Kings and Governours of Israel from al Kings & Governors of the world. First, they were all members of the Church. Excellent Talents vouchsafed by God to unregenerate persons. A doctrine contrary to all true Piety and Humanity it selfe.

men that have not heard of *God* nor *Christ*, certainly their *Officers*, *Ministers*, and *Governours* must be lawfull also.

<small>The Papists doctrine of deposing Magistrates confessed in effect to be true by the Protestants.</small>
Fourthly, it is notoriously knowne to be the dangerous *doctrine* profest by some *Papists*, that *Princes* degenerating from their *Religion*, and turning *Heretickes*, are to be deposed, and their *Subjects* actually discharged from their obedience.[1] Which *doctrine* all such must necessarily hold (however most loath to owne it) that hold the *Magistrate Guardian* of both *Tables*, and consequently such an one as is inabled to judge, yea and to demonstrate to all men the *worship* of *God:* yea and being thus *Governor* and *Head* of the *Church* he must necessarily be a part of it himselfe: which when by *Heresie* he falls from (though it may be by *Truth*, miscalled *Heresie*) he falls from his calling of *Magistracy*, and is utterly disabled from his (pretended) *guardianship* and *government* of the Church.

<small>No civill Magistrate Christian in Chrifts time.</small>
Lastly, we may remember the practice of the *Lord Iesus* and his *followers*, commanding and practising *obedience* to the *Higher Powers*, though we finde not one *Civill Magistrate* a *Christian* in all the *first*

---

[1] The Oath of Allegiance required by James I. after the Gunpowder Plot of course produced considerable controversy respecting its lawfulness. The oath declared "that the pope, neither of himself, nor by any authority of the church or see of *Rome*, or by any other means with any other, hath any power or authority to depose the King, or to dispose of any of his majesty's kingdoms or dominions; or to discharge any of his subjects of their allegiance and obedience to his majesty, &c." Against this Paul V. issued two Briefs. Cardinal Bellarmin also wrote against it on the Papal side. For the Oath and the Briefs, with an account of the controversy, and the Declaration of the Gallican church in 1682 against the Pope's Deposing Power, see Butler's *Memoirs of English Catholics*, xlvii–l. vol. 2, 184–223.

Churches. But contrarily the *civill Magistrate* at that time was the bloody *Beast*, made up (as *Daniel* seemes to imply concerning the *Romane State*, Dan. 7. 7.) of the *Lion*, the *Beare*, and the *Leopard*, Rev. 13. 2.

CHAP. CXV.

Peace. BY these waights wee may try the waight of that commonly received and not questioned *opinion, viz.* That the *civill state* and the *spirituall*, the *Church* and *Commonweale*, they are like *Hippocrates twinnes*, they are borne together, grow up together, laugh together, weepe together, sicken and die together.

Truth. A witty, yet a most dangerous *Fiction* of the *Father* of *Lies*, who hardned in *Rebellion* against *God*, perswades *Gods* people to drinke downe such deadly poison, though he knowes the truth of these five particulars, which I shall reminde you of.

First, many flourishing States in the World have beene and are at this day, which heare not of *Iesus Christ*, and therefore have not [190] the *presence* and *concurrence* of a *Church* of *Christ* with them.

Secondly, there have beene many thousands of *Gods* people, who in their personall estate and life of grace were awake to *God*, but in respect of *Church* estate they knew no other then a Church of dead stones, the Parish Church; or though some light be of late come in through some cranny, yet they seeke not after, or least of all are joyned to any true Church of *God*, consisting of living and beleeving stones.

So that by these *New English Ministers* principles,

Five demonstrative arguments proving the unsoundnesse of that Maxime: The Church and Commonwealth are like Hypocrates twins.

Many flourishing States without a true Church. Many of Gods people farre off from a true Church state.

Yet fit for civill services.

not onely is the doore of calling to *Magiſtracy* ſhut againſt *naturall* and unregenerate *men* (though excellently fitted for *civill* offices) but alſo againſt the beſt and ableſt ſervants of *God*, except they be entred into Church eſtate; ſo that thouſands of *Gods* owne people (excellently qualified) not knowing, or not entring into ſuch a Church eſtate, ſhall not be accounted fit for civill ſervices.

Thirdly, admit that a *civill Magiſtrate* be neither a member of a true Church of *Chriſt* (if any bee in his *dominions*) nor in his perſon feare *God*, yet may he (poſſibly) give free *permiſſion* without *moleſtation*, yea and ſometimes incouragement and aſſiſtance to the ſervice and *Church* of *God*. Thus wee finde *Abraham* permitted to build and ſet up an *Altar* to his *God* whereſoever hee came amongſt the idolatrous Nations in the Land of *Canaan*. Thus *Cyrus* proclaims liberty to all the people of God in his Dominions, freely to goe up and build the *Temple* of God at *Jeruſalem*, and *Artaxerxes* after him confirmed it.

Gods people permitted and favoured by Idolaters.

Thus the *Romane Emperours* and *Governours* under him permitted the *Church* of *God* [,] the *Jewes* in the *Lord Chriſts* time, their *Temple* and *Worſhip*, although in *Civill* things they were ſubject to the *Romanes*.

Chriſts church gathered and governed without the helpe of an arme of fleſh.

Fourthly, the Scriptures of *Truth* and the *Records* of Time concurre in this, that the firſt *Churches* of *Chriſt Jeſus*, the *lights, patternes* and *preſidents* to all ſucceeding Ages, were gathered and governed without the aid, aſſiſtance, or countenance of any Civill Authoritie, from which they ſuffered great perſecutions for the name of the *Lord Jeſus* profeſſed amongſt them.

The *Nations*, *Rulers*, and *Kings* of the Earth tumultuously rage againſt the *Lord* and his Anointed, *Pſal.* 2. 1. 2. Yet *verſ.* 6. it hath pleaſed the *Father* to ſet the *Lord Jeſus* King upon his holy Hill of *Zion*.
191] *Chriſt Jeſus* would not be pleaſed to make uſe of the *Civill Magiſtrate* to aſſiſt him in his Spirituall *Kingdome:* nor would he yet be daunted or diſcouraged in his Servants by all their *threats* and *terrours:* for *Love* is ſtrong as *death*, and the coales thereof give a moſt vehement *flame*, and are not quenched by all the waters and *flouds* of mightieſt oppoſition, *Cant.* 8. _{Chriſts true Spouſe chaſte and faithfull to Chriſt Jeſus in the midſt of feares or favours from the World.}

Chriſts *Church* is like a chaſte and loving *wife*, in whoſe *heart* is fixed her *Husbands love*, who hath found the tenderneſſe of his *love* towards her, and hath been made fruitfull by him, and therefore ſeekes ſhe not the *ſmiles*, nor feares the *frownes* of all the *Emperours* in the *World* to bring her *Chriſt* unto her, or keep him from her.

Laſtly, we finde in the tyrannicall uſurpations of the *Romiſh Antichriſt*, the 10 hornes (which ſome of good note conceive to be the 10 Kingdomes, into which the Romane Empire was quartred and divided) are expreſly ſaid *Revel.* 17. 13. to have one minde to give their power and ſtrength unto the *Beaſt*, yea (*ver.* 17.) their *Kingdome* unto the *Beaſt*, untill the Words of *God* ſhall be fulfilled: whence it followes, that all thoſe *Nations* that are guilded over with the name of *Chriſt*, have under that *mask* or *vizard* (as ſome *Executioners* and *Tormentors* in the *Inquiſition* uſe to torment) perſecuted the *Lord Jeſus Chriſt*, either with a more open, groſſe and bloody, or with a more ſubtle, ſecret and gentle violence. _{The 10 horns, Revel. 13. & 17.}

The great mysterie of Persecution unfolded.

Let us cast our eyes about, turne over the *Records*, and examine the experience of past and present *Generations*, and see if all particular *observations* amount not to this summe, viz. that the great *whore* hath committed fornication with the *Kings* of the *Earth*, and made drunke thereof Nations with the cup of the wine of her *fornications*: In which *drunkennes* and *whoredome* (as *whores* use to practice) she hath robbed the *Kings* and *Nations* of their *power* and strength, and (*Iesabel* like) having procured the *Kings* names and *seales*, she drinks drunk, *Revel.* 17. with

Christian Naboths slaughtered.

the blood of *Naboth*, who (because he dares not part with his rightfull *inheritance* in the land of *Canaan*, the blessed land of promise and salvation in *Christ*) as a *Traitour* to the *civill State*, and *Blasphemer* against *God*, she (under the colour of a day of *humiliation* in Prayer and *Fasting*) stones to death.

192]   CHAP. CXVI.

Peace. DEare *Truth*, how art thou hidden from the eyes of men, in these *mysteries?* how should men weep abundantly with *Iohn*, that the Lambe may please to open these blessed *seales* unto them?

Truth. O that Men more prized their makers feare! then should they be more acquainted with their *Makers councells*, for his *Secret* is with them that feare him, *Psal.* 25.

2. *Difference.*

I passe on to a second *Difference*.

The mysterie of

The *Kings* of *Israel* and *Iudah* were all solemnly annointed with oyle, *Psal.* 39. 20. *I have found David my servant, with my holy Oile have I annointed him.* ^{the anointing the Kings of Israel and Judah.} Whence the *Kings* of *Israel* and *Iudah* were honoured with that myſticall and glorious Title of the *Anointed,* or *Chriſt* of the *Lord*, Lam. 4. 20. the *Breath of our Noſtrils,* the *Anointed of Iehovah was taken in their pits,* &c.

Which *anoynting* and *title,* however[,] the *Man* of Sinne, together with the Crowne and *Diademe* of Spirituall *Iſrael,* the *C*hurch of *God,* he hath given to ſome of the *Kings* of the *Earth*, that ſo he may in lieu thereof diſpoſe of their Civill Crownes the eaſier: yet ſhall we finde it an incommunicable priviledge and prerogative of of the *Saints* and people of *God*.

For as the *Lord Jeſus* himſelfe in the *Antitype* was not annointed with materiall but *ſpirituall* oyle, *Pſal*. 45. with the oyle of *Gladnes,* and *Luke* 4. 14. from *Iſa*. 61. 1. with the ſpirit of *God.* The ſpirit of the *Lord* is upon me, the *Lord* hath annointed me to preach good tidings, &c. So alſo all his members are annointed with the holy *ſpirit* of *God*, 2 Cor. 1. 21. & 1 John 2. ^{The Name Chriſtian or Anointed.}

Hence is it that *Chriſtians* rejoyce in that name, as carrying the very expreſſe title of the *Anointed* of the *Lord*; which moſt ſuperſtitiouſly and ſacrilegiouſly hath been applied only unto *Kings.*

Peace. O deare Truth, how doth the great *Searcher* of all Hearts finde out the thefts of the *Antichriſtian* World? how are men caried in the darke they know not whither? How is that heavenly charge, Touch not mine Anointed, &c. (*Pſal*. 105.) common to all *Chriſtians* (or anointed with) *Chriſt* their Head, by ^{A Sacrilegious Monopolie of the Name Chriſtian.}

way of *Monopoly* or priviledge appropriated to *Kings* and *Princes?*

Truth. It will not be here unseasonable to call to minde that [193] admirable *Prophecie, Ezek.* 21. 26, 27. Thus faith *Jehovah God,* Remove the D*iadem,* take away the *Crowne,* this shall not be the same, exalt him that is low, and abase him that is high: I will overturne, overturne, overturne, untill he come whose right it is, and I will give it him. The matter is a *Crown* and D*iadem* to be taken from an *Usurpers* head, and set upon the head of the right *Owner.*

<small>The Crown of Chrifts Kingly power.</small>

Peace. Doubtlesse this myftically intends the spirituall Crowne of the Lord Jesus, for these many hundreth yeares set upon the *heads* of the *Competitours* and *Corrivals* of the *Lord Jesus,* upon whose glorious head in his *Messengers* and *Churches,* the *Crown* shall be established; The *anointing,* the *title,* and the *crown* and power muft returne to the *Lord Jesus* in his *Saints,* unto whom alone belongs his *power* and *authoritie* in *Ecclefiasticall* or *Spirituall* cases.

CHAP. CXVII.

<small>3. The Kings of Ifrael and Judah invefted with a Spirituall power.</small>

Truth. I Therefore proceed to a third difference between those *Kings* and *Governours* of *Ifrael* and *Judah,* and all other *Kings* and *Rulers* of the *Earth.* Looke upon the Adminiftrations of the *Kings* of *Ifrael* and *Judah,* and well weigh the *Power* and *Authoritie* which those *Kings* of *Ifrael* and *Judah* exercised in *Ecclefiasticall* and *spirituall* causes, and upon a due search we shall not find the same *Scepter* of *Spirituall power* in the hand of *Civill Authoritie*, which was setled in the hands of the *Kings* of *Israel* and *Judah*.

David appointed the *Orders* of the *Priests* & *Singers*, he brought the *Arke* to *Jerusalem*, he prepared for the building of the *Temple*, the *patterne* whereof he delivered to *Salomon*: yet *David* herein could not be a type of the *Kings* and *Rulers* of the Earth, but of the *King* of Heaven, *Christ Iesus*: for,

First, *David*, as he was a *King*, so was he also a Prophet, *Acts* 2. 30. and therefore a type (as *Moses* also was, of that great *Prophet* the Son of *God*. And they that plead for *Davids* Kingly power, must also by the same rule plead for his Propheticall, by which he swayed the Scepter of *Israel* in *Church* affaires.

Secondly, it is expresly said, 1 *Cron.* 28. 11. 12. 13. *verses*, that the patterne which *David* gave to *Salomon* (concerning the matter of the *Temple* and *Worship* of *God*, he had it by the *Spirit*, which was no other but a figure of the immediate inspiration of the *spirit* of *God*, unto the *Lord Iesus* the true Spirituall *King* of *Israel*, John. 1. [194] 49, *Rabbi*, thou art the Son of *God*; *Rabbi*, thou art the *King* of *Israel*. ^{David immediately inspired by the Spirit of God, in his ordering of Church matters.}

Againe, What Civill *Magistrate* may now act as *Salomon* (a type of *Christ*) doth act, 1 *King.* 2. 26. 27.? *Salomon* thrust out *Abiathar* from being *Priest* unto *Iehovah*. ^{Salomons deposing Abiathar (1 Kings 2. 26. 27.) discussed.}

Peace. Some object that *Abiathar* was a man of *death*, ver. 26. worthy to die, as having followed *Adonijah*; and therefore *Salomon* executed no more then Civill *justice* upon him.

Truth. *Salomon* remits the *Civill* punishment, and ^{Salomon his putting}

inflicts upon him a *spirituall*, but by what *right*, but as he was *King* of the *Church*, a figure of *Christ?*

Abiathar his Life is spared with respect to his former good service in following after *David*; but yet he is turned out from the Priesthood.

But now put the case: suppose that any of the Officers of the *New-England Churches* should prove false to the *State*, and be discovered joyning with a *French Monsieur*, or *Spanish Don*, (thirsting after *conquest* and *dominion*) to further their *invasions* of that Countrey; yet for some former faithfull service to the State, he should not be adjudged to Civill punishment: I aske now, might their *Governours* or their *Generall Court* (their *Parliament*) depose such a man, a *Pastour*, *Teacher*, or *Elder*, from his holy Calling or office in *Gods* House?

Or suppose in a *partiall* and *corrupt* State, a *Member* or *Officer* of a *Church* should escape with his life upon the commission of *murther*, ought not a Church of *Christ* upon *repentance* to receive him? I suppose it will not be said that he ought to *execute* himselfe; or that the *Church* may use a *Civill sword* against him. In these cases may such persons (spar'd in *civill* punishments for some reason of, or by partialitie of State) be punished spiritually by the *Civill Magistrate*, as *Abiathar* was? Let the very Enemies of *Zion* be Judges.

Secondly, If S*alomon* in thrusting out of *Abiathar* was a *patterne* and *president* unto all *Civill Magistrates*, why not also in putting *Zadok* in his roome, *ver.* 35. But against this the *Pope*, the *Bishops*, the *Presbyterians*, and the *Independents* will all cry out against

Abiathar from the Priesthood, examined.

A case put upon occasion of Abiathars case.

Another case.

such a practice in their feverall refpective *claimes* and *challenges* for their *Miniftries*.

We find the *Libertie* of the *fubjects* of *Chrift* in the choice of an [195] *Apoftle, Act.* 1. of a *Deacon, Act.* 6. of *Elders, Act.* 14. and guided by the *affiftance* either of the *Apoftles* or *Evangelifts,* 1 *Tim.* 1. *Tit.* 1. without the leaft influence of any *civill Magiftrate,* which fhewes the *beauty* of their *liberty.* _{The liberties of Chrifts Churches in the choice of their officers.}

The *Parliaments* of *England* have by right free choice of their *Speaker*, yet fome *Princes* have thus farre beene gratified as to nominate, yea and implicitely to commend a *Speaker* to them.¹ *Wife men* have feene the evill *confequences* of thofe *influences* (though but in *civill* things) how much farre greater and ftronger are thofe fnares, when the golden *Keyes* of the Sonne of *God* are delivered into the hands of *civill Authority?* _{A civill influence dangerous to the Saints liberties.}

Peace. You know the noife raifed concerning thofe famous *acts* of *Afa, Hezekiah, Iehofaphat, Iofiah*. What thinke you of the Faft proclaimed by *Iehofaphat?* 2. *Chron.* 20. 3.

Truth. I finde it to be the duty of *Kings* and all in *authority,* to incourage *Chrifts Meffengers* of *Truth* proclaiming *Repentance, &c.*

But under the *Gofpel* to enforce all *naturall* and *unregenerate* people to *acts* of *worfhip,* what prefident hath *Chrift Iefus* given us?

Firft, tis true *Iehofaphat* proclaimed a *Faft, &c.* _{Jehofa-}

---

¹ "As foon as his majefty [Charles I.] had refolved upon the calling of a Parliament, he confidered of a fit fpeaker (the election of whom in all times had been by the defignation of the King.)" Clarendon, *Hiftory of Rebellion,* vi: 281, App. D.

phats fast examined. but was he not in matters *spirituall* a *type* of *Christ,* the true *King* of *Israel?*

Secondly, *Iehosaphat* calls the members of the true *Church* to *Church* service and *worship* of God.

If civill powers may injoyne the time of the Churches worship, they may also forbid her times.
But consider, if *civill Powers* now may judge of and determine the actions of *worship* proper to the *Saints:* If they may appoint the time of the *Churches worship,* Fasting and Prayer, &c. why may they not as wel forbid those times which a Church of *Christ* shall make choice of, seeing it is a branch of the same *Root* to forbid what liketh not, as well as to injoyne what pleaseth?

And if in those most solemne *duties* and *exercises,* why not also in other ordinary *meetings* and *worships?* And if so, where is the power of the *Lord Iesus* bequeathed to his *Ministers* and *Churches,* of which the *power* of those *Kings* was but a shadow?

CHAP. CXVIII.

Peace. THe liberty of the *Subject* sounds most sweet, *London* and *Oxford* both professe to fight for it: How much infinitly more sweet is that true soule *liberty* according to *Christ Iesus?*

God will not wrong Cæsar, and Cæsar should not wrong God.
I know you would not take from *Cæsar* ought, although it were [196] to give to *God:* And what is *Gods* and his *peoples* I wish that *Cæsar* may not take. Yet for the satisfaction of some, be pleased to glance upon *Iosiah* his famous *Acts* in the Church of *God* concerning the *worship* of God, the *Priests, Levites,* and their *Services,* compelling the people to keepe the *Passeover,* making himselfe a *covenant* before the

Lord, and compelling all that were found in *Ierusalem* and *Benjamin* to stand to it.

Truth. To these famous practices of *Iosiah* I shall parallell the practices of Englands Kings: and first *de jure*, a word or two of their right: then *de facto*, discusse what hath been done.

First, *de jure*: *Iosiah* was a precious branch of that Royall Root King *David*, who was immediately designed by God: and when the golden linkes of the Royall chaine broke in the usurpations of the Romane Conquerour, it pleased the most wise God to send a Sonne of *David*, a Sonne of God, to beginne againe that Royall Line, to sit upon the Throne of his Father D*avid*, *Luc.* 1. 32. *Acts* 2. 30. The famous acts of Josiah examined.

It is not so with the Gentile Princes, Rulers and Magistrates, (whether *Monarchicall*, *Aristocraticall*, or *Democraticall*) who (though *government* in generall be from *God*, yet) receive their *callings*, *power* and *authority*, (both *Kings* and *Parliaments*) mediately from the people. Magistracy in generall from God, the particular formes from the people.

Secondly, *Iosiah* and those *Kings* were *Kings* and *Governours* over the then true and onely Church of *God Nationall*, brought into the *Covenant* of *God* in *Abraham*, and so downward: and they might well be forced to stand to that *Covenant* into which with such immediate *signes* and miracles they had beene brought.

But what Commission from *Christ Iesus* had *Henry* the eight, *Edward* the 6. or any (*Iosiah* like) to force the many hundred thousands of *English* men and women, without such immediate *signes* and *miracles* that Israel had to enter into an holy and spirituall Israel confirmed in a Nationall Covenant by revelations, *signes, and miracles, but so not England.*

Covenant with the invisible *God*, the *Father* of *Spirits*, or upon paine of death (as in I*osiahs* time) to *stand* to that which they never made, nor before *Evangelicall Repentance* are possibly capable of.

Henry 8. the first head and governour of the Church of England.

Now secondly *de facto*, let it be well remembered concerning the Kings of *England* professing *Reformation*. The *foundation* of all was laid in *Henry* the 8. The *Pope* chalengeth to be the *Vicar* of *Christ* I*esus* here upon earth, to have power of reforming the Church, redressing abuses, &c. *Henry* 8. falls out with the *Pope*, and chalengeth [197] that very power to himself of which he had despoiled the *Pope*, as appeares by that *Act* of *Parliament* establishing *Henry* 8. the supreme *Head* and *Governour* in all cases Ecclesiasticall,[1] &c. It pleased the most *High God* to plague the *Pope* by *Henry* the 8. his means: but neither *Pope* nor *King* can ever prove such power from *Christ* derived to either of them.

The wonderfull formings and re-

Secondly, (as before intimated) let us view the *Workes* and *Acts* of *Englands* imitation of I*osiahs* practice. *Henry* the 7. leaves *England* under the

---

[1] "Be it enacted by authority of this present Parliament, that the King our Sovereign Lord, his heirs and successors, Kings of this realm, shall be taken, accepted and reputed the only supreme Head in earth of the Church of England, &c."

The Act of Supremacy is quoted in full by Froude, *Hist. of England*, ii : 324, who adds : "Considerable sarcasm has been levelled at the assumption by Henry of his title; and on the accession of Elizabeth, the crown, while reclaiming the authority, thought it prudent to retire from the designation. Yet it answered a purpose in marking the nature of the revolution, and the emphasis of the name carried home the change into the mind of the country. It was the epitome of all the measures which had been passed against the encroachments of the spiritual powers within and without the realm ; it was at once the symbol of the independence of England, and the declaration that thenceforth the civil magistrate was supreme within the English dominions over church as well as state."

flavish bondage of the *Popes* yoake. *Henry* the 8. reformes all *England* to a new fashion, halfe *Papist*, halfe *Protestant*. King *Edward* the 6. turnes about the Wheele of the *State*, and workes the whole Land to absolute *Protestanisme*. Queene *Mary* succeeding to the Helme, steeres a direct contrary course, breakes in peeces all that *Edward* wrought, and brings forth an old *edition* of *Englands Reformation* all *Popish*. *Mary* not living out halfe her dayes (as the Prophet speakes of bloudy persons) *Elizabeth* (like I*oseph*) advanced from the Prison to the *Palace*, and from the *irons* to the *Crowne*, she pluckes up all her sister *Maries* plants, and founds a *Trumpet* all *Protestant*.

<small>formings of Religion by Englands Kings.</small>

<small>Kings and States often plant and often pluck up Religions.</small>

What sober man stands not amazed at these *Revolutions?* and yet like Mother like Daughter: and how zealous are we their off-spring for another *impression* and better *edition* of a *Nationall Canaan* (in imitation of I*udah* and I*osiah*) which if attained, who knowes how soone succeeding Kings or Parliaments will quite pull downe and abrogate?[1]

Thirdly, in all these *formings* and *reformings*, a *Nationall Church* of *naturall* unregenerate men was (like wax) the subject matter of all these formes and *changes*, whether *Popish* or *Protestant:* concerning which Nationall State the time is yet to come when ever the Lord Jesus hath given a word of *institution* and appointment.

<small>A Nationall Church ever subject to turne and returne, &c.</small>

---

[1] The Westminster Assembly was then in session. The Solemn League and Covenant was subscribed Sept. 25, 1643, not long after Williams's arrival in England. The Directory of Public Worship which was established by an ordinance of Parliament, dated January 3, 1644-6, was already in preparation while *The Bloudy Tenent* was going to press, the committee having it in charge being appointed Oct. 17, 1643. Neal, *Hist. of Puritans*, i: 495. Events soon justified the author's anticipations of its short continuance, and of another revolution.

CHAP. CXIX.

A woman Papissa or head of the Church.
Peace. YOu bring to minde (deare *Truth*) a plea of some wiser *Papists* for the *Popes supremacy*, *viz.* that it was no such exorbitant or unheard of power and *jurisdiction* which the *Pope* chalenged, but the very same which a *Woman*, Queene *Elizabeth* her selfe chalenged, stiling her *Papissa*, or *she Pope*: withall pleading that in point of *Reason* it was far more suitable that the Lord Jesus [198] delegate his power rather to a *Clergie man* then a *Lay man,* as *Henry* the 8. or a woman, as his daughter *Elizabeth*.

The Papists neerer to the Truth concerning the government of the Church then most Protestants.
Truth. I beleeve that neither one nor t'other hit the white,[1] yet I beleeve the *Papists* arrowes fall the nearest to it in this particular, *viz.* That the *government* of the *Church* of *Christ* should rather belong to such as professe a *Ministry* or *Office* Spirituall, then to such as are meerly *Temporall* and *Civill.*

So that in conclusion, the whole *controversie* concerning the *government* of *Christs Kingdome* or *Church*, will be found to lye between the true and false *Ministry*, both chalenging the true *commission, power* and *keyes* from *Christ.*

The Kingly power of the Lord Jesus troubles all the Kings and Rulers
Peace. This all glorious *diadem* of the *Kingly* power of the *Lord Jesus* hath beene the eye-sore of the *World*, and that which the *Kings* and *Rulers* of the *World* have alwayes lift up their hands unto.

The first report of a new *King* of the *Jewes* puts *Herod* and all *Jerusalem* into *frights*; and the power

---

[1] The centre of the butt in archery was formerly painted white. "'Twas I won the wager, though you hit the white." Shakespeare, *Taming of the Shrew*, v. 5.

of this most glorious *King* of *Kings* over the *Soules* of the *World*. and *Consciences* of men, or over their *lives* and *worships*, is still the *white* that all the *Princes* of this *World* shoot at, and are enraged at the tidings of the true *Heire* the *Lord Jesus* in his servants.

Truth. You well minde (deare *Peace*) a twofold exaltation of the *Lord Jesus*, one in the *Soules* and *Spirits* of men, and so he is exalted by all that truly love him, though yet remaining in *Babels captivity*, and before they hearken to the voyce of the *Lord*, Come forth of *Babel* my people.

<small>A twofold exaltation of Christ.</small>

A second *exaltation* of *Christ Jesus* upon the *Throne* of *David* his *Father* in his *Church* and *Congregation*, which is his Spirituall *Kingdome* here below.

I confesse there is a tumultuous *rage* at his *entrance* into his *Throne* in the *Soule* and *Consciences* of any of his chosen; but against his second *exaltation* in his true *Kingly power* and *government*, either *Monarchicall* in himself, or *Ministeriall* in the hands of his *Ministers* and *Churches*, are mustred up and shall be in the *battels* of *Christ* yet to be *fought*, all the *powers* of the *gates* of *Earth* and *Hell*.

<small>The world stormeth at both.</small>

But I shall mention one difference more between the *Kings* of *Israel* and *Judah*, and all other *Kings* and *Rulers* of the *Gentiles*.

<small>A fourth difference. Kings of Israel types.</small>

Those *Kings* as *Kings* of *Israel* were all invested with a *typicall* and figurative respect, with which now no Civill power in the World can be invested.

199] They wore a double *Crowne*, First, *Civill:* Secondly, *Spirituall*, in which respect they typed out the *Spirituall King* of *Israel*, *Christ Jesus*.

<small>They wore a double Crown.</small>

When I say they were *types*, I make them not in

The Bloudy Tenent.

all respect so to be, but as *Kings* and *Governours* over the Church and Kingdome of *God*, therein types.

The Saviours of the Jewes, figures of the Saviour of the World.

Hence all those *Saviours* and *Deliverers*, which it pleased *God* to stirre up extraordinarily to his people, *Gideon, Baruc, Sampson*, &c. in that respect of their being *Saviours, Judges*, and *Deliverers* of *Gods* people, so were they types of *Iesus Christ*, either *Monarchically* ruling by himself immediately, or *Ministerially* by such whom he pleaseth to send to *vindicate* the *liberties* and *inheritances* of his people.

CHAP. CXX.

Peace. IT must needs be confest that since the *Kings* of *Israel* were ceremonially anointed with Oile : and

Secondly, in that they sat upon the Throne of *David* (which is expressely applied to *Christ Iesus, Luc.* 1. 32. *Acts* 2. 30. *Iohn* 1. 49.) their Crownes were figurative and ceremoniall : but some here question whether or no they were not types of *civill Powers* and *Rulers* now, when *Kings* and *Queens* shall be nursing Fathers and nursing Mothers, &c.

The Monarchicall and Ministeriall power of Christ.

Truth. For answer unto such, let them first remember that the dispute lyes not concerning the *Monarchicall* power of the *Lord Iesus*, the power of making *Lawes*, and making *Ordinances* to his Saints and Subjects : But concerning a deputed and Ministeriall power, and this distinction the very *Pope* himself acknowledgeth.

3 Great Competi-

There are three great Competitours for this deputed or Ministeriall power of the *Lord Iesus.*

First, the *Arch-vicar* or *Sathan,* the pretended *Vicar* of *Christ* on *Earth,* who sits as *God* over the *Temple* of *God,* exalting himselfe not only above all that is called *God,* but over the *soules* and *consciences* of all his *vassals,* yea over the *Spirit* of *Christ,* over the holy *Scriptures,* yea and *God* himselfe, *Dan.* 8. & 11 chap. & *Rev.* 15. together with 2 *Thes.* 2.

tours for the Ministeriall power of Christ. ThePopes great pretenders for the Ministeriall power of Christ. They also upon the point chalenge the Monarchicall also.

This pretender although he professeth to claime but the Ministeriall power of Christ, to declare his Ordinances, to preach, baptise, [200] ordaine Ministers, and yet doth he upon the point challenge the Monarchicall or absolute power also, being full of selfe exalting and blaspheming, *Dan.* 7. 25. & 11. 36. *Rev.* 13. 6. speaking blasphemies against the God of Heaven, thinking to change times and *Lawes:* but he is the sonne of perdition arising out of the bottomlesse pit, and comes to destruction, *Revel.* 17. for so hath the Lord Jesus decreed to consume him by the breath of his mouth, 2 *Thes.* 2.

The second great Competitour to this Crowne of the Lord Jesus is the Civill Magistrate, whether Emperours, Kings, or other inferiour Officers of State who are made to beleeve by the false Prophets of the World that they are the Antitypes of the Kings of Israel and Judah, and weare the Crowne of Christ.

The second great pretender the Civill Magistrate

Under the wing of the Civill Magistrate doe three great factions shelter themselves, and mutually oppose each other, striving as for life, who shall sit downe under the shadow of that Arme of Flesh.

3 Great factions chalenging an Arme of Flesh.

First, the *Prelacie,* who (though some extravagants of late have inclined to wave the *King,* and to creepe under the wings of the *Pope,* yet) so far depends upon

1. The Prelacie.

the *King*, that it is juſtly ſaid they are the *Kings Biſhops*.

<small>2. The Preſbyterie.</small>

Secondly, the *Preſbyterie*, who (though in truth they aſcribe not ſo much to the *civill Magiſtrate* as ſome too groſſely do, yet they) give ſo much to the *civill Magiſtrate* as to make him abſolutely the Head of the Church: For, if they make him the Reformer of the Church, the Suppreſſour of Schiſmaticks and Hereticks, the Protectour and defendour of the Church, &c. what is this in true plain Engliſh but to make him the Judge of the true and falſe Church, Judge of what is *truth*, and what *errour*; who is Schiſmaticall, who Hereticall, unleſſe they make him only an *Executioner*, as the *Pope* doth in his puniſhing of Hereticks?

<small>The Pope and Preſbyterie make uſe of the Civill Magiſtrate but as of an Executioner.</small>

I doubt not but the Ariſtocraticall government of Presbyterians may well ſubſiſt in a Monarchie (not only regulated but alſo tyrannicall) yet doth it more naturally delight in the element of an Ariſtocraticall government of State, and ſo may properly be ſaid to be (as the Prelates, the Kings ſo theſe) the States Biſhops.

<small>3. Independents.</small>

The third, though not ſo great, yet growing faction is that (ſo called) Independent: I prejudice not the perſonall worth of any of the three ſorts: This latter (as I beleeve this Diſcourſe hath [201] maniſeſted) jumpes with the *Prelates*, and (though not more fully, yet) more explicitely then the Presbyterians caſt down the *Crowne* of the *Lord Jeſus* at the feet of the *Civill Magiſtrate*: And although they pretend to receive their *Miniſtrie* from the choice of 2 or 3 private *perſons* in *Church-covenant*, yet would

<small>The Independents: who come neereſt to the Biſhops.</small>

they faine perfwade the Mother *Old England* to imitate her Daughter *New England's* practice, viz. to keep out the *Presbyterians*, and only to embrace themfelves, both as the *States* and the *Peoples* Bifhops.[1]

The third *competition* for this *Crown* and *power* of the *Lord Jefus* is of thofe that *feparate* both from one and t'other, yet divided alfo amongft themfelves into many feverall *profeffions*.

The third competition, of thofe that feparate.

---

[1] This picture of the religious parties of that time is fomewhat more unfavorable to the Independents than the judgment which hiftory has paffed upon them. Williams judged them from his own advanced point of view, and perhaps juftly, as holding effentially the fame view of the power of the civil magiftrate with the Prefbyterians, and only competing with them for the poffeffion of that power. The open connection between them and the perfons in New England who had fent him into exile, and whofe views he knew fo well, might have led him to think that there was little to choofe between the two. His judgment he evidently refts on thofe views of the New England minifters which he is here controverting,—"as I believe this difcourfe hath manifefted." The Prefbyterians in their difcuffion with the Independents in the Weftminfter Affembly, while trying to fettle fome fcheme of accommodation for tender confciences, fay in the paper prefented December 25, 1645, "As for fuch a toleration as our brethren defire, we apprehend it will open a door to all fects; and though the Independents, now plead for it, their brethren in New England do not allow it." Neal, *Hift. of Puritans*, ii: 17.

But it is evident from their language that the Prefbyterians underftood, or at leaft wifhed to make it appear, that the Independents were feeking for a toleration which would cover more than themfelves. "They plead for an accommodation to other fects as well as to themfelves," faid Robert Baylie, defcribing the difcuffion with the Independents in the Committee for Accommodation. *Letters*, ii: 172. They at leaft were bitter enough againft any fort of indulgence. The Scottifh Parliament wrote (Feb. 3, 1645–6) to Weftminfter that "it was perfuaded That the Piety and Wifdom of the Honourable Houfes will never admit Toleration of any Sects or Schifms contrary to our Solemn and Sacred Covenant." Rufhworth, *Hiftorical Collections*, vi: 234. Edmund Calamy faid to Parliament, in a fermon in 1644, "If you do not labor according to your duty and power to fupprefs the errors thereby that are fpread in the Kingdom, all thofe errors are your errors, and thofe herefies are your herefies. You are the Anabaptifts, you are the Antinomians, and 'tis you that hold that all religions are to be tolerated." Crofby, *Hift. of Baptifts*, i: 176.

Baylie hated the Independents with all the vigor of a good hater, but it was becaufe he hated their doctrines. In the preface to a Sermon before the Houfe of Lords in 1645, he fays: "It is more, at

Of these, they that goe furthest, professe they must yet come neerer to the wayes of the Son of *God:* And doubtlesse, so farre as they have gone, they bid the *most*, and make the *fairest* plea for the *puritie* and *power* of *Christ Jesus*, let the rest of the Inhabitants of the World be Judges.

Their neerer conformitie to Christ.

Let all the former well be viewed in their externall State, pomp, riches, conformitie to the World, &c. And on the other side, let the latter be considered, in their more through departure from *sinne* and *sinfull Worship*, their condescending (generally) to the lowest and meanest *contentments* of this *life*,

The Churches of the Seperation ought in Humanitie and Subjects Libertie not to be oppressed, but (at least) permitted.

their exposing of themselves for *Christ* to greater sufferings, and their desiring no Civill sword nor Arme of Flesh, but the two-edged sword of Gods Spirit to try out the matter by: and then let the Inhabitants of the World judge, which come neerest to the doctrine, holines, povertie, patience and practice of the Lord Jesus Christ; and whether or no these later deserve not so much of Humanitie, and the Subjects Libertie, as (not offending the Civill State) in the freedome of their Soules, to enjoy the common aire to breath in.

least not less, unlawful for a Christian State to give any liberty or toleration to errors, than to set up, in every city or parish of their dominions, bordels for uncleanness, stages for plays and lists for duels. That so much extolled Independency wherein many religious souls for the time do wander, is the chief hand that opened at first, and keepeth open to this day, the door to all the other errors that plague us." Quoted by Palfrey, *Hist. of New England*, ii: 89.

CHAP. CXX.[1]

Peace. DEare *Truth*, you have shewne me a little draught of Zions sorrowes, her children tearing out their mothers bowels: O when will Hee that stablisheth, comforteth, and builds up Zion, looke downe from Heaven, and have mercy on her? &c.

Truth. The Vision yet doth tarry (saith *Habacuk*) but will most [202] surely come: and therefore the patient and believing must wait for it.

But to your last Proposition, whether the Kings of Israel and Judah were not types of Civill Magistrates? now I suppose by what hath been already spoken, these things will be evident.

First, that those former *types* of the *Land*, of the *People*, of their *Worships*, were *types* and *figures* of a *spirituall Land, spirituall People*, and *spirituall Worship* under *Christ*. Therefore consequently, their *Saviours, Redeemers, Deliverers, Judges, Kings*, must also have their *spirituall Antitypes*, and so consequently not *civill* but *spirituall Governours* and *Rulers*; lest the very *essentiall nature* of *Types, Figures* and *Shadowes* be overthrowue.

Secondly, although the Magistrate by a Civill sword might well compell that Nationall Church to the externall exercise of their Naturall Worship: yet it is not possible (according to the rule of the New Testament) to compell whole Nations to true Repentance and Regeneration, without which (so farre as

[side note: 7 Reasons proving that the Kings of Israel and Judah cannot have any other but a Spirituall Antitype. Civill Types and figures must needs be answered by Spirituall Antitypes. Civill compulsion was proper in the Nationall Church of the*]*

---
[1] By misprint there are two chapters numbered alike.

354   *The Bloudy Tenent.*

Jewes, but most improper in the Christian, which is not Nationall.

may be difcerned true) the Worfhip and holy Name of God is prophaned and blafphemed.

An Arme of Flefh, and Sword of Steele cannot reach to cut the darkneffe of the Mind, the hardneffe and unbeleefe of the Heart, and kindely operate upon the Soules affections to forfake a long continued Fathers worfhip, and to imbrace a new, though the beft and trueft. This worke performes alone that fword out of the mouth of Chrift, with two edges, *Rev.* 1. & 3.

Neither Chrift Jefus nor his Meffengers have made the Civill Magiftrate Ifraels Antitype, but the contrary.

Thirdly, we have not one tittle in the New Teftament of *Chrift Jefus* concerning fuch a *parallel*, neither from *Himfelfe*, nor from his *Minifters*, with whom he converfed fourty dayes after his *Refurrection*, inftructing them in the matters of his *Kingdome*, *Acts* 1.

Neither find we any fuch *commiffion* or *direction* given to the *Civill Magiftrate* to this purpofe, nor to the *Saints* for their *fubmiffion* in matters fpirituall, but the contrary, *Acts* 4. & 5. 1 *Cor.* 7. 23. *Coloff.* 2. 18.

Civill Magiftracie effentially civill and the fame in all parts of the World

Fourthly, we have formerly viewed[1] the very nature and effence of a *Civill Magiftrate*, and find it the fame in all parts of the *World*, where ever people live upon the face of the *Earth*, agreeing together in *Townes*, *Cities*, *Provinces*, *Kingdomes*: I fay the fame effentially Civill, both from, 1. the *rife* and *fountaine* whence it [203] fprings, to wit, the *peoples* choice and free confent. 2. The Object of it, viz. the *common-weale* or *fafety* of fuch a *people* in their *bodies* and *goods*, as the *Authours* of this *Modell* have themfelves confeffed.

[1] Chap. xcii.

This *civill* Nature of the *Magistrate* we have proved to receive no *addition* of *power* from the *Magistrates* being a *Christian*, no more then it receives *diminution* from his not being a *Christian*: even as the *Common-weale* is a true *Common-weale*, although it have not heard of *Christianitie*; and *Christianitie* professed in it (as in *Pergamus*, *Ephesus*, *&c*.) makes it ne're no more a Commonweale, and *Christianitie* taken away, and the *candlestick* removed, makes it ne're the lesse a Commonweale. Christianitie adds not to the nature of a Civill Commonweale, nor doth want of Christianitie diminish it.

Fifthly, the S*pirit* of *God* expresly relates the worke of the *civill Magistrate* under the *Gospel*, Rom. 13. expresly mentioning (as the *Magistrates* object) the duties of the *second Table*, concerning the *bodies* and *goods* of the *subject*. Rom. 13. evidently proves the Civill work and wages of the Civill Magistrate

2. The *reward* or *wages* which people owe for such a worke, to wit, (not the *contribution* of the *Church* for any *spirituall* work, but) *tribute, toll, custome* which are *wages* payable by all sorts of men, *Natives* and *Forreigners*, who enjoy the same benefit of *publick peace* and *commerce* in the *Nation*.

Sixthly, Since the *civill Magistrate*, whether *Kings* or *Parliaments*, *States*, and *Governours*, can receive no more in *justice* then what the People give, and are therefore but the *eyes* and *hands* and *instruments* of the people (simply considered, without respect to this or that *Religion*) it must inevitably follow (as formerly I have touched) that if *Magistrates* have received their power from the *people*, then the greatest number of the people of every Land have received from *Christ Iesus* a power to *establish*, *correct*, *reforme* his S*aints* and *servants*, his *wife* and *spowse*, the Most strange, yet most true consequences from the Civill Magistrates now being the Antitype

Church: And she that by the expresse *word* of the *Lord* (*Psal.* 149.) binds *Kings* in *chaines*, and *Nobles* in *links* of *iron*, must her selfe be subject to the changeable pleasures of the people of the *World* (which lies in *wickednesse*, 1 *Iohn* 5.) even in matters of Heavenly and *spirituall* Nature.

<small>of the Kings of Israel and Judah.</small>

Hence therefore in all controversies concerning the Church, Ministrie and worship, the last Appeale must come to the Bar of the People or Commonweal, where all may personally meet, as in some Commonweales of small number, or in greater by their Representatives.

204] Hence then no person esteemed a beleever, and added to the Church.

No Officer chosen and ordained.

No person cast forth and excommunicated, but as the Commonweale and people please, and in conclusion, no Church of Christ in this Land or World, and consequently no visibly Christ the Head of it. Yea yet higher, consequently no God in the World worshipped according to the institutions of Christ Jesus, except the severall peoples of the Nations of the World shall give allowance.

<small>If no Religion but that which the Commonweal approves the no Christ, no God, but at the pleasure of this world 2. Ep. Jo. 9.</small>

Peace. Deare Truth, Oh whither have our Forefathers and teachers led us? higher then to God himselfe (by these doctrines driven out of the World) you cannot rise: and yet so high must the inevitable and undeniable consequences of these their doctrines reach, if men walke by their owne common Principles.

Truth. I may therefore here seasonably adde a seventh, which is a necessary consequence of all the

<small>The true antitype</small>

former *Arguments*, and an *Argument* it felfe: *viz.* we finde exprefly a fpirituall power of *Chrift Jefus* in the hands of his *Saints, Minifters* and *Churches,* to bee the true *Antitype* of thofe former figures in all the *Prophecies* concerning *Chrift* his *fpirituall power,* Ifa. 9. Dan. 7. Mich. 4. *&c.* compared with Luc. 1. 32. Act. 2. 30. 1 Cor. 5. Math. 18. Marc. 13. 34. &c.

<small>of the Kings of Ifrael and Judah.</small>

CHAP. CXXI.

Peace. GLorious and conquering Truth, mee thinkes I fee moft evidently thy glorious conquefts: how mighty are thy fpirituall weapons (2 *Cor.* 10.) to breake downe thofe mighty and ftrong Holds and Caftles, which men have fortified themfelves withall againft thee? O that even the thoughts of men may fubmit and bow downe to the captivity of Jefus Chrift!

Truth. Your kinde incouragement makes mee proceed more cheerfully to a fourth difference from the Lawes and Statutes of this Land, different from all the Lawes and Statutes of the World, and parallel'd onely by the Lawes and Ordinances of fpirituall Ifrael. <small>A fourth difference of Lawes and Statutes from all others.</small>

Firft then confider we the *Law-maker,* or rather the *Law-publifher* or *Prophet,* as *Mofes* calls himfelfe, *Deut.* 18. and *Act.* 3. he is [205] exprefly called that Prophet who figured out *Chrift Jefus* who was to come, like unto *Mofes,* greater then *Mofes,* as the fon is greater then the fervant. <small>Mofes a type of Chrift.</small>

Such *Law-givers* or *Law-publifhers* never had any *State* or *People* as *Mofes* the *type,* or *Chrift Jefus,* miraculoufly ftirred up and fent as the mouth of *God* betweene *God* and his people.

The Lawes of Ifrael unparallel'd.

Secondly, concerning the *Lawes* themfelves: It is true, the fecond *Table* containes the *Law* of *Nature*, the *Law Morall* and *Civill*, yet fuch a *Law* was alfo given to this people as never to any people in the *World*: fuch was the *Law* of *worfhip*, *Pfal.* 147. peculiarly given to *Jacob*, and *God* did not deale fo with other *Nations*: which *Lawes* for the *matter* of the *worfhip* in all thofe wonderfull fignificant *Sacrifices*, and for the manner by fuch a *Priefthood*, fuch a *place* of *Tabernacle*, and afterward of *Temple*, fuch *times* and *folemnities* of *Feftivals*, were never to be parallel'd by any other *Nation*, but onely by the true *Chriftian Ifrael* eftablifhed by *Jefus Chrift* amongft *Jewes* and *Gentiles* throughout the *World*.

Gods owne finger penn'd Lawes for Ifrael.

Thirdly, the *Law* of the tenne Words (*Deut.* 10.) the *Epitome* of all the reft, it pleafed the moft high *God* to frame and pen twice with his owne moft holy and dreadfull *finger* upon *Mount Sinai*, which he never did to any other *Nation* before or fince, but onely to that fpirituall *Ifrael*, the *people* and *Church* of *God*, in whofe hearts of *flefh* he writes his *Lawes*, according to *Jer.* 31. *Heb.* 8. and 10.

Peace. Such *promulgation* of fuch *Lawes*, by fuch a *Prophet*, muft needs be *matchleffe* and *unparallel'd*.

Fift difference Temporall profperity moft proper to the temporall National

Truth. In the fift place confider we the *punifhments* and *rewards* annexed to the *breach* or *obfervation* of thefe *Lawes*.

Firft, thofe which were of a *temporall* and prefent confideration of this *life*: *Bleffings* and *Curfes* of all forts opened at large, *Levit.* 26. and *Deut.* 28. which cannot possibly be made good in any *State, Countrey* or *Kingdome*, but in a *spirituall* sense in the *Church* and *Kingdome* of *Christ*. ^{State of the Jewes.}

The reason is this, such a temporall *prosperity* of outward *peace* and *plenty* of all things, of *increase* of *children*, of *cattell*, of *honour*, of *health*, of *successe*, of *victory*, suits not temporally with the afflicted and persecuted estate of *Gods people* now: And therefore *spirituall* and soule *blessednesse* must be the Antitype, *viz*. In the midst of *revilings*, and all manner of evill speeches for *Christs* sake, soule *blessednesse*. In the midst of *afflictions* and *persecutions*, soule *blessednesse*, 206] Math. 5. and Luc. 6. And yet herein the *Israel* of God should enjoy their spirituall peace, *Gal*. 6. 16. ^{The spirituall prosperity of Gods people, now, the antitype.}

Out of that blessed *temporall estate* to be cast or caried *captive*, was their *excommunication* or casting out of *Gods sight*, 2 *King*. 17. 23. Therefore was the *blasphemer*, the *false Prophet*, the *idolater*, to bee cast out or cut off from this *holy Land*: which *punishment* cannot be parallel'd by the punishment of any *State* or *Kingdome* in the *world*, but onely by the *excommunicating* or outcasting of *person* or *Church* from the fellowship of the *Saints* and *Churches* of *Christ Jesus* in the *Gospel*. ^{What Israels excommunication was.}

And therefore (as before I have noted) the putting away of the false *prophet*, by stoning him to *death*, Deut. 13. is fitly answered (and that in the very same words) in the *Antitype*, when by the generall *consent* or *stoning* of the whole *Assembly*, any *wicked person* is put away from amongst them, that is, spiritually *cut off* out of the *Land* of the spiritually living, the people or *Church* of God, 1 *Cor*. 5. Galat. 5. ^{The corporall stoning in the Law, typed out spirituall stoning in the Gospell.}

The Bloudy Tenent.

The rewards or punishments of the Lawes of Israel not to be parallel'd.

Laſtly, the great and high *reward* or *puniſhment* of the keeping or breach of theſe Lawes to Iſrael, was ſuch as cannot ſuit with any State or Kingdome in World beſide: the *Reward* of the *Obſervation* was *Life, Eternall Life.* The *Breach* of any one of theſe *Lawes* was *death, Eternall death* or *damnation* from the preſence of the Lord. So *Rom.* 10. *Iam.* 2. Such a *Covenant God* made not before nor ſince with any State or People in the world. For, *Chriſt* is the *end* of the *Law* for *righteouſneſſe* to every one that beleeveth, *Rom.* 10. 4. And he that beleeveth in that Son of *God*, hath eternall life; hee that beleeveth not hath not life, but is condemned already, John 3. and 1 John 5.

CHAP. CXXII.

The wars of Iſrael typicall.

Peace. DEare *Truth*, you have moſt lively ſet forth the *unparallel'd* ſtate of that *typicall Land* and people of the Iewes in their *peace* and quiet government: Let mee now requeſt you in the laſt place to glance at the *difference* of the *wars* of this people from the *wars* of other *Nations*, and of their having no *Antitype* but the *Churches* of *Chriſt Ieſus*.

[*Truth.*] Firſt, all *Nations* round about *Iſrael* more or leſſe, ſometime or other, had indignation againſt this people, *Ægyptians, Edomites,* [207] *Moabites, Ammonites, Midians, Philiſtians, Aſſyrians* and *Babylonians*, &c. as appeares in the Hiſtory of *Moſes, Samuel, Iudges* and *Kings*, and in all the *Prophets*: You have an expreſſe Catalogue of them, *Pſal.* 83. ſometimes many

Iſraels Enemies round about.

hundred thousand Enemies in pitcht field against them: of *Ethiopians* ten hundred thousand at once in the dayes of *Asa*, 2 Chron. 14. and at other times as the sand upon the Sea shoare.

Such Enemies the *Lord Iesus* foretold his *Israel*, The World shall hate you, *Iohn* 16. You shall be hated of all men for my Names sake, *Matth.* 24. All that will live godly in *Christ Iesus* must be persecuted or hunted, 1 *Tim.* 4. And not only by *flesh* and *bloud*, but also by *Principalities*, Powers, Spirituall wickednesse in high places (*Ephes.* 6.) by the whole *Pagan World* under the *Roman Emperours*, and the whole *Antichristian World* under the *Roman Popes*, Rev. 12. & 13. Chap. by the *Kings* of the *Earth*, Rev. 17. And *Gog* and *Magog*, like the sand upon the Sea shoare (Rev. 20.) *[The Enemies of mysticall Israel.]*

Peace. Such *Enemies*, such *Armies*, no History, no experience proves ever to have come against one poore *Nation* as against *Israel* in the *type*; and never was nor shall be knowne to come against any State or Country now, but the *Israel* of God the *Spirituall Jewes*, *Christs* true followers in all parts and quarters of the World.

[*Truth.*] Beside all these without, *Israel* is betraied *within* her owne bowels, bloudy *Sauls*, *Absaloms*, *Shebaes*, *Adonijahs*, *Ieroboams*, *Athaliahs* raising *insurrections, conspiracies, tumults*, in the *Antitype*, and *Parallell*[,] the Spirituall state of the Christian Church. *[Enemies against Israel in her owne bowells.]*

Secondly, consider we the famous and wonderfull *battells, victories, captivities, deliverances*, which it pleased the *God* of *Israel* to dispence to that people and *Nation*, and let us search if they can be paralleld by any State or people, but myftically and Spiritually the true *Chriftian Ifrael* of God, Gal. 6.

The famous typically captivities of the Jews.
How famous was the bondage and flavery of that people and Nation 430 yeares in the Land of *Ægypt*, and as famous, glorious and miraculous was their *returne* through the *Red Sea* (a figure of *Baptifme*, 1 Corinth. 10. and *Ægypt* a figure of an *Ægypt* now, *Rev.* 11. 8 ?)

How famous was the 70 yeares *captivity* of the *Iewes* in *Babel* tranfported from that Land of *Canaan*, and at the full period returned againe to *Ierufalem*, a type of the *captivity* of Gods people [208] now Spiritually captivated in myfticall *Babel*, Rev. 18. 4?

Their wonderfull victories.
Time would faile me to fpeake of *Iofhua's* conqueft of literall *Canaan*, the flaughter of 31 Kings, of the miraculous taking of *Iericho* and other Cities; *Gideon* his miraculous battell againft the *Midianites*; *Ionathan* and his Armour bearer againft the *Philiftims*; *David* by his 5 fmooth ftones againft *Goliah*; *Afa*, *Iehofaphat*, *Hezechia*, their mighty and miraculous *victories* againft fo many hundred thoufand Enemies, and that fometimes without a blow given.

What State, what Kingdome, what warres and combats, victories and deliverances can parallel this people, but the Spirituall and myfticall *Ifrael of God* in every *Nation* and *Country* of the *World*, typed out by that fmall typicall handfull, in that little fpot of ground the land of *Canaan?*

The myfticall battells of Gods Ifrael now.
The *Ifrael* of God now, men and women, fight under the Great *Lord Generall*, the *Lord Iefus Chrift*: Their *Weapons, Armour*, and *Artillery*, is like themfelves *Spirituall*, fet forth from *top* to *toe*, Ephef. 6.

So mighty and so potent that they breake downe the strongest *holds* and *Castles*, yea in the very soules of men and carry into *captivity* the very thoughts of men, subjecting them to *Christ Iesus:* They are Spirituall *conquerours*, as in all the 7 Churches of *Asia*, He that overcommeth: He that overcommeth, Rev. 2. & 3.

Their *victories* and *conquests* in this are contrary to those of this *World*, for when they are slaine and slaughtered, yet then they conquer: So overcame they the *Divell* in the *Roman Emperours*, Rev. 12. By the *bloud* of the *Lambe*: 2. By the *word* of their *Testimony:* 3. The cheerfull spilling of their owne *bloud* for *Christ*; for they loved not their lives unto the death: And in all this they are *more* then *Conquerors* through him that loved them, *Rom*. 8.

This glorious *Armie* of *white Troopers*, horses and harnesse (*Christ Iesus* and his true *Israel*) Rev. 19. gloriously conquer and overcome the *Beast*, the false *Prophet* and the *Kings* of the Earth up in Armes against them, *Rev*. 19. and lastly, raigning with *Christ* a thousand yeares they conquer the *Divell* himselfe and the numberlesse *Armies* (like the sand on the Sea shoare) of *Gog* and *Magog*, and yet not a tittle of mention of any *sword, helmet, breastplate, shield* or *horse*, but what is *Spirituall* and of a *heavenly nature:* All which Warres of *Israel* have been, may be, and shall be fulfilled mystically and Spiritually.

The mysticall Army of white troopers R. 19.

209] I could further insist on other particulars of *Israels* unparalled state, and might display those excellent passages which it pleaseth *God* to mention, *Nehem*. 9.

CHAP. CXXIII.

Peace. YOu have (deare *Truth*) as in a glaſſe preſented the face of *Old* and *New Iſrael*, and as in water, face anſwereth to face, ſo doth the face of typicall *Iſrael* to the face of the *Antitype*, between whom, and not between *Canaan* and the *Civill Nations* and Countries of the *World* now, there is an admirable conſent and harmony: But I have heard ſome ſay, was not the *civill ſtate* and Judicialls of that people preſidentiall?

<small>Whether the Civill ſtate of Iſrael was preſidentiall.</small>   *Truth.* I have in part, and might further diſcover, that from the *King* upon his *Throne*, to the very *Beaſts*, yea the *excrements* of their *bodies* (as we ſee in their going to War, *Deut.* 23. 12.) their *civills, moralls*, and *naturalls* were carried on in types: and however I acknowledge that what was ſimply *morall, civill*, and *naturall* in *Iſraels ſtate*, in their *conſtitutions, Lawes, puniſhments*, may be imitated and followed by the *States, Countries, Cities* and *Kingdomes* of the World: Yet who can queſtion the *lawfulneſſe* of other formes of *Government, Lawes* and *puniſhments* which differ, ſince *civill conſtitutions* are mens *Ordinances* (or creation, 2 *Pet.* 2. 13.) unto which *Gods* people are commanded even for the *Lords* ſake to ſubmit themſelves, which if they were unlawfull they ought not to do?

Peace. Having thus far proceeded in examining whether God hath charged the Civill State with the eſtabliſhing of the Spirituall and Religious, what conceive you of that next aſſertion, *viz.* "It is well "knowne that the remiſſenes of Princes in Chriſten-

"dome in matters of Religion and Worſhip, divolv-
"ing the care thereof only to the Clergie, and ſo
"ſetting their Hornes upon the Churches head, hath
"been the cauſe of Antichriſtian invention, uſurpa-
"tion and corruption in the Worſhip and Temple of
"God.

Truth. It is lamentably come to paſſe by *Gods* juſt *permiſſion, Sathans* policie, the *peoples* ſinne, and the *malice* of the *wicked* againſt *Chriſt*, and the *corruption* of *Princes* and *Magiſtrates*, that ſo many *inventions, uſurpations*, and *corruptions* are riſen in the *Worſhip* and *Temple* of *God* throughout that part of the World which is called *Chriſtian*, and may moſt properly be called the *Popes Chriſtendome*, [210] in oppoſition to *Chriſt Jeſus* his true *Chriſtian Commonweale*, or *Church* the true *Chriſtendome:* But that this hath ariſen from *Princes* remiſſeneſſe in not keeping their watch, to eſtabliſh the *Purity* of *Religion, Doctrine* and *Worſhip*, and to puniſh (according to Iſraels patterne) all falſe Miniſters, by rooting them and their worſhips out of the *World*, that, I ſay, can never bee evinced; and the many thouſands of glorious *Soules* under the *Altar*, (whoſe blood hath beene ſpilt by this *poſition*) and the many hundred thouſand ſoules, driven out of their bodies by *Civill Warres*, and the many millions of ſoules forced to *hypocriſie* and *ruine* eternall, by inforced *Vniformities* in *Worſhip*, will to all Eternity proclaime the contrary. <small>The true Chriſtendome.</small>

Indeed it ſhewes a moſt injurious *idlenes* and *unfaithfulnes* in ſuch as profeſſe to be *Meſſengers* of *Chriſt Jeſus*, to caſt the heavieſt weight of their care upon the *Kings* and *Rulers* of the *Earth*, yea, upon the very <small>Great unfaithfulneſſe in Miniſters to caſt the</small>

Common-weales, Bodies of People, (that is, the *World* it selfe) who have fundamentally in themselves the *Root* of *Power*, to set up what *Government* and *Govenours* they shall agree upon.

<small>chiefest burden of judging and establishing true Christianity upon the Commonweal or world it selfe.</small>

Secondly, it shewes abundance of carnall *diffidence* and distrust of the glorious *power* and gracious *presence* of the *Lord Jesus*, who hath given his *promise* and Word, to bee with such his *messengers* to the end of the *world*, Matth. 28.

That *Dog* that feares to meet a man in the path, runnes on with boldnes at his masters comming and *presence* at his backe.

Thirdly, what imprudence and *indiscretion* is it in the most common affaires of Life, to conceive that *Emperours*, *Kings* and *Rulers* of the earth must not only be qualified with *politicall* and *state abilities* to make and execute such *Civill Lawes* which may concerne the common *rights*, *peace* and *safety* (which is worke and businesse, load and burthen enough for the ablest shoulders in the *Commonweal*) but also furnished with such *spirituall* and heavenly *abilities* to governe the *Spirituall* and *Christian Commonweale*, the *flocke* and *Church* of *Christ*, to *pull downe*, and *set up Religion*, to *judge*, *determine* and *punish* in *Spirituall controversies*, even to *death* or *banishment*: And beside, that not only the severall sorts of *civill Officers* (which the people shall choose and set up) must be so authorised, but that all respective *Commonweales* or *Bodies* of people are charged (much more) by *God* with this *worke* and *busines*, radically and fundamentally, because all true *civill Magistrates*, have not the least *inch* of *civill power*, but what is measured out to them from

<small>To governe & judge in civill affaires load enough on the Civill Magistrate</small>

<small>Magistrates can have no more power then the common consent of the people shall betrust them with.</small>

the free consent of the [211] *whole:* even as a *Committee* of *Parliament,* cannot further act then the power of the *House* shall arme and enable them.

    Concerning that Objection which may arise from the Kings of *Israel* and *Judah,* who were borne members of *Gods Church,* and trained up therein all their dayes, (which thousands of lawfull *Magistrates* in the *world,* possibly borne and bred in false Worships, *Pagan* or *Antichristian,* never heard of) and were therein *types* of the great anointed, the *King of Israel,* I have spoken sufficiently to such as have an eare to heare: and therefore *(margin: Thousands of lawfull Magistrates who never heare of the true church of God.)*

    Lastly, so unsutable is the commixing and intangling of the C*ivill* with the *Spirituall* charge and *Government,* that (except it was for subsistence, as we see in *Paul* and *Barnabas,* working with their owne hands) the Lord *Jesus,* and his *Apostles,* kept themselves to one: If ever any in this world was able to manage both the Spirituall and Civill, Church and Commonweale, it was the Lord Jesus, (wisedome it selfe:) Yea hee was the true Heire to the Crowne of Israel, being the Sonne of David: yet being sought for by the people to be made a King, Joh. 5. he refused, and would not give a president to any King, Prince, or Ruler, to manage both swords, and to assume the charge of both Tables. *(margin: The Spirituall and Civill Sword can not be managed by one and the same person.)* *(margin: The Lord Jesus refused to manage both.)*

    Now concerning Princes, I desire it may bee remembred, who were most injurious and dangerous to Christianity, whether *Nero, Domitian, Julian,* &c. *Persecuters,* or *Constantine, Theodosius,* &c. who assumed this Power and *Authority,* in and over the *Church* in *Spirituall* things: It is confest by the *(margin: Nero and the persecuting Emperours not so injurious to Christianity, as Con-)*

stantine and others who assumed a power in Spirituall things. Under Constantine Christianity fell into corruption, and Christians fell asleep.

Answerer and others of note, that under these later, the Church, the Christian State, Religion, and Worship, were most corrupted: under *Constantine*, *Christians* fell asleepe on the beds of carnall ease and Liberty: insomuch that some apply to his times, that sleepe of the *Church*, Cant. 5. 2. I sleep though mine heart waketh.[1]

CHAP. CXXIV.

Peace. YEa, but some will say, this was not through their assuming of this power, but the ill managing of it.

Truth. Yet are they commonly brought as the great *Presidents* for all succeeding Princes and Rulers in after Ages: and in this very controvesie, their practices are brought as presidentiall to establish *persecution* for *conscience*.

---

[1] A Brief Exposition of the whole Book of Canticles, or, Song of Solomon; Lively describing the Estate of the Church in all the Ages thereof, &c. &c. Written by that Learned and Godly Divine *John Cotton*, etc. London. 1642.

"This Song containes the estate of the Church, as well in the worst as best times." p. 7. "This booke was chiefly penned to bee an historicall prophecie or propheticall history." p. 10. Following this application of it, chap. 4, ver. 16. *Let my beloved come into his garden, and eat of his pleasant fruits,* he explains: "Let *Constantine* come to them, and partake of the benefits of the Churches serviceable graces to God and him." Proceeding, he continues the application in chap. 5. "*Constantine* came into the Church, enjoyed the fellowship of it, did partake in all the parts of it, yea and richly endowed it; so that the Church and all her friends did eat and drinke, yea and did drink abundantly of wealth, preferments, &c. whence it was that shee fell into a deepe sleepe. ver. 2. to chap. 6. ver. 4. Now followeth the description of the Church from Constantines time to the time of the restoring of the Gospell." pp. 139, 141.

212] Secondly, those *Emperours* and other *Princes* and *Magistrates* acted in *Religion* according to their *consciences* perswasion, (and beyond the light and perswasion of *conscience* can no man living walk in any feare of God.) Hence have they forced their *subjects* to *uniformitie* and *conformitie* unto their own *consciences* (what ever they were) though not willing to have been forced themselves in the matters of *God* and *Conscience*. ^{Who force the consciences of others, yet are not willing to be forced themselves.}

Thirdly, Had not the *light* of their *eye* of *conscience*, and the *consciences* also of their *Teachers* been darkned, they could not have been condemned for want of heavenly *affection*, rare *devotion*, wonderfull care and *diligence*, propounding to themselves the best *patternes* of the *Kings* of *Judah*, *David*, *Salomon*, *Asa*, *Jehosaphat*, *Josiah*, *Hezekiah*: But here they lost the path, and *themselves*, in perswading *themselves* to be the *parallels* and *antytipes* to those *figurative* and *typicall* Princes: whence they conceived themselves bound to make their *Cities*, *Kingdomes*, *Empires* new holy lands of *Canaan*, and themselves *Governours* and *Judges* in *spirituall* causes, compelling all *consciences* to *Christ*, and persecuting the contrary with fire and sword. ^{Constantine and others wanted not so much affection as information of conscience}

Upon these *rootes*, how was, how is it possible but that such *bitter fruits* should grow of *corruption of Christianitie*, *Persecution* (of such *godly*, who happily see more of *Christ* then such *Rulers* themselves) their Dominions and Jurisdictions being overwhelmed with inforced *dissimulation* and *hypocrisie*, and (where power of *resistance*) with flames of *civill combustion*, as at this very day, he that *runs* may *read* and tremble at. ^{Sad consequences of charging the Civill powers with the care of Spiritualls.}

Peace. They adde further, that the *Princes* of *Christendome* setting their *Hornes* upon the *Churches* head, have been the cause of *Antichristian inventions*, &c.

Truth. If they mean that the *Princes* of *Europe* giving their power and *authoritie* to the *seven-headed* and *ten-horned Beast* of *Rome*, have been the cause, &c. I confesse it to be one concurring cause: yet withall it must be remembred, that even before such *Princes* set their *hornes* or *authoritie* upon the *Beasts* head, even when they did (as I may say) but *lend* their *hornes* to the *Bishops*, even then rose up many *Antichristian abominations*. And though I confesse there is but small difference (in some respect) betweene the *setting* their *hornes* upon the *Priests* heads (whereby they are inabled immediately to push and gore whoever crosse their *doctrine* and *practice*) [213] and the *lending* of their *hornes*, that is, *pushing* and *goring* such themselves, as are declared by their *Bishops* and *Priests* to be *hereticall*, as was and is practised in some *Countries* before and since the *Pope* rose: yet I confidently affirme, that neither the *Lord Jesus* nor his first ordained *Ministers* and *Churches* (gathered by such *Ministers*) did ever weare, or crave the helpe of such *hornes* in Spirituall and *Christian* affaires: The *spirituall power* of the *Lord Jesus* in the hands of his true *Ministers* and *Churches* (according to *Balaams* prophesie *Num.* 23.) is the horne of that *Unicorne* or *Rhinocerot* (*Psal.* 92.) which is the strongest *horne* in the *world*, in comparison of which the strongest hornes of the *Bulls* of *Basan* breake as *sticks* and *reeds*. *Historie* tells us how that *Unicorne* or one-horned *Beast* the *Rhinocerot*, tooke up a *Bull* like a *Tennis ball*, in

Civill Rulers giving and lending their Horns or Authority to Bishops, both dangerous to the truth of Christ.

The Spirituall power of the Lord Jesus compared in Scripture to the incomparable horne of

the *Theater* at *Rome* before the *Emperour*, according to that record of the *Poet* :[1]   *the Rhi-nocerot.*

Quantus erat cornu cui pila Taurus erat?

Unto this Spirituall power of the Lord *Jesus*, the *soules* and *thoughts* of the highest *Kings* and *Emperours* must [be] subject, *Math.* 16. & 18. 1 *Cor.* 5. & 10. chapters.

CHAP. CXXV.

Peace. DEare *Truth*, You know the noyse is made from those *prophecies*, Isa. 46. *Kings* and *Queenes* shall be nursing *Fathers, &c.* and *Revel.* 21. the *Kings* of the Earth shall bring their *Glory* and Honour to new *Jerusalem*, &c.

Truth. I answer with that mournfull *Prophet*, Psal. 74. I see not that man, that Prophet, that can tell us how long. How many excellent *Pen-men* fight each against other with their *pens* (like *swords*) in the application of those prophecies of *David, Isa, Jer. Ezekiel, Daniel, Zacharie, John,* when and how those Prophecies shall be fulfilled!   *A time when Gods people are wholly at a losse for Gods worship.*

Secondly, When ever those prophecies are fulfilled, yet shall those Kings not be Heads, Governours, and   *Nursing fathers*

---

[1] Martial, *De Spectaculis Libellus*, Ep. ix.

Præstitit exhibitus tota tibi, Cæsar, arena,
Quæ non promisit, prælia rhinoceros.
O quam terribiles exarsit pronus in iras!
Quantus erat cornu, cui pila taurus erat!

He, who with armed nostril wildly glar'd,
Has fought the battles, he had not declar'd.
How did his headlong rage the pit appall!
How flasht the horn, that made a bull a ball!

Transl. of James Elphinston.

and mothers. Judges in Ecclefiafticall or Spirituall caufes, but be themfelves judged and ruled (if within the Church) by the power of the Lord Jefus therein. Hence faith *Ifaiah*, thofe Kings and Queenes fhall lick the Duft of thy feet, &c.

214] *Peace.* Some will here aske, What may the Magiftrate then lawfully doe with his Civill horne or power in matters of Religion?

Truth. His horne not being the horne of that *Unicorne* or *Rhinocerot*, the power of the *Lord Jefus* in *Spirituall cafes*, his *fword* not the *two-edged fword* of the *Spirit*, the word of *God* (hanging not about the *loines* or *fide*, but at the *lips*, and proceeding out of the *mouth* of his *Minifters*) but of an humane and Civill nature and conftitution, it muft confequently be of a humane and Civill *operation*, for who knowes not that *operation* followes *conftitution?* and therefore I fhall end this paffage with this *confideration*:

The Civill horne or power being of a humane conftitution cannot but be of a humane operation.

The *Civill Magiftrate* either refpecteth that *Religion* and *Worfhip* which his *confcience* is perfwaded is true, and upon which he ventures his Soule: or elfe that and thofe which he is perfwaded are *falfe*.

The Civill power owes 3 things to the true Church of Chrift.

Concerning the firft, if that which the *Magiftrate* believeth to be true, be true, I fay he owes a threefold dutie unto it:

1. Approbation.

Firft, *approbation* and *countenance*, a reverent efteeme and honorable *Teftimonie*, according to *Ifa.* 49. *Revel.* 21.) with a tender refpect of *Truth*, and the *profeffours* of it.

2. Submiffion.

Secondly, Perfonall *fubmiffion* of his owne Soule to the power of the *Lord Jefus* in that *fpirituall Government* and *Kingdome*, according to *Mat.* 18. 1 *Cor.* 5

Thirdly, *Protection* of such true *professours* of *Christ*, whether apart, or met together, as also of their *estates* from violence and injurie, according to *Rom.* 13.   3. Protection.

Now secondly, if it be a false *Religion* (unto which the *Civill Magistrate* dare not adjoyne, yet) he owes,   The Civill Magistrate owes to false worshippers.

First, *permission* (for *approbation* he owes not to what is evill) and this according to *Matthew* 13. 30. for publike peace and quiet sake.   1. Permission.

Secondly he owes *protection* to the persons of his Subjects, (though of a false *worship*) that no injurie be offered either to the persons or goods of any, *Rom.* 13.   2. Protection.

Peace. Deare *Truth*, in this 11 head concerning the *Magistrates* power in *Worship*, you have examined what is affirmed:[1] that the *Magistrate* may doe in point of *Worship*, there remaines a second; to wit, that which they say the *Magistrate* may not doe in *Worship*.

215] They say, "The *Magistrate* may not bring in "set *formes* of *prayer*: Nor secondly, bring in *signifi*- "*cant ceremonies:* Nor thirdly, not *governe* and rule "the *acts* of *worship* in the *Church* of God, for which "they bring an excellent *similitude* of a *Prince* or "*Magistrate* in a *ship*, where he hath no *governing* "*power* over the *actions* of the *mariners:* and sec- "ondly, that excellent *prophecie* concerning *Christ* "*Iesus*, that his *government* should be upon his *shoul*- "*ders*, *Isa.* 9. 6, 7.

Truth. Unto all this I willingly subscribe: Yet can I not passe by a most injurious and unequall practice toward the *Civill Magistrate*: *Ceremonies, Holy dayes, Common Prayer,* and what ever else dislikes their *con-*   The Civill Magistrates conscience torne and

---

[1] The colon should follow the subsequent word "worship."

sciences, that the *Magistrate* must not bring in: Others againe as learned, as godly, as wise, have conceived the *Magistrate* may approve or permit these in the *Church*, and all men are bound in obedience to obey him. How shal the *Magistrates conscience* be herein (between both) torn and distracted, if indeed the power either of *establishing* or *abolishing* in *Church* matters bee committed to him?

<small>*distracted between the divers and contrary affirmations even of the most godly Reformers.*</small>

Secondly, me thinkes in this case they deale with the *Civill Magistrate* as the Souldiers dealt with the *Lord Jesus*: First they take off his owne clothes, and put upon him a *purple Robe*, plat a *Crowne of Thornes* on his head, bow the knee, and salute him by the name of *King of the Jewes*.

<small>*The Authors of these positions deal with the Civill Magistrate as the souldiers dealt with the Lord Jesus.*</small>

They tell him that he is the *Keeper* of both *Tables*, he must see the *Church* doe her duty, he must establish the true *Church*, true *Ministry*, true *Ordinances*, he must keepe her in this purity. Againe, hee must abolish *superstition*, and punish false *Churches*, false *Ministers*, even to *banishment*, and *death*.

Thus indeed doe they make the blood run downe the head of the *civill Magistrate*, from the *thorny* vexation of that *power* which sometimes they crowne him with (whence in great *States*, *Kingdoms* or *Monarchies*, necessarily arise *delegations* of that *spirituall power*, *High Commissions*[1]) &c.

<small>*The rise of high Commissions. &c.*</small>

---

[1] The High Commission sprung from the Act of Supremacy passed in the first year of Queen Elizabeth. Burnet says, (*Hist. of Reformation*, ii: 599.) "The power that was added for the Queen's commissionating some to execute her supremacy gave the rise to that Court, which was commonly called the High Commission Court." Hallam (*Constitutional History*, i: 272, note.) says, "The germ of the high commission court seems to have been a commission granted by Mary (Feb. 1557) to certain bishops and others to inquire after all heresies, punish persons misbehaving at church, &c. Burnet, ii: 347. But the primary model

Anon againe they take off this purple robe, put him into his own clothes, and tell him that he hath no power to command what is againſt their *con-ſcience*. They cannot conforme to a *ſet form* of *prayer*, nor to *Ceremonies*, nor *Holy dayes*, &c. although the civill *Magiſtrate* (that moſt pious *Prince Edw.* 6. and his famous *Biſhops* (afterwards burnt for Chriſt) were of another *conſcience:* which of theſe two *conſciences* ſhall ſtand, if either *Magiſtrate* muſt put forth his civill [216] *power* in theſe caſes, the ſtrongeſt *arme* of *fleſh* and moſt conquering bloody *ſword* of Steele can alone decide the Queſtion.

Pious Magiſtrates and Miniſters conſciences are perſwaded for that, which other Magiſtrates conſciences condemne.

I confeſſe it is moſt true, that no *Magiſtrate* (as no other ſuperiour) is to be obeyed in any matter diſpleaſing to *God:* yet, when in matters of *worſhip* we aſcribe the abſolute *headſhip* and *government* to the *Magiſtrate*, (as to keepe the *Church* pure, and force her to her duty, *Miniſters* and *People*) and yet take unto our ſelves power to *judge* what is right in our owne eyes, and to judge the *Magiſtrate* in and for thoſe very things, wherein we confeſſe he hath power to ſee us doe our duty, and therefore conſequently muſt *judge* what our duty is: what is this but to play with *Magiſtrates*, with the *ſoules* of men, with *Heaven*, with *God*, with *Chriſt Ieſus? &c.*

To profeſſe the Magiſtrate muſt force the Church to her duty and yet muſt not judge what that is, what is it but to play in Spirituall things?

was the inquiſition itſelf." Lingard ſays, (*Hiſtory of England*, viii: 88, note,) "Whoever will compare the powers given to this tribunal with thoſe of the inquiſition, which Philip II. endeavoured to eſtabliſh in the Low Countries, will find that the chief difference between the two courts conſiſted in their names." It was aboliſhed in 1641. Clarendon, *Hiſt. of Rebellion*, i: 412.

CHAP. CXXVI.

An apt fimilitude difcuffed concerning the Civill Magiftrate.

Peace. Paffe on (holy *Truth*) to that *fimilitude* whereby they illuftrate that *Negative Affertion:* "The Prince in the Ship (fay they) is *governour* over "the bodies of all in the Ship, but hee hath no power "to governe the *Ship* or the *Mariners* in the *Actions* "of it: If the *Pilot* manifeftly erre in his *Action,* the "*Prince* may reprove him, (and fo fay they may any "*paffenger*) if hee offend againft the *life* or *goods* of "any, the *Prince* may in due time and place punifh "him, which no private perfon may.

Truth. Although (deare *Peace*) wee both agree that *civill powers* may not injoyne fuch devices, no nor inforce on any *Gods Inftitutions,* fince *Chrift Iefus* his comming: Yet for further *illuftration* I fhall propofe fome *Quæries* concerning the *civill Magiftrates* paffing in the fhip of the *Church,* wherein *Chrift Iefus* hath appointed his *Minifters* and *Officers.* as *Governours* and *Pilots,* &c.

Firft quærie: what if the Prince command the Mr. or Pilot to fteere fuch a courfe which they know will never bring them to the harbour.

If in a fhip at Sea, wherein the *Governour* or *Pilot* of a fhip undertakes to carry the fhip to fuch a Port, the *civill Magiftrate* (fuppofe a *King* or *Emperour*) fhall command the *Mafter* fuch and fuch a courfe, to fteere upon fuch or fuch a point, which the *Mafter* knowes is not their courfe, and which if they fteere he fhall never bring the *Ship* to that *Port* or harbour: what fhall the *Mafter* doe? Surely all men will fay, the *Mafter* of the *Ship* or *Pilot* is to prefent *Reafons* and *Arguments* from his *Mariners* Art (if the Prince bee capable of them) or elfe in humble and fubmiffive manner to perfwade the *Prince* not to interrupt them in their courfe and duty properly [217] belonging to them, to wit, *governing* of the *fhip*, *fteering* of the *courfe*, &c.

If the *Mafter* of the Ship command the *Mariners* thus and thus, in *cunning*[1] the *fhip*, *managing* the *helme*, *trimming* the *faile*, and the *Prince* command the *Mariners* a different or contrary courfe, who is to be obeyed? *2. Quærie. If the Mr. of the Ship command the mariners thus, & the Prince command the contrary, who is to be obeyed?*

It is confeft that the *Mariners* may lawfully difobey the *Prince*, and obey the *governour* of the *fhip* in the *actions* of the *fhip*.

Thirdly, what if the *Prince* have as much skill (which is rare) as the *Pilot* himfelfe? I conceive it will be anfwered, that the *Mafter* of the fhip and *Pilot*, in what concernes the fhip, are *chiefe* and above (in refpect of their office) the *Prince* himfelfe, and their commands ought to be attended by all the *Mariners*: unleffe it bee in manifeft errour, wherein tis granted any paffenger may reprove the *Pilot*. *If the Prince have as much skill as the Mr. or Pilot, &c.*

Fourthly, I aske if the *Prince* and his *Attendants* be unskilfull in the *fhips* affaires, whether every *Sayler* and *Mariner*, the youngeft and loweft, be not (fo farre as concernes the fhip) to be preferred before the *Princes followers*, and the *Prince* himfelfe? and their *counfell* and advice more to be attended to, and their *fervice* more to bee defired and refpected, and the *Prince* to bee requefted to ftand by and let the *bufineffe* alone in their hands. *4. Quærie.*

---

[1] "The Cunning of a Ship is the Directing the Perfon at Helm how to fteer her." Bailey, *Dictionarium Britannicum*, ed. 1736.

"Cond, v. To conduct. *Chaucer*." Wright, *Dict. of Obfolete and Provincial Englifh*.

"Cunning" evidently carries the meaning of "conduct," and probably comes from "Cond."

5. Quærie.
Whether the meanest faylor (in respect of his skill and service) be not to be preferred before the Prince himself.

Fifthly, in case a wilfull *King* and his *Attendants*, out of opinion of their *skill,* or wilfulnesse of *passion,* would so steere the course, trim sayle, &c. as that in the judgement of the *Master* and *Seamen* the ship and lives shall bee indangered: whether (in case humble perswasions prevaile not) ought not the *Ships company* to refuse to act in such a course, yea and (in case power be in their hands) resist and suppresse these dangerous *practices* of the *Prince* and his *followers,* and so save the *ship?*

6. Quærie.
Whether if the Mr. of the ship gratifie the Prince to the casting away of the ship and Prince &c. he be not guilty and liable to answer?

Lastly, suppose the Master out of base feare and cowardise, or covetous desire of reward, shall yeeld to gratifie the minde of the Prince, contrary to the rules of Art and Experience, &c. and the ship come in danger, and perish, and the Prince with it: if the Master get to shore, whether may he not be justly questioned, yea and suffer as guilty of the Princes death, and those that perished with him? These cases are cleare, wherein according to this similitude, the Prince ought not to governe and rule the actions of the ship, but such whose office and charge and skill it is.

The application in generall of the ship to the Church, &c.

218] The result of all is this: The Church of Christ is the Ship, wherein the Prince (if a member, for otherwise the case is altred) is a passenger. In this ship the Officers and Governours, such as are appointed by the Lord Jesus, they are the chiefe, and (in those respects) above the Prince himselfe, and are to bee obeyed and submitted to in their works and administrations, even before the Prince himselfe.

The meanest Christian

In this respect every Christian in the Church, man or woman (if of more knowledge and grace of Christ) ought to be of higher esteeme (concerning *Religion* and *Christianity*) then all the Princes in the world, who have either none or lesse *grace* or *knowledge* of *Christ*: although in *civill* things all *civill reverence*, *honour* and *obedience* ought to be yeelded by all men.

according to his knowledg and grace, to bee preferred before the highest who have received none or lesse grace of Christ.

Therefore, if in matters of *Religion* the *King* command what is contrary to *Chrifts* rule (though according to his *perfwasion* and *confcience*) who fees not that (according to the fimilitude) he ought not to be obeyed? yea, and (in cafe) boldly with fpirituall force and power he ought to be refisted: And if any Officer of the *Church* of *Christ* shall out of basenesse yeeld to the command of the *Prince*, to the danger of the *Church*, and foules committed to his charge, the foules that perish (notwithstanding the *Princes* command) shall be laid to his charge.

A true Minister of Christ ought to walk by another rule then the command of Civill Authority in Spirituall caufes.

If fo then, I rejoyne thus: How agree thefe truths of this fimilitude with thofe former pofitions, *viz.* that the Civill Magistrate is keeper of both Tables, That he is to fee the Church doe her duty, That he ought to eftablish the true Religion, fuppreffe and punish the falfe, and fo confequently muft difcerne, judge and determine what the true gathering and governing of the *Church* is; what the *dutie* of every *Minister* of *Christ* is; what the true *Ordinances* are, and what the true *Administrations* of them; and where men faile, correct, punish, and reforme by the *Civill Sword:* I defire it may be anfwered in the feare and prefence of him whofe *eyes* are as a *flame of fire*, if this be not (according to the fimilitude, though contrary to their fcope in propofing of it) to be *Governour* of the *Ship* of the *Church*, to fee the *Master*,

Former pofitions compared with this fimilitude, and found to contradict each other.

Pilot, and *Mariners* do their duty, in setting the course, steering the ship, trimming the sailes, keeping the watch, &c. and where they faile, to *punish* them; and therefore by undeniable consequence, to *judge* and *determine* what their *duties* are, when they doe *right*, and when they doe *wrong*: and this not 219] only in *manifest Errour*, (for then they say every passenger may reprove) but in their *ordinary* course and practice.

<small>The similitude of the Magistrate prescribing to the Physitian in civill things but the Physitian to the Magistrate concerning his body.</small>

The similitude of a *Physitian* obeying the *Prince* in the *Body* politick; but prescribing to the *Prince* concerning the *Princes body*, wherein the *Prince* (unlesse the *Physitian* manifestly erre) is to be obedient to the *Physitian*, and not to be *Judge* of the *Physitian* in his *Art*, but to be ruled and judged (as touching the state of his *body*) by the *Physitian*: I say this similitude and many others suiting with the former of a *ship*, might be alleadged to prove the *distinction* of the *Civill* and *Spirituall* estate, and that according to the rule of the *Lord Jesus* in the *Gospel*, the *Civill Magistrate* is only to attend the Calling of the *Civill Magistracie*, concerning the *bodies* and *goods* of the *Subjects*, and is himselfe (if a *member* of the *Church* and within) subject to the power of the *Lord Jesus* therein, as any member of the *Church* is, 1 Cor. 5.

CHAP. CXXVII.

Peace. Deare *Truth*, you have uprightly and aptly untied the *knots* of that 11 Head, let me present you with the 12 Head, which is

Concerning the Magistrates power in the Censures of the Church.

"First (say they) he hath no power to execute or to substitute any Civill officer to execute any Church censure, under the notion of Civill or Ecclesiasticall men. *The 12 Head examined.*

"Secondly, Though a Magistrate may immediately Civilly censure such an offender, whose secret sinnes are made manifest by their casting out, to be injurious to the good of the State; yet such offences of excommunicate persons, which manifestly hurt not the good of the State, he ought not to proceed against them, sooner or later, untill the Church hath made her complaint to him, and given in their just Reasons for helpe from them: For to give libertie to Magistrates without exception to punish all excommunicate persons within so many moneths, may prove injurious to the person who needs, to the Church who may desire, & to God who cals for longer indulgence from the hands of thé.[them]

"Thirdly, for persons not excommunicate, the Magistrate hath no power immediately to censure such offences of Church members by the power of the Sword, but onely for such as doe immediately hurt the peace of the State: Because the proper end of Civill Government being the preservation of the peace and welfare of the State, they ought not to breake downe those bounds, and so to censure immediately for such sins which hurt not their peace.

"Hence, first, Magistrates have no power to censure for secret sinnes, as deadnesse, [or] unbeleefe, because they are secret, and not yet come forth immediately

" to hurt the peace of the State; we fay immediately,
" for every finne, even originall finne, remotely hurts
" the Civill State.

" Secondly, hence they have no power to cenfure
" for fuch private finnes in Church members, which
" being not hainous may be beft healed in a private
" way by the Churches themfelves. For that which
" may be beft healed by the Church, and yet is prof-
" ecuted by the State, may make a deeper wound and
" greater rent in the peace both of Church and State:
" the Magiftrates alfo being members of the Church,
" are bound to the rule of Chrift, *viz*. not to pro-
" duce any thing in publike againft a brother, which
" may bee beft healed in a private way.

" Now we call that private,

" Firft, which is only remaining in Families, not
" knowne of others: and therefore a Magiftrate to
" heare and profecute the complaint of children
" againft their parents, fervants againft mafters, wives
" againft their husbands, without acquainting the
" Church firft, tranfgreffeth the rule of Chrift.

" Secondly, that which is between members of the
" fame Church or of divers Churches: for, it was a
" double fault of the Corinthians (1 *Cor*. 6.) firft to
" goe to Law, fecondly to doe it before an Infidell,
" feeing the Church was able to judge of fuch kinde
" of differences by fome Arbitratours among them-
" felves: So that the Magiftrates fhould referre the
" differences of Church members to private healing,
" and try that way firft: By meanes whereof the
" Churches fhould be free from much fcandall, and
" the State from much trouble, and the hearts of the
" godly from much griefe in beholding fuch breaches.

"Thirdly, such offences which the Conscience of "a Brother dealing with another privately, dares not "as yet publish openly, comming to the notice of the "Magistrate accidentally, he ought not to make pub-"lique as yet, nor to require the Grand Jurie to 221] "present the same, no more then the other pri-"vate brother, who is dealing with him, untill hee "see some issue of the private way.

"Thirdly, hence they have no power to put any "to an oath *ex officio,* to accuse themselves, or the "brethren, in case either *criminis suspecti,* or *prætensi,* "because this preserves not, but hurts many wayes "the peace of the State, and abuseth the ordinance "of an Oath, which is ordained to end controversies, "not to begin them, Heb. 6. 16.

"Fourthly, hence they have no power to censure "any for such offences as breake either no Civill Law "of God, or Law of the State published according to "it, for the peace of the State being preserved by "wholesome Laws, when they are not hurt, the peace "is not hurt.

Truth. In this passage (as I said before) I observe how weakly and partially they deale with the soules of *Magistrates* in telling them they are the *Guardians* of both *Tables,* must see the C*hurch* doe her duty, punish, &c. and yet in this passage the *Elders* or *Ministers* of the C*hurches* not only sit *Judges* over the *Magistrates* actions in C*hurch* affaires, but in *civill* also, straitning and inlarging his *commission* according to the particular interests of their owne ends or (at the best) their Consciences.

I grant the *Word* of the *Lord* is the only *rule, light*

and *lanthorn,* in all cafes concerning *God* or Man: and that the *Minifters* of the *Gofpell* are to teach this way, hold out this *Lanthorne* unto the feete of all men: but to give fuch an abfolute power in *Spirituall* things to the *Civill Magiftrate,* and yet after their owne ends or *Confciences* to abridge it, is but the former fporting with holy things, and to walk in *Contradictions,* as before I noted.

Many of the particulars, I acknowledge true, where the *Magiftrate* is a *Member* of the *Church:* yet fome paffages call for *Explication,* and fome for *Obfervation.*

Firft, in that they fay, the *Civill Magiftrate* ought not to proceed againft the offences of an *Excommunicate* perfon, which manifeftly hurt not the good of the *ftate,* untill the *Church* hath made her complaint for helpe from them, I obferve 2 things:

Firft, a cleare grant, that when the *Church* complayneth for helpe, then the *Magiftrate* may punifh fuch *offences* as hurt not the good of the *ftate:* and yet in a few lines after, they fay, the *Magiftrates* have no power to cenfure fuch *offences* of *Church* members [222] by the power of the *civill fword,* but only fuch, as doe immediately hurt the *peace* of the *civill ftate*; and they adde the *Reafon,* becaufe the proper end of the *civill Government,* being the prefervation of the *peace* and *welfare* of the *ftate,* they ought not to breake downe thofe *bounds,* and fo to cenfure immediately for fuch *finnes* which hurt not their *peace.* And in the laft place, they acknowledge the *Magiftrate* hath no power to punifh any, for any fuch offences as breake no *civill Law* of *God,* or *Law* of the *ftate,* publifhed according to it: For the *peace*

To give the government of the Church to the Civill Magiftrate (as before) and yet to abridge his confcience what is it but to fport with holy things? &c.

An evident contradiction.

An excellent confeffion of the proper end of Civill Government. Lawes are not broken, it is confeft of the *ſtate*, (ſay they) being preſerved by wholeſome *Lawes*, when they are not hurt, the *Peace* is not hurt.   *that Civill Peace is not hurt.*

CHAP. CXXVIII.

Peace. Deare *Truth*, here are excellent confeſſions unto which both *Truth* and *Grace* may gladly aſſent: but what is your ſecond Obſervation from hence?

Truth. I obſerve ſecondly, what a deepe charge of *weaknes* is layd upon the *Church* of *Chriſt*, the *Lawes*, *Government* and *Officers* thereof, and conſequently upon the *Lord Jeſus* himſelfe: to wit, that the *Church* is not enabled with all the power of *Chriſt*, to cenſure ſufficiently an *offendour* (on whom yet they have executed the *deepeſt cenſure* in the world, to wit, *cutting* off from *Chriſt*, *ſhutting* out of *Heaven*, *caſting* to the *Divell*) which offendours crime reacheth not to hurt the good of the *civill ſtate*, but that ſhe is forced to make *complaint* to the *civill ſtate*, and the Officers thereof, for their helpe.   *A grievous charge againſt the Chriſtian Church, and the King of it.*

O let not this be told in *Gath*, nor heard in *Aſhkalon*! and O! how dimme muſt needs that *eye* be, which is *blood ſhot*, with that *bloody* and cruell *Tenent* of *Perſecution* for cauſe of *Conſcience*?

Peace. But what ſhould be meant by this paſſage? *viz.* "That they cannot give *liberty* to the *Magiſtrate* " to puniſh without exception all *excommunicate* per- " ſons, within ſo many *months*.

Truth. It may be this hath reference to a *Law* made formerly in *New England*, that if an excom-   *A ſtrange law in New Eng-*

land formerly against Excommuni- municate perſon repented not within (as I have heard) three *months* after ſentence of *excommunication*, then the *Civill Magiſtrate* might proceed with him.[1]

[1] "It is therefore ordered, that whoſoever ſhall ſtand excommunicate for the ſpace of 6 months, without laboring what in him or her lyeth to bee reſtored, ſuch perſon ſhall bee preſented to the Court of Aſſiſtants, and there proceeded with by fine, impriſonment, or further, &c." *Maſs. Colonial Records*, i: 242. Sept. 6, 1638. This was repealed Sept. 9, 1639. *Records*, i: 271.

Cotton was oppoſed to uſing the civil power to ſuch extent, and, it may be, had influence in the repeal of this ſtatute. For he ſays early in 1640, "It was a matter in queſtion here not long agoe, whether the Court ſhould not take a courſe to puniſh ſuch perſons as ſtood excommunicate out of the Church, if they ſhould ſtand long excommunicate, but it was a good providence of God that ſuch a thing was prevented: Let not any Court, *ipſo facto*, take things from the Church." *An Expoſition upon the Thirteenth Chap. of the Revelation*, p. 19. But he would not allow communication with ſuch. "The Jews would not eat with a publican, nor ſhould we with an excommunicate." *Way of the Churches*, p. 93. (1645.)

Francis Hutchinſon, ſon of the famous Anne, after the family removed to Aquidneck wrote to the Church in Boſton for a letter of diſmiſſion. Cotton wrote "with the reſt of the elders, in the name of the Church," declining to diſmiſs him "to no church," &c. He then proceeds to explain what the Teacher of the Church was reported to have ſaid about Hutchinſon's holding any connection with his mother. "For in general, he ſaid indeed, that with excommunicate perſons no religious communion is to be held, nor any civil familiar connexion as fitting at table. But yet he did put a difference between other brethren in church fellowſhip, and ſuch as were joined in natural or civil near relations, as parents and children, huſband and wife, &c. God did allow them that liberty which he denies others." *Maſs. Hiſt. Coll.*, 2d Series, x: 186.

Lechford, writing in 1641, ſays, "The excommunicate is held *as an Heathen and Publican*. Yet it hath been declared in *Boſton* in divers caſes, that children may eate with their parents excommunicate; that an elected Magiſtrate excommunicate may hold his place, but better another were choſen; that an hereditary Magiſtrate, though excommunicate, is to be obeyed ſtill in civill things; that the excommunicate perſon may come and heare the Word, and be preſent at Prayer, ſo that he give not publique offence, by taking up an eminent place in the Aſſembly." *Plain Dealing*, p. 32.

The Synod at Cambridge in 1649 agreed as follows: "5. While the offender remains excommunicate, the church is to refrain from all member-like communion with him in ſpiritual things, and alſo from all familiar communion with him in civil things farther than the neceſſity of natural or domeſtical or civil relations do require; and are therefore to forbear to eat and drink with him, that he may be aſhamed. 6. Excommunication being a ſpirituall puniſhment, it doth not prejudice the excommunicat

These *worthy men* see cause to question this *Law* cate persons. upon good *reasons* rendred, though it appears not by their words that they wholly condemne it, only they desire a longer time, implying that after [223] some longer time the Magistrate may proceed: and indeed I see not, but according to such *principles*, if the *Magistrate* himselfe should be cast out, he ought to be proceeded against by the *Civill state*, and consequently deposed and punished (as the *Pope* teacheth) yea though *happily* he had not offended against either *bodies* or *goods* of any subject.

<small>A dangerous doctrine against all civill Magistrates.</small>

Thirdly, from this true *confession* that the *Magistrate* ought not to punish for many sinnes above mentioned: I observe how they crosse the *plea* which commonly they bring for the *Magistrates* punishing of false *Doctrines, Heretiques*, &c. [*viz.* Rom. 13. The *Magistrate* is to punish them that doe evill:] and when it is answered, True, evill against the *Second Table*, which is there onely spoken of, and against the *Bodies* and *Goods* of the *Subject*, which are the proper *object* of the *Civill Magistrate*, (as they confesse:) It is replied, why is not *Idolatry* sinne? *Heresie* sinne? *Schisme* and false *Worship* sinne? Yet

<small>Many sins prohibited to be punished by the Magistrate and yet they also charge him to punish all sin, Rom. 13.</small>

---

in, or deprive him of his *civil rights*, and therefore toucheth not Princes, or other Magistrates, in point of their civil dignity or authority." *Cambridge Platform*, xiv. p. 22.

In England till quite a recent period excommunication worked civil disqualification quite beyond any known here. "Formerly an excommunicated man was disabled to do any act that was required to be done by a *probus et legalis homo*. He could not serve upon juries, could not be a witness in any court, and what was worst of all, could not bring an action, either real or personal, to recover lands or money due to him. But now by 53 Geo. III. C. 127, S. 3, no person who shall be pronounced excommunicate shall incur thereby any civil penalty or incapacity whatever, save such imprisonment, not exceeding six months, as the court so excommunicating such person shall pronounce." Stephen, *Commentaries*, iv: 17.

heere in this paſſage many *evils*, many *ſins*, even of *Parents* againſt their *Children*, *Maſters* againſt their *Servants*, *Husbands* againſt their *Wives*, the *Magiſtrate* ought not to meddle with.

<small>Originall ſin charged to hurt remotely (but falſely) the civill ſtate.</small>

Fourthly, I dare not aſſent to that aſſertion, "*That even originall ſinne remotely hurts the civill State*. Tis true, ſome doe, as *inclinations* to *murther*, *theft*, *whoredome*, *ſlander*, *diſobedience* to *Parents* and *Magiſtrates*: but *blindnes* of *minds*, *hardnes* of *heart*, *inclination* to chooſe or worſhip this or that *God*, this or that *Chriſt*, beſide the true, theſe hurt not remotely the *civill ſtate*, as not concerning it, but the *ſpirituall*.

<small>Magiſtrates ſtrangely forbidden to hear civill complaints.</small>

Peace. Let me (in the laſt place) remind you of their charge againſt the *Magiſtrate*, and which will neceſſarily turne to my wrong and prejudice: They ſay, the *Magiſtrate* in hearing and proſecuting the *complaints* of *children* againſt their *parents*, of *ſervants* againſt their *maſters*, of *wives* againſt their *huſbands*, without acquainting the *Church* firſt, tranſgreſſeth the rule of *Chriſt*.

Truth. Sweet *Peace*, they that pretend to be thy deareſt friends, will prove thy bitter enemies.

Firſt, I ask for one *rule* out of the *Teſtament* of the Lord *Jeſus*, to prove this deepe *charge* and accuſation againſt the *Civill Magiſtrate*?

<small>Thouſands of Commonweales where no true church of Chriſt.</small>

Secondly, This is built upon a ſuppoſition of what rarely falls out in the World, to wit, that there muſt neceſſarily be a true [224] Church of Chriſt (in every lawfull State) unto whom theſe complaints muſt goe: whereas how many thouſand Common-weales have been and are, where the name of Chriſt hath not (or not truly) been founded.

Thirdly, The Magistrates office (according to their own grant) properly respecting the bodies and goods of their *Subjects*, and the whole *body* of the *Commonweale* being made up of *Families* (as the *members* constituting that *body*) I see not how (according to the rule of *Christ* (*Rom.* 13.) the *Magistrate* may refuse to heare and helpe the just *complaints* of any such *petitioners*, Children, Wives, and Servants, against *oppression*, &c.

The complaints of families properly fall into the cognizance of the civill Magistrate.

Peace. I have long observed that such as have been ready to ascribe to the *Civill Magistrate* and his *Sword* more then *God* hath ascribed, have also been most ready to cut off the skirts, and (in case of his inclining to another *conscience* then their owne) to spoile him of the robe of that due *Authoritie* with which it hath pleased God and the People to invest and cloath him.

They who give to Magistrates more then is due, are most apt to disrobe them of what is theirs.

But I shall now present you with the 13. Head: whose Title is,

CHAP. CXXIX.

What power Magistrates have in publike Assemblies of Churches.

13. Head.

" First (say they) the Churches have power to
" assemble and continue such Assemblies for the
" performance of all Gods Ordinances, without or
" against the consent of the Magistrate, *renuente Magistratu*, because
" Christians are commanded so to doe, *Matth.* 28.
" 18. 19. 20.

"Alſo becauſe an Angel from God commanded
"the Apoſtles ſo to doe, *Acts* 5. 20.

"Likewiſe from the practice of the Apoſtles, who
"were not rebellious or ſeditious, yet they did ſo,
"*Act*. 4. 18. 19. 20. *Act*. 5. 27. 28.

"Further from the practice of the Primitive Church
"at Jeruſalem, who did meet, preach, pray, miniſter
"Sacraments, cenſures, *Act*. 4. 23. *renuente Magiſtratu*.
225] "Moreover from the exhortation to the
"Hebrewes, 10. 25. not to forſake their Aſſemblies,
"though it were in dangerous times, and if they
"might doe this under profeſſed Enemies, then we
"may much more under Chriſtian Magiſtrates; elſe
"we were worſe under Chriſtian Magiſtrates then
"Heathen: therefore Magiſtrates may not hinder
"them herein, as *Pharaoh* did the people from ſac-
"rifiſing, for Wrath will be upon the Realme, and
"the King and his Sons, *Ezra* 7. 23.

Secondly, it hath been a uſurpation of forraigne
"Countries and Magiſtrates to take upon them to
"determine times and places of Worſhip: rather let
"the Churches be left herein to their inoffenſive
"Libertie.

Thirdly, concerning their power of Synod Aſſemblies:
"Firſt in corrupt times, the Magiſtrate deſirous to
"make Reformation of Religion, may and ſhould
"call thoſe who are moſt fit in ſeverall Churches, to
"aſſemble together in a Synod, to diſcuſſe and declare
"from the Word of God, matters of Doctrine and
"Worſhip, and to helpe forward the Reformation of
"the Churches [of] God: Thus did *Joſiah*.

Secondly, in the reformed times he ought to give

"Libertie to the Elders of feverall Churches to affem-
"ble themfelves by their owne mutuall and voluntary
"agreement, at convenient times, as the meanes
"appointed by God, whereby he may mediately
"reform matters amiffe in Churches, which imme-
"diately he cannot nor ought not to doe.

Thirdly, Thofe meetings for this end we conceive
"may be of two forts.

"1. Monthly, of fome of the Elders and Meffen-
"gers of the Churches.

"2. Annuall, of all the Meffengers and Elders of
"the Churches.

"Firft monthly of fome: Firft, thofe members of
"Churches which are neereft together, and fo may
"moft conveniently affemble together, may by mutu-
"all agreement once in a moneth confult of fuch
"things as make for the good of the Churches.

"Secondly, the time of this meeting may be fome-
"times at one place, fometimes at another, upon the
"Lecture day of every Church where Lectures are:
"and let the Lecture that day be ended by eleven of
"the clock.

"Thirdly, let the end of this Affembly be to
"doe nothing by way of Authoritie, but by way of
"Councell, as the need of Churches fhall require.

Secondly Annuall, of all the Elders within our
"jurifdiction or others, whereto the Churches may
"fend once in the yeare to confult together for the
"publike welfare of all the Churches.

"Firft, let the place be fometimes at one Church,
"fometimes at another, as Reafons for the prefent
"may require.

"Secondly, let all the Churches send their waighty questions and cases six weeks or a month before the set time, to the Church where the Assembly is to be held, and the Officers thereof disperse them speedily to all the Churches, that so they may have time to come prepared to the discussing of them.

"Thirdly, let this Assembly doe nothing by Author-itie, but only by Councell, in all cases which fall out, leaving the determination of all things to particular Churches within themselves, who are to judge, and so to receive all doctrines and directions agreeing only with the Word of God.

The grounds of these Assemblies.

"First, need of each others helpe, in regard of dayly emergent troubles, doubts, and controversies.

"Secondly, love of each others fellowship.

"Thirdly, of Gods glory out of a publike spirit to seeke the welfare of the Churches, as well as their owne, 1 *Cor.* 10. 33. 2 *Cor.* 11. 23.

Fourthly, The great blessing and speciall presence of God upon such Assemblies hitherto.

Fifthly, the good Report the Elders and Brethren of Churches shall have hereby, by whose communion of Love others shall know they are the Disciples of Christ.

CHAP. CXXX.

A strange double picture.

Truth. I May well compare this *passage* to a double *picture:* on the first part or side of it a most faire and beautifull *countenance* of the pure and holy

Word of *God*: on the later side or part, a most sowre and uncomely deformed *looke* of a meere humane invention.

227] Concerning the former, they prove the true and unquestionable *power* and *priviledge* of the *Churches* of *Christ* to assemble and practise all the holy *Ordinances* of *God*, without or against the consent of the *Magistrate*. *The great priviledge of the true Spouse or Church of Christ.*

Their Arguments from *Christs* and the *Angels* voyce, from the *Apostles* and *Churches* practice, I desire may take deepe *impression* written by the point of a *diamond*, the finger of *Gods spirit*, in all hearts whom it may concerne.

This *Libertie* of the *Churches* of *Christ* he inlargeth and amplifieth so far, that he calls it an *usurpation* of some *Magistrates* to determine the time and place of *Worship*: and say, that rather the *Churches* should be left to their inoffensive *libertie*.

Upon which Grant I must renew my former *Quærie*, Whether this be not to walke in *contradictions*, to hold with *light*, yet walke in *darknes*? for *To hold with light and walk in darknesse.*

How can they say the *Magistrate* is appointed by *God* and *Christ* the *Guardian* of the *Christian Church* and *Worship*, bound to set up the true *Church, Ministrie* and *Ordinances*, to see the *Church* doe her duty, that is, to force her to it by the *Civill sword:* bound to suppresse the false *Church, Ministrie* and *Ordinances*, and therefore consequently, to judge and determine which is the true *Church*, which is the false, and what is the duty of the *Church officers* and *members* of it, and what not: and yet (say they) the *Churches* must assemble, and practice all *Ordinances*, without his *consent*, yea against it: Yea and he hath *The Magistrate lift up to be the chief governour of the Church, and yet cast downe not to have power to appoint the place or time of meeting.*

not so much power as to *judge* what is a convenient *time* and *place* for the *Churches* to assemble in; which if he should doe, he should be an *usurper*, and should abridge the *Church* of her inoffensive *libertie*.

2 Similitudes illustrating the Magistrate cannot be both governor of the Church and yet usurper in commanding.

As if the *Master* or *Governour* of a Ship had power to judge who were true and fit officers, mariners, &c. for the managing of the Ship, and were bound to see them each performe his duty, and to force them thereunto, and yet he should be an *usurper* if hee should abridge them of *meeting* and *managing* the *vessel* at their pleasure, when they please, and how they please, without and against his *consent*: Certainly if a *Physitian* have power to judge the *disease* of his *patient*, and what course of *Physicke* he must use, can he bee counted an *usurper* unlesse the *patient* might take what *physicke* himselfe pleased, day or night, summer or winter, at home in his chamber, or abroad in the aire?

If a Church may assemble without and against the Magistrates consent (as is affirmed) then much more constitute and become a Church, &c.

228] Secondly, by their *grant* in this passage that *Gods* people may thus assemble and practice *ordinances* without and against the consent of the *Magistrate* I infer, then also may they become a *Church*, *constitute* and *gather* without or against the consent of the *Magistrate*: Therefore may the *Messengers* of *Christ*, *preach* and *baptise*, that is, make *disciples* and *wash* them into the true profession of *Christianity* according to the *commission*, though the *Magistrate* determine and publikly declare, such *Ministers*, such *baptismes*, such *Churches* to be hereticall.

Thirdly, it may here be questioned what power is now given to the *Civill Magistrate* in *Church* matters and Spirituall affairs?

If it be anſwered that although *Gods people* may doe thus againſt the *Magiſtrates* conſent, yet others may not.

I anſwer (as before) who ſees not herein partiality to themſelves: *Gods* people muſt enjoy their *Liberty* of *Conſcience*, and not be forced; but all the Subjects in a *Kingdome* or *Monarchie*, or the whole world beſide, muſt be compelled by the power of the *Civill Sword* to aſſemble thus and thus. *{Groſſe partiality.}*

Secondly, I demand who ſhall judge whether they are *Gods people* or no, for they ſay whether the *Magiſtrate conſent* or *conſent* not, that is *judge* ſo or not, they ought to goe on in the Ordinances *renuente Magiſtratu?* *{If the Civill Magiſtrate be to build the Spirituall or Chriſtian houſe, he muſt judge of the matter.}*

How agrees this with their former and generall *aſſertion*, that the *Civill Magiſtrate* muſt ſet up the *Chriſtian Church* and *Worſhip*, therefore by their owne grant he muſt judge the godly themſelves, he muſt diſcerne who are fit matter for the Houſe of *God*, *living ſtones*, and what unfit matter, *traſh* and *rubbiſh*?

Thoſe *worthy men*, the *Authours* of theſe *poſitions*, and others of their *judgement* have cauſe to examine their ſoules with feare and trembling in the preſence of *God* upon this *intergatory*, viz. whether or no this be not the *bottome* and *root* of the matter: If they could have the ſame ſupply of maintenance without the helpe of the *Civill Sword*, or were perſwaded to live upon the voluntary *contribution* of poore Saints, or their owne *labour*, as the *Lord Jeſus* and his firſt *Meſſengers* did: I ſay, if this lay not in the *bottom*, whether or no they could not be willingly ſhut of *{A cloſe and faithfull interrogatory to the conſciences of the auuthors of theſe poſitions.}*

the *Civill power*, and left only to their *inoffensive liberties?*

<small>A sad quærie to some concerning their practice.</small>
I could also put a sad *Quærie* to the *consciences* of some, viz. what should be the *reason* why in their *native Country* where the *Magistrate* [229] consented not, they forbore to practice such *Ordinances* as now they doe and intended to doe, so soone as they got into another place where they might set up *Magistrates* of their owne, and a *Civill Sword*, &c. How much is it to be feared that in case their *Magistracie* should alter, or their persons be cast under a *Magistracie* prohibiting their practice, whether they would then maintaine their *separate* meetings without and against the consent of the Magistrate, *renuente Magistratu?*

<small>A marvailous challenge of more Libertie to Christians under a Christian Magistrate then under the Heathen.</small>
Lastly, it may be questioned how it comes to passe that in pleading for the *Churches liberty* more now under the *Christian Magistrate*, since the *Christians* tooke that *liberty* in dangerous times under the *Heathen*, why he quotes to prove such liberty, *Pharaohs* hindring the *Israelites* from *worship*, and *Ezra* 7. 23. *Artaxerxes* his feare of wrath upon the Realme?

Are not all their hopes and arguments built upon the *Christian Magistrate,* whom (say they) the first *Christians* wanted, and yet do they scare the *Christian Magistrate* (whom they account the *governour* of the *Church*) with *Pharaoh* and *Artaxerxes* that knew not God, expecting that the *Christian Magistrate* should act and command no more in Gods worship then they?

But what can those instances of *Pharaohs* evill in hindring the *Israelites* worshipping of *God,* and *Arta-*

xerxes giving liberty to *Israel* to worship *God*, and build the *Temple*, what can they prove but a duty in all *Princes* and *Civill Magistrates* to take off the yoake of *bondage*, which commonly they lay on the necks of the soules of their *subjects* in matters of *Conscience* and *Religion*?

CHAP. CXXXI.

Peace. IT is plausible, but not reasonable that *Gods* people should (considering the drift of these positions) expect more liberty under a *Christian* then under a *Heathen Magistrate:* Have *Gods* people more liberty to breake the command of a *Christian* then an *Heathen governour?* and so to set up *Christs Church* and *Ordinances* after their owne *conscience* against his consent more then against the consent of an *Heathen* or unbeleeving *Magistrate?* what is become of all the great expectation what a *Christian Magistrate* may and ought to doe in establishing the *Church*, in reforming the *Church*, and in punishing the contrary? 'Tis true (say [230] men) in *Christs* time and in the time of the first *Ministers* and *Churches* there were no *Christian Magistrates*, and therefore in that case, it was in vaine for *Christians* to seeke unto the *Heathen Magistrates* to governe the *Church*, suppresse *Hereticks*, &c. but now we enjoy *Christian Magistrates*, &c.

If Magistrates were appointed by Christ Jesus Governours of his Kingdome, it were not reasonable that Christians should more freely breake the commands of the Christian, then of the Heathen Magistrate.

Truth. All *Reason* and *Religion* would now expect more submission therefore (in matters concerning *Christ*) to a *Christian Magistrate*, then to a *Pagan* or *Antichristian* ruler! But (deare *Peace*) the day will discover, the fire will trie, 1 *Cor.* 3. what is but wood, hay, and stubble, though built (in mens upright intention) on that foundation *Jesus Christ*.

The necessity of Civill government in generall of God, but the speciall kindes of men, 1 Pet. 2. 13.

But (to winde up all) as it is most true that *Magistracy* in generall is of God (Rom. 13.) for the preservation of Mankinde in *civill order* and *peace*, (the *World* otherwise would bee like the *Sea*, wherein Men, like *Fishes* would hunt and devoure each other, and the greater devour the lesse:) So also it is true, that *Magistracy* in speciall for the severall kindes of it is of Man, 1. Pet. 2. 13. Now what kinde of *Magistrate* soever the people shall agree to set up, whether he receive *Christianity* before he be set in office, or whether he receive *Christianity* after, hee receives no more power of *Magistracy*, then a *Magistrate* that hath received no *Christianity*. For neither of them both can receive more, then the *Commonweal*, the *Body* of People and *civill State*, as men, communicate unto them, and betrust with them.

Civill Magistrates are derivatives from the fountaines or bodies of people.

All lawfull *Magistrates* in the World, both before the comming of *Christ Jesus*, and since, (excepting those unparaleld *typicall Magistrates* of the *Church* of *Israel*) are but *Derivatives* and *Agents* immediately derived and employed as *eyes* and *hands*, serving for the good of the whole: Hence they have and can have no more *Power*, then fundamentally lies in the *Bodies* or *Fountaines* themselves, which *Power*, *Might*, or *Authority*, is not *Religious*, *Christian*, &c. but naturall, humane and civill.

A beleeving Magistrate no more a Magistrate

And hence it is true, that a *Christian Captaine*, *Christian*, *Merchant*, *Physitian*, *Lawyer*, *Pilot*, *Father*, *Master*, and (so consequently) *Magistrate*, &c. is no more a *Captaine*, *Merchant*, *Physitian*, *Lawyer*, *Pilot*,

Father, *Master*, *Magistrate*, &c. then a *Captaine*, *Marchant*, &c. of any other Conscience or Religion.

then an unbeleeving.

Tis true, Christianity teacheth all these to act in their severall callings, to an higher ultimate end, from higher principles, in a [231] more heavenly and spirituall manner, &c.

The excellencie of Christianity in all callings.

CHAP. CXXXII.

Peace. O that thy *Light* and *Brightnes* (deare Truth) might shine to the darke World in this particular: let it not therefore be grievous, if I request a little further illustration of it.

Truth. In his season *God* will glorifie himselfe in all his *Truths*: but to gratifie thy desire, thus: A *Pagan* or *Antichristian Pilot* may be as skilfull to carry the Ship to its desired Port, as any *Christian Mariner* or *Pilot* in the World, and may performe that worke with as much safety and speed: yet have they not command over the *soules* and *consciences* of their *passengers* or *mariners* under them, although they may justly see to the labour of the one, and the *civill* behaviour of all in the *ship:* A *Christian Pilot* he performes the same worke, (as likewise doth the Metaphoricall *Pilot* in the ship of the *Commonweale*) from a principle of *knowledge* and *experience:* but more then this, he acts from a roote of the feare of *God* and love to *mankind*, in his whole course. Secondly, his *aime* is more to glorifie *God* then to gaine his pay, or make his voyage. Thirdly, he walkes heavenly with Men, and *God,* in a constant observa-

The Magistrate like a Pilot in the Ship of the Commonweale.

Christianitie steeres a Christian Pilots course.

<small>The Christian Pilot hath no more power over the soules of his Mariners or passengers, then the unchristian or Pagan Pilot.</small> tion of *Gods* hand in *stormes, calmes,* &c. So that the thread of *Navigation* being equally spun by a *believing* or *unbelieving Pilot*, yet is it drawn over with the gold of *Godlines* and *Christianitie* by a *Christian Pilot*, while he is holy in all manner of *Christianitie*, 1 Pet. 1. 15. But lastly, the *Christian Pilots* power over the Soules and *consciences* of his *Sailers* and *Passengers* is not greater then that of the *Antichristian*, otherwise then he can subdue the soules of any by the two-edged sword of the *Spirit*, the Word of *God*, and by his holy demeanour in his place, &c.

Peace. I shall present you with no other consideratioon in this first part of the Picture, but this only:

<small>The tearmes Heathen and Christian Magistrate.</small> Although the tearme *Heathen* is most commonly appropriated to the wilde naked *Americans*, &c. yet these worthy men justly apply it even to the civilized *Romanes* &c. and consequently must it be applied to the most *civilized Antichristians*, who are not the Church and people of *God* in *Christ*.

Truth. The Word גוים in the *Hebrew*, and ἔθνη in the *Greeke*, signifie no more then the *Gentiles* or *Nations* of the Earth, which [232] were without and not within, the true typicall nationall *Church* of the *Jewes* before *Christ*, and since his comming, the *Gentiles* or *Nations* of the *World*, who are without that one holy Nation of the *Christian Israel* the Church gathered unto *Christ Jesus* in particular and distinct *congregations* all the World over.

<small>All out of Christ are heathens, that is of the Nations or Gentiles.</small> *Translatours* promiscuously render the words *Gentiles, Heathens, Nations*: whence it is evident that even such as professe the Name of *Christ* in an unregenerate and impenitent estate, whether *Papist* or

Proteſtant are yet without, that is *Heathen, Gentiles* or of the *Nations*.

CHAP. CXXXIII.

Peace. Deare *Truth*, it is now time to caſt your eye on the ſecond part of this *Head* or picture uncomely and deformed.

Truth. It containes two ſorts of Religious meetings or aſſemblies.

Firſt, more extraordinary and occaſionall, for which he quotes the practice of *Joſiah*.

An. *Joſiah* was in the type, ſo are not now the ſeverall Governours of Commonweales, *Kings* or *Governours* of the *Church* or *Iſrael*, whoſe ſtate I have proved to be a *None-ſuch*, and not to bee parallel'd but in the *Antitype* the particular *Church* of *Chriſt*, where *Chriſt Jeſus* alone ſits *King* in his owne moſt holy *Government*. Joſiah a type of Chriſt Jeſus the King of the Church

Secondly, they propound meetings or *aſſemblings ordinarily ſtated* and *conſtant, yearly* and *monthly* unto which the *civill Magiſtrate* ſhould give *liberty*. For theſe meetings they propound plauſible arguments from the *neceſſity* of them from *Chriſtian fellowſhip* from *Gods glory*, from the experience of the benefit of them, and from the good report of them, as alſo thoſe two Scriptures, 1 Cor. 10. 33. 2 Cor. 11. 38.

To theſe I anſwer, If they intend that the *civill Magiſtrate* ſhould permit *liberty* to the free and voluntary Spirituall meetings of their Subjects, I ſhall ſubſcribe unto them; but if they intend that the *Magiſtrate* ſhould give *liberty* only unto themſelves, An unjuſt and partiall deſire of liberty to ſome conſciences, &

<small>bondage unto all others.</small> and not to the reft of their *fubjects*, that is to defire their owne *foules* only to be free, and all other *foules* of their *fubjects* to be kept in *bondage*.[:]

233] Secondly, if they intend that the *Magiftrate* fhould inforce all the *Elders* of fuch *Churches* under their *Jurifdiction*, to keepe *correfpondencie* with them in fuch meetings, then I fay (as before) it is to caufe him to give *Libertie* with a *partiall* hand, and *unequall Ballance*: for thus I argue: If the *Civill State* and *Civill officers* be of their *Religion* and *Confcience*, it is not proper for them to give *libertie* or *freedome*, but to give honourable *teftimonie* and *approbation*, and their own perfonall *fubmiffion* to the *Churches*. But if the *civill State* and *Officers* be of another *confcience* and *worfhip*, and fhall be bound to grant permiffion and libertie to them, their *confciences* and *meetings*, and not to thofe of his own *Religion* and *Confcience* alfo, how will this appeare to be equall in the very eye of Common *peace* and *righteoufneffe*?

For thofe *yearely* and *monthly* meetings, as we find not any fuch in the firft *Churches*; So neither will thofe generall *arguments* from the plaufible pretence of *Chriftian* fellowfhip, *Gods* glory, &c. prove fuch particular wayes of *glorifying God*, without fome *precept* or *prefident* of fuch a kind.

For thofe *Scriptures*, 1 Cor. 10. 33. & 2 Cor. 11. 38. expreffing the Apoftle *Paul* his zeale for glorifying *God*, and his care for all the *Churches*, it is cleere <small>The Commiffion Mat. 28. of preaching and</small> they concerne fuch as are indeed *Pauls fucceffors*, fent forth by *Chrift Jefus* to preach and gather *Churches*: but thofe Scriptures concerne not the *Churches* themfelves, nor the *Paftours* of the *Churches* properly,

leaſt of all the *Civill State* and *Commonwealth*, neither *baptizing not properly directed to the Churches, or fixed Teachers of it, leaſt of al to the Commonweale.*
of which (the *Churches*, the *Paſtours*, or *Commonwealth*) doe goe forth perſonally with that *commiſſion*, *Matth.* 28. to *preach* and *baptize*, that is, to gather *Churches* unto *Chriſt.*

 For as for the firſt, the *Churches* are not *Miniſters* of the *Goſpel:* the *Angels* or *Meſſengers* of the *Churches*, and the *Churches* themſelves were diſtinct, *Revel.* 2. & 3.

 As for the ſecond, the *paſtours* and *Elders* of the *Church*, their worke is not to *gather* Churches, but to *governe* and *feed* them, *Acts* 20. & 1 *Pet.* 5. *A quærie, who have now the care of all the Churches?*

 As for the *civill Magiſtrate*, it is a *Miniſtry* indeed: (*Magiſtrates* are Gods *Miniſters*, *Rom.* 13.) but it is of another Nature, and therefore none of theſe, the *Churches* of *Chriſt*, the *Shepherds* of thoſe *Churches*, nor the *civill Magiſtrate*, ſucceeding the *Apoſtles* or firſt *Meſſengers*, theſe Scriptures alleadged concerne not any of [234] theſe to have care of all the *Churches*.

 Peace. Deare *Truth*, who can heare this Word, but will preſently cry out, Who then may rightly challenge that *commiſſion*, and that *promiſe*, *Math.* 28. &c.

 Truth. Sweet *Peace*, in due place and ſeaſon, that *Queſtion* may be reſolved; but doubtles the true *ſucceſſours* muſt precede or goe before the *Church*, making *Diſciples*, and *baptizing* as the *Apoſtles* did, who were neither the *Churches*, nor the *Paſtours* and fixed *Teachers* of them, but as they gathered, ſo had the care of the *Churches*. *A Miniſtrie before the Church*

CHAP. CXXXIV.

Peace. I Ceafe to urge this further; and, in the laft place, marvell what fhould be the reafon of that Conclufion, "viz. There is no power of deter-"mination in any of thefe meetings, but that all muft "be left to the particular determination of the "Churches.[1]

Acts 15. commonly mifapplied

Truth. At the meeting at *Jerufalem*, when *Paul* and *Barnabas* and others were fent thither from the *Church* of *Chrift* at *Antioch*, the *Apoftles* and *Elders* did not only *confult* and advife, but particularly *determined* the *Queftion* which the *Church* of *Antioch* fent

---

[1] The doctrine of the "Model" in regard to the determinative power of Councils and Synods is about the fame as that laid down in the "Anfwer to Two and Thirty Queftions &c.," written by Richard Mather fome four years later. That quotes with approbation from Ames, "The fentence of a Synod is onely a certaine enquiring and giving of fentence by way of Miniftery, and with limitation; fo that the decree of the Councell hath fo much force as there is force in the reafon of it." Alfo from Junius, "The fentence of a Councell is of itfelfe onely of advice, not of compulfion or conftraint, and brings with it a judgement minifteriall, not authority of it felfe, nor neceffity." *Anfwer, &c.* p. 66.

The "Body of Liberties" drawn up by Ward of Ipfwich, and adopted by the General Court in 1641, in the 95th claufe, eleventh fection, provides "That once in every month of the yeare (when the feafon will bear it) It fhall be lawfull for the Minifters and Elders of the Churches neere adjoyneing together, with any other of the breetheren, with the confent of the churches to affemble by courfe in each feverall Church one after an other. Provided that the whole action be guided and moderated by the Elders of the Church where the Affemblie is helde, or by fuch others as they fhall appoint. And that no thing be concluded and impofed by way of Authoritie from one or more churches upon an other, but onely by way of Brotherly conference and confultaticn." 3 *Mafs. Hift. Coll.*, viii: 235, 236.

The Cambridge Platform allows fomewhat more authority to fuch bodies. "The Synod's directions and determinations, fo far as confonant to the Word of God, are to be received with reverence and fubmiffion: not only for their agreement therewith (which is the principal ground thereof, and without which they bind not at all) but alfo fecondarily, for the power, whereby they are made, as being an ordinance of God appointed thereunto in his word." *Platform*, xvi: 5.

to them, about *Acts* 15. and send their particular *determinations* or *decrees* to the *Churches* afterward.

So that if these *Assemblies* were of the nature of that *pattern* or *president* (as is generally pretended) and had such a *promise* of the *assistance* and *concurrence* of the *Spirit*, as that *Assembly* had, they might then say as that *Assembly* did, *Acts* 15. *It seemeth good to the holy Spirit and to us:* and should not leave particular *determinations* to the particular Churches, in which sometimes are very few able *Guides* and *Leaders*.

Peace. But what should be the Reason to perswade these worthy men to conceive the *particular Congregations* or *Churches* to be more fit and competent *Judges* in such high points, then an *Assembly* of so excellent and choice persons, who must only consult and advise, &c.? *[Christs promise and presence only makes an Assembly blessed.]*

Truth. Doubtlesse there is a strong conviction in their Soules of a professed promised *presence* of the Lord *Jesus* in the midst of his *Church* gathered after his mind and will, more then unto such kind [235] of *Assemblies*, though consisting of far more able persons, even the *flower* and *creame* of all the *Churches*.

Peace. It is generally conceived, that the promise of *Chrifts presence* to the end of the World (*Matth.* 28.) is made to the *Church*.

Truth. There is doubtlesse a promise of Chrifts presence in the midst of his Church and Congregation, *Matth*. 18. but the promise of Chrifts presence, *Matth*. 28. cannot properly and immediately belong to the *Church* constituted and gathered, but to such *Ministers* or *Messengers* of *Chrift Jesus*, whom he is *[The promise of Chrifts presence, Mat. 18. distinct from that, Mat. 28.]*

pleased to imploy to gather and constitute the C*hurch* by *converting* and *baptizing:* unto which *Messengers* (if Christ Jesus will be pleased to send such forth) that passage, *Acts* 15. will be *presidentiall.*

14. Position examined.

Peace. The 14. generall head is this, *viz*. What power particular C*hurches* have particularly over *Magistrates.*

"First (say they) they may censure any Member
" (though a Magistrate) if by sinne he deserve it.

"First, because Magistrates must be subject to
" Christ, but Christ censures all offenders, 1 Cor. 5.
" 4. 5.

Secondly, Every Brother must be subject to Christs censure, *Mat.* 18. 15, 16, 17. But Magistrates are brethren, *Deut,* 17. 15.

Thirdly, They may censure all within the Church, 1 Cor. 5. 12.

"But the Magistrates are within the Church, for
" they are either without, or within, or above the
" Church: not the first, nor the last, for so Christ is
" only above it.

"Fourthly, The Church hath a charge of all the
" Soules of the members, and must give account
" thereof, *Heb.* 13. 17.

"Fifthly, Christs censures are for the good of
" Soules, 1 Cor. 5. 6. but Magistrates must not be
" denied any priviledge for their Soules, for then they
" must lose a priviledge of Christ by being Magis-
" trates.

"Sixthly, In Church priviledges Christians are all
" one, *Gal.* 2. 28. Col. 3. 11.

2. Magistrates may be censured for apparent and

"manifeft finne againft any Morall Law of God, in
"their judiciall proceedings, or in the execution of
"their office. Courts are not Sanctuaries for fin; and
"if for no fin, then not for fuch efpecially.

"Firft, becaufe finnes of Magiftrates in Court are
"as hatefull to God. 2. And as much fpoken againft,
"*Ifa.* 10. 1. *Mic.* 3. 1. [236] Thirdly, God hath no
"where granted fuch immunity to them. Fourthly,
"what a brother may doe privately in cafe of private
"offence, that the Church may doe publikely in cafe
"of publike fcandall. But a private brother may
"admonifh and reprove privately in cafe of any pri-
"vate offence, *Mat.* 18. 15. *Luc.* 19. 17. *Pfal.* 141. 5.

"Laftly, Civill Magiftracy doth not exempt any
"Church from faithfull watchfulneffe over any mem-
"ber, nor deprive a Church of her due power, nor a
"Church member of his due priviledge, which is to
"partake of every Ordinance of God, needfull and
"requifite to their winning and falvation. *Ergò,*

CHAP. CXXXV.

Truth. THefe Arguments to prove the *Magiftrate* fubject (even for finne committed in judiciall proceeding) I judge, like Mount *Zion,* immoveable, and every true *Chriftian* that is a Magiftrate will judge fo with mee: Yet a Quærie or two will not be unfeafonable.

Firft, where they name the *Church* in this whole paffage, whether they meane the *Church* without the *Miniftry* or *Governours* of it, or with the *Elders* and *Governours* joyntly? and if the latter, why name they _{Church adminiftrations are charged firftly upon}

<small>the Ministers thereof.</small> not the *Governours* at all, since that in all *administrations* of the *Church* the duty lies not upon the *body* of the *Church*, but firstly and properly upon the *Elders*

It is true in case of the *Elders* obstinacy in apparent sinne, the *Church* hath power over him, having as much power to take down as to set up, *Col.* 4. Say to *Archippus, &c.* Yet in the ordinary dispensations and administrations of the *Ordinances*, the *Ministers* or *Elders* thereof are first charged with duty, &c.

<small>The Ministers or Governors of Chrifts Church to be acknowledged in their dispensations</small> Hence first for the *Apostles*, who converted, gathered & espoused the *Churches* to *Christ*, I question whether their *power* to *edification* was not a *power* over the *Churches*, as many *Scriptures* seem to imply.

Secondly, for the ordinary *Officers* ordained for the ordinary and constant guiding, feeding, and governing the *Church*, they were *Rulers, Shepheards, Bishops,* or *Overseers,* and to them was every *letter* and *charge, commendation* or *reproofe* directed, *Revel.* 2. 3. *Acts* 20. And that place by them quoted for the submission of the *Magistrates* to the *Church,* it mentions only *submission* to the *Rulers* therof, *Heb.* 13. 17. Those excellent men concealed not this out of *ignorance,* and therefore most certainly in a silent way confesse that their *doctrine* concerning the *Magistrates*

<small>A paradox, Magistrates made the Judges of the Churches, and Governours of them, yet</small> power in *Church* causes would [237] seem too grosse, if they should not have named the whole *Church,* and but silently implyed the *Governours* of it: And is it not wonderfull in any sober eye, how the same persons (*Magistrates*) can be exalted over the *Ministers* and *Members,* as being bound to *establish, reforme, suppresse* by the *civill sword* in punishing the *body* or

goods, and yet for the same actions (if the Church and Governours thereof so conceive) be liable to a punishment ten thousand times more transcendent, to wit, *excommunication*, a punishment reaching to their *soules* and *consciences*, and eternall estate, and this not only for *common* sins, but for those *actions* which immediately concerne the *execution* of their *civill* office, in *judiciall* proceeding. *censurable by them.*

Peace. The *Prelates* in Q. *Elizabeths* dayes, kept with more plainnesse to their principles, for acknowledging the *Queen* to be Supreme in all *Church causes*, (according to the Title and Power of *Henry* the 8. her Father, taken from the *Pope*, and given to him by the *Parliament*) they professed that the *Queen* was not a *sheepe*, but under *Christ* the chiefe *Shepheard*, and that the *Church* had not power to *excommunicate* the *Queen*. *Queene Eliz. Bishops truer to their principles, then many of a better spirit and profession.*

Truth. Therefore (sweet *Peace*) it was esteemed *capitall* (in that faithfull *witnesse* of so much *truth* as he saw, even unto *death*, Mr. *Barrow*) to maintaine before the *Lords* of the *Councell*, that the *Queen* herselfe was subject to the power of *Christ Jesus* in the *Church*: which *Truth* overthrew that other *Tenent*, that the *Queene* should be *Head* and *Supreme* in all *Church* causes.[1] *Mr. Barrowes profession concerning Queen Elizabeth.*

---

[1] Henry Barrowe was executed at Tyburn, April 6, 1593. He had been kept in close prison for many years. He studied at Cambridge and was a lawyer of Gray's Inn. He was at the head of the stricter Puritans who were called Brownists or Barrowists. Strype, *Life of Whitgift*, ii: 191.

An account of his examination with Penry and Greenwood before the High Commissioners, "penned by the prisoners themselves, before their deaths," was printed in 1586. One of the questions was "Whither he thinketh the Queene's Majestie be supreme governour of the Church; and whither she may make lawes for the church which are not contrary to the Word of God, or no?

Peace. Thofe Bifhops according to their principles (though bad and falfe) dealt plainly (though cruelly) with Mr. *Barrow:* but thefe *Authors,* whofe *principles* are the fame with the *Bifhops* (concerning the *power* of the *Magiftrate* in *Church* affaires) though they wave the *Title,* and will not call them *Heads* or *Governors* (which now in lighter times feems too groffe) yet give they as much *fpirituall power* and *authoritie* to the *civill Magiftrate* to the full, as ever the *Bifhops* gave unto them, although they yet alfo with the fame breath lay all their *honour* in the *duft,* and make them to lick the *duft* of the feet of the Churches, as it is prophefied, the *Kings* and *Queens* of the *Earth* fhall doe, when Chrift makes them nurfing *fathers,* and nurfing *mothers,* Ifa. 49. The *truth* is, Chrift Jefus is honoured, when the *civill Magiftrate* a member of the Church, punifheth any member or *Elder* of the Church with the *civill fword,* even to the *death,* for any crime againft the *civill State* fo deferving it; for he beares not the fword in vain.

_{Is not this too like the Popes profeffion of *fervus fervorum Dei,* yet holding out his flipper to the lips of Princes, Kings and Emperours?}

238] And *Chrift Jefus* is againe moft highly honoured, when for apparent finne in the *Magiftrate,* being a member of the *Church* (for otherwife they have not to meddle with him) the *Elders* with the *Church,* admonifh him and recover his Soule, or if *obftinate* in fin, caft him forth of their *Spirituall* and *Chriftian* fellowfhip, which doubtleffe they could not doe, were the *Magiftrate fupreme Governour* under

---

Anfw. I thinke the Queene's Majeftie fupreme governour of the whole land, and over the church alfo, bodies and goods: but I thinke that no prince, neither the whole world, neither the church itfelf, may make any lawes for the church, other than Chrift hath already left in his worde." *Harleian Mifcellany,* iv: 348. Brook, *Lives of Puritans* ii: 30. Neal, *Hift. of Puritans,* i: 201.

Chriſt in *Eccleſiaſticall* or *Church* cauſes, and ſo conſequently the true heire and ſucceſſour of the *Apoſtles*.

CHAP. CXXXVI.

Peace. THe 15. Head runs thus: viz. In what caſes muſt Churches proceed with Magiſtrates in caſe of offence. ^{15. Head examined.}

"We like it well, that Churches be ſlower in pro-
"ceeding to excommunication, as of all other, ſo of
"Civill Magiſtrates eſpecially in point of their Judi-
"ciall proceedings, unleſſe it be in ſcandalous breach
"of a manifeſt Law of God, and that after notorious
"evidence of the fact, and that after due ſeeking and
"waiting for ſatisfaction in a previous Advertiſement.
"And though each particular Church in reſpect of
"the Government of Chriſt be independent and abſo-
"lute within it ſelfe, yet where the Commonweale
"conſiſts of Church members, it may be a point of
"Chriſtian wiſedome to conſider and conſult with
"the Court alſo, ſo far as any thing may ſeeme doubt-
"full to them in the Magiſtrates caſe, wch may be
"further cleered by intelligence given from them;
"but otherwiſe we dare not leave it in the power of
"any Church to forbear to proceed & agree upon
"that on Earth, which they plainly ſee Chriſt hath
"reſolved in his Word, and will ratifie in Heaven.

Truth. If the ſcope of this Head be to qualifie and adorne *chriſtian impartialitie* and *faithfulnes* with *chriſtian wiſdome* and *tenderneſſe*, I honour and applaud ſuch a *Chriſtian* motion: but whereas that caſe is put, which is no where found in the *patterne* of the firſt

Churches, nor suiting with the Rule of *Christianitie,* to wit, that the *Commonweale* should consist of *Church members,* which must be taken *privatively,* to wit, that none should be admitted members of the *Commonweale,* but such as are first members of the Church (which must necessarily run the *Church* upon that *Temptation* to feele the pulse of the *Court* concerning a *delinquent Magistrate,* before they dare proceed) I say let such Practices be brought to [239] the *Touchstone* of the true frame of a *civill commonweale,* and the true frame of the *Spirituall* or *Christian commonweale,* the *Church* of *Christ,* and it will be seen what *wood, hay,* and *stubble* of *carnall policie* and *humane inventions* in *Christs* matters are put in place of the *precious stones, gold* and *silver* of the *Ordinances* of the most *High* and only wise *God.*

The inventions of men in swarving from the true essentialls of Civill and Spirituall Commonweales.

CHAP. CXXXVII.

16. and last Head examined.

Peace. DEare *Truth,* We are now arrived at their last Head: the Title is this, *viz.*

Their power in the Liberties and Priviledges of these Churches.

" First, all Magistrates ought to be chosen out of
" Church-members, *Exod.* 18. 21. *Deut.* 17. 15. *Prov.*
" 29. 2. When the Righteous rule, the people rejoyce.

" Secondly, that all free men elected, be only
" Church-members.

1. Because if none but Church members should
" rule, then others should not choose, because they

"may elect others beside Church members.

2. From the patterne of *Israel*, where none had "power to choose but only Israel, or such as were "joyned to the people of God.

3. If it shall fall out, that in the Court consisting "of *Magistrates* and *Deputies*, there be a dissent "between them which may hinder the common "good, that they now returne for ending the same, "to their first principles, which are the Free men, "and let them be consulted with.

Truth. In this *Head* are 2 branches: First concerning the choice of *Magistrates*, that such ought to be chosen as are *Church members*: for which is quoted, *Exod*. 18. 21. *Dut*. 17. 15. *Proverbs* 19. 29.

Unto which I answer: It were to be wished, that since the point is so weighty, as concerning the *Pilots* and *Steeresmen* of *Kingdoms* and *Nations*, &c. on whose *abilitie*, *care* and *faithfulnesse* depends most commonly the *peace* and *safety* of the *commonweales* they fail in: I say it were to be wished that they had more fully explained what [240] they intend by this *Affirmative*, viz. *Magistrates* ought to be chosen out of *Church members*.

For if they intend by this [*Ought to be chosen*] a *necessitie* of *convenience*, viz. that for the greater advancement of *common utilitie* and *rejoycing* of the people, according to the place quoted (*Prov*. 29. 2.) it were to be desired, prayed for, and peaceably endeavored, then I readily assent unto them.

But if by this [*Ought*] they intend such a *necessitie* as those Scriptures quoted imply, viz. that people shall sin by choosing such for *Magistrates* as are not

A great Quegion, viz. Whether only Church members (that is as is intended) Godly persons in a particular Church estate, be only eligible or to be chosen for Magistrates.

members of *Churches*; as the *Israelites* should have sinned, if they had not (according to *Jethro's* counsell, *Exod.* 18. and according to the *command* of God, Deut. 18.) chosen their *Judges* and *Kings* within themselves in *Israel*: then I propose these necessary *Quæries*.

<small>Lawfull Civil States, where Churches of Christ are not.</small>
First whether those are not lawfull *Civill combinations, societies,* and *communions* of men, in *Townes, Cities, States* or *Kingdoms,* where no *Church* of *Christ* is resident, yea where his name was never yet heard of: I adde to this, that Men of no small note, skilfull in the *state* of the *World,* acknowledge, that the *World* divided into 30 parts, 25 of that 30 have never yet heard of the name of *Christ*:[1] If their *Civill polities* and *combinations* be not lawfull, (because they are not *Churches,* and their *Magistrates Church* members) then *disorder, confusion,* and all *unrighteousnes* is lawfull, and pleasing to *God.*

<small>Theworld being divided into 30 parts, 25 never heard of Christ.</small>

<small>Lawfull heires of Crownes & Civill Government, although not Christian and godly.</small>
Secondly, whether in such States or Commonweales, where a Church or Churches of Christ are resident, such persons may not lawfully succeed to the Crown or Government, in whom the feare of God (according to *Jethroes* councell) cannot be discerned, nor are brethren of the Church, according to *Deut.* 17.) but only are fitted with Civill and Morall abilities, to manage rhe Civill affaires of the Civill State.

<small>Few Christians wise and noble, and qualified for affaires of State.</small>
Thirdly, since not many *Wise* and *Noble* are called, but the *poore* receive the *Gospel,* as *God* hath chosen the *poore* of the *World* to be *rich* in *Faith,* 1 Cor. 1. Jam. 2. Whether it may not ordinarily come to passe, that there may not be found in a true *Church*

---

[1] *Hireling Ministry,* p. 3. See *supra* p. 321.

of *Chrift* (which sometimes consisteth but of few persons) persons fit to be either *Kings* or *Governours, &c.* whose *civill office* is no lesse difficult then the office of a *Doctor* of *Physick*, a *Master* or *Pilot* of a *Ship*, or a *Captaine* or *Commander* of a *Band* or *Army* of men: for [241] which services, the children of *God* may be no wayes *qualified*, though otherwise excellent for the *feare* of *God*, and the *knowledge* and *Grace* of the *Lord Iesus*.

4. If *Magistrates* ought (that is, ought only) to be chosen out of the *Church*, I demand if they ought not also to be *dethroned* and *depofed*, when they cease to be of the *Church*, either by voluntary departure from it, or by *excommunication* out of it, according to the bloody *tenents* and *practice* of some *Papists*, with whom the *Protestants* (according to their *principles*) although they seeme to abhor it, doe absolutely agree? _{Some Papists and some Protestants agree in depofing of Magistrates.}

5. Therefore laftly, I ask if this be not to turne the *World* upfide down, to turne the *World* out of the *World*, to pluck up the *roots* and *foundations* of all *common focietie* in the *World*? to turne the *Garden* and *Paradice* of the *Church* and *Saints* into the *Field* of the *Civill State* of the *World*, and to reduce the *World* to the firft *chaos* or *confufion*.

CHAP. CXXXVIII.

Peace. DEare *Truth*, thou *conquereft*, and fhalt triumph in feafon: but fome will fay, How anfwer you thofe Scriptures alleadged?

Truth. I have fully and at large declared the vaft

differences between that holy *Nation* of typicall *Israel*, and all other *Lands* and *Countries*, how unmatchable then and now, and never to be parallel'd, but by the true *Israel* and particular *Churches* of *Christ*, residing in all parts (and under the severall *civill Governments*) of the *world:*[1] In which *Churches*, the *Israel* of *God*, and *Kingdome* of *Christ Iesus*, such only are to be chosen spirituall *Officers* and *Governours*, to manage his *Kingly* power and *authoritie* in the *Church*, as are (according to the Scriptures quoted, not *Pope*, *Bishops*, or *Civill powers*, but) from amongst themselves, *Brethren*, fearing *God*, hating *covetousnesse* or filthy *lucre*, according to those golden *Rules* given by the Lord *Iesus*, 1 Tim. 3. & Tit. 1.

<small>Those Scriptures Exod. 18. Deut. 17. & 18. &c. parallel'd in the true spirituall Israel, by 1 Tim. 3. & Tit. 1.</small>

The want of discerning this true *parallel*, between *Israel* in the *type* then, and *Israel* the *antitype* now, is that *rock* whereon (through the *Lords* righteous *jealousie*, punishing the *World*, and chastising his people) thousands dash, and make wofull *Shipwrack*. 242] The second branch, viz. that all *Freemen* elected be only *Church* members, I have before shewne to be built on that sandy and dangerous *Ground* of *Israels patterne:* O that it may please the *Father* of *Lights* to discover this to all that fear his name! then would they not sin to save a *Kingdome*, nor run into the lamentable *breach* of *civill peace* and *order* in the *world*, nor be guilty of forcing *thousands* to *Hypocrisie*, in a *State worship*, nor of *prophaning* the holy name of *God* and *Christ*, by putting their *Names* and *Ordinances* upon *uncleane* and *unholy* persons: nor of shedding the *blood* of such *Hereticks*, &c. whom

---

[1] Chapters cx.–cxiv.

Chrift would have enjoy longer *patience* and *permiſ-ſion* untill the *Harveſt:* nor of the *blood* of the *Lord Ieſus* himſelfe, in his faithfull *Witneſſes* of *Truth:* nor laſtly, of the blood of ſo many hundred thouſands ſlaughtred men, women, and children, by ſuch *uncivill* and *unchriſtian wars* and *combuſtions* about the *Chriſtian faith* and *Religion.*

Peace. Deare *Truth:* before we part, I aske your faithfull helpe once more, to 2 or 3 Scriptures, which many alleadge, and yet we have not ſpoken of. The Ninevites Faſt examined.

Truth. Speake on; here is ſome ſand left in this our houre glaſſe of mercifull *opportunitie:* One *graine* of *Times* ineſtimable ſand is worth a golden *mountaine*; let's not loſe it.

Peace. The firſt is that of the *Ninevites* faſt, commanded by the *King* of *Ninevie* and his *Nobles,* upon the preaching of *Jonah*; ſucceeded by *Gods mercifull anſwer* in ſparing of the Citie; and quoted with honorable *approbation* by the Lord *Jeſus Chriſt*, Jonah 3. & Math. 12.

Truth. I have before proved,[1] that even *Jehoſaphats* faſt (he being *King* of that *Nationall Church* and people of *Iſrael*) could not poſſibly be a *type* or *warrant* for every *King* or *Magiſtrate* in the *World* (whoſe Nations, Countries or Cities cannot be *Churches* of *God,* now in the *Goſpel,* according to *Chriſt Jeſus:*

Much leſſe can this patterne of the *King* of *Ninevie* and his *Nobles,* be a ground for *Kings* and *Magiſtrates* now, to force all their Subjects under them in the matters of *Worſhip.*

[1] See Chap. cxvii. p. 342, *ſupra.*

Peace. It will be said, why did *God* thus anſwer them?

Truth. Gods mercy in hearing doth not prove an *action* right and according to rule.

It pleaſed God to heare the *Iſraelites* cry for *Fleſh*, and afterward for a *King*, given both in *anger* to them.

243] It pleaſed God to heare *Ahabs* prayer, yea and the prayer of the *Devils* (Luc. 8.) although their *perſons* and *prayers* in themſelves abominable.

Object. If it be ſaid, why did *Chriſt* approve this example?

Anſw. I anſwer, the *Lord Jeſus Chriſt* did not approve the *King* of *Ninevies* compelling all to Worſhip, but the men of *Ninevies* repentance at the preaching of *Ionah*.

Peace. It will be ſaid, what ſhall *Kings* and *Magiſtrates* now doe in the plagues of *ſword, famine, peſtilence*?

Truth. Kings and Magiſtrates muſt be conſidered (as formerly) inveſted with no more *power* then the *people* betruſt them with.

But no People can betruſt them with any *ſpirituall* power in matters of *worſhip*, but with a Civill power belonging to their *goods* and *bodies*.

2. *Kings* and *Magiſtrates* muſt be conſidered as either *godly* or *ungodly*.

If *ungodly*, his own and peoples duty is *Repentance*, and reconciling of their perſons unto God, before their *ſacrifice* can be accepted. Without *Repentance* what have any to doe with the *covenant* or *promiſe* of *God*? Pſal. 50.

Againe, if *Godly*, they are to humble themſelves, and beg mercies for themſelves and *people*.

Secondly, upon this *advantage* & *occasion*, they are to ftir up their people (as poffibly they may) to *Repentance*: but not to force the *confciences* of *people* to *worfhip*.

If it be faid, What muft be attended to in this example? *Object. Anfw.*

Two things are moft *eminent* in this *example*.

Firft, the great worke of *Repentance*, which *God* calls all men unto, upon the true preaching of his *Word*.

Secondly, the nature of that true *repentance* whether *Legall* or *Evangelicall*: The people of *Ninevie* turned from the *violence* that was in their hands: And confident I am, if this *Nation* fhall turne (though but with a *Legall* repentance) from that violent perfecuting or hunting each of other for *Religion* fake, (the greateft violence and hunting in the *wildernefſe* of the whole *World*) even as *Sodome* and *Gomorrah* upon a *Legall repentance*, had continued untill *Chrifts* day; fo confequently might *England, London*, &c. continue free from a generall *deſtruction* (upon fuch a turning from their *violence*) untill the *Heavens* and the whole *World* be with fire confumed.

How England and London may yet be fpared.

244] *Peace*. The fecond Scripture is that fpeech of the *Lord Chrift, Luc.* 22. 36. He that hath not a *fword*, let him fell his coat, and buy one.

Truth. For the cleering of this *Scripture*, I muft propofe and reconcile that feeming contrary command of the *Lord Jefus* to *Peter* (*Mat.* 2. 6.) Put up thy *fword* into his place, for all that take the *fword*, fhall perifh by it.

Luc. 22. the felling of the Coat, to buy a Sword, difcuffed.

In the former Scripture (*Luc.* 22.) it pleafed the

Lord Jesus, speaking of his present trouble, to compare his former sending forth of his *Disciples* without scrip, &c. with that present condition and triall comming upon them, wherein they should provide both scrip and sword, &c.

Yet now, first, when they tell him of two *swords*, he answers, It is *enough:* which shewes his former meaning was not literall, but figurative, foreshewing his present danger above his former.

Secondly, in the same case at the same time (*Mat.* 26.) commanding *Peter* to put on his sword, he gives a threefold *Reason* thereof.

1. (*vers.* 52.) from the *event* of it: for all that take the sword, shall perish by it.

2. The *needlesnes* of it: for with a word to his *Father*, he could have 12 *legions* of *Angels*.

3. The councell of *God* to be fulfilled in the Scripture: *Thus it ought to be.*

Peace. It is much questioned by some, what should be the meaning of *Christ Jesus* in that speech, All that take the *sword*, shall perish by the *sword*.

Truth. There is a threefold taking of the *sword*: First, by *murtherous crueltie*, either of private persons, or secondly, publike States or Societies, in wrath or revenge each against other.

A threefold taking of the Sword.

Secondly, a just and righteous taking of the *sword* in punishing offenders against the *Civill peace*, either more *personall*, private and ordinary; or more *publike*, Oppressors, Tyrants, Ships, Navies, &c. Neither of these can it be imagined that *Christ Jesus* intended to *Peter*.

Thirdly, There is therefore a 3. taking of the *sword*,

forbidden to *Peter*, that is, for *Chrift* and the Gofpels caufe, when Chrift is in danger: which made *Peter* ftrike, &c.

Peace. It feemes to fome moft contrary to all true reafon, that [245] *Chrift Jefus*, Innocencie it felfe, fhould not be defended.

Truth. The foolifhnes of *God* is wifer then the wifedome of Man.

It is not the purpofe of *God*, that the Spirituall *battailes* of his *Son* fhall be fought by *carnall weapons* and *perfons*.

It is not his pleafure that the *World* fhall flame on fire with *civill combuftions*, for his *Sons* fake. It is directly contrary to the *nature* of *Chrift Jefus*, his *Saints* and *Truths*, that *throats* of men (which is the higheft *contrarietie* to *civill converfe*) fhould be torne out for his fake, who moft delighted to converfe with the greateft finners.

It is the councell of *God*, that his fervants fhall overcome by 3 *weapons*, of a fpirituall nature, *Revel.* 12. 11. And that all that take the *fword* of fteele, fhall perifh.

Laftly, it is the Councell of *God*, that *Chrift Jefus* fhall fhortly appeare a moft glorious *Iudge* and *Revenger* againft all his Enemies, when the *Heavens* and the *Earth* fhall flee before his moft glorious prefence.

Peace. I fhall propofe the laft *Scripture* much infifted on by many, for carnall weapons in fpirituall cafes, *Revel.* 17. 16. The 10 *hornes* which thou faweft upon the *Beaft*, thefe fhall hate the *whore*, and fhall make her defolate and naked, and fhall eat her *flefh*, and fhall burne her with *fire*.

_{Revel. 17. 16. the Kings hating of the Whore, difcuffed.}

Truth. Not to controvert with some, whether or no the *Beast* be yet risen and extant.

Nor secondly, whether either the *Beast*, or the *Hornes*, or the *Whore* may be taken literally for any corporall *Beast* or *Whore*.

Or thirdly, whether these 10 *Hornes* be punctually and exactly 10 *Kings*.

Or fourthly, whether those 10 *Hornes* signifie those many *Kings*, *Kingdomes*, and *Governments*, who have bowed down to the *Popes* yoake, and have committed fornication with that great *Whore* the *Church* of *Rome*.

Let this last be admitted (which yet will cost some work to cleer against all opposites:) Yet,

First, can the *Time* be now cleerly demonstrated to be come, &c?

Secondly, how will it be proved, that this hatred of this *Whore* shall be a true, *chaste, Christian* hatred against *Antichristian whorish* practices, &c?

246] Thirdly, or rather that this *hating* and *desolating* and *making naked* and *burning* shall arise, not by way of an *ordinance* warranted by the *institution* of *Christ Jesus*, but by way of *providence* when (as it useth to be with all *whores* and their *lovers*) the *Church* of *Rome* and her great *lovers* shall fall out, and by the righteous vengeance of *God* upon her, drunke with the *blood* of *Saints* or holy Ones, these mighty *fornicators* shall turne their *love* into *hatred*, which *hatred* shall make her a poore desolate naked Whore, torne and consumed, &c.

Peace. You know it is a great controversie how the *Kings* of the *Earth* shall thus deale with the

Whore in the 17 Chap. and yet so bewaile her in the 18 Chapter.

Truth. If we take it that these *Kings* of the *Earth* shall first *hate*, and *plunder*, and *teare*, and *burne* this Whore, and yet afterward shall relent and bewaile their cruell dealing toward her: Or else, that as some Kings deale so terribly with her, yet others of those Kings shall bewaile her.

If either of these two answers stand, or a better be given, yet none of them can prove it lawfull for people to give power to their *Kings* and *Magistrates* thus to deale with them their subjects[,] for their *conscience*; nor for *Magistrates* to assume a title more then the people betrust them with; nor for one people out of *conscience* to *God*, and for *Christ* his sake, thus to kill and slaughter and burne each other: However it may please the Righteous Judge, according to the famous types of *Gideons* and *Jehosaphats* battells, to permit in *Justice*, and to order in *Wisdome* these mighty and mutuall slaughters each of other.

Peace. We have now (deare *Truth*) through the gracious hand of God clambered up to the top of this our tedious Discourse.

Truth. O 'tis mercy unexpressible that either *Thou* or *I* have had so long a breathing time, and that together!

Peace. If *English ground* must yet be *drunk* with *English blood*, O where shall *Peace* repose her wearied *head* and heavy *heart*?

Truth. Deare *Peace*, if thou finde welcome, and the *God* of *peace* miraculously please to quench these all-devouring flames, yet where shall *Truth* finde rest from cruell *persecutions?*

Peace. Oh, will not the *Authority* of holy *Scriptures*, the Commands and Declarations of the Sonne of *God*, therein produced by thee, together with all the lamentable *experiences* of former and [247] present slaughters prevaile with the Sons of *Men* (especially with the *Sons* of *Peace*) to depart from the *dens* of *Lyons*, and mountaines of *Leopards*,[1] and to put on the *bowels* (if not of *Christianitie*, yet) of *Humanitie* each to other!

Truth. Deare *Peace*, *Habacucks* Fishes[2] keep their constant bloody game of *Persecutions* in the Worlds mighty *Ocean*; the greater taking, plundring, swallowing up the lesser: O happy he whose portion is the *God* of *Iacob!* who hath nothing to lose under the *Sun*, but hath a *State*, a *House*, an *Inheritance*, a *Name*, a *Crowne*, a *Life*, past all the *Plunderers*, *Ravishers*, *Murtherers* reach and furie!

Peace. But loe! Who's here?

Truth. Our Sister *Patience*, whose desired company is as needfull as delightfull: 'Tis like the *Wolfe* will send the scattered *Sheep* in one: the common *Pirate* gathers up the loose and scattered *Navie:* the slaughter of the *Witnesses* by that bloody *Beast* unite the *Independents* and *Presbyterians*. The *God of Peace*,

---

[1] "Come with me from Lebanon, my spouse, with me from Lebanon: look from the top of Amana, from the top of Shenir and Hermon, from the lions' dens, from the mountains of the leopards." *Song of Solomon*, iv: 8.

[2] "Wherefore lookest thou upon them that deal treacherously, and holdest thy tongue when the wicked devoureth the man that is more righteous than he? and makest men as the fishes of the sea, as the creeping things, that have no ruler over them? *Habakkuk*, i: 13, 14.

the *God* of *Truth* will shortly seale this *Truth*, and confirme this *Witnes*, and make it evident to the whole *World*,

That the Doctrine of *Persecution* for cause of *Conscience*, is most evidently and lamentably contrary to the doctrine of *Christ Iesus* the *Prince* of *Peace*. Amen.

FINIS.

Errata.[1]

PAge 23. line 28. *for* this, *read* that. p. 31. l. alt. his soule. p. 32. l. 12. *read* mouth. ibid. *r.* person. p. 35. l. 16. *r.* turned off, or loosed from. p. 37. l. 8. *for* to, *read* doe. p. 38 l. 2. *dele* affirme. p. 41. l. 22. his perilous soule. p. 43. l. 20. *r.* or l. ult. Answerer. p. 44. l. 28. be closer. p. 49. l. 1. last. p 57. l. 22. cut. l. 24. I affirme that Justice. p. 58. l. 5. the lying. p 98. l. 6. *read*, or doe these p. 114. l. 29. *r.* the 31 question. p. 119 l. 10. *r.* members. p. 139. l. 9. immunitie. p. 161. l. 28. or Christ. p. 214. l. 36. *dele* shall. p. 225. l. 19. the Churches of God. 225. l. 25. nor might not.

---

[1] On page 52 the reference to R. Wallace, *Antitrinitarian Biography*, i. 352, should be ii: 103, 112, and to Jac. Spon, *Histoire de Généve*, should be tom. 1, p. 301, Généve, 1730. The reference to C. C. Sand, *Biblioth. Antitrin.* is to the edition *Freistadii*, 1684.

On page 233 the reference in the margin to "Chamer de Eccles." is to a work of Daniel Chamier, the French Protestant polemic. The only work of his I have been able to consult is his principal one, *Panstrateiæ Catholicæ*, Genevæ, 1626. Tom. 3, lib. 15, cap. 8–17, is De constitutionibus Ecclesiæ. But I cannot verify the allusion of the text. The reference to "Park. part. polit." is to *De Politeia Ecclesiastica Christi et Hierarchica opposita* of Robert Parker. It is often quoted by Mather in the "Answer of the Elders, &c.," and by Cotton, who acknowledges that he first received light from him as to the true structure of a Church. *Way of Cong. Churches Cleared*, p. 14.

DATE DUE			
~~APR 23 69~~			
GAYLORD			PRINTED IN U.S.A.